AF725478

Thomas Jefferson, Legal History, and the Art of Recollection

In this innovative book, historian Matthew Crow unpacks the legal and political thought of Thomas Jefferson as a tool for thinking about constitutional transformation, settler colonialism, and race and civic identity in the era of the American Revolution. Thomas Jefferson's practices of reading, writing, and collecting legal history grew out of broader histories of early modern empire and political thought. As a result of the peculiar ways in which he theorized and experienced the imperial crisis and revolutionary constitutionalism, Jefferson came to understand a republican constitution as requiring a textual, material culture of law shared by citizens with the cultivated capacity to participate in such a culture. At the center of the story in *Thomas Jefferson, Legal History, and the Art of Recollection*, Crow concludes, we find legal history as a mode of organizing and governing collective memory, and a way of instituting a particular kind of legal subjectivity.

MATTHEW CROW is an assistant professor of History at Hobart and William Smith Colleges in Geneva, New York.

Cambridge Historical Studies in American Law and Society

Recognizing legal history's growing importance and influence, the goal of this series is to chart legal history's continuing development by publishing innovative scholarship across the discipline's broadening range of perspectives and subjects. It encourages empirically creative works that take legal history into unexplored subject areas, or that fundamentally revise our thinking about familiar topics; it also encourages methodologically innovative works that bring new disciplinary perspectives and techniques to the historical analysis of legal subjects.

Series Editor

Christopher Tomlins, *University of California, Berkeley*

Previously Published in the Series

Oren Bracha, *Owning Ideas: The Intellectual Origins of American Intellectual Property, 1790–1909*
Anne Twitty, *Before Dred Scott: Slavery and Legal Culture in the American Confluence, 1787–1857*
Castañeda Anastacio, Anna Leah Fidelis T., *The Foundations of the Modern Philippine State: Imperial Rule and the American Constitutional Tradition in the Philippine Islands, 1898–1935*
Robert Deal, *The Law of the Whale Hunt: Dispute Resolution, Property Law, and American Whalers, 1780–1880*
Sandra F. Vanburkleo, *Gender Remade: Citizenship, Suffrage, and Public Power in the New Northwest, 1879–1912*
Reuel Schiller, *Forging Rivals: Race, Class, Law, and the Collapse of Postwar Liberalism*
Ely Aaronson, *From Slave Abuse to Hate Crime: The Criminalization of Racial Violence in American History*
Stuart Chinn, *Recalibrating Reform: The Limits of Political Change*
Ajay K. Mehrotra, *Making the Modern American Fiscal State*
Yvonne Pitts, *Family, Law, and Inheritance in America: A Social and Legal History of Nineteenth-Century Kentucky*
David M. Rabban, *Law's History*
Kunal M. Parker, *Common Law, History, and Democracy in America, 1790–1900*
Steven Wilf, *Law's Imagined Republic*
James D. Schmidt, *Industrial Violence and the Legal Origins of Child Labor*
Rebecca M. McLennan, *The Crisis of Imprisonment: Protest, Politics, and the Making of the American Penal State, 1776–1941*
Tony A. Freyer, *Antitrust and Global Capitalism, 1930–2004*
Davison Douglas, *Jim Crow Moves North*
Andrew Wender Cohen, *The Racketeer's Progress*
Michael Willrich, *City of Courts, Socializing Justice in Progressive Era Chicago*
Barbara Young Welke, *Recasting American Liberty: Gender, Law and the Railroad Revolution, 1865–1920*
Michael Vorenberg, *Final Freedom: The Civil War, the Abolition of Slavery, and the Thirteenth Amendment*
Robert J. Steinfeld, *Coercion, Contract, and Free Labor in Nineteenth Century America*
David M. Rabban, *Free Speech in Its Forgotten Years*
Jenny Wahl, *The Bondsman's Burden: An Economic Analysis of the Common Law of Southern Slavery*
Michael Grossberg, *A Judgment for Solomon: The d'Hauteville Case and Legal Experience in the Antebellum South*

Thomas Jefferson, Legal History, and the Art of Recollection

MATTHEW CROW

Hobart and William Smith Colleges, New York

CAMBRIDGE
UNIVERSITY PRESS

CAMBRIDGE
UNIVERSITY PRESS

University Printing House, Cambridge CB2 8BS, United Kingdom

One Liberty Plaza, 20th Floor, New York, NY 10006, USA

477 Williamstown Road, Port Melbourne, VIC 3207, Australia

314-321, 3rd Floor, Plot 3, Splendor Forum, Jasola District Centre, New Delhi - 110025, India

79 Anson Road, #06-04/06, Singapore 079906

Cambridge University Press is part of the University of Cambridge.

It furthers the University's mission by disseminating knowledge in the pursuit of education, learning and research at the highest international levels of excellence.

www.cambridge.org
Information on this title: www.cambridge.org/9781107161931
DOI: 10.1017/9781316676776

© Matthew Crow 2017

This publication is in copyright. Subject to statutory exception and to the provisions of relevant collective licensing agreements, no reproduction of any part may take place without the written permission of Cambridge University Press.

First published 2017

A catalogue record for this publication is available from the British Library

Library of Congress Cataloging in Publication data
NAMES: Crow, Matthew, 1982– author.
TITLE: Thomas Jefferson, legal history, and the art of recollection / Matthew Crow, Hobart and William Smith Colleges, New York.
DESCRIPTION: New York : Cambridge University Press, 2016. |
Includes bibliographical references and index.
IDENTIFIERS: LCCN 2016044620 | ISBN 9781107161931 (Hardback)
SUBJECTS: LCSH: Jefferson, Thomas, 1743-1826. | Law–Virginia–History. |
Lawyers–Virginia–Biography.
CLASSIFICATION: LCC KF363.J4 C76 2016 | DDC 340.092 [B] –dc23 LC record available at https://lccn.loc.gov/2016044620

ISBN 978-1-107-16193-1 Hardback
ISBN 978-1-316-61412-9 Paperback

Cambridge University Press has no responsibility for the persistence or accuracy of URLs for external or third-party internet websites referred to in this publication, and does not guarantee that any content on such websites is, or will remain, accurate or appropriate.

For Sarah

Forms of the Land, the flow of water, the occurrence of what us'd to be call'd Miracles, all are Text,– to be attended to, manipulated, read, remember'd.

– Copyright © 1997 by Thomas Pynchon. From *Mason & Dixon* (Henry Holt and Co.). Reprinted with permission by Melanie Jackson Agency, LLC.

Contents

Acknowledgments

In a book that is at least in part about selectively inheriting, borrowing, and using history, it feels a little funny and not a little daunting to acknowledge the incredible support I have received in completing it. This book is a product of multiple histories of inspiration, disagreement, influence, use, frustration, labor, and love, and it is exciting to now acknowledge those that have been a part of making those histories.

Several organizations have given financial and other forms of support to this project. I would not have been able to complete it without generous support from Hobart and William Smith Colleges, especially from Pat McGuire and Provost Titi Ufomata. I am also grateful to Judy Mahoney-Benzer for all of her work. From the beginning, my gratitude goes to the Department of History and the Graduate Division at UCLA. The Library of the American Philosophical Society provided a Mellon research fellowship, and at the APS, I owe a special debt to Earle Spamer and Roy Goodman for their time and hospitality. The Robert H. Smith International Center for Jefferson Studies further provided generous support through a research fellowship and accommodations at Kenwood. For reference assistance and conversation, I am indebted to Anna Berkes, Endrina Tay, Eric Johnson, Andrew O'Shaughnessy, and Joan Hairfield. The Rockefeller Library of the Colonial Williamsburg Foundation provided a Robert M. & Annetta J. Coffelt and Robert M. Coffelt Jr. Fellowship, and I am grateful for help from Bennie Brown, Doug Mayo, the special collections and research staff at the Rockefeller Library, and for fruitful conversations with Fredrika Teute, Nadine Zimmerli, Taylor Stoermer, Alexandre Dubé, and other members of the Williamsburg community. Further thanks go to the Special Collections staff at the

University of Virginia, Susan Riggs and Special Collections at the Swem Library, College of William and Mary, Brent Tarter and the Special Collections staff at the Library of Virginia, Lee Shepard and the staff of the Virginia Historical Society, the Rare Book Department of the Free Library of Philadelphia, the Rare Book and Special Collections Division of the Library of Congress, and finally to the Huntington Library for a Mellon fellowship in 2011 and another one in 2016, which, at the time of this writing, is allowing me to journey into other seas. I thank successive directors of research at the Huntington, Roy Ritchie and Steve Hindle, and the academic support staff of the Huntington, especially Juan Gomez, Olga Tsapina, and Ed Rinderle.

For discourse at conferences and colloquia, as well as the chance to present my work, I thank colleagues in the History, Philosophy, English, and Political Science Departments at Hobart and William Smith Colleges; the Central New York Early Modern Seminar and especially Rachel Weil and Heather Welland; the British Legal History Conference and Holly Brewer, Sally Hadden, and Dan Hulsebosch; the Colombia Early American History Seminar and Brian Murphy and Zara Anishanslin for their invitation; the members of the 2014 Jack Miller Center Summer Institute, David Lieberman; the "Jeffersonian Democracy: From Theory to Practice" conference at Princeton in 2012 and Lo Faber, Jessica Lowe, Barbara Oberg, Hendrik Hartog, Christopher Curtis, and Mark Schmeller; the Society of Early Americanists and Timothy Sweet; the 2013 Legal Theory and Legal History Conference at Queen Mary, University of London and Maksymilian Del Mar; the University Center for Human Values at Princeton, Quentin Skinner; the Society for Historians of the Early American Republic; the fellow's forums at the Rockefeller Library of Colonial Williamsburg and The Robert H. Smith Center for Jefferson Studies at Monticello; the Clark Library and the Center for Seventeenth and Eighteenth Century Studies at UCLA; the History Department Graduate Student Colloquium at UCLA; the W.G. Hart Legal Workshop at the Institute for Advanced Legal Studies, University College, London; Bernard Bailyn, Mary Sarah Bilder, and the members of the 2010 Seminar on the History of the Atlantic World at Harvard; and the attendees of the 2011 "Inscriptions" conference at UC Riverside. I also wish to thank the staff and readers of *Republics of Letters* and *Law and History Review*, especially *Law and History Review* editor Elizabeth Dale.

Material in the first and second chapter of this book appeared in earlier forms as, respectively, "Thomas Jefferson and the Uses of Equity" in the February 2015 issue of *Law and History Review*, and as "Jefferson, Pocock, and the Temporality of Law in a Republic" in the December 15, 2010 issue of *Republics of Letters: A Journal for the Study of Knowledge, Politics, and the Arts*. Thanks on the latter go to the editors Margaret Jacob, Jacob Soll, and Dan Edelstein. Reference to, quotation from, and otherwise reproduction of manuscript material appears in this book courtesy of the Library of Congress, Special Collections of the University of Virginia Library, Special Collections at the Swem Library of the College of William and Mary, the Rockefeller Library of Colonial Williamsburg, the Virginia Historical Society, the Library of the American Philosophical Society, and the Huntington Library.

I want to sincerely thank my current and former colleagues in the History Department at Hobart and William Smith: Clif Hood, Derek Linton, Dan Singal, Susanne McNally, Lisa Yoshikawa, Will Harris, Stephen Frug, Laura Free, Liz Thornberry, and most especially for their friendship and understanding Colby Ristow, Matt Kadane, Maureen Flynn, whose grace and sense of intellectual exploration will always be sorely missed, and Sarah Whitten. From my time at UCLA I will always be grateful to Ruth Bloch, Naomi Lamoreaux, Mary Yeager, Lynn Hunt, Joyce Appleby, Mary Terrall, Pete Stacey, Anthony Pagden, Andrew Sabl, Joan Waugh, Jesse Sadler, Naomi Taback, Jake Collins, Melanie Arias, Stephanie Amerian, Ned Schoolman, and to Christopher Looby, Lowell Gallagher, Saree Makdisi, and Helen Deutsch in the English Department. I am grateful to Peter Martland and to Emile Perreau-Saussine, sadly gone, at Cambridge, and to Sophia Rosenfeld and the other attendees of the Clark Library conference that Michael Meranze and I hosted in October of 2014, "The Civic Arts: Enlightenment and the Subjects of Liberal Learning." In the world of Jefferson studies, I am indebted and particularly grateful to David Konig, Annette Gordon-Reed, Peter Onuf, Frank Cogliano, Kevin Hayes, Jeff Looney, Jessica Walker, Christa Dierksheide, Hannah Spahn, and above all to Brian Steele. I will always be grateful to David Waldstreicher, Andrew Robertson, Martha King, Kevin Butterfield, Billy Wayson, Keith Thomson, Frank Shuffleton, also sadly gone, to Al Brophy, and to Ken Owen and Tom Cutterham at the Junto blog. This book and its author have happily and substantially benefited from the learning, support, and friendship of Rachel Weil and Aziz Rana at Cornell, and I am forever in their debt.

Again at UCLA, for her support I am deeply and forever grateful to Margaret Jacob. I thank Perry Anderson and Kirstie McClure for the seminars that provided the space in which a good deal of this project was initially explored and conceptualized, and for all of our discussions about the work of J.G.A. Pocock, among others. I also wish to thank John Pocock. Craig Yirush welcomed me to UCLA and was always available for critical back and forth, and so I will always be grateful to him. At Cambridge University Press, I want to thank Deborah Gershenowitz, Kristina Deusch, Sarah Lambert, Anup Kumar, the copy editors and the management team, two anonymous readers, and Christopher Tomlins, without whose work and support this book would not be possible. Any errors are my own.

Finally, and most importantly, to call what I owe Michael Meranze "debt" would be such an understatement it could cause an economic crisis, and we would have to call it the 405 bubble. First at UC San Diego and then at UCLA, and just about every day since, I have found my way in no small part with the help of his critical feedback, guidance, conversation, support, and I think more than anything else a sense of what is at stake in histories of intellectual practice, including those in which we are currently acting. Thank you.

For room and board as well as support and encouragement, I want to thank Margaret and Joel Watson, Kathy Whitten, Barry and Rita Whitten, Barbara and Nick Tennant, Ted Prim and Marian Johnston. I owe my sense that politics and history matter and for many of the same reasons to my parents, Michael and Katherine Crow, and in that I am grateful not only for life but for my sense of what it means to live it in a world made and shared with others. It has been the blessing of my life to become a father while completing this book, and I will always be in loving awe of Felicity Elizabeth Crow. You cannot know how much you mean to us. As to us, Sarah, I love you, and this book belongs to you.

I

Introduction

"in the course of human events..."

Novelists and their readers, or perhaps poets, painters, performers and their audiences, might move back and forth between the distant and the recent past, playing with time as a way of making it both alien and tangible. Politicians, lawyers, judges, or the general public might seek to robe themselves in the comfort and majesty of a monumental past and put a particular figure, image, or quotation to use in the legitimation of particular interests and ideas in the present. Historians will generally think of themselves as doing something very different from either of these activities, distancing themselves from the power of the playful, the idolatrous, and the cynically manipulative in a wider culture of seemingly uncritical historical consciousness. The intensely felt and powerful assumption informing that distancing would be that of a clear line separating the study of history from its use. Even to acknowledge that all history is a history of the present, as many historians might, would reinforce this basic and almost instinctual sense of what it is historians tell themselves they are doing when they do history. The same could be said for any student-scholar engaged in a kind of critically reflective, historically inflected and focused mode of intellectual practice.

If the legitimating assumption of contemporary humanistic practice is an equally passionate opposition to the mere use of historical material and to questions about the use of the humanities, then the work of study, in this assumption, gets constructed as a kind of policing of the boundaries of collective currency in the language and imagery of the past. It is one of the primary goals of this book to use Thomas Jefferson as a way of *questioning* that assumption, and to clear some conceptual space for understanding historical practices as particular modes of use.

Use, I want to suggest, goes all the way down. Jefferson is useful for efforts to rethink history and historiography because his self-conscious and purposeful, if wandering, exploration of the use of history in law and politics puts questions of use at the center of inquiry, where, at least for the time being, such questions belong.[1] Historians use the past to ask questions, to make arguments, to find themselves, to justify themselves, to make political arguments, to bother lawyers, political theorists, and literary critics with pesky points about context, to insist that certain things should be remembered, and last but certainly not least to get jobs, money, better jobs, and to impress each other and their audiences. There is nothing wrong with any of that, except insofar as it all goes unacknowledged as use, as use of history, and as a particular mode or modes of use among many possible others. As has become increasingly clear from recent scholarship, the study of history and the study of law have been and in many ways continue to be mutually constitutive of one another. They share a history rooted in the conjoined trajectories of early modern empire, legal humanism, and historical and political thought. In his own practices of self-formation and his thinking about the nature of law and constituted authority in a republic, Jefferson put himself in that shared history. His thinking, his awareness of his own self-situating in material histories of bodies, words, and things, grants us a unique vantage point on the history of the relationships between legal, political, and historical thought. He anchored himself in the intellectual history of early modern legal humanism, and he marshalled that inheritance, and ideas about inheritance, in an effort to think about the use of history in constructions of law, race, and civic identity.

In this book I take up these anchoring and marshalling activities as pieces of a wider history of intellectual and constitutional change. I see these activities as distinctive instantiations of what can be called the art of recollection, of seeing and working with the presence of histories as contexts, some chosen, others not, and so as productive environments from which collective life gets made and remade in time. History practiced as recollection in this particularly civic and material sense, and as distinct

[1] On this point and a few others I take up and build on the work of Giorgio Agamben, *The Highest Poverty: Monastic Rules and Form-of-Life*, Adam Kotsko, trans. (Stanford: Stanford University Press, 2013), and *The Use of Bodies*, Adam Kotsko, trans. (Stanford: Stanford University Press, 2016); on conceptualizations of intellectual practice and use in the present, see also Paul Rabinow, *The Accompaniment: Assembling the Contemporary* (Chicago: University of Chicago Press, 2011); Hayden White, *The Practical Past* (Evanston: Northwestern University Press, 2014).

from the weighty valences of the term in the western philosophical canon, would be the art of attending to the availability of the past to the present. My goal here is to recollect Jefferson's thinking and the histories in which he acted and helped construct, to make them available, and to offer my own thinking about what the uses of this kind of activity are, have been, and might be.

JEFFERSON IN PIECES

The history of Thomas Jefferson's thinking is useful, but in contrast to what scholars have made of his, James Madison's, James Wilson's, or John Marshall's thought, it is not always particularly edifying. Nor, it should be said, has it always been taken to be in histories of legal and constitutional thought, where Jefferson remains a somewhat marginal figure.[2] Just two years before his death in July 1826, Jefferson wrote to British radical John Cartwright as part of a dialogue on constitutional politics in their respective countries. Turning to what in 1776 had become his own nation's history, Jefferson suggested the following comparison with the English Glorious Revolution of 1688:

> Our Revolution commenced on more favorable ground. It presented us an album on which we were free to write what we pleased. We had no occasion to search into any musty records, to hunt up royal parchments, or to investigate the laws and institutions of a semi-barbarous ancestry. We appealed to those of nature, and found them engraved on our hearts.[3]

[2] It is the very strangeness of Jefferson's thinking, and the fruit it can bear for historical understanding when rubbed against the grain, that warrants attention here; see Mary Sarah Bilder, "James Madison, Law-Student and Demi-Lawyer," *Law and History Review*, Vol. 28, No. 2 (May 2010), pp. 389–449; David Thomas Konig, "James Madison and Common-Law Constitutionalism," *Law and History Review*, Vol. 28, No. 2 (May 2010), pp. 507–14; their notes on law and legal reading show Madison and Marshall, for example, to have had in many ways more typical legal minds, but we should not take that to mean they were simply legal and historical in a way that Jefferson's in fact far more wide-ranging and deep reading in law, legal history, and legal theory was not; see John Marshall, *Accounts and Law Notes*, 39:1 M34 M-105 Box 8, Swem Library Special Collections, College of William and Mary, 1776; while it is possible to locate thinkers more committed to concepts of unified popular sovereignty in politics, Jefferson's attentions to the local availability of the law as text to be touched and handled by its users was, once again, unique, and radically so; see Christopher Tomlins, "Republican Law," in *The Oxford Handbook of the American Revolution*, Edward G. Gray and Jane Kamensky, ed. (Oxford: Oxford University Press, 2012), pp. 540–59.

[3] Thomas Jefferson to Major John Cartwright, June 5, 1824, *Writings*, Merrill D. Peterson, ed. (New York: Library of America, 1984), p. 1491. Jefferson's language evoked the natural rights rhetoric of the late imperial crisis and outbreak of the American

Forty-eight years after the Declaration of Independence, Jefferson comfortably denied the importance of a legal culture of historical texts and manuscripts, and thus apparently of history, to American revolutionary thought, but the passage betrays its author's narrative. With the use of the pronoun "those" in the last sentence, Jefferson imported the language of civil history, "laws and institutions," into the supposedly separate domain of nature, which he in turn valorized as antithetical to being bogged down by civil history. Likewise, he retained a language that was thoroughly textual to describe the apparent absence of texts in American revolutionary political action: "an *album* on which we were free to *write* what we pleased." While the Whigs of the Glorious Revolution had to make due with inked-up folios of history, so the argument went, the Americans could open a new book and start at the top of an empty first page. Jefferson's forthright declaration was complete nonsense, but in this as in many other cases it is important to try and get at what Jefferson was not able, or willing, to see about himself and the histories in which he found himself, and why.

Certainly, this rhetorical naturalization of the collective historical experience of one polity and the assumption of its consequent superiority to that of others was an important part of legal justifications for conquest.[4] The putting aside of the assemblage of historical record and representation that made up complex bodies of inherited concepts and materials allowed the organizer to locate themselves in a unique position of power and authority. Practices of representing legal history were part of wider histories of law and empire, histories of which Jefferson was keenly aware. In his own practices of historical representation and his thinking about the politics of such practice, he participated in these histories and played a significant role in their transformation. There was a strong link between ways of recognizing and forgetting the constructed character of historical, civic identity on the one hand and the intensification and expansion of power on the other.

Revolution and, either consciously or unconsciously, rehearsed nearly exactly the words of Alexander Hamilton's 1775 pamphlet, *The Farmer Refuted*, depicting American colonial opposition to metropolitan policy as having stood on an uncontested foundation; see Alexander Hamilton, "The Farmer Refuted," in *The Revolutionary Writings of Alexander Hamilton*, Richard B. Vernier, ed. (Indianapolis: Liberty Fund, 2008).

4 See James Tully, *Public Philosophy in a New Key, Volume II: Imperialism and Civic Freedom* (Cambridge: Cambridge University Press, 2008), pp. 246–56. Tully sees modern, mainstream liberal constitutionalism as an outgrowth of precisely this kind of theory and its applications. Critique of empire and the modern state, then, begins with decoupling historical edifices of law from their image as natural or logically necessary, see Tully, *ibid*, pp. 257–309.

That being said, Jefferson as liberal optimist and the plotter of settler colonialism and commercial empire in the American west is not the only image with which a look at his life of legal and political theorizing leaves us. Leading up to and during the revolution, Jefferson was a ringleader of efforts to "search into any musty records," "hunt up royal parchments," and "investigate the laws and institutions" of what he considered a "semi-barbarous ancestry." He was a vociferous collector of the manuscript copies of the Virginia Company records and the Laws of the Assembly. From the estate of Peyton Randolph, Jefferson acquired pieces of the library of his father Sir John Randolph, who had been the King's Attorney in Virginia and had assembled a collection for the purpose of writing a history and constructing an English colonial jurisprudence for Virginia. These included notes on English decisions regarding Virginia, the elder Randolph's commonplace book, and records from the establishment of Virginia as a royal colony in 1624. From the estate of Richard Bland, another noted collector of Virginia legal manuscripts, Jefferson acquired records of the Virginia Company from as early as 1606 and 1607, when English colonizers first successfully landed at Jamestown, records that included manuscript copies of the original charters and subsequent laws passed by the General Assembly. Jefferson also acquired personal manuscripts and early printed editions of Virginia laws from his peers, including a manuscript copy of Thomas Mathew's contemporaneous history of the rebellion of western settlers led by Nathaniel Bacon in 1676.

Jefferson rescued other manuscript copies of laws and other records from neglect in county court houses and even from the trash heaps of taverns, where he found handwritten copies of Virginia laws being used as scrap paper, copies which bear doodles of stick figures and horses by an anonymous illustrator, or perhaps several.[5] The assembled archive represented the continuous history of legal government in the provincial context and as such was the material guarantee of property and legal status of the subjects there, documenting as it did the establishment of English colonialism in North America and the rigid binding of indentured servitude and chattel slavery. And yet the dispersed, fragile, and fragmented character of these palimpsests, and their material history of variable uses, from the most authoritative to the most profane, was not lost on Jefferson, and the manifest tensions inherent in such practices of historical

[5] Thomas Jefferson Papers, Library of Congress Special Collections, Manuscripts Division, Series VIII, Manuscript Vol. 9.

representation would prove to play an enormous role in his thinking about law and constitutionalism in a republic.

The fate of these manuscripts is a fitting testament to their place in the trajectory of Jefferson's thinking and the wider history of which it was a part, becoming as they did a part of his property, property burdened with not only a complicated history but with Jefferson's heavy debts, his failed efforts to alleviate those debts, and his reluctance to surrender the illusion of masterly independence and self-possession. Even so, Jefferson spent a good deal of energy over the course of his life trying to secure external funding for the printing and public distribution of his private manuscript collections, assuming as he did that widespread access to textual records of law was a critical component of constitutionalism in any republican polity. He experimented with instituting a constitutional order where law was understood as an assembled archive of text and use, and as only safely held in the hands of a properly cultivated laity. Jefferson was the principal inheritor of efforts on the part of elite legal actors in Virginia over the course of the previous century to collect the legal and constitutional history of the colony. The purpose guiding this project was to make possible the articulation of a civil history that balanced metropolitan constitutional inheritance and a distinctly provincial identity, and in so doing secure a narrative of legitimate and stable Anglicization within the contested and increasingly uncertain constitution of early modern empire in the British Atlantic world. It was from the failure of that project during the imperial crisis of the mid- to late eighteenth century that Jefferson's peculiarly material, historical, and textual sense of constitutional design and practice sprang. And it was in his thinking about such material constitutional culture that Jefferson found it necessary to turn his attention to thinking about thinking as material and embodied practice, as reading and writing, as collecting and recollecting. He went on to expand his concern with the design of texts and institutions to include the habits and practices of the people whose responsibility it was to use those texts and contexts well.

Convinced as he was of the necessity of widely constituted participation in the formation of legal and political judgment in such a polity, Jefferson's project became the institution of a particular kind of citizen, a mode of legal and historical subjectivity that conceived of the citizen as a cultivated user and shaper of inherited materials.[6] It

[6] On Jefferson as a theorist of subjectivity and history, I am indebted to Lee Quinby, *Freedom, Foucault, and the Subject of America* (Boston: Northeastern University Press, 1991); and Jonathan Elmer, *On Lingering and Being Last: Race and Sovereignty in the*

was in this project that Jefferson confronted the inextricable plurality of these modes and the histories of which they were made. And that plurality directly challenged his imagined settler subject's form of life, in which self-government rested on self-ownership and mastery. In pursuit of this project and the territory necessary to provide for it, Jefferson gradually reformulated the actively situated participant in the rich textuality of republican law as a more passive member of civil society, whose role in the circulation of words and things was limited to their participation in expanding networks of print culture and commercial exchange. The attempt to secure a particular mode of subjectivity not only carried great costs for those not counted among its subjects but hollowed out the very conceptualization of political life that was meant to be secured. As a retiree, Jefferson returned to many of his early concerns with the politics of humanist intellectual practice, but he did so largely on his own. Only then could Jefferson assert the promise of the American Revolution as driven by its lack of dependence on the troubled inheritance of multiple histories.

We live, I suggest, with and in fragments of these histories, of these efforts to inscribe arts of historical representation within a particular kind of civic thought and practice. This matters to how we might think about ourselves and about history, law, and politics today. Jefferson's historical constructions of legal subjectivity can get us access to the power of such constructions, but they cannot simply be restored or remembered as edifying memorials. Rather, they can be approached as fragments, as material ruins underneath a good deal of our modern conceptual architecture. Jefferson's thinking is available and potentially useful, I want to suggest, but not solely on conditions of his or our own making, not in a vacuum or unattached to other pieces of history, and not without some substantial risk. As the work of Raymond Geuss on political thought and judgment warns, specific constructions of history and politics are powerful tools, even weapons, and they are as often used to harm and kill as they are to persuade, inspire, or assist. To this hard fact of historical and political life Jefferson proves no exception.[7]

New World (New York: Fordham University Press, 2008). While I find a more particular, purposive logic driving Jefferson's interest in historical representation, a work that nevertheless appreciates that interest as eccentric and troubled is Michael Knox Beran, *Jefferson's Demons: Portrait of a Restless Mind* (New York: Free Press, 2003).

7 Raymond Geuss, *Philosophy and Real Politics* (Princeton: Princeton University Press, 2008), *Politics and the Imagination* (Princeton: Princeton University Press, 2010); see also Friedrich Nietzsche, "On the Uses and Disadvantages of History for Life," in *Untimely*

JEFFERSON'S HISTORIES

Jefferson's various and consequential occlusions of civic identity grew out of the particular ways in which he thought about historical subjectivity as a key aspect of civic capacity. He described African Americans and Native Americans as lacking in the cultivated capacity to be other than creatures of their conditioned histories. The imagined critically thinking citizen of what we would later call Jeffersonian democracy was thus nervously constructed and creatively secured from its beginning as an exclusionary form of political life. The records of plantation oversight that scholars of Jefferson's life have used to understand him also illuminate a particular kind of self-management rooted in not only the government but the ownership and mastery of self and others, with all of its attendant tensions, insecurities, and cold calculations of human life caught up in the violence of slavery and conquest on both a personal and continental scale.[8] American slavery was biopolitics.[9]

Meditations, R.J. Hollingdale, trans., (Cambridge: Cambridge University Press, 1984); Bernard Williams, *In the Beginning Was the Deed* (Princeton: Princeton University Press, 2005), ch. 3. In legal theory, the richness of attending to law as a constructed image of the legal and constitutional past has been fruitfully explored in different ways by Norman W. Spaulding, "Constitution as Countermonument: Federalism, Reconstruction, and the Problem of Collective Memory," *Columbia Law Review*, Vol. 38, No. 8 (December, 2003), pp. 1992–2051; Alexandre Lefebvre, *The Image of Law: Deleuze, Bergson, Spinoza* (Stanford: Stanford University Press, 2008).

8 On slavery at Monticello, see Annette Gordon-Reed, *The Hemingses of Monticello: An American Family* (New York: Norton, 2008); Lucia Stanton, *"Those Who Labor for My Happiness:" Slavery at Thomas Jefferson's Monticello* (Charlottesville: University of Virginia Press, 2012); Annette Gordon-Reed and Peter S. Onuf, *Most Blessed of the Patriarchs: Thomas Jefferson and the Empire of the Imagination* (New York: Liveright, 2016); on a broader scale, in a series of notes to George Washington as Secretary of State, Jefferson calculated the labor costs and productivity of white and enslaved black labor in Virginia, weighting his calculations with his belief that "the negro does not perform quite as much work, nor with as much intelligence." He went on to estimate comparative labor costs of free and enslaved labor, judging the latter to be more profitable due to assumed natural population growth offering a greater return on the initial higher investment in purchasing the slaves, see Thomas Jefferson, "Notes on Arthur Young's Letter to George Washington," June 18, 1792, *The Papers of Thomas Jefferson*, John Catanzariti, ed. (Princeton: Princeton University Press, 1990), Vol. 24, pp. 95–9; see John Chester Miller, *The Wolf By the Ears: Thomas Jefferson and Slavery* (New York: Free Press, 1977); Paul Finkelman, *Slavery and the Founders: Race and Liberty in the Age of Jefferson* (Armonk, NY: M.E. Sharpe, 1996); Henry Wieneck, *The Master of the Mountain* (New York: Farrar, Straus, and Giroux, 2012).

9 On the growth of "biopolitics" in neoliberal economic theory and its origins in the modern form of subjective governmental practice that grew out of the discourse of political economy, see Michel Foucault, *Security, Territory, and Population: Lectures at*

Law and more specifically legal study as a distinct kind of historical practice played a determinative role in these wider historical processes of revolution, founding, and empire. The goal of this book is constructive: to see Jefferson as an engaged theorist of the politics of historical representation and a powerful wielder of those constructions; to suggest at once his distance and his apparent proximity to us, and in short, to take advantage of this situation and put him to work. His unique attentions to the problematically transmitted and assembled quality of law configured law itself as constructed history, or histories, and for this reason legal personhood was a question for Jefferson of imposed conceptions of what it meant to have a history and the freedom to know and use it. This assembled and constructed understanding of law and history was made possible by a historically particular mode of textual practice and the context of that practice in the peripheral reception of English law and British imperial governance in the eighteenth century, but its implications both in its time and ours run deeper than that immediate context would suggest.

Jefferson's construction of the criteria for acknowledging legal and political subjectivity in others builds on this idealized vision of the citizen as a cultivated and self-possessed agent capable of taking the materials of history and submitting them to the possibility of new use. In his revolutionary-era proposals for legal and constitutional reform, Jefferson was determined to hold on to an "ancient" and customary understanding of constitutions as collections of ordinary law as opposed to foundational text.[10] Uniquely among leading figures of the Founding era, Jefferson actively retained a profoundly English understanding of constitutionalism as the history of accumulated use, and his constitutional theorizing in the

the College de France, 1977–1978, Graham Burchell, trans., Michel Senellart, ed. (New York: Palgrave Macmillan, 2007); *The Birth of Biopolitics: Lectures at the Collège de France, 1978–1979*, Michael Sennelart, ed., Graham Burchell, trans. (New York: Palgrave Macmillan, 2008); on antebellum slavery as a form of capitalism predicated on the capitalization of the enslaved body, see Walter Johnson, *River of Dark Dreams: Slavery and Empire in the Cotton Kingdom* (Cambridge, MA: Harvard University Press, 2013); Elizabeth Maddock Dillon, *New World Drama: The Performative Commons in the Atlantic World, 1649–1849* (Durham: Duke University Press, 2014).

[10] J.G.A. Pocock, *The Ancient Constitution and the Feudal Law: A Study of English Historical Thought in the Seventeenth Century, A Reissue with Retrospect* (Cambridge: Cambridge University Press, 1987); James Tully, *Strange Multiplicity: Constitutionalism in an Age of Diversity* (Cambridge: Cambridge University Press, 1995); Jefferson argued against the production of a fundamental code of law for Virginia, as "it was thought dangerous to attempt to reduce" the body of law "to a text: it was therefore left to be collected from the usual monuments of it," *Notes on the State of Virginia*, p. 144.

Notes on the State of Virginia represents an ambivalent radicalization of his own deep reading in the common law tradition. Jefferson railed against the legislature for its assumption of the power to adopt a constitution for the state without calling a convention or canvassing the text among the people.[11] His 1776 draft of a constitution for Virginia included proposals to have amendments circulated among citizens called together in their counties to collectively edit the text of the proposed change and send it back to the legislature.[12] Late in life, he wrote to Samuel Kercheval, belittling those "who look at constitutions with sanctimonious reverence, and deem them like the arc of the covenant, too sacred to be touched," reflecting on a life engaged in exploring a republican, even democratic politics of the availability of constitutional text to the touch of the people.[13] Political participation was thus framed as a deeply textual experience, and Jefferson's project amounted to a nervous attempt at a nevertheless radical democratization of an aristocratic mode of reading that came out of the world of legal and historical practice of Jefferson's own intellectual development.

In Jefferson's vision, the responsibility and power of judgment was activated by use and found its truest expression in the ability to participate in the making and remaking of the text of the law. That responsibility, in turn, needed to be established and maintained by what he called "a plurality of hands."[14] He evaluated historical subjectivity as nothing less than a capacity for use – use of language to be sure but at the same time use of land through labor and use of law through interpretation, argument, and judgment. As Jefferson famously put the point to Madison, "the earth belongs in usufruct to the living."[15] In seeking to relocate the responsibilities and powers of political and even legal judgment into

[11] Jefferson, *Notes on the State of Virginia*, pp. 127–36.

[12] Thomas Jefferson, "Third Draft," *Papers of Thomas Jefferson*, Boyd, ed. (Princeton: Princeton University Press, 1951), Vol. 1, p. 364; Jefferson would later complain to James Madison about the lack of a similar process in the ratification of the US Constitution, "To James Madison from Thomas Jefferson, 20 December 1787," Founders Online, National Archives (http://founders.archives.gov/documents/Madison/01–10-02–0210, ver. 2013-06-26), accessed August 1, 2013.

[13] Jefferson to Samuel Kercheval, July 12, 1816, *Papers of Thomas Jefferson: Retirement Series*, J. Jefferson Looney, ed. (Princeton: Princeton University Press, 2013), p. 226.

[14] Jefferson, *Notes on the State of Virginia*, p. 133; on the legal and political theory of Jefferson's constitutional proposals and extended thinking about law and constitutionalism, see Shannon C. Stimson, *The American Revolution in the Law: Anglo-American Jurisprudence before John Marshall* (Princeton: Princeton University Press, 1990).

[15] Jefferson to James Madison, September 6, 1789, *The Papers of Thomas Jefferson*, Julian P. Boyd, ed. (Princeton: Princeton University Press, 1958), Vol. 15, p. 392.

constituted spaces of public assembly, Jefferson was reformulating the substance of his reading in early modern law and legal theory in both common law and equity jurisprudence, and putting it to new use.

Like the late medieval and early modern glossators and reporters of the law in whose writings he immersed himself and encouraged students to do the same, Jefferson compiled and assembled more than he authored, and he characteristically continued to do so with the text of the *Notes* itself for the rest of his life. He thought and worked genealogically and at times archaeologically as suited his purposes, and like the writing of the law or the rules of language or the rights of property, he found the symbolic value of money was likewise the product not of some underlying natural order but of a history of collecting and recollecting, reading and rereading, and assembling and reassembling. The Jeffersonian project was to equip a cultivated and cultivating citizenry with the conditions and the capacity to find and constitute themselves in history, natural and civil, to exercise critically reflective judgment on their surroundings, their inheritances, and their influences, to prepare themselves for the burden of self-government. Jefferson's own mode of intellectual work and textual construction shaped his understanding of how subjects constituted themselves in and through active embedment in histories. His constitutional program was predicated on the assumption that a republican constitutional culture would require an assembled, workable, and open material textual culture to support it. This was a question of memory, and in the sense that Jefferson frequently discussed it: as recollection, a common enough word for the act of memory in the eighteenth century, but Jefferson's use captures the Latin root of the word, *recoligere*, to gather back up or reassemble. Jefferson explored how it might become possible to have a constitutional order that actively declined to enlist origin, authorship, or intent as useful categories of practice. Far from being an imagined escape from history, this exploration grew out of his legal study and in response to questions about the legal status of his colonial society to be found in competing narratives of early modern British jurisprudence and constitutional history. To understand Jefferson's textuality, it is important to understand the conceptual background of debates over the historical and textual authority of written law in seventeenth-century England.

LAW AND HISTORY

Jefferson's theorization of this textual, material idea of constitutionalism was rooted in his uniquely extensive reading in the law, but in seeing himself at the colonial receiving end of a tradition of specifically English legal humanism, he was not alone. The colonial Virginian legal mind could be said to have constituted itself in its relation to the writings of Sir Edward Coke, who provided a representation of the past of the law as authoritatively constructed through centuries of unbroken tradition and transmission. At the Court of Common Pleas and later the Lord Chief Justice at the Court of King's Bench and a member of Parliament, Coke (1552–1634) sought to consolidate a legal and parliamentary basis for balancing the power of the Crown in an institutional narrative of the development of a mixed British constitution over time. Coke's jurisprudence played a foundational role in seventeenth-century English law and constitutional conflict, and for colonial law, constitutional conflict, and historical self-understanding well into the eighteenth century. His famous decision in *Calvin's Case* in 1608 confirming the common law protections of the *post-nati*, Scots born after the ascension of James VI as James I, outlined a customary basis not only for that legal protection but for the legal status of all peoples living under the Crown's authority.

The decision formed the basis for subsequent articulations of the legal theory of the British Empire in the early modern period. Even so, it was less any particular case or idea than the narrative of unbroken historical development and the description of that narrative's proper mode of study that most appealed to elite Virginians. With rare and limited opportunities to procure the latest court reports and treatises and in the context of an even cloudier jurisdictional structure and unsystematic legal culture than had existed in England before the eighteenth century, Virginians grounded their legal study in seventeenth-century law books, and Coke's in particular, up to the eve of the revolution. It has been argued that in different ways colonists carried into the conflict of the imperial crisis what amounted to a seventeenth-century understanding of English constitutional arrangements, one predicated on bounded conflict of Crown and Parliament rather than the revolutionary settlement of 1689, and that makes a lot of sense – colonists were anchoring their understanding of themselves in their reading of seventeenth-century books and arguments.[16] Just as importantly, elite colonists were

[16] Jack P. Greene, *Negotiated Authorities: Essays in Colonial Political and Constitutional History* (Charlottesville: University of Virginia Press, 1994); "Law and the Origins of the American Revolution," *Cambridge History of Law in America: Volume I*, Bruce H. Mann and Christopher Tomlins, ed. (Cambridge: Cambridge University Press, 2008), pp. 447–81; *The Constitutional Origins of the American Revolution* (Cambridge: Cambridge University Press, 2010); Eric Nelson, *The Royal Revolution:*

compelled to demonstrate to themselves and colonial and metropolitan audiences alike their own sharing in the history of English law and legal learning. The anxieties surrounding this effort produced the nervous constructions of law and history that characterized colonial constitutional argument, and exercised a formative influence on Jefferson's thought.

Looking back from Jefferson's vantage point, it would be difficult to overstate the importance of the philosophical and historiographical issues that characterized seventeenth-century English constitutional conflict to subsequent debates about law and sovereignty in the Atlantic world. In his voluminous writings on the English common law, Coke painted a picture of legal learning as an almost impossible exercise in antiquarian erudition, an adventure into the rolls and records that marked the development of the common law through judicial decisions. These records, Coke asserted, bore witness to a continuous historical experience that dated back before the Norman Conquest to the practice and principles of the ancient constitution.[17] Such a framing of his narrative of legal history placed Coke in a continental discourse of historically informed legal

Monarchy and the American Founding (Cambridge: MA, Harvard University Press, 2013). On the jurisprudence of the imperial constitution as a formative context, see Charles McIlwain, *The American Revolution; A Constitutional Interpretation* (New York: Macmillan, 1924); Charles McLean Andrews, *The Colonial Background to the American Revolution: Four Essays in Colonial History* (New Haven: Yale University Press, 1924); Barbara A. Black, "The Constitution of Empire: The Case for the Colonists," *University of Pennsylvania Law Review*, Vol. 124, No. 5 (May, 1976), pp. 1157–1211; Mary Sarah Bilder, *The Transatlantic Constitution: Colonial Legal Culture and the Empire* (Cambridge, MA: Harvard University Press, 2004); Daniel J. Hulsebosch, *Constituting Empire: New York and the Transformation of Constitutionalism in the Atlantic World, 1664–1830* (Chapel Hill: University of North Carolina Press, 2005); Alison LaCroix, *The Ideological Origins of American Federalism* (Cambridge, MA: Harvard University Press, 2010); Aziz Rana, *The Two Faces of American Freedom* (Cambridge, MA: Harvard University Press, 2010); Craig Yirush, *Settlers, Liberty, and Empire: The Roots of Early American Political Theory, 1675–1775* (Cambridge: Cambridge University Press, 2011); Andrew Fitzmaurice, *Sovereignty, Property, and Empire, 1500–2000* (Cambridge: Cambridge University Press, 2014).

17 Stephen D. White, *Sir Edward Coke and the "Grievances of the Commonwealth," 1621–1628* (Chapel Hill: University of North Carolina Press, 1979); Pocock, *The Ancient Constitution and the Feudal Law*; J.W. Tubbs, *The Common Law Mind: Medieval and Early Modern Conceptions* (Baltimore: Johns Hopkins University Press, 2000); Michael Lobban, *A History of the Philosophy of Law in the Common Law World, 1600–1900* (Heidelberg: Springer, 2005); Alan Cromartie, *The Constitutionalist Revolution: An Essay on the History of England, 1450–1642* (Cambridge: Cambridge University Press, 2006); Kunal M. Parker, *Common Law, History, and Democracy in America, 1790–1900* (Cambridge: Cambridge University Press, 2011); David Chan Smith, *Sir Edward Coke and the Reformation of the Laws: Religion, Politics, and Jurisprudence, 1578–1616* (Cambridge: Cambridge University Press, 2014).

criticism and humanism that, in respective local contexts, had sought to provide a historical and institutional basis for local constitutional order that had existed independently of the Roman Empire and its more contemporary incarnation in the authority claimed over the earth by the Roman Catholic Church. Coke's aims in the performance of his erudition were squarely in the present. His image of the judge as antiquarian-in-chief communicated an intensely textual experience of law and legal learning, painting the practice of law as a sacred discipline of immersion, transformation, and retrieval.[18] Likewise, the antiquity and continuity of the common law and the corresponding assertion of the antiquity of parliament configured sovereignty as made in history rather than given by nature, and as inherently split across intertwined institutions. The historical erudition claimed for practitioners of the law by Coke carried with it a performative edge, cloaking his judicial authority in a narrative that because of its antiquity and continuity was carefully configured as unassailable.[19]

Crucial to Coke's narrative as developed in his four-volume *Institutes of the Laws of England* (1628–44) was the assertion of the insularity of

[18] In this Coke, and even more so his followers, were not unlike his critical predecessors in Bartolus of Sassoferrato (1314–57), Lorenzo Valla (1407–57), the Gallic theorist Francois Hotman (1524–90), and the German Herman Corning (1606–81); see Quentin Skinner, *Foundations of Modern Political Thought, Volume I: The Renaissance* (Cambridge: Cambridge University Press, 1978); Donald R. Kelley, *Foundations of Modern Historical Scholarship: Language, Law and History in the French Renaissance* (New York: Columbia University Press, 1970); *Francois Hotman: A Revolutionary's Ordeal* (Princeton: Princeton University Press, 1973); *The Human Measure: Social Thought in the Western Legal Tradition* (Cambridge, MA: Harvard University Press, 1990); Constantin Fasolt, *The Limits of History* (Chicago: University of Chicago Press, 1994).

[19] Pocock, The Ancient Constitution and the Feudal Law; see also Pocock, "The Origins of the Study of the Past: A Comparative Approach," (1962) reprinted in J.G.A. Pocock, *Political Thought and History: Essays on Theory and Method* (Cambridge: Cambridge University Press, 2009), pp. 145–86; others have argued that Coke's wider project was even more directly political and more explicitly engaged with defining his terms in more narrowly suited purposes relative a more politically contested discursive context, see Quentin Skinner, "History and Ideology in the English Revolution," (1965) reprinted in Skinner, *Visions of Politics, Volume III: Hobbes and Civil Science* (Cambridge: Cambridge University Press, 2002), pp. 238–63; Howard Nenner, *By Colour of Law: Legal Culture and Constitutional Politics in England, 1660–1689* (Chicago: University of Chicago Press, 1977); Glenn Burgess, *The Politics of the Ancient Constitution: An Introduction to English Political Thought, 1603–1642* (State College: Penn State University Press, 1993); Janelle Greenberg, *The Radical Face of the Ancient Constitution: St. Edward's 'Laws' in Early Modern Political Thought* (Cambridge: Cambridge University Press, 2001).

the English common law and its historical development. To the extent that he could, Coke was compelled to marginalize evidence of the legal consequences of the Norman Conquest, namely the development of what would later come to be called the feudal laws.[20] Coke's most famous work, *Commentary upon Littleton*, the first volume of the *Institutes*, consisted of marginal glosses on the fifteenth-century tract of Thomas Littleton on land tenures in English law, and served to monumentalize Littleton's assertion of the antiquity of what would later be called "feudal" laws of property at the expense of previous core texts.[21] Outlining the distinct branches of English law and the courts that exercised jurisdiction over them, Coke established an intellectual and institutional continuity underwriting the laws of land tenure recorded by Littleton.[22] This was a narrative of continuity of constitutional order and laws relating to customary rights and property transmission that assumed the pre-Conquest, ancient origins of much of what previous authors had described in terms of Roman and feudal legal concepts. The second volume of the *Institutes*, on Magna Carta and written or statute law, carried out a similar project of establishing secure continuity, providing

[20] This entailed marginalizing linguistic evidence, too. Bradin Cormack has described as the "embarrassment" of the presence of law-French and recourse to Roman juridical concepts (particularly in real property law) in the traditional signposts of English law and in alternative jurisdictions of Chancery and ecclesiastical jurisprudence; see Bradin Cormack, *A Power to Do Justice: Jurisdiction, English Literature, and the Rise of the Common Law* (Chicago: University of Chicago Press, 2008).

[21] Namely, the medieval works of "Glanville" and the collection under the name of Henry de Bracton's *De legibus et consuetudinibus Angliae*. In the text historically attributed to Bracton, the chief justice of the court that would become King's Bench and a member of the clergy, several authors outline a relatively immediately post-Conquest, comprehensive picture of the English legal system within the framework of the Roman civil law and ecclesiastical law that were the predominant modes of legal education in thirteenth century England; see Frederick Pollock and Frederic William Maitland, *The History of English Law Before the Time of Edward I*, S.F.C. Milsom, ed. (Cambridge: Cambridge University Press, 2nd edn., 1968), Vol. 1, ch. 5–7; James A. Brundage, *The Medieval Origins of the Legal Profession: Canonists, Civilians, and Courts* (Chicago: University of Chicago Press, 2008); Thomas McSweeney, "English Judges and Roman Jurists: The Civilian Learning Behind England's First Case Law," *Temple Law Review* Vol. 84, No. 4 (Summer, 2012), pp. 827–62.

[22] On the composition of the first volume of the *Institutes* and the 13 volumes of Coke's *Reports*, and in particular Coke's own reading and note-taking practices, see J.H. Baker, "Coke's Note-Books and the Sources of His Reports," *The Cambridge Law Journal* Vol. 30, No. 1 (Apr., 1972), pp. 59–86, and Allen D. Boyer, "Sir Edward Coke, Ciceronianus: Classical Rhetoric and the Common Law Tradition," *International Journal for the Semiotics of Law* Vol. 10, No. 28 (1997), pp. 3–36.

glosses on the baronial document that selectively traced its continuous use in Parliament up to Coke's present. As a Member of Parliament and an eloquent defender of Parliament's constitutional authority, Coke anchored his arguments in the debates leading to the Petition of Right in 1628 in the legal authority of Magna Carta.[23]

This articulation of a "common law mind" relied on the assertion of a legal continuity, the origins of which lay in time immemorial. There was little if any apparent need to acknowledge the reality of constitutional revolution amid dramatic social and political change as had occurred under the Norman Conquest, and was again occurring in the transition from a "feudal" to post-enclosure, mercantilist, and commercial society.[24] Coke's conventionalism was intended to monumentalize custom and convention, and locate the legitimate understanding of the authoritative common law in the intellectual labor of the common law judge. In his tracing of the different branches of jurisdiction in the first volume of the *Institutes*, Coke had defined and developed English common law as "artificial reason." Reason, Coke wrote, "is the life of the Law, nay the Common Law itself is nothing but reason, which is to be understood as an artificial perfection of reason, gotten by long study, observation, and experience, and not of every man's natural reason." Likewise, Coke defined equity as "the assemblage of things that make equality among all people," and "the perfection of that reason [i.e., that artificial reason] that interprets and improves the written law."[25] Previous authorities had also defined equity as the application of principles of natural justice to the final interpretation of written law, equally amenable to and indeed a constituent component of the common law, and as such an essential tool

[23] Stephen D. White, *Sir Edward Coke and the "Grievances of the Commonwealth," 1621–1628* (Chapel Hill: University of North Carolina Press, 1979); James R. Stoner, Jr., *Common Law and Liberal Theory: Coke, Hobbes, and the Origins of American Constitutionalism* (Lawrence: University of Kansas Press, 1992); Alan Cromartie, *The Constitutionalist Revolution: An Essay on the History of England, 1450–1642* (Cambridge: Cambridge University Press, 2006); Paul D. Halliday, *Habeas Corpus: From England to Empire* (Cambridge, MA: Harvard University Press, 2010).

[24] On the ideological configuration, and in fact invention, of feudalism in jurisprudence as a category against which early modern and modern law and historical thought could measure itself and define the legitimacy of its own specifically modern history and power relations, see Kathleen Davis, *Periodization and Sovereignty: How Ideas of Feudalism and Secularism Govern the Politics of Time* (Philadelphia: University of Pennsylvania Press, 2008).

[25] Sir Edward Coke, *Selected Writings and Speeches of Sir Edward Coke*, Vol. 2, Steve Sheppard, ed. (Indianapolis: Liberty Fund, 2005), p. 701.

in the hands of the common law judge.[26] But for Coke, equity was firmly in the hands overseeing the supreme jurisdiction of the common law, and not a rival or even coequal jurisdiction of conscience and natural law in its own right.

If equitable interpretation was the province of the common law judge, the precise function of the Chancellor's jurisdiction as an institutional representation of the King's conscience was drastically reduced. This was certainly part of Coke's project at the Court of King's Bench: in 1616, Coke directly challenged the power of then Lord Chancellor Ellesmere by accusing him of committing *praemunire*, the recognition of foreign ecclesiastical jurisdiction, in Ellesmere's granting of injunctions against decisions at common law. Coke only relented when James I intervened, precipitating the end of Coke's tenure and three tumultuous years of jurisdictional conflict with the Chancery.[27] Certainly, Coke wanted to avoid ceding the high ground of judicature to the office of the Chancellor, but if the common law together with the statute law was the embodiment of reason, perfecting itself naturally over time, Coke's dramatically innovative arguments about his own power raised the question of why equity would need to be a separate branch of interpretation at all. If the common law in its pristine, ancient form had been the acknowledged

[26] Sir John Fortescue, *On the Laws and Governance of England*, Shelly Lockwood, ed. (Cambridge: Cambridge University Press, 1997); Christopher St. German, *St. German's Doctor and Student*, T.F.T. Plunkett and J.L. Barton, ed. (London: Selden Society, 1974); Cromartie, *The Constitutionalist Revolution*, ch. 1–2. Aristotle had defined *epieikeia* as the rules of an unchanging natural order that subsisted amid the processes of change that characterized politics and civil law, lending itself in particular cases to the "rectification of legal justice." Focusing on institutions, the author of the *Rhetorica ad Herennium* understood *aequitas* as the totality of justice that encompassed all of the legal and political strands of Roman life – maxims that guaranteed "each his own right, for the dignity of all;" see Aristotle, *Nicomachean Ethics*, H. Rackham, trans. (Cambridge, MA: Harvard University Press, 1934), pp. 11–13; "Cicero," *Rhetorica ad Herennium*, Harry Caplan, trans. (Cambridge, MA: Harvard University Press, 1954); Aldo Schiavone, *The Invention of Law in the West*, Jeremy Carden and Anthony Shugaar, trans. (Cambridge, MA: Harvard University Press, 2012), pp. 299–305; on the development of equity as supplementary to the English common law and dealings with wills and trusts, see F.W. Maitland, *Equity: A Course of Lectures*, John Brunyate, ed. (Cambridge: Cambridge University Press, 1939), pp. 1–42; "right" in this case was class-specific, and corresponded not to an anonymous equality before the law, but to a consideration of what general principles of justice were due to particular members of a polity in particular cases. This tension between universal, natural justice and contextual, case-specific particularity would prove a persistent one.

[27] Louis A. Knafla, *Law and Politics in Jacobean England: The Tracts of Lord Chancellor Ellesmere* (Cambridge: Cambridge University Press, 1977); Cromartie, *The Constitutionalist Revolution*, ch. 6–7.

application of reason at the time of the ancient constitution, and added upon and reauthorized as such ever since, what kind of reason did equity provide that a legal tradition described by its champions and authorities as the perfect embodiment of reason could not? These questions plagued jurists of the early seventeenth century, and served as the vocabulary through which legal and political theorists confronted and articulated fundamental issues of the location and origin of sovereignty in the English constitutional edifice.

The consolidation of state power in the Crown that took place during the reign of Tudor monarchs in the sixteenth century brought to the fore fundamental issues of the stability, legitimacy, and historical primacy of the English common law. Francis Bacon (1561–1626), a clerk of the controversial Star Chamber, Queen's Counsel to Elizabeth I and Lord Chancellor for James I, used his own position as an advisor to the Crown and the chief legal officer of the realm to argue for the necessity of strengthening royal prerogative and the independence of the crown from the normal operation of the common law and parliamentary oversight.[28] The chief instruments for Bacon's vision of an enlightened state apparatus were a broad program of legal reform that included codification of the worrying volume and complexity of the various yearbooks, treatises, statutes, and reports that made up the English legal edifice. He also sought to strengthen the jurisdiction of Chancery over which he presided as the Chancellor in the name of the Crown. Both of these projects would remove considerable interpretive power from the common law judges that Coke understood to be the final arbiters of the law. Legal reform and consolidated statutes, in theory, would remove the image of arcane erudition attached to the interpretive power of the judge, and a strengthened Chancery would be in a better position to compete with the Court of King's Bench and thus enable the Chancellor to more directly protect and assert the interests of the Crown in legal and constitutional disputes.

For Bacon, the triumph of reason over mysticism and superstition required a close relationship between natural philosophy and the activities of the state.[29] A sovereign ruler, versed in philosophically informed

[28] Perez Zagorin, *Francis Bacon* (Princeton: Princeton University Press, 1998); see also Michael J. Braddick, *State Formation in Early Modern England, c. 1550–1700* (Cambridge: Cambridge University Press, 2000).

[29] Doing research in archives, most notably the manuscripts in the library of Sir John Cotton, perhaps the greatest English antiquarian of the seventeenth century, Bacon deployed the methodology appropriate to the humanistic culture of the Renaissance,

discourses of the reason of state, and advised by men who could straddle the gap between philosophy and politics, would be in a position to master the uncertainty of international politics and calculations of national interest. Only such a prince could wield the image of an enlightened state with a single head against domestic challenges from the growing power of the judiciary and its strong historical relationship to Parliament. Bacon's *Elements of the Common Lawes of England*, written in the 1590s for Queen Elizabeth, set down basic principles of law and constitutional order as groundwork to his advocacy for a general project of law reform. His *Essays, or Counsels Civil and Moral*, composed earlier but not published until 1625, amounted to a series of similar principles, maxims, and lessons of prudent conduct and statecraft, a set of conceptual tools for the prince that defined law as amenable to the methods of natural and not artificial reason.

Thomas Hobbes (1588–1679), for all of Coke's legal conservatism, astutely saw in Coke's framing of the transmission of legal language over time a threat to the ordering of speech, of signs, and therefore of law and politics. Coke had found it necessary to distinguish artificial and natural reason, but left the cleanliness of this crucial distinction in question. In his most famous work, *Leviathan*, Hobbes attacked the notion of the customary origins of law and language in developing and continuous usage. "Ignorance of the causes, and originall constitution of Right, Equity, Law, and Justice, disposeth a man to make Custome and Example the rule of his actions," he asserted. The idea that precedent was a reliable basis for deciding right and wrong ignored the fact that

sifting through source material to build an empirical basis for narratives of civil government for his *History of the Reign of Henry VII*; see Richard Tuck, *Philosophy and Government, 1572–1621* (Cambridge: Cambridge University Press, 1993); Markku Peltonen, *Classical Humanism and Republicanism in English Political Thought, 1570–1640* (Cambridge: Cambridge University Press, 1995); Anthony Musson, "Myth, Mistake, and Invention: Excavating the Foundations of the English Legal Tradition," *Law and History: Current Legal Issues* Vol. 6 (2003), pp. 63–81; Michael Lobban, "Custom, Nature, and Authority: The Origins of English Legal Positivism," *The British and their Laws in the Eighteenth Century*, David Lemmings, ed. (London: Boydell, 2005), pp. 27–58; Cromartie, *The Constitutionalist Revolution*, ch. 7, Jennifer Summit, *Memory's Library: Medieval Books in Early Modern England* (Chicago: University of Chicago Press, 2008); on print and legal change in common law thought, see Richard J. Ross, "The Memorial Culture of Early Modern English Lawyers: Memory as Keyword, Shelter, and Identity, c. 1560–1640," *Yale Journal of Law and Humanities* Vol. 10 (Summer, 1998), pp. 229–324; Ian Williams, "'He Creditted More the Printed Booke': Common Lawyers' Receptivity to Print, c. 1550–1640)," *Law and History Review* Vol. 28, No. 1 (Feb., 2010), 39–70.

people "appeale from custome to reason, and from reason to custome, as it serves their turn..., Which is the cause, that the doctrine of Right and Wrong, is perpetually disputed, both by the Pen and the Sword."[30] Tradition and the grounding of one's thought in it was a rhetorical move, and the instability and contingency of naming, defining, and interpreting made the sacred authority of precedent a dangerous public myth.

At stake in this critique of Coke was the location and character of sovereignty, or the recognized power to make and decide the law. "The Sovereign of a Common-wealth, be it an Assembly, or one Man, is not Subject to the Civill Lawes," as a consequence of the ability to make and repeal them. It followed that "the Law of Nature and the Civill Law, contain each other, and are of equal extent. For the Lawes of Nature, which consist in Equity, Justice, Gratitude, and other morall Vertues" depend on the establishment of the civil law, which in turn depends on the natural laws that cause men to seek peace and obey for purposes of self-preservation.[31] Just so, natural law enforced civil law, and civil law constituted the natural law as law in the commonwealth. This squaring of natural and civil law made the distinction between equity and common law, or between natural and artificial reason, nothing but a grievous error. Citing Coke's tract on Littleton, Hobbes reasoned that if "law can never be against reason," as it was only reasonable to obey the law, then the reason that decided on and applied the law could not be the "artificiall Perfection of Reason," gotten not from the study of the cumulative wisdom of judges, but the point of singular reason the artifice authorized as the head of the body politic, the sovereign.

In his later *Dialogue between a Philosopher and a Student of the Common Laws of England*, Hobbes delivered an extended battering of Coke's failure to square the relationship between equity and the common law. As the student suggests, "seeing all Judges in all Courts out to Judge according to Equity, which is the Law of Reason, a distinct Court of Equity seemeth to me to be unnecessary." Indeed, responds Hobbes, the philosopher, "if Judges could not err; but since they may err, and that the King is not Bound to any other Law but that of Equity, it belongs to him alone to give Remedy to them that by the Ignorance, or Corruption of a

[30] Thomas Hobbes, *Leviathan* (1651), Noel Malcolm, ed. (Oxford: Oxford University Press, *Clarendon Edition of the Works of Thomas Hobbes*, Vol. 4, 2012), Vol. 2, p. 158.

[31] Hobbes, *ibid*, pp. 416–18.

Judge shall suffer damage."[32] Law, or equity, in this logic was nothing other than the published command of the sovereign. Hobbes enshrined equitable interpretation as the key to the sole and superior jurisdiction of the sovereign. In doing so he radicalized Bacon's project of using Chancery jurisdiction to further the interests of the royal prerogative into an understanding of equity as the conceptual and constitutional superior to the highest branch of the common law. The conscience of the sovereign alone was the final arbiter of legal meaning.[33]

In his critique, Hobbes affirmed a body of research into legal history that cast doubt on Coke's narrative of the untroubled continuity of the common law. Historical theorists of English law pursued Coke's depiction of law as in large part an antiquarian discipline, and did so with much greater accuracy than Coke had been able or willing to carry out himself. Hobbes' skeptical critique of customary concepts of law, which went hand in hand in with his critique of republican concepts of liberty, picked up on the work of the royalist scholar Henry Spelman, who argued contra Coke and his successors that the Norman Conquest had

32 Hobbes, *A Dialogue between a philosopher and a student of the common laws of England* (printed 1681), in *Thomas Hobbes: Writings on Common Law and Hereditary Right*, Alan Cromartie and Quentin Skinner, ed. (Oxford: Oxford University Press, *Clarendon Edition of the Works of Thomas Hobbes*, Vol. 11, 2005), p. 31; see Richard Tuck, *Natural Rights Theories: Their Origin and Development* (Cambridge: Cambridge University Press, 1979); David Johnston, *The Rhetoric of Leviathan: Thomas Hobbes and the Politics of Cultural Transformation* (Princeton: Princeton University Press, 1986); Deborah Baumgold, *Hobbes' Political Theory* (Cambridge: Cambridge University Press, 1988); Noberto Bobbio, *Thomas Hobbes and the Natural Law Tradition*, Daniela Gobetti, trans. (Chicago: University of Chicago Press, 1993); Quentin Skinner, *Reason and Rhetoric in the Philosophy of Hobbes* (Cambridge: Cambridge University Press, 1997); for the importance of the organization of speech and writing to Hobbes' political philosophy, see Tracy B. Strong, "How to Write Scripture: Words, Authority, and Politics in Thomas Hobbes," *Critical Inquiry* Vol. 20, No. 1 (Autumn, 1993), pp. 128–29; Noel Malcom, *Aspects of Hobbes* (Oxford: Oxford University Press, 2002); Philip Pettit, *Made with Words: Hobbes on Language, Mind, and Politics* (Princeton: Princeton University Press, 2009); on Hobbes and legal thought, see James R. Stoner, Jr., *Common Law and Liberal Theory: Coke, Hobbes, and the Origins of American Constitutionalism* (Lawrence: University of Kansas Press, 1992); *Hobbes and the Law*, David Dyzenhaus and Thomas Poole, ed. (Cambridge: Cambridge University Press, 2012); Paul Downes, *Hobbes, Sovereignty, and Early American Literature* (Cambridge: Cambridge University Press, 2015).

33 And as Paul Halliday has shown in his study of *habeas corpus*, the equitable power of the prerogative was claimed by King's Bench judges, including Coke, in their own assertions of jurisdictional superiority over other courts, illustrating the centrality of that power across formal jurisdictional boundaries, even in a context of jurisdictional conflict; see Paul D. Halliday, *Habeas Corpus: From England to Empire* (Cambridge, MA: Harvard University Press, 2010).

indeed brought about a revolution in both private and public law, introducing feudal land tenures and the historical primacy of the Crown.[34] Finding linguistic evidence of the European origins of the laws governing real property and inheritance from even before the Norman Conquest up to the recent past (and the use of Chancery jurisdiction to get around feudal constraints on increasingly commercial, moveable property), Spelman employed historical critique to cast doubt on the common law tradition.[35] This constitutional skepticism was at least partially incorporated by the common lawyers of the Stuart period and beyond into a revised, more complicated picture of the development of

[34] Pocock, *The Ancient Constitution and the Feudal Law*, pp. 94–103; Kunal Parker's study of the concepts of time in British and American jurisprudence before legal realism builds on Pocock's analysis of the mythical, even ahistorical character of the common law mind before the nineteenth century, but we risk overlooking how important antiquarian intellectual culture was to the self-image of the common lawyer, and how beset that self-image was by alternative political uses of historical narration on both the Leveller left and the Royalist right; Kunal M. Parker, *Common Law, History, and Democracy in America, 1790–1900: Legal Thought before Modernism* (Cambridge: Cambridge University Press, 2011), ch. 1. One could go so far as to say that the historicality of the common law mind, in the midst of the upheavals of constitutional politics from 1628 through the Interregnum, forced on its adherents a confrontation with historicity and a participation in a politics of historiography.

[35] On the use of Chancery courts, see Charles M. Gray, *Copy-Hold, Equity, and the Common Law* (Cambridge, MA: Harvard University Press, 1963); on the role of civil and natural law concepts more broadly, see D.J. Ibbetson, *A Historical Introduction to the Law of Obligations* (Oxford: Oxford University Press, 1999); "Natural Law and Common Law," *Edinburgh Law Review* 5 (2001), pp. 4–20; R.H. Helmholz, *Natural Law in Court: A History of Legal Theory in Practice* (Cambridge, MA: Harvard University Press, 2015). As the Whig ascendency and the Glorious Revolution solidified Parliamentary sovereignty and the basis of the language of the common law as the *lingua franca* of English jurisprudence and constitutional politics, it was nevertheless possible in the eighteenth century to attach to the independence of equitable jurisdiction the threat of the undoing of the structural integrity of the entire British constitutional edifice as it was by then understood. Equity, John Selden wrote in the posthumously published *Table Talk*, is in law "the same that the Spirit is in Religion, what everyone pleases to make it." It was in fact a "Rouguish thing," nearly the direct opposite of law, where "we have a measure" and "know what to trust to." Indeed, as John Fortescue-Aland, whose edition of the writings of the early theorist of English law John Fortescue Jefferson recorded in his legal commonplace book, suggested, "to have no rule to decide controversies, but the rule of Equity, is to begin the world again." Equity threatened to unravel "the fine and close texture of the law which has been so many hundred years in the making;" see John Selden, *The Table-Talk of John Selden: With Biographical Preface and Notes* (Cambridge: Cambridge University Press, 2015); John Fortescue-Aland, preface to *The Difference between an Absolute and Limited Monarchy; As it more particularly regards the English Constitution. Being a Treatise written by Sir John Fortescue, Kt.* (London: William Bowyer, 2nd edn, 1719), p. xii.

the institution of Parliament and the historical inseparability of written from immemorial or natural, unwritten law.

Indeed, legal antiquarians and historians of the common law and judges such as John Selden (1558–1654) and Sir Matthew Hale (1609–76) remained driven to refute the absolutist doubt of the antiquity of Parliament and with it the primacy of the customary grounds of law, even as they complicated Coke's narrative of the principled continuity of the ancient constitution and the sole province of its interpretation in common law adjudication, or for that matter in Parliament.[36] Selden, an antiquarian and polymath, made the recognition of the historical reality of legal and jurisdictional transformation, particularly after 1066, safe for the common law, defending royal claims to possession of the English Channel as having been customarily established by principles of the law of nature and nations which governed acquisitions of landed territory, and arguing on a more philosophical level that the common law itself was infused with natural law. This made it possible to construct the common law as kind of an idealized instantiation of natural law. As J.G.A. Pocock notes, "custom might be idealized and described as perfect equity," at the same time that it made it possible to bind the use of equity as an extension of the prerogative with custom, observing a history of it having been so.[37] Like canons and digests of the civil law, Hale argued in his *History of the Common Law of England*, the ancient and unwritten laws of the common law, as distinguished from written statutes, were known to the present through records and histories and so themselves formed part of the written body of material that made up law and its history. "All those Laws," Hale wrote of the *lex non scripta*, "have their several Monuments in Writing, whereby they are transferr'd from one Age to another, and without which they would soon lose all kind of Certainty."[38] The effect of this historical approach was a depiction of jurisdictional authority and even

[36] Alan Cromartie, *Sir Matthew Hale, 1609–1676: Law, Religion, and Natural Philosophy* (Cambridge: Cambridge University Press, 1995), pp. 103–17; Pocock, *The Ancient Constitution and the Feudal Law*, pp. 170–8; Julia Rudolph, *Common Law and Enlightenment in England, 1689–1750* (Woodbridge: Boydell Press, 2013).

[37] Pocock, *Ancient Constitution and the Feudal Law*, p. 24; indeed, this was the work of Hale's *Historia placitae coronoam*, circulated in manuscript and not published until 1726, much like *The History of the Common Law of England*, not published until 1713.

[38] Sir Matthew Hale, *History of the Common Law of England*, Charles M. Gray, ed. (Chicago: University of Chicago Press, 1971), p. 16.

sovereignty itself as a kind of contract perpetually, if tacitly, enacted. It was "long and immemorial Usage, and by the strength of Custom and Reception in this Kingdom," that made the common law the law – the substance of these laws was in writing, but "the formal and obliging Force and Power of them grows by long Custom and Use."[39] Common law adjudication was for Hale and his successors a historical tool for the extended negotiation and enforcement of binding promises and agreements between the crown, the people, and the judges.

The effect of the increasingly historical studies through which common lawyers situated their subject in the political and intellectual currents of their time was the construction of a historically inflected framework for political theory. This was a set of available conjunctions of law and history in which even republicans and revolutionaries like Algernon Sidney (1623–83) and John Locke (1632–1704) could both find inspiration. Both argued that legitimate authority was rooted in historical agreements about the bounds of that authority between rulers and ruled, and both sought to grant greater legitimacy to the at once jurisprudential and constitutional role of the ruled as final judges of the terms of their contracts.[40] It cannot be doubted that this combination of

[39] Hale, *ibid*, p. 17; see Cromartie, *Sir Matthew Hale, 1609–1676*, pp. 30–9. For Hale, this involved a rebuke of the collapsing of common law and equity, and a redefinition of appropriate intellectual activity not as creature as a kind of craftsmanship of custom and habit, "taken complexedly when the reasonable facultie is in Conjunction with the reasonable Subject, and habituated to it by Use and Exercise," and so in a significant sense not the same kind of certain knowledge aimed at by the mathematician or in any use of natural faculty of reason on its own: "And upon all this that hath been said it appears that men are not borne Comon Lawyers, neither can the bare Exerciss of the Faculty of Reason give a man a Sufficient Knowledge of it, but it must be gained by the habituateing and accustomeing and Exerciseing that Faculty by reading, Study, and observation to give a Man a compleate Knowledge thereof. And although a man that hath long and Industriously Exercised himself in that Study cannot p'tend either to Infallibilitie in his Judgment or to a full attainment of all that is attaineable toucheing the Laws of England, yett he will be much better fitted for right Judgment therein...," Hale, "Reflections by the Lord Chiefe Justice Hale on Mr. Hobbes his Dialogue of the Lawe," printed in W.S. Holdsworth, *A History of English Law: Volume V* (London: Methuen and Co., 2nd edn., 1937), p. 501, p. 505, see pp. 499–513.

[40] Caroline Robbins, *The Eighteenth Century Commonwealthman* (Cambridge, MA: Harvard University Press, 1961); Bernard Bailyn, *The Ideological Origins of the American Revolution* (Cambridge, MA: Harvard University Press, 1967); Gordon S. Wood, *The Creation of the American Republic, 1776–1787* (Chapel Hill: University of North Carolina Press, 1968); J.G.A. Pocock, *The Machiavellian Moment: Florentine Political Thought and the Atlantic Republican Tradition* (Princeton: Princeton University Press, 1975); J.G.A. Pocock and Richard Ashcraft, *John Locke: Papers Read at a Clark Library Seminar, 10 December 1977* (Los Angeles: Clark Memorial Library, 1980), Richard

rights discourse and civic, even popular constitutionalism exercised a powerful influence on eighteenth-century political thought and on that of the American Revolution in particular. That being said, at least for Jefferson, as a result of how the legal status of colonies came to be contested and defined, and of how he came to think about law and history himself in these respective contexts, the earlier history of English legal learning and British constitutionalism show up in his thought in two important and distinct ways. First, the settler response to the imperial crisis that preceded the war for colonial independence took the form of a variety of attempts to establish access to the history of customary liberty recounted and developed by Coke and Hale. Jefferson was more attuned than most to the fact that Americans found themselves in a heated political contest over history, and that like the common lawyers before them they found themselves in a contest over historiography, over the criteria for establishing the variable narratives of continuity and discontinuity in play. For Jefferson, this made revolutionary politics a question of the affirmation and possession of a collective history. Secondly, Jefferson pushed on this awareness of the conjunction of law, equity, history, and constitutional politics. In his effort to think through how republican law and constitutionalism could be put into practice, he would turn his attention to the project of constituting a very particular kind of historical subjectivity, one imagined in turn as a particular kind of use. This attention is important for understanding Jefferson's thought, but it is equally important in drawing our own renewed attention to the conjunctions of law and history at work in the political thought of the American Revolution and founding, and to the histories of these conjunctions to be observed and represented in the present.

Ashcraft, *Revolutionary Politics and Locke's Two Treatises of Government* (Princeton: Princeton University Press, 1986); Jonathan Scott, *Algernon Sidney and the English Republic, 1623–1677* (Cambridge: Cambridge University Press, 1988); and *Algernon Sidney and the Restoration Crisis, 1677–1683* (Cambridge: Cambridge University Press, 1991); Alan Houston, *Algernon Sidney and the Republican Heritage in England and America* (Princeton: Princeton University Press, 1991); Annabel Patterson, *Early Modern Liberalism* (Cambridge: Cambridge University Press, 1997); Lee Ward, *The Politics of Liberty in England and Revolutionary America* (Cambridge: Cambridge University Press, 2004); John Marshall, *John Locke: Resistance, Religion, and Responsibility* (Cambridge: Cambridge University Press, 1994), and *John Locke, Toleration, and Early Enlightenment Culture* (Cambridge: Cambridge University Press, 2010); Steve Pincus, *1688: The First Modern Revolution* (New Haven: Yale University Press, 2009).

JEFFERSON'S USES

J.G.A. Pocock describes this particular strand of historical consciousness and its lasting impact on early modern Atlantic political thought in *The Machiavellian Moment*: "when in the course of human events, unstable and fluctuating in time as they were, a contingency arose which was not already integrated into usage, the first steps must be taken toward attending to that integration."[41] Experience, mediated and represented in custom, stitched together the inherent instability and fragmentation of finite political life carried out in historical time. For Pocock, in examining the history of such experience as theorized and articulated in the history of legal, political, and historical thought, we are clued into something elemental about belonging to a particular polity: "Societies exist in time, and conserve images of themselves as continuously so existing," and so "the understanding of time, and of human life as experienced in time, disseminated in a society, is an important part of that society's understanding of itself—of its structure and what legitimates it, of the modes of action which are possible to it and in it."[42] Tradition, the "handing on of formed ways of acting, a formed way of living" constitutes the structure

[41] Pocock, The Machiavellian Moment, p. 25.

[42] Pocock, "Time, Institutions, and Action: An Essay on Traditions and Their Understanding," (1968) reprinted in Pocock, *Political Thought and History*, p. 187, see pp. 187–216; and it is in this attention to conditions and trajectories of intellectual practice, to transmission and use as practice, that I have found the work of Pocock on the history and politics of historiography to be useful in understanding Jefferson's place in this history, and perhaps surprisingly and counter-intuitively, in asserting that Jefferson has a place in that history at all; and it is also in this attention that I have found Pocock's thinking amenable, or at least in potential conversation with, materialist and radical as well as conservative attention to these processes and practices; see Hannah Arendt, "Walter Benjamin, 1892–1940," in Walter Benjamin, *Illuminations: Essays and Reflections* (New York: Schocken, 1968), pp. 1–58; Walter Benjamin, "Edward Fuchs, Collector and Historian," *Selected Writings, Volume 3: 1935–1938*, Howard Eiland and Michael W. Jennings, ed., trans. (Cambridge, MA: Harvard University Press, 2002); pp. 260–302; "On the Concept of History," and "Paralipomena to 'On the Concept of History," *Selected Writings, Volume 4: 1938–1940*, Howard Eiland and Michael W. Jennings, ed., trans. (Cambridge, MA: Harvard University Press, 2003), pp. 389–400, pp. 401–11; Henry S. Kariel, "Creating Political Reality," *American Political Science Review* Vol. 64, No. 4 (1970), pp. 1088–98; Raymond Williams, *Culture and Materialism* (London: Verso, 1980), Raphael Samuel, *Theaters of Memory: Volume 1: Past and Present in Contemporary Culture* (London: Verso, 1994); Norman W. Spaulding, "The Historical Consciousness of the Resistant Subject," *UC Irvine Law Review*, Vol. 1, No. 3 (Feb., 2012), pp. 101–15; Timothy Brennan, *Borrowed Light: Vico, Hegel, and the Colonies* (Stanford: Stanford University Press, 2014); see also Michael Oakeshott, *Rationalism in Politics and Other Essays* (London: Methuen, 1981); Bruce James Smith,

of the transmission of these constructed images of time, which unlike cosmic or geological time in which we also find ourselves, are "social and subjective" in origin. The thinking that Jefferson did in his life, this book argues, emerged in the context of a crisis in the structure of transmission of historically constituted identity through law. That thinking, eccentric and even marginal as it was, had a profound impact on the trajectory of United States history, and, "in the course of human events," it provides an opportunity to address ourselves to collected images of the past, some transmitted and others forgotten, but all having their origin in the context of a breakdown in the very processes of transmission and the practices that had guaranteed their meaning by attachment to the continuity of those processes in time.

If what gave provocation to Jefferson's thinking about the politics of law and history was fragmentation in the customary constitutionalism that underwrote civic identity for English colonials, what Jefferson confronted in his project of new-modeling law and government in the wake of that fragmentation was the problem of subjectivity, of what kind of participatory historical consciousness would be appropriate in a polity that had lost its access to the privilege of thinking of itself strictly in terms of the transmission of inherited practice through time.[43] In this context, Jefferson was compelled to think creatively about law and about the question of in whose hands it could be entrusted. Jefferson confronted the fundamental fact of plurality, of the multiplicity of laws, customs, usages, and histories that actually existed within the newly formed United

Politics and Remembrance: Republican Themes in Machiavelli, Burke, and Tocqueville (Princeton: Princeton University Press, 1985).

43 And in this sense, what I describe in the following two chapters of the book as the experience of a kind of cracked open historical consciousness can make Jefferson out to be something like Pocock's reference to Humpty Dumpty in Lewis Carroll's *Alice Through the Looking Glass*, who tells Alice he is master of his words, that he retains control of the meaning of his words and deeds, independently of the shared context of discourse, institutions, or what Pocock calls the "multivalence" of this context; for Jefferson, however, the more anxious securing of the condition of mastery follows from as much as it brings about kinds of fragmentation that become irrevocable, and Pocock relates his discussion of mastery directly to the history of the master-slave relationship. Stanley Cavell illuminates this point further, for it would indeed be a mistake to think that our only options are authoritative convention and sovereign mastery, or as he puts it: "Is W.C. Fields our only alternative to Humpty Dumpty?" See Pocock, "Verbalizing a Political Act," in *Political Thought and History: Essays on Theory and Method*, pp. 40–3; "Time Institutions, and Action: An Essay on Traditions and Their Understanding," pp. 202–11; Stanley Cavell, *Emerson's Transcendental Etudes* (Stanford: Stanford University Press, 2003), p. 96.

States. And it was in that context that Jefferson would come to frame his project as one of measuring and securing that particular subjectivity from its confrontation with others, and of circumscribing and defining the boundaries of historical capacity itself.

As a result, this book argues, not only the liberties and political lives of people and peoples with whom Jefferson shared a continent, a country, and a home but the liberties of the settler beneficiaries of his project were to a significant extent hollowed out. We are left with the brittle pieces of these histories. And we are left with the problem of how to remember and use them, together, and to see if it is possible to do so without falling further into readjusted traps of possession and mastery. This book uses Jefferson and with him the histories in which he participated and that he thought about and helped shape in exploring the possibility of a kind of historical practice tied to a direct awareness of itself as consisting in various modes of use, and as an activity of thought that is best carried out collectively. The fragile image of the past this project seeks to make available is that of a constitution: a community established in its laws and relations as embarked on the difficult task of working with and on its histories.[44] This book insists

[44] The direction of a good deal of recent work, in contrast to contextualist approaches to the history of political thought and critical legal studies, has been renewed interest in the philosophy of history not as critique, critical theory, or critical self-reflection but as the recovery of a kind of first philosophy or metaphysics of time, presence, and even of law, or at least, as the firm suggestion that historical practice, postmodern or otherwise, has a lot of trouble defining itself against these concerns without, ironically uncritically, assuming some of its own; on distinctive elaborations of context and political thought in history, see Quentin Skinner, *Meaning and Context: Quentin Skinner and His Critics*, James Tully, ed. (Princeton: Princeton University Press, 1988); James Tully, *Public Philosophy in a New Key* (Cambridge: Cambridge University Press, 2008), 2 vols.; Raymond Geuss, *Philosophy and Real Politics* (Princeton: Princeton University Press, 2008); Pocock, *Political Thought and History*; on critical legal studies as critical and historical method in legal thought, see Morton Horwitz, *The Transformation of American Law* (Oxford: Oxford University Press, 1977), 2 vols.; Robert W. Gordon, "Critical Legal Histories," *Stanford Law Review* 36 (1984), pp. 57–125; Roberto Mangabeira Unger, *The Critical Legal Studies Movement* (Cambridge, MA: Harvard University Press, 1986); Wendy Brown and Janet Halley ed., *Left Legalism/Left Critique* (Durham: Duke University Press, 2002); Austin Sarat and Jonathan Simon, ed., *Cultural Analysis, Cultural Studies, and the Law: Moving Beyond Legal Realism* (Durham: Duke University Press, 2003). On this emerging criticism, see Panu Minkkinen, *Thinking without Desire: A First Philosophy of Law* (London: Hart, 1999); Constantin Fasolt, *The Limits of History* (Chicago: University of Chicago Press, 2004); Christopher Tomlins, "The Threepenny Constitution (and the Question of Justice)," 58 *Alabama Law Review* (2006), pp. 979–1008; "What Is Left of the Law and Society Paradigm after Critique? Revisiting Gordon's 'Critical Legal Histories'," *Law and Social Inquiry*, Vol. 37, No. 1 (Winter 2012), pp. 155–66; Kunal M. Parker, *Common Law, History, and Democracy in America, 1790–1900: Legal Thought Before*

on the possibility of entertaining conjunctions of law, politics, and history that do not subsume any to either, and so on a historical practice that can contribute not just to jurisprudence but in a democratic spirit to the necessary intersection of jurisprudence with constitutionalism and political life. This is a direction in which Jefferson's conjoined legal, political, and historical thinking can point us. Any assumption of law as an autonomous zone of concepts and practice simply does not make sense of Jefferson's immersive engagement with it as history.[45] Jefferson managed to do without rigid distinctions between legal and critically historical uses of the past, or for that matter between law and the usual subject matter of intellectual history. This book challenges attempts to police the boundaries of those distinctions today.[46]

Modernism (Cambridge: Cambridge University Press, 2011); see also Reinhart Koselleck, *Critique and Crisis: Enlightenment and the Pathogenesis of Modern Society* (Cambridge, MA: MIT Press, 1988).

45 Here I mean to problematize, at least in accounting for Jefferson's legal and historical thought, the strict and clear difference between law's use of history and historical writing in the seventeenth and eighteenth centuries; see John Philip Reid, "The Jurisprudence of Liberty: The Ancient Constitution in the Legal Historiography of the Seventeenth and Eighteenth Centuries," in *The Roots of Liberty: Magna Carta, Ancient Constitution, and the Anglo-American Tradition of Rule of Law*, Ellis Sandoz, ed. (Indianapolis: Liberty Fund, 1993), pp. 185–308.

46 This is to take Jefferson intellectually seriously as a legal and political thinker, although not in a traditional academic or philosophical sense; in the light of his deep and abiding engagements with the textuality and historicity of law and what that meant for law and legal subjectivity in a republican polity, prevalent depictions of his thought as fundamentalist, ahistorical, or anti-constitutional are unconvincing; see Morton Horwitz, "Foreword: The Constitution of Change- Legal Fundamentality without Fundamentalism," 107 *Harv. L. Rev.* 30 (1993–4); Stephen Holmes, *Passions and Constraint: On the Theory of Liberal Democracy* (Chicago: University of Chicago Press, 1995), pp. 140–6; Jed Rubenfeld, *Freedom and Time: A Theory of Constitutional Self-Government* (New Haven: Yale University Press, 2001); David A. Strauss, "Common Law, Common Ground, and Jefferson's Principle," *Yale Law Journal* Vol. 112, No. 7 (May, 2003), pp. 1717–55; for more positive appraisals of Jefferson's constitutional thought and its relevance, to both of which this book is indebted, see Richard K. Matthews, *The Radical Politics of Thomas Jefferson: A Revisionist View* (Lawrence: University of Kansas, 1984); Sanford Levinson, *Constitutional Faith* (Princeton: Princeton University Press, 1988); in contrast to Michael Hardt's "radical Jefferson," this book does not proceed by separating what is inspirational from Jefferson's political thought from what is not, and it finds Jefferson to have been committed to the possibility of democratic institutions, of jurisprudence and constitutionalism, and not constituent power as such; indeed, to see Jefferson as positing constituent power against constitutions, or constitutions as only constituent power, is to miss the institutional quality of his thought; see Michael Hardt, "Jefferson and Democracy," *American Quarterly*, Vol. 59, No. 1 (March 2007), pp. 41–78; see also Besty Erkkila, "Radical Jefferson," and Berry Shank, "Jefferson, the Impossible," *American Quarterly*, Vol. 59, No. 2 (June 2007), pp. 277–89, pp. 291–9.

While concerns with empire, legal protections of property, and the rights of settler populations to enjoy them can be found in the history of law and political thought before and after the American Revolution, Jefferson's thinking about race and expansion suggests that the conceptual underpinnings of these concerns were shifting in the context of domestic and international commerce and the ideological imperatives of using commerce as an explanation for territorial conquest. Scholarship has seen fit to discuss these transformations as either shifts from republicanism to liberalism, elitism to democracy, or mercantilism and colonialism to liberal political economy and the modern state, and from colonial to national identity, or on the other hand as discursive shifts constructed on top of underlying continuities of imperial ambition, racial hierarchy, and what C.B. Macpherson famously called "possessive individualism."[47] This book argues that Jefferson augmented

[47] C.B. Macpherson, *The Political Theory of Possessive Individualism: Hobbes to Locke* (Oxford: Oxford University Press, 1962); Drew R. McCoy, *The Elusive Republic: Political Economy in Jeffersonian America* (Chapel Hill: University of North Carolina Press, 1980); Steven Watts, *The Republic Reborn: War and the Making of Liberal America, 1790–1820* (Baltimore: Johns Hopkins University Press, 1987); Joyce Appleby, *Liberalism and Republicanism in the Historical Imagination* (Cambridge, MA: Harvard University Press, 1992); Michael Meranze, *Laboratories of Virtue: Punishment, Revolution, and Authority in Philadelphia, 1760–1835* (Chapel Hill: University of North Carolina Press, 1996); James T. Kloppenberg, *The Virtues of Liberalism* (Cambridge, MA: Harvard University Press, 1998); ch. 2; Ruth H. Bloch, *Gender and Morality in Anglo-American Culture, 1650–1800* (Berkeley and Los Angeles: University of California Press, 2003); Patrick Griffin, *American Leviathan: Empire, Nation, and Revolutionary Frontier* (New York: Hill and Wang, 2007); Sarah Knott, *Sensibility in the American Revolution* (Chapel Hill: University of North Carolina Press, 2009); Carroll Smith-Rosenberg, *This Violent Empire: The Birth of an American National Identity* (Chapel Hill: University of North Carolina Press, 2010); Eliga H. Gould, *Among the Powers of the Earth: The American Revolution and the Making of a New World Empire* (Cambridge, MA: Harvard University Press, 2012); Max M. Edling, *A Revolution in Favor of Government: Origins of the U.S. Constitution and the Making of the American State* (Oxford: Oxford University Press, 2003); *A Hercules in the Cradle: War, Money, and the American State, 1783–1867* (Chicago: University of Chicago Press, 2014). On the importance of legal history to the transformation of scholarship on the origins of trajectory of revolutionary politics, see Hendrik Hartog, ed., *Law in the American Revolution and the American Revolution in the Law* (New York: NYU Press, 1981); John Philip Reid, *The Constitutional History of the American Revolution* (Madison: University of Wisconsin Press, 1987–1991), 4 vols.; Christopher Tomlins and Bruce H. Mann, *The Many Legalities of Early America* (Chapel Hill: University of North Carolina Press, 2001); Mary Sarah Bilder, *The Transatlantic Constitution: Colonial Legal Culture and the Empire* (Cambridge, MA: Harvard University Press, 2004); Daniel J. Hulsebosch, *Constituting Empire: New York and the Transformation of Constitutionalism in the Atlantic World, 1664–1830* (Chapel Hill: University of North Carolina Press, 2005); Holly Brewer, *By Birth or Consent: Children, Law, and the Anglo-American Revolution in Authority*

these wider histories of intellectual transformation from early modern to modern empire, and so from jurisprudence to political economy as the organizing framework for political thought and the principal justification for conquest.[48] These shifts matter here not only because Jefferson was a part of them but because they point to the fact that the exercise of legally endowed authority over subject peoples, while continuous, needed to change in justification and operation in response to newly arising problems inherent in the founding of the American republic. In the context of slavery and the settler project of removing Native American title to desired western land, for Jefferson these shifts entailed further transformations of racial subjection from legal status to ascribed capacities for a particular kind of legal and historical subjectivity, and of the textual culture within which that subjectivity was situated from law and constitutionalism to a flattened and expansive plane of commerce and national print culture.

The portrait of Jefferson painted here is of an actor in time, a reflexively engaged and participant theorist of constitutional transformations in the revolutionary world of the late eighteenth and early nineteenth centuries.[49] It suggests that Jefferson's own project of self-constitution was

(Chapel Hill: University of North Carolina Press, 2005); Alison LaCroix, *The Ideological Origins of American Federalism* (Cambridge, MA: Harvard University Press, 2010); Jack P. Greene, *The Constitutional Origins of the American Revolution* (Cambridge: Cambridge University Press, 2010); Christopher Tomlins, *Freedom Bound: Law, Labor, and Civic Identity in the Colonizing of English America, 1580–1865* (Cambridge: Cambridge University Press, 2010).

48 Michel Foucault, *Security, Territory, and Population: Lectures at the College de France, 1977–1978*, Graham Burchell, trans., Michel Senellart, ed. (New York: Palgrave Macmillan, 2007); James Tully, *Public Philosophy in a New Key, Volume II: Imperialism and Civic Freedom* (Cambridge: Cambridge University Press, 2008); Istvan Hont, *Jealousy of Trade: International Competition and the Nation State in Historical Perspective* (Cambridge, MA: Harvard University Press, 2010); Andrew Fitzmaurice, *Sovereignty, Property, and Empire, 1500–1800* (Cambridge: Cambridge University Press, 2014); for work on Jefferson in particular that place his political career in the context of nation-building and empire, see Robert W. Tucker and David C. Hendrickson, *Empire of Liberty: The Statecraft of Thomas Jefferson* (Charlottesville: University of Virginia Press, 1990); Anthony F.C. Wallce, *Jefferson and the Indians: The Tragic Fate of the First Americans* (Cambridge, MA: Harvard University Press, 1999); Peter S. Onuf, *Jefferson's Empire: The Language of American Nationhood* (Charlottesville: University of Virginia Press, 2000); Brian Steele, *Thomas Jefferson and American Nationhood* (Cambridge: Cambridge University Press, 2012); Francis D. Cogliano, *Emperor of Liberty: Thomas Jefferson's Foreign Policy* (New Haven: Yale University Press, 2014).

49 In this, I take inspiration from Jay Fliegelman, *Declaring Independence: Jefferson, Natural Language, and the Culture of Performance* (Stanford: Stanford University Press,

inextricably linked with a project of imagining and instituting a particular legal and historical subjectivity appropriate to republican political life. It further suggests that Jefferson was neither the passive conduit of paradigms or doctrines nor simply the product of his era or his contexts, but was rather an inveterate user of inherited concepts and practices.[50] And in his use, and in his thinking about use, he opened up and constructed new problems and issues, and responded to them, and in doing so not only acted in but on the contexts in which he found himself. This is an important fact to understand about Jefferson and how it was possible for him to think the things that he did. It is equally important for us to understand the conditions and limits as well as the power and possibilities of what Jefferson called "that mode of action called thinking."[51]

The goal of this first, introductory chapter has been to outline the argument and argumentative stakes of the book, and to situate Jefferson in the contexts of early modern legal humanism and colonial identity in

1993); on Jefferson's experience of his world and his thinking about it, see Fawn M. Brodie, *Thomas Jefferson: An Intimate Portrait* (New York: Norton, 1974); Joseph J. Ellis, *American Sphynx: The Character of Thomas Jefferson* (New York: Knopf, 1997); Annette Gordon-Reed and Peter S. Onuf, *Most Blessed of the Patriarchs: Thomas Jefferson and the Empire of the Imagination* (New York: Liveright, 2016).

50 In this aspect the book differs from a good deal of recent scholarship on Jefferson's thought, which has tended to reconstruct Jefferson's intellectual life in conversation with the history of ideas and Jefferson as a kind of philosopher, or at least studious applicant of the philosophy, political or natural, that he read, suggesting that Jefferson either absorbed the doctrines of others or came up with a kind of doctrine or system on his own that can be traced consistently throughout his life. While deeply indebted to much of this work, I argue that such an approach risks overlooking the power and significance of Jefferson's wandering and creative uses of words and things, which in turn risks leaving us with an incomplete sense not only of Jefferson's thinking but of what counts as the history of thought, and of the other histories to which the history of the activity of thinking can be related in the present. See Steven M. Dworetz, *The Unvarnished Doctrine: Locke, Liberalism, and the American Revolution* (Durham: Duke University Press, 1989); David N. Mayer, *The Constitutional Thought of Thomas Jefferson* (Charlottesville: University of Virginia Press, 1994); Michael P. Zuckert, *The Natural Rights Republic: Studies in the Foundation of the American Political Tradition* (South Bend: University of Notre Dame Press, 1996); and more recently, Hannah Spahn, *Thomas Jefferson, Time, and History* (Charlottesville: University of Virginia Press, 2011); Maurizio Valsania, *The Limits of Optimism: Thomas Jefferson's Dualistic Enlightenment* (Charlottesville: University of Virginia Press, 2011); *Nature's Man: Thomas Jefferson's Philosophical Anthropology* (Charlottesville: University of Virginia Press, 2013); Ari Helo, *Thomas Jefferson's Ethics and the Politics of Human Progress: The Morality of a Slaveholder* (Cambridge: Cambridge University Press, 2014).

51 Jefferson to John Adams, August 15, 1820, *The Adams-Jefferson Letters: The Complete Correspondence between Thomas Jefferson and John and Abigail Adams*, Lester J. Cappon, ed. (Chapel Hill: University of North Carolina Press, 1959), p. 568.

the British Atlantic world. Chapter 2 locates Jefferson's legal education and his collections of legal books and manuscripts in the context of the intellectual culture of eighteenth-century Virginia's planter elite. Jefferson inherited a concern to collect, narrate, and represent a history of law and constitutional authority in Virginia that both connected governance to the continuity of English law and liberty and allowed for provincial self-government. Jefferson's revolutionary constitutionalism, I argue, grew out of a productive awareness of the fragility of foundational histories. In Chapter 3, I examine Jefferson's revolutionary-era proposals for legal and constitutional reform, and argue that Jefferson's project consisted of an effort to constitute a mode of active and historically situated legal subjectivity. A republican constitution demanded a republican subject possessed of the cultivated capacity for participation in it. Chapter 4 turns to a close reading of the *Notes on the State of Virginia* as an extended essay in constitutional criticism, and a theorization of the legal and historical subjectivities that actually existed in Virginia, the United States, and on the North American continent. In his book, Jefferson confronted the problem of plurality, and specifically, the problem of a plurality of collective histories from which legal and political judgment would follow, and it was in this confrontation with the histories of others, I argue, that Jefferson proceeded to explicitly restrict the racial and gendered boundaries of civic identity. Recognizing plurality, even among the indigenous and enslaved populations that fell under his gaze, Jefferson was unwilling to institutionalize it at the expense of the security of the white settler subject's exclusive and possessive use that conditioned the form of life appropriate to Jefferson's vision of politics.

Chapter 5 continues to put Jefferson's racial thinking in the context of these concerns for the security of a particular mode of subjectivity and the anchoring of that subjectivity in conditions of self-possession and self-government. I follow Jefferson's intellectual and political career as a politician and correspondent with the American Philosophical Society, and argue that the cancellation of Native title to western land and the legal and political theory of expansion emerged in Jefferson's thinking as solutions to problems that had plagued the project of instituting a republican constitution. In cooperation with James Madison and in conversation with French social thought, Jefferson turned to political economy and print culture as ways of governing the plurality and unpredictability of political judgment, in effect attempting to coordinate and discipline the possible uses of law, land, and language for the sake of governability in an expansive and expanding republic. Chapter 6 looks at the consequences of Jefferson's articulation of a liberal, modern argument for racial hierarchy and empire. It considers Jefferson's intellectual projects in his retirement, understands them as in part mournful returns to exploring the valence of a kind of early modern humanist and historical practice, and the connections of these practices to imagined forms of idealized legal and political life. A brief conclusion relocates the issues of law, civic identity, and historical practice in the present.

2

Jurisdiction and British Legal Memory in Colonial Virginia

In 1701, an anonymous Virginian published a pamphlet in London that contested the uncertain legal status of the colony within the constitutional and economic structure of imperial governance. The text, *An Essay upon the Government of the English Plantations on the Continent of America*, was in part a response to the argument of Charles Davenant in his *Discourses on the Public Revenues, and on the Trade of England* of 1698 that among other things urged the Board of Trade to consider colonial unification under a common government. In the wake of the Glorious Revolution and the removal of the much-hated Dominion of New England from the northern colonies by the new royal government under William III, Davenant's proposal for a colonial assembly and his praise for the bustling and productive commercial societies characteristic of northern colonies threatened the unique political and economic power of Virginia, the oldest, wealthiest, and most populous of Britain's North American colonies. The political economy informing Davenant's arguments suggested a developmental theory of feudal breakdown and commercial progress, an emerging narrative in eighteenth-century social theory that relegated, or at least purported to relegate, the primacy of the political and economic power of the traditional landed gentry to the past.[1] The author of the pamphlet took aim at that narrative, defending

[1] J.G.A. Pocock, *The Machiavellian Moment: Florentine Political Thought and the Atlantic Republican Tradition* (Princeton: Princeton University Press, 1975), ch. 13–14; Istvan Hont, *Jealousy of Trade: International Competition and the Nation-State in Historical Perspective* (Cambridge, MA: Harvard University Press, 2005), ch. 2; David Armitage, *The Ideological Origins of the British Empire* (Cambridge: Cambridge University Press, 2000), ch. 5–6.

the heavily stratified society that had developed in Virginia as the established loyal centerpiece of England's colonial possessions in North America.

That the Board of Trade would consider proposals that showed so little respect for Virginia's special status and so little memory of the conflicts that had characterized colonial history elsewhere was troubling. A royal colony since 1624, a loyal supporter of the cause of the Crown in the English Civil War, and the most denominationally, culturally, and institutionally Anglicized colony, Virginia expected special consideration in light of their contrast with northern colonies, where rebellious Puritans in Massachusetts had existed uneasily under imperial governance since the colony's origins and where profits were allegedly made from smuggling that flaunted the minimally enforced Navigation Acts. Virginia was the most populous and richest colony, but that was threatened in the foreseeable future by natural population growth in Massachusetts and expansive settlement in Pennsylvania, disputes and possible contractions of its southern and western borders, and declining immigration rates in Virginia. In his later *History of the Dividing Line betwixt Virginia and North Carolina* and the more personal *Secret History of the Dividing Line*, which related his experiences of the 1728 survey of the colonial border by agents of both colonies, William Byrd II, of Westover plantation on the James River, repeatedly made it clear to his intended English audience that North Carolina was an undeveloped backwater with little potential for impressive development, in stark contrast to the strength of Virginia.[2] Virginia's leaders felt the need to be constantly on guard against policy proposals and developments that could threaten the future interests of its planter class, the viability of Virginia's tobacco trade, and their preeminence in intercolonial affairs.

The *Essay* took special care to defend the potential of Virginia's future development and the wealth-generating promises of fertile soil made fruitful by the proprietorship of a planter elite and an institutional structure built on the emerging importance of slavery.[3] It was logical for a

[2] As Byrd says of North Carolina, "...for want of Navigation and Commerce, the best Estate affords little more than a coarse Subsistence," and later, "the Government there is so Loose and the Laws so feebly executed" that "everyone just does what seems good in his own eyes," William Byrd, *The Dividing Line Histories of William Byrd II of Westover* (Chapel Hill: University of North Carolina Press, 2013), pp. 87, 112.

[3] Rhys Isaac, *The Transformation of Virginia, 1740–1790* (Chapel Hill: University of North Carolina Press, 1982); Anthony S. Parent, Jr. *Foul Means: The Formation of a Slave Society in Virginia* (Chapel Hill: University of North Carolina Press, 2003);

Virginia planter to be concerned with the affairs of Virginia in London, and to be anxious about the viability of the enormous power and privilege made possible by such a hierarchical society. In many ways, the pamphlet and its articulated anxieties of both individual security and collective colonial status anticipated the fraught nature of the power exercised by colonial planters that underlay their willingness to contemplate independence several decades later. In fact, the debates over the status of colonial Virginia within the empire anticipated the urgency with which Southern political elites in the founding and antebellum periods would seek to protect and expand the place of slaveholding states within the federal union established by the United States Constitution.[4] Even so, at a deeper level the *Essay* reveals a powerful current of thought on both sides of the Atlantic surrounding the legal and historical construction of civic identity.[5] Actors in transatlantic disputations over the nature of sovereignty in the imperial constitution were having an argument over history. Elite Virginians carefully guarded the possible representations of that history in local, colonial, and imperial contests over where the powers to assemble and represent such histories were understood to be located.

Creating a framework of historical self-understanding that proved to have a formative impact on how Jefferson thought about law and politics, from his own legal study and practice to his thinking about republican

Emory G. Evans, *A Topping People: The Rise and Decline of Virginia's Old Political Elite, 1680–1790* (Charlottesville: University of Virginia Press, 2009).

[4] Kathleen M. Brown, *Good Wives, Nasty Wenches, and Anxious Patriarchs: Gender, Race, and Power in Colonial Virginia* (Chapel Hill: University of North Carolina Press, 1996); April Lee Hatfield, *Atlantic Virginia: Intercolonial Relations in the Seventeenth Century* (Philadelphia: University of Pennsylvania Press, 2004); on later years, see Woody Holton, *Forced Founders: Indians, Debtors, Slaves, and the Making of the American Revolution in Virginia* (Chapel Hill: University of North Carolina Press, 1999); Matthew Mason, *Slavery and American Politics in the Early American Republic* (Chapel Hill: University of North Carolina Press, 2006); Michael A. McDonnell, *The Politics of War: Race, Class, and Conflict in Revolutionary Virginia* (Chapel Hill: University of North Carolina Press, 2007); David Waldstreicher, *Slavery's Constitution: From Revolution to Ratification* (New York: Hill and Wang, 2009); George William Van Cleve, *A Slaveholder's Union: Slavery, Politics, and the Constitution in the Early American Republic* (Chicago: University of Chicago Press, 2010).

[5] Jack P. Greene, *The Intellectual Construction of America: Exceptionalism and Identity from 1492 to 1800* (Chapel Hill: University of North Carolina Press, 1993); *Negotiated Authorities: Essays in Colonial Political and Constitutional History* (Charlottesville: University of Virginia Press, 1994), ch. 1–3; Christopher Tomlins, *Freedom Bound: Law, Labor, and Civic Identity in the Colonizing of English America, 1580–1865* (Cambridge: Cambridge University Press, 2010).

constitutionalism, these elite Virginians were under pressure to represent a legitimate provincial legal and constitutional history to metropolitan officials. Seeking to control the image of the at once inherited English and distinctly Virginian institutional development that had been taking place, Virginia's leaders combated English characterizations of colonial governments as undeveloped, incomplete, and in the case of royal colonies like Virginia, as dependent on the strong power of the Governor and his selected Council. They did so by constructing different histories that emphasized three key points: the degree to which the creole planter elite in the colonies were capable of sharing and furthering the project of empire in the Atlantic world, the degree to which in doing so thousands of miles away from the imperial center they had been compelled to develop a distinct set of practices and institutions that legitimately departed from English precedent but not from the spirit of English law or the British Constitution, and finally, and most crucially, their exclusive access to and possession of the records that documented this history.

This concern with records was self-interested, to be sure. One of the probable authors of the *Essay*, Robert Beverley, took over from his father the task of managing the official records of Virginia's colonial government, in 1698 becoming the keeper of the Governor's Council records, and going on to become the clerk of the General Court and the House of Burgesses. He trained himself in Virginia legal history and the management of state records, and, as Susan Scott Parrish points out, in the politics of historical representation in political argument.[6] His experience in the politics of colonial history crystalizes what was at stake for other planter elites. The younger Beverley corresponded with his brother-in-law William Byrd II and could have sent the essay to his friend who was serving as a colonial agent in London on one of his many extended stays across the Atlantic. Both men were anxious to personally advance their own political careers and the economic basis of their power. Byrd had gone to London to study law at Middle Temple in the Inns of Court, but returned home when he failed to procure more prestigious appointments within the colonial governing structure. Beverley was in London to appeal a land dispute before the Privy Council, and it was there that he became

[6] Robert Beverley, *The History and Present State of Virginia*, Susan Scott Parrish, ed. (Chapel Hill: University of North Carolina Press, 2013), see Introduction; on Byrd, Beverley, and their intellectual lives, see Louis B. Wright, *The First Gentlemen of Virginia: Intellectual Qualities of the Early Colonial Ruling Class* (Charlottesville: University of Virginia Press, 1964); Richard Beale Davis, *Literature and Society in Early Virginia, 1608–1740* (Baton Rouge: Louisiana State University Press, 1973).

alerted to the true state of discourse about the colony, coming into contact with letters from the sitting Governor, Francis Nicholson, urging further increase in royal control that had been tightening since the aftermath of Bacon's Rebellion in 1676. In attacking Nicholson directly, Beverley invited the Governor's wrath and was removed from his clerkship.

Both Byrd and Beverley came to understand their personal frustrations and the confusions about the legal and constitutional status of the colony and its governance within the empire as consequences of undue monopoly on the representations of the colony prevalent in England. Both men along with their peers responded to this situation by collecting and narrating a different history, a history that depicted the continuity of English law and good order in the colonies as safely in the hands of a cultivated governing elite, schooled in English law and politics, familiar with the situation on the ground in the colony, and mediating between the office of the Governor's personification of royal prerogative and the population of small planters, farmers, Indians, and slaves who lived in Virginia. Seizing on his intricate knowledge of the colonial records, Beverley wrote *The History and Present State of Virginia*, published in London 1705, for just such a purpose and with just such a history in mind. He placed great emphasis on his local knowledge, his erudition, and his access to original manuscripts, as would subsequent authors of Virginian histories. He was in a sense founding a tradition of locating, collecting, and securing access to these records, a project that would occupy the attentions of particular members of Virginia's legal and political elite up to the outbreak of the American Revolution, and for Jefferson, far beyond it. This chapter reconstructs the intellectual culture out of which Jefferson's concerns for collecting and reading legal history emerged.

CONTEXTS OF LEGAL KNOWLEDGE

Establishing and defining civic identity in the lives of eighteenth-century Virginia elites was a problem they confronted in numerous aspects of their lives, but rarely more intensely than in their methods of reading, copying, learning, writing law and building legal knowledge. This drama of self-constitution, of locating oneself in constitutional place and time, played itself out in libraries, margins, and commonplace books. It was a drama that would unravel in the outbreak of the American Revolution. Projects of self-constitution, understood as practices of self-collection, were a crucial component of consolidating political and social authority in the colony, and articulating an imperial constitutional vision that allowed for limited participation in sovereignty, and so in the power of making and defining law.[7] The self being constructed through such acts of collecting was a self that needed to be autonomous and stable for the sake of an active, public life, a life led in the assembly or before the court, and a life fit to be measured for its place in a wider historical framework defined by metropolitan norms.

In constituting themselves in this particularly early modern fashion, elite Virginians like William Byrd II and Thomas Jefferson played significant roles in the creation of a mode of subjectivity that was characterized as much by their anxious defining of the subjectivities of others as it was of securing the racialized and gendered boundaries for their own authority.[8] Boundaries of the particular historical subjectivity constructed in the libraries, collections, and writings of the creole planter elite extended to the libraries themselves. In the pages of his secret diaries, William Byrd raged against women who refused his entices, and later against his wife for intruding on or interrupting him in his library. He retreated back to the library to read Coke on Littleton and to enjoy the space that not only grounded the exclusivity of his position but provided him with the very stuff with which he constructed and cared for the discipline of governing, and owning, self and others. Likewise, Jefferson would later respond to his own travails as a country gentleman and bachelor circulating among the Tidewater gentry by recording extensive passages of emotional defeat and frustration in the pages of his literary commonplace book. Both men

[7] See Kenneth A. Lockridge, "The Commonplace Book of a Colonial Gentleman in Crisis: An Essay," in *The Commonplace Book of William Byrd of Westover*; Kevin Barland, Jan Kirsten Gilliam and Kenneth A. Lockridge, eds. (Chapel Hill: University of North Carolina Press, 2001), p. 93. Here, Lockridge builds on the Foucault's late study of modes of self-care in ancient Greek and Roman ethics; see Michel Foucault, *Hermeneutics of the Subject*, Graham Burchell, trans. (New York: Picador, 2005); *The Government of Self and Others*; Graham Burchell, trans. (New York: Palgrave Macmillan, 2010). See also Sean Silver, *The Mind is a Collection: Case Studies in Eighteenth Century Thought* (Philadelphia: University of Pennsylvania Press, 2015), who builds on the work of Pierre Bourdieu and to a greater extent Bruno Latour, which while possibly illuminating on the history and theory of intellectual practice in other contexts, does not to my mind capture the historical specificity of the human power dynamics constructed in these purposeful uses of material texts and contexts.

[8] The literary entries of their respective commonplace books, as Kenneth Lockridge has shown, reveal a fundamental insecurity of their mastery over themselves and the white women and enslaved people over whom they were also supposed to exercise that mastery; see Lockridge, *On the Sources of Patriarchal Rage: The Commonplace Books of William Byrd and Thomas Jefferson and the Gendering of Power in the Eighteenth Century* (New York: New York University Press, 1992).

carried on their careers from a home that was surrounded by an increasing number of slaves whose labor was necessary to the existence of the colony but whose numbers and historically uncertain legal status presented serious risks to the security of the planter elite. Government of the colony, management of the plantation household and labor force, and careful historical construction of legal subjectivity for themselves and for their place in the structure of the empire were inextricably linked projects.

The tremendous cultural value placed on establishing the legal and historical grounds of their legitimate authority followed a particularly provincial constitutional logic. Virginians defending their privileges from home in Virginia and in London as emissaries made every effort to secure both the continuity of their legal structures and customary rights from the authority of the English common law and the freedom of their own laws, customs, and usages to develop in different but not antithetical directions. In particular, Virginians were anxious to establish the legitimacy of their court system, customary checks on the power of the Governor, rights and privileges of the landed gentry, and the status of slaves as inheritable along with estates like serfs or villeins, but not possessing any of the minimal customary rights of laborers attached to landed property.[9] At least since the late seventeenth century, Virginians were anxious to hold these records and put them to use as material support for their distinct legal culture and as the basis for claiming legitimacy for that culture within the structures of imperial governance. Copies of colonial charters established Virginia land claims in unsettled and disputed territory, and it is important to note that users of these manuscripts like William Byrd and later George Mason, a stakeholder in the Ohio Company and its land speculation schemes in the Ohio River Valley, west of Virginia, were looking to argue that Virginia's original letters patent and charters granted Virginians exclusive rights of settlement and control of contested border regions with other colonies. Jefferson was as much a partisan of Virginia's interests in the Empire and later in the federal union as any of his fellows.

Their collections of their records and their histories were intended to further these interests and the broader goal of securing their distinct status within the constitution of the empire and colony alike, but it would be a mistake to understand their historical and constitutional arguments as merely instrumental. The records and their various representations as

9 Robert Beverley, *History and Present State of Virginia*, Susan Scott Parrish, ed. (Chapel Hill: University of North Carolina Press, 2013), p. 216.

evidence of authoritative custom constituted the materials with which it was possible to theorize law and constitutionalism in a colonial legal context. Law as collected history was the very stuff of civic identity.[10] What we see in the legal and intellectual culture of colonial Virginia is a growing and at the same time ambivalent defense of what the members of the creole planter elite were keenly aware of as the punctured, uneven, and assembled quality of the provinces and jurisdictions that made up the empire. They collected and defended themselves as inhabiting a specific historically constituted time and space within the patchwork of imperial governance. Internally, as Rhys Isaac has shown, low literacy and the limited, costly availability of printed matter in Virginia allowed the ritualistically acknowledged ability to read in public from the pulpit and the bench to serve as a key element of constructing and maintaining cultural authority. The same was true for the means to enjoy the freedom to own, read, and interpret in private.[11] Surrounded by cultures of the indentured and the enslaved that were understood as cultures of orality, for male elites literacy and textuality advertised mastery to distinct audiences in the home, colonial society, and in Westminster.

In this framework, practices of reading and collecting law books and manuscripts among political actors formed critical components of defining a balance between the particular narratives of civil government in Virginia and those of the wider context of British constitutionalism throughout the empire. In these practices, elite Virginians configured law as a fragile assemblage, far more fragile and more consciously assembled than traditional interpretations have recognized.[12] The importance

[10] Lauren Benton has called attention to early modern imperial legal space and the efforts at "legal posturing" of actors within or on the borders of that space as multi-layered and pluralistic, punctured by the necessary incompleteness of any attempt to impose legal uniformity on the varied contexts and spaces within the cultural and jurisdictional plurality of early modern empires; see Lauren Benton, *A Search for Sovereignty: Law and Geography in European Empires* (Cambridge: Cambridge University Press, 2010), p. 24. Kunal Parker has discussed the early modern common law as a vehicle for the creation of times, of the temporalities appropriate to legal and political argument; see Kunal M. Parker, *Common Law, History, and Democracy in America, 1790–1900* (Cambridge: Cambridge University Press, 2011).

[11] Rhys Isaac, *The Transformation of Virginia: 1740–1790* (Chapel Hill: University of North Carolina Press, 1982), pp. 121–4.

[12] Arguments about the centrality, stability and authority of the English common law as an ideological framework, see William M. Oufutt, "The Atlantic Rules: The Legalistic Turn in Colonial British America," *The Creation of the British Atlantic World*, Elizabeth Mancke and Carole Shammas, eds. (Baltimore: Johns Hopkins University Press, 2005), pp. 160–81; John Philip Reid, *The Ancient Constitution and the Origins*

of a jurisprudential framework for the practices involved in forging historical identity underscores the mixed and uncertain character of colonial constitutional culture. The lack of clear and uncontested jurisdictional boundaries and systematic organization in English legal structures during the seventeenth century became intensified in the colonies. This was particularly the case in Virginia, where the General Court met on different occasions with different jurisdictional authority. Even in Virginia, the most Anglicized colony, forms of law were not nearly as settled or organized as they were in England.[13] The General Court in Williamsburg, formed of appointees by the Governor from the Governor's Council, who were selected by the Governor, was bound by the English common law as it pertained in the colonies (an uncertain issue in and of itself), but when necessary the same body exercised both equity and ecclesiastical jurisdiction, forms of law that over time had developed into separate branches of the court system in England.

In the eighteenth century, equity practice before the General Court and principles of equity jurisprudence more generally were an important though disputed part of legal knowledge.[14] The idea of equity allowed

of Anglo-American Liberty (DeKalb: University of Northern Illinois Press, 2005), and "The Irrelevance of the Declaration," *Law in the American Revolution and Revolution in the Law*, Hendrik Hartog, ed. (New York: New York University Press, 1981); Kevin R.C. Gutzman, *Virginia's American Revolution: From Dominion to Republic, 1776–1840* (Lanham: Lexington Books, 2007), ch. 1–2; William E. Nelson, *The Common Law of Colonial America: The Chesapeake and New England, 1607–1660* (Oxford: Oxford University Press, 2008); traditionally attention to English liberty has been synthesized with an even broader framework of a Whig political tradition, Gordon S. Wood, *The Creation of the American Republic: 1776–1787* (Chapel Hill: University of North Carolina Press, 1969); H. Trevor Colbourn, *The Lamp of Experience: Whig History and the Intellectual Origins of the American Revolution* (Chapel Hill: University of North Carolina Press, 1965).

13 The authoritative study of county court and General Court practice is A.G. Roeber, *Faithful Magistrates and Republican Lawyers: Creators of Virginia Legal Culture, 1680–1810* (Chapel Hill: University of North Carolina Press, 1981).

14 William Hamilton Bryson, *Census of Law Books in Colonial Virginia* (Charlottesville: University of Virginia Press, 1978), finds twenty-nine copies of eighteen titles concerning equity in a representative survey of eighteenth-century library cataloges, and while none of the single titles are among the most widely held, the vast majority of equity treatises are held in extremely large libraries like that of John Mercer, or in later libraries like those of Dabney Carr, Robert W. Carter, the lesser-known John Edmunds, and Patrick Henry and Thomas Jefferson, suggesting that the perceived necessity of reading equity was increasing in the late eighteenth century; C. Malcolm Watkins, ed., *The Cultural History of Marlborough, VA* (Washington, DC: Smithsonian, 1968), appendixes E, K; "Library of Dabney Carr, (1773)," *The Virginia Magazine of History and Biography*, Vol. 2 (1894), pp. 221–8; *The Journal of Philip Vickers Fithian, 1773–1774: A Plantation Tutor*

for a degree of laxity in judicial observance of the finer points of law and procedure, and so could serve as an extension of the Governor's prerogative, a complaint made by the author of the *Essay on the Government of the English Plantations on the Continent of America*. While adjudicating matters of ecclesiastical concern usually fell to the county courts, the intertwining of church and state and the common legal issue of wills and testaments points to the importance of ecclesiastical law before the Court as well. The presence of both Roman civil law and the use of natural law arguments further complicated the amalgamation that characterized legal practice.[15] Provincial elites confronted the question of how the British Constitution pertained to their own settings where common law existed alongside other forms. In efforts to resolve such issues, legal thinkers turned to a historical language of jurisprudence in legal argument and wider constitutional debates within Virginia and across the Atlantic in order to frame coherent narratives of the origins and operation of their institutions. Because of their mixed constitutional backgrounds, and the provincial and already uncertain legal and constitutional status of the colonies within imperial governance, arguments from precedent and custom were never totally conceptually distinct from narratives of civil history.

Judge and lawyer alike therefore had to be able to draw on multiple traditions at any one time or for any one case, and the question of which tradition was appropriate was often just as important as the legal dispute itself. Because the General Court consisted of members of the Governor's Council, law was inseparable from constitutionalism, and both law and politics were inseparable from their enmeshment in constructions of historical subjectivity. Later in the eighteenth century, county court

of the Old Dominion (Charlottesville: University of Virginia Press, 1968), pp. 221–9; "Inventory of the Estate of John Edmunds," August 16, 1770, Sussex Co. Will Book, Pt. 2, pp. 253–66; "Extract from an Inventory of the Estate of Patrick Henry, July 1799," Manuscripts, Virginia Historical Society, and E. Millicent Sowerby, ed., *The Catalogue of the Library of Thomas Jefferson* (Washington, DC, 1953), Vol. 2, pp. 193–209.

15 Bryson's survey demonstrates that the second and third most widely held law books in the colony were editions of Swinburne's *Brief Treatise on Testaments and Last Wills*, covering a branch of ecclesiastical jurisprudence, and George Webb's *Virginia Justice* (1736), which amounted to a survey of basic legal principles for the use of county justices of the peace, and included law as it pertained to ecclesiastical discipline, church land, as well as testaments and wills; see *Census of Law Books in Colonial Virginia*, pp. xvi–xvii; Herbert A. Johnson, *Imported Eighteenth Century Law Treatises in American Libraries, 1700–1799* (Knoxville: University of Tennessee Press, 1978), introduction. On civil law books, see Bryson, "Roman Law in Virginia Courts," *The American Journal of Legal History*, Vol. 28, No. 2 (April 1984), pp. 145–56.

justices like Landon Carter often tacitly inherited their seat, and held the position for life as a consequence of their social standing, regardless of their legal training. However much colonial Virginians strived to carry out a culture of "political mimesis," the constitutional structure and the means of organizing legal knowledge gave the experience of law and politics in Virginia its own unique, provincial character. Constitutional development, then, was broader than strict models of Anglicization and relations to the English common law would suggest.[16] Provincial subjects of the eighteenth-century British Empire inhabited a richer if more uncertain world of historical thought than that.[17]

Understandings of law as inseparable from history and in particular from the history of its use and representation as history had even by Jefferson's career in public life been a long time in the making. Among the items Jefferson purchased from the estate of Peyton Randolph was the legal commonplace book and written legal opinions of Sir John Randolph. Manifest in the reading and collecting practices of the elder Randolph was a particular way of thinking about the law. His commonplace book, which he purchased already used from the estate of Benjamin Harrison, was bound with a short manual for organizing legal commonplace books, printed in London in 1680.[18] The author of the pamphlet makes an explicit connection between law and memory, both individual and collective:

[16] Jack Greene has described eighteenth-century Virginian political identity as characterized by a process of "political mimesis" of seventeenth-century English constitutional balance between executive and legislative authority, although a more recent study has shown the degree to which colonial elites both in and out of Virginia felt compelled to assert provincial distinctiveness as much as attachment to England, Jack P. Greene, *Negotiated Authorities: Essays in Colonial Political and Constitutional History* (Charlottesville: University of Virginia Press, 1994), p. 190; Peter C. Messer, *Stories of Independence: Identity, Ideology, and History in Eighteenth Century America* (Dekalb: Northern Illinois University Press, 2005).

[17] The work of Lauren Benton and Alison LaCroix has drawn attention to the varied, fragmented, and rich world of jurisdictional space in the early modern Atlantic, but it is as at least as important to note that the textual practices of legal actors who lived in that world illustrates a multifaceted universe of legal and civil histories within and alongside spaces of law and constitutionalism; see Lauren Benton, *A Search for Sovereignty: Law and Geography in European Empires, 1400–1900* (Cambridge: Cambridge University Press, 2009); Alison LaCroix, *The Ideological Origins of American Federalism* (Cambridge, MA: Harvard University Press, 2010).

[18] *A Brief Method of the Law, Being an Exact Alphabetical Disposition of All the Heads Necessary for a Perfect Common-Place* (London: Richard Atkins and Edward Atkins, 1680).

> We have not always the command of our Memory, when most we stand in need of its assistance, it is treacherous and very apt to deceive, and I believe that only Consideration gave the first original to Books, a desire that our Ancient Fore-Fathers had to instill into their posterity the Wisdom of their long Experience, after they themselves were lost in the Dust ... Books introduced a Method, and that [made] plain and easy the darker Mysteries of Arts and Sciences. This, by succession of Time, found out new, more ready ways to bring up Youth... We must attribute the happiness of it to their laborious, instructive writings, which have cut short those long and tedious forms which they were forced to take, e're they could attain the Proficiencies which we so soon attain to.[19]

The author of the pamphlet identifies books, and in this particular case law books, as articles that carry civic memory through time, and identifies the problem of the student as the digestion of the material so transmitted. Filling a commonplace book, the author suggests, reduces the vast compendium of knowledge involved in these books to a manageable project. Parallel to the linear arch of time created by the passing down of knowledge in the form of books, there is a narrative of progress that speaks of the growing capacity of students to deal with increasingly large rolls of history. The key to that progress, the author implies, is reorganizing legal knowledge into terms, organized alphabetically, and the manual provides a suggested list of those terms. "I have laid out utmost Efforts," he says, "to fix my Genus right in all the Terms, and to reduce all the Species under their particular Heads." At stake here was a tension between two ways of viewing the law: as a historical compendium, in all of its complexity, or as a rationalization and reorganization of that complexity into an easily referenced, stable body of knowledge, unquestionably a distinction that echoed the competing visions of Coke and Bacon. Tellingly, the pages of the commonplace book are for the most part empty, and in an attached fragment, Randolph ascribes most of the writing in it to the original owner, adding that a few of the entries were "placed under the wrong heads, as if he did not know to what Genus the particular Species did belong." It is appropriate to read a mocking tone here; Randolph apparently had little time for the author's suggestions on how to organize legal knowledge and the idea that legal

[19] Sir John Randolph's Commonplace Book, The Thomas Jefferson Papers at the Library of Congress, Series 8, Vol. 4, and Sowerby, *Catalogue of the Library of Thomas Jefferson*, Vol. 2, pp. 193–209, #1798; the purchase included the King's Bench reports of Randolph from his time in England. Jefferson would later come into possession of some of Randolph's General Court case reports from Virginia through a personal gift from Edmund Randolph.

knowledge should or could be so organized at all. Too much codification, organization, and systematization threatened the elite and antiquarian identity of the early modern common lawyer as described by the writings of Sir Edward Coke.

Coke's tract on Thomas Littleton's *Tenures*, the most widely held law book in the colony, earned recognition not as a systematic theory, or even a commentary on one, but as a kind of collection of historical researches. As the antiquarian John Aubrey would record, "the world expected from Coke a Commentary on Littleton's Tenures; and he left them with his Common-place book."[20] Again, with his promise to provide students with the "signification" of the "ancient books, charters, deeds, and records" of the law, Coke gave an enticingly textual experience of gaining legal knowledge. While Coke's narrative of long continuity has always come under criticism as English national mythology, it was not so much the historical argument as its open, assembled, unsystematic historicality and the elite, almost sacerdotal sense of individual status that gave it special meaning to Virginians who were looking for narratives of legal history in which they could locate themselves.

For Randolph, a Speaker of the House of Burgesses, the only colonial Virginian to be knighted, a rarely successful negotiator of the balance between provincial identity and metropolitan attachment, and who returned from his time in England with his own case reports from the Court of King's Bench and set upon the same practice for cases before the General Court, legal learning was an essential act of self-construction. There was a performative aspect to the private practice of reading law, reporting, and filling notebooks. The capacity to lay claim to the full protection of English liberty, participation in British history, as well as the full legitimacy of provincial land tenures within this framework depended on the display of cultivation in the restricted arena of the law. Efforts on the part of imperial officials to reorganize and rationalize colonial governance in the late seventeenth and early eighteenth centuries prompted increasing colonial assertions of full participation in a commonwealth of the British Atlantic and the relative historical independence of colonial politics.[21]

[20] John Aubrey, *Aubrey's Brief Lives* (New York: Penguin, 1949), p. 163.

[21] In this Randolph played a crucial role; see Speeches of Sir John Randolph, August 24, 1734, August 6, 1736, *Journals of the House of Burgesses of Virginia, 1727–1740* , John Pendleton Kennedy and Henry R. McIlwain, eds. (Richmond: Virginia State Library, 1910), pp. 175–7, 241–3.

HISTORIES IN PLAY

Before moving on to discuss the emergence of Jefferson's legal thinking, and the role that a politics of records and historical representation played in that thinking, the provenance of his concern with records and historical representations warrants appreciation. Late-seventeenth and early eighteenth-century Virginians pursued the project of writing the history of the colony from consultation of the colonial archive. Not only did Virginians seek to craft an image of attached and continuous but distinct legal development; they had to establish the legitimate authority of their own institutions, their own histories, at the same time that they argued that their present situation with tightening royal control, increasing parliamentary authority to enforce the taxation of goods, and expanded prerogative in the office of the Governor was untenable, even unconstitutional. By the lights of the author of the *Essay on the Government of the English Plantations on the Continent of America* and the more extensive formal histories written by Virginians that came after it in the early decades of the eighteenth century, the solution to this untenable situation for Virginians was greater royal oversight of colonial affairs in the form of a guarantee of rights and powers, rights and powers that were necessary to act with some degree of latitude in developing their own laws, customs, and usages. Pleading for royal intervention to guarantee relative independence, in this aspect too Virginians were anticipating the constitutional arguments of the years leading up the Declaration of Independence.[22] The tension between wanting to be acknowledged by English governing elites as at once more English and as members of a distinctly provincial Virginian elite would dominate the historical sense of that same elite for the rest of the colonial period.

Whoever wrote the anonymous *Essay* certainly exhibited the characteristic concerns of the Virginia elite, and placed the text in a significant and at times acrimonious debate between metropolitan theorists of empire and colonial representatives. The themes of confusion of the precise legal status of the colonies within the empire and of the legitimacy of the jurisdictional authority of colonial institutions abound in the short pamphlet, as they would go on to in subsequent exchanges over imperial constitutionalism from William Byrd II and Robert Beverley to Richard

[22] On the assertion of the centrality of this turn to royal power within the imperial constitution in revolutionary thought, see Eric Nelson, *The Royalist Revolution: Monarchy and the American Founding* (Cambridge, MA: Harvard University Press, 2014).

Bland and Thomas Jefferson. Taking aim at the expansion of the power of royal governors that was felt to be taking place, the author directly charged these tendencies with undermining royal authority. The disastrous turn of Edmund Andros as Governor of the Dominion of New England proved that royal power belonged in only one place, and that was with the Crown.[23] Lesser representatives wielding such power were bound to pursue their own interests with the unmitigated power of royal prerogative in their hands. Migration to the colony had slowed (not, according to the author, because of the rigid social hierarchy or the turn to chattel slavery for labor, but because of the awareness in England of the arbitrary government potentially practiced by its governors), and so the interests of the Crown had been hurt as a result. Appealing to reason of state, the author suggested in effect that any reading of the royal colonial charters that concluded that the colonies were dependent on the Crown and so were "Subject to such Laws as the King shall please to Impose" was circulating an innovation.[24] Such had never been the case, claimed the author, and while agents on both sides of the Atlantic were agreed that change was needed, it was only a "free constitution" that guaranteed the liberties and interests of colonial subjects and the rights and interests of the Crown. A free constitution, the author asserted, such that "the Inhabitants of the Plantations may enjoy their Liberties and Estates, and have Justice equally and impartially administered to them; and it should not be in the power of any Governour to prevent this."[25] Prerogative needed to be checked by local institutions, custom, and the free spirit of the British Constitution in the colonies, just as had been recently achieved in Britain itself.

[23] *An Essay upon the Government of the English Plantations on the Continent of America*, Louis B. Wright, ed. (San Marino: The Huntington Library, 1945), p. 18.

[24] *An Essay upon the Government of the English Plantations on the Continent of America*, pp. 18, 18–21. The 1624 Royal Charter of Virginia lent itself to similar ambiguities as Sir Edward Coke's decision in *Calvin's Case*, for the charter stipulated that the colonists would enjoy the full liberties subjects, but by the grace of the Crown – it is not made clear at all that the colonists had any natural claim to the continuance of these rights should the judgments and interests of the Crown change; on the earlier charters and the place of Coke in subsequent legal and historical understanding, see Mary Sarah Bilder, "Charter Constitutionalism: The Myth of Edward Coke and the Virginia Charter," 94 *North Carolina Law Review* (2016), pp. 1545–98.

[25] *An Essay upon the Government of the English Plantations on the Continent of America*, pp. 20–1. On the prevalence of civic humanist language of free states and the corrupting force of private interest in colonial discourse, see Andrew Fitzmaurice, *Humanism and America: An Intellectual History of English Colonization, 1500–1625* (Cambridge: Cambridge University Press, 2003).

The author of the *Essay* presumed a narrative of the events of the Glorious Revolution in England that retained an understanding of royal sovereignty at the center of British constitutionalism, and in that the author was characteristic of later colonial ignorance or disavowal of the rise of parliamentary supremacy. In fact, the author made their plea for the erection and recognition of a free constitution in the colonies through a plea for greater direct royal oversight of colonial law and governance. The history of law in the colonies, the author suggested, had been a reckless and confusing one, it being "a great Unhappiness, that no one can tell what is Law, and what is not, in the Plantations."[26] Nor could anyone seem to define who exactly had the responsibility to say what law was and what law was not in the colonies. Rehearsing the variable interpretations of the legal status of the colonies, whether the colonies were bound by the English common law, whether Acts of Parliament since colonization were binding, and if so, perhaps only if the colonies are named in the Acts, the author concluded that whatever the case has been, it was simply untenable. "Thus are we left in the dark, in one of the most considerable Points of our Rights," the author argued, too often dependent on judicial discretion alone. As the General Court was appointed by the Governor and consisted of members of his Council, in Virginia in particular it was hardly the case that legal decisions were made with a degree of certainty or independence.[27] This state of affairs and the laxity of jurisdictional boundaries made possible in such a context had been characteristic of colonial law since the beginning, argued the author, hardly making the case for the historical existence of an independently developed legal and constitutional culture as subsequent authors would go on to do.

The author of the *Essay* argued for greater metropolitan regulation, asking for rules that lay out precisely what law was in the colonies, definitions of legitimate colonial institutions and appropriate jurisdictional authority for those respective institutions, the ability to appeal significant disputes (more than 500 Pounds in sterling) to English courts, and royal confirmation of private land title, in particular.[28] Needless to say, the appeal to the Crown and to the Board of Trade to effectively intervene on behalf of Virginia's planter elite in its intermittent spats with royally appointed governors was largely unsuccessful

[26] *An Essay upon the Government of the English Plantations on the Continent of America*, p. 23.

[27] *Ibid*, p. 23.

[28] *Ibid*, pp. 39–40.

(although much to the later disliking of that same planter elite, the power of the Board of Trade and the Privy Council over colonial affairs did dramatically increase in the eighteenth century, just as colonial law was felt by its users and defenders to be coming into its own). What the essay forecasted was a constitutional dispute that was increasingly framed by theorists on both sides of the Atlantic as an argument over history, and for colonists in particular, over control of the constitutional implications of narratives of colonial history.

To establish their particular understanding of their own status in the empire, colonial elites would need to establish a particular civil and specifically legal history to represent it, and Robert Beverley, who might well have been the author of the *Essay*, was, along with his father, a leader of this project.[29] His *History and Present State of Virginia* was published in London in 1705, in a revised edition in 1722, and the book marked a fundamental turning point in the production of provincial historical consciousness. Beverley's father Major Robert Beverley had been a justice of the peace, the attorney general for the colonial government, and the clerk of the House of Burgesses, whose job it was to oversee the production of manuscript copies of house journals and legislation. In 1677, the senior Beverley refused an order of the lieutenant governor, Herbert Jeffreys, to hand over copies of the laws and records of the House of Burgesses. The records were seized, although Beverley would never actually surrender his post. The clerkship was an office that Beverley, Jr. would basically inherit, appointed to the role in 1703, having previously served in the office of the colonial secretary, as the clerk of King and Queen County, and as the clerk of the General Court. When he traveled to London in 1703 to unsuccessfully appeal a lost land dispute, Beverley became even more aware than he must have already been of the importance of controlling the flow of information to metropolitan authorities.[30]

29 F. H. Harrison, "Robert Beverley, the Historian of Virginia," *The Virginia Magazine of History and Biography*, Vol. 36, No. 4 (October 1928), pp. 333–44; Jon Kukla, "Robert Beverly Assailed: Appellate Jurisdiction and the Problem of Bicameralism in Seventeenth Century Virginia," *The Virginia Magazine of History and Biography*, Vol. 88, No. 4 (October 1980), pp. 415–29.

30 Susan Scott Parrish, "Introduction," to Robert Beverley's *The History and Present State of Virginia*, Parrish, ed. (Chapel Hill: University of North Carolina Press, 2013), pp. xvi–xxi. Captain John Purvis was the merchant sea captain ordered in 1682 to repossess the subsequent records of the House that Major Robert Beverley had refused to hand over, and to arrest him for allegedly participating in a scheme to raise the price of tobacco by destroying crops. While predated by the Francis Moryson and Henry Randolph edition of 1662, "*Lawes of Virginia now in Force*" (London: E. Cotes, A. Seile, 1662) and earlier

For his arguments and correspondence against the sitting Governor, Francis Nicholson, and Nicholson's carrying out of plans to regularize and strengthen imperial control of the colonial governments, Beverley was removed from his clerkships over protest from the House of Burgesses. As Susan Scott Parrish suggests in introducing the modern scholarly edition of the text, it was an imperative for the planter elite to gain control of representations of themselves and their capacity for lawful and ordered government before English audiences, and this was precisely the goal of Beverley's *History* and his subsequent work in collecting and publishing a Virginian edition of the laws of Virginia.

The contexts in which *The History and Present State of Virginia* was written allowed its author and his peers to understand their goals as the representation and defense of a particularly provincial history in which they were the primary actors. Beverley problematized theories of creole degeneracy, depicting a vibrant colonial world of abundant natural resources, Native peoples in possession of their own history, if not entirely in his eyes of the land on and with which they had been making that history, and of the progress of English colonial civilization under the stewardship of colonial landholders themselves. In this they were interrupted only by the unwarranted intrusions of power-hungry governors, and Beverley was as convinced as any other colonial representative that if only the Crown understood their version of realities on the ground, the situation of the colonies would improve. Secondly, in the wake of the events of Bacon's Rebellion in Virginia and the Glorious Revolution in England, both of which provided occasions for strengthening royal authority in the colony, Beverley needed to craft a historical identity of settlement that included disaffected smaller planters and western farmers, constructing an image of a broad, united, and orderly proprietary class protecting and expanding the empire by resisting self-interested corruption from appointed officials and

smaller compilations of laws and orders going back to William Strachey's, *For the Colony Virginea Brittania. Lawes Divine, Morall and Martiall, &c* (London: Walter Burre, 1612), a new and widely disparaged as incomplete printed edition of the Laws of Virginia was published circa 1684 for "J.P." in London, and the "Purvis" edition, as it was called by its users in Virginia, and despite it being condemned for publication without license, to their consternation remained the most readily available printed copy of the laws for decades; see William Waller Hening, *Statutes at Large: Being a Collection of all the Laws of Virginia from the First Session of the Legislature, in the Year 1619* (Philadelphia: Thomas Desilver, 1823), Vol. 3, pp. 547–9.

forcefully subduing and governing dwindling populations of Natives and expanding populations of African slaves.

In his presentation of history, Robert Beverley was anxious to let his readers know that he had exclusive access to records that others involved in colonial disputes did not, and that he had the cultivated erudition in the relevant history to be acknowledged as an authority on the subject, on either side of the Atlantic. Through successive sections on the history of colonization, the natural history of Virginia, the Native American population, and the present state of government and society, Beverley offers a "faithful Account," careful to not publish anything not verifiable by "Authentique Testimony," or that is justified by "my own Knowledge, or by credible Information," and avoiding "Partiality," sharing with his audience both the "Inconveniences" and the "Excellencies" of what he did not hesitate to call his country.[31] Claiming a space in the emergent culture of enlightened transatlantic exchange of information as well as in the constitution of the British Empire in the early modern Atlantic world, Beverley established his unique ability to offer a history. In fitting with the chorographic imperatives of early modern governmental knowledge production, that history needed to shift and back and forth from natural to civil history, defending both the particular social and institutional development that had taken place under the agency of the creole planter elite and the natural resources that had supported and would continue to support future development.

Of course, this put the impetus on the author to distinguish the use made of those resources by English settlers from the image of the Native American as having at best an inferior claim to their land because they had not cultivated it. Offering a settler narrative of what earlier English settlers had found in Virginia upon their arrival, Beverley introduced the native peoples of the Powhatan Confederacy as in full possession of their "Primitive Innocence," if nothing else, for they "were without Boundaries to their Land; and without Property in Cattle, and seem'd do have escaped, or rather not to have been concern'd in the first Curse, *Of getting their Bread by the Sweat of their Brows*."[32] The depiction of Native Americans has "Living without Labour" was a crucial part of justifications of British conquest in North America, although Beverley's appraisal of their form of life was a complex one. Checked by the need to defend the materials at hand for building empire in Virginia, Beverley was concerned

[31] Beverley, *The History and Present State of Virginia*, pp. 8–9. [32] *Ibid*, p. 14.

later in the text to argue that Native Americans were not wandering savages of the woods but people with a society and a history of which they were aware. This was a crucial point for Beverley and for other eighteenth-century Virginians fitting the strange plurality of life in the colonies into a coherent narrative with themselves at the center of it. The legal humanism that they practiced and wanted to put on display, after all, implied a minimal awareness of human communities as historically constructed and kept alive by memory of the continuity of their history.[33] Beverley painted a picture of a successful and civilizing colonial project, and to say the least a justifiable one, but he also aimed to represent a Virginia that was made up of a plurality of peoples and their histories. And he did so as part of a broader attempt to achieve metropolitan acknowledgment of alternative historical processes and practices occurring in the colonies than those of creole degeneracy.

Beverley proceeded with a large part of that argument by insisting that the recent decades of Virginia's legal and political history were examples of tyranny and corruption threatening the liberties of English subjects there and so the potential of the colonial enterprise itself. The arrival of Sir Thomas Culpeper as royal governor in 1679 had brought with it a series of legal changes that challenged the power of the House of Burgesses and its leaders. These were part of an effort to shore up imperial authority in the colonies, and they included penalties of 500 pounds and a year imprisonment for speaking or writing ill of the Governor, slightly less severe penalties for speaking ill of members of the Council (100 pounds and three months imprisonment), moves which Beverley described as "such a Safeguard to Tyranny" as to make any disagreement or appeal impossibly dangerous.[34] At the same time, the Governor began making the tax rates based on wealth regular and perpetual, and enforced and collected by the Governor and Council as opposed to the House of Burgesses. Amid declines in the price of tobacco and other exported goods, and enforcement of the Navigation

[33] J.G.A. Pocock, *The Ancient Constitution and the Feudal Law: A Study of English Historical Thought in the Seventeenth Century* (Cambridge: Cambridge University Press, 1957, 1987); "Time, Institutions, and Action: An Essay on Traditions and Their Understanding," *Politics, Language, and Time: Essays on Political Thought and History* (New York: Atheneum, 1971), 233–72; James Tully, *Strange Multiplicity: Constitutionalism in an Age of Diversity* (Cambridge: Cambridge University Press, 1995). In this as in so many other cases, the nominally distinct traditions of civic humanism and juridical discourse concerning rights of possession were hardly incompatible.

[34] Beverley, *The History and Present State of Virginia*, p. 67.

Acts and other laws passed in Parliament restricting trade and manufacturing in the colonies, these changes hit men like Beverley personally, threatening their almost complete control of economic if not political life in Virginia. The collection of quitrents became another hot-button point of contention between planters and the royal government. The paradox that by the time of Beverley's writing Parliament was gaining in constitutional power in England while what Virginians considered their own legislative body in the form of the House of Burgesses gradually lost constitutional power was not lost on him, or others. Indeed, constitutional issues and disputes over jurisdictional authority of colonial governing institutions were another major bone of contention.

Culpeper mandated changes in the recording of legal decisions before the General Court and in the authority of the Court itself. Listing a "useful Thing which his Lordship was pleased to do," describing how it seemed that "Nicety of Pleading, with all of the Juggle of *Westminster Hall*, was creeping into the Courts," Beverley wrote of the Governor's instructions to the clerk of the court system to cease recording arguments and reasons given for decisions. The aim of the shift, as Beverley noted, was to keep the General Court in particular away from "pretending to set Precedents of inviolable Form to be observed in all future Proceedings," hoping to keep decisions speedy and direct, "according to the Innocence of former Times." Beverley displayed a subtle but significant ambivalence about what was at stake in this shift, for while he celebrated the jurisdictional flexibility of the General Court and the necessary simplicity of its jurisprudence, if it could be said to have one at all, the implications of the shift ran deeper.[35] The Governor found the court system to be lacking in the historical authority to participate in the making of common law for the polity it served, "alledging, that their Courts were not of so great Experience, as to be able to make Precedents to Posterity; who ought to be left at Liberty to determine, according to the Equity of the Controversie before them."[36] Equity was a particularly potent matter of both legal and more broadly constitutional significance in English legal discourse given the previous century of sometimes direct conflict over the appropriate powers of equitable consideration in the complexity of English legal structures.

[35] See David Thomas Konig, "Virginia and the Imperial State: Law, Enlightenment, and 'the crooked cord of discretion'" *The British and Their Laws in The Eighteenth Century*, David Lemmings ed. (London: Boydell, 2005), pp. 206–29.

[36] Beverley, *The History and Present State of Virginia*, p. 2.

The power of the Lord Chancellor's Court of Chancery and the Star Chamber to overrule common law courts in the name of the Crown had become a symbol of Stuart absolutism, and the denigration of common law proceedings in Virginia and the strengthening of chancery powers served to confirm for Beverley the dangerous direction in which the fate of English liberty was headed in the empire. When Baron Howard of Effingham was appointed Governor in 1684, Beverley continued, "though he pretended no great Skill in Legal Proceedings, yet he made great Innovations in their Courts, pretending to follow the *English* Forms. Thus he created a new Court of Chancery, distinct from the General Court, who had ever before claim'd that Jurisdiction. He erected himself into a Lord Chancellor," Beverley explained, taking the Council as mere advisors to discretionary power in the Court, holding that Court outside of the State-House in Jamestown, and accessing court fees arbitrarily. It was only when Effingham's brief tenure came to an end that the chancery jurisdiction returned to the General Court.[37] Over the course of the eighteenth century, that jurisdiction would come to play a significant role in the legal practice and conceptualization of colonial constitutionalism of Virginia's governing class both on their own terms and in their ongoing dialogue with metropolitan officials and British legal theory over their place in the empire.

While Beverley defended the rights of Virginians to the particular rights and protections of English liberty, he also defended the provincial distinctiveness of its legal edifice, defending in point of fact nothing less than the actuality and legitimacy of a colonial legal edifice in the first place. The establishment and enforcement of the body of English statutory law passed in Parliament since colonization as binding for Virginia courts, as Governor Edmund Andros decreed upon his arrival in 1692, could be just as arbitrary and uncertain a legal condition for the colonists as being entirely at the discretion of the Crown's appointees, denying as that idea did the particular legal system that had developed legitimately and customarily in the civil history of the colony. The assemblage, preservation, and representation of that history was part of the peculiar civic identity they were constructing. Beverley, with the spirit of a clerk, went out of his way to praise Andros for his dutiful efforts to maintain the colonial records in the State-House, keeping them dry and ordered, and even taking special care to restore those that survived the fire of 1698. No

[37] *Ibid*, p. 73.

doubt settling scores by demonstrating the consequences of his own removal from the offices of the colonial secretary and clerkship, Beverley held up Andros, who he deemed far from perfect, for his unique attention to the material record of land title and legislation that for Beverley and his fellows guaranteed their particular place atop colonial society and within the broader governing structure of the empire.

Beverley's estimation of colonial governors was almost entirely rooted in their acknowledgment of the rights and privileges of participation in governance on the part of the planter elite, and for Beverley the tenure of Francis Nicholson served as an example of how bad things could get without these acts of acknowledgment. Much of what Beverley records from Nicholson is gossip, but the gossip serves to confirm a wider narrative Beverley wanted to tell about Nicholson's imprudent dismissal of the interests and concerns of Virginia's creole leaders. Given to "excessive Passions," Beverley related, "in the General Court, of which he is Chief Judge, he has often behaved in that boisterous manner, that neither the rest of Judges on the Bench, nor the Lawyers at the Bar, cou'd use their just Freedom."[38] When the Attorney General or anyone else questioned his decisions, Beverley continued, they ran the grave risk of being "ill used" by the Governor, met with exclusion or even civil punishment. Indeed, "ill usage" runs throughout Beverley's *History* as a trope that measures the flux of acknowledged colonial access to and possession of a history of law, custom, and usage, and Nicholson's lack of attention to the good uses being made of both English inheritance and the resources of the colonial context was for Beverley and his peers intolerable. When his abuses were resisted, Beverley told his readers, on the grounds that such treatment was not to be born in any country "that had the Happiness to be govern'd by the Laws of England ... he has been heard to reply, *That they had no Right at all to the Liberties of English Subjects, and that he wou'd hang up those that should presume to oppose him, with* Magna Charta *about their Necks*."[39] Whether Nicholson actually said such a thing or not, it was a statement that represented the antithesis of everything colonial Virginians historically understood themselves to be.

Nicholson's "ill usage" and the mentality he represented threatened the exclusivity of planter elite power, the security of their gendered self-mastery, their sense of racial consanguinity and status within the empire, the profitability of the plantation system for those that felt

[38] *Ibid*, p. 80. [39] *Ibid*, p. 81.

themselves to be on its front lines, and the security of unchallenged ownership of large tracts of land and further acquisition – all to be sure – but it threatened something else, too.[40] It threatened the particular historical narrative that Virginians told themselves about their unique place in the empire. That narrative was constructed in part by a claim to the possession of records and a legal archive that established both continuity and distinctiveness from English legal culture, but it was also measured against the histories of others. Uniquely among eighteenth-century Virginian historians, Beverley gave extended attention to Native Americans. While he contrasted the cultivating and civilized settler population with the roaming Natives, Beverley was also compelled to establish the land of Virginia as having the potential for further and future development, and not as degenerate. Describing Native sacred and funerary rites, and the especially erected altars to commemorate people or events in their history, Beverley suggests "that their careful observance of these Traditions, proves as good a Memorial of such Antiquities, as any Written Records; especially for so long as the people continue to inhabit in, or near the same place."[41] The lack of an archive as such distinguishes Beverley's English Virginia from Native America, but the recognition of a recorded and maintained historical awareness also marks similarities if not a shared understanding of what makes people *a people*. "The *Indians* having no sort of Letters among them, as has been before observ'd, they can haven no Written Laws;" Beverley says of political authority among them, "nor did the Constitution in which we found them, seem to need any."[42] They obey "one Chief" who decides all disputes, and custom and interconnectivity seemed to Beverley to take care of a great deal of the other work one would normally expect of law and government.

[40] Beverley also records Nicholson as having said to the governors of the College of William and Mary in an argument that "*they were all Dogs, and their Wives were Bitches; that he knew how to govern the Moors, and would beat them into better Manners*," for Beverley took every chance of reminding his reader that Nicholson's previous colonial post was in Morocco and that this hardly qualified him to be governing the self-assured civil polity of Virginia, as Beverley continued, "*he knew how to govern the Country without Assemblies; and if they should deny him anything, after he had obtain'd a standing Army, he wou'd bring them to Reason, with Halters about their Necks*," Beverley, *ibid*, p. 81; as the book was published in London in 1705, the House of Burgesses was approving legislation further strengthening the security of slave property, making the politics of racial hierarchy in the colony all the more central to the concerns of its master class; on the laws of slavery and labor as described in the 1722 edition, see Beverley, *ibid*, p. 216.

[41] *Ibid*, p. 168.

[42] *Ibid*, p. 177.

There was a tone of appreciation and even admiration in Beverley's text. Beverley acknowledged the Powhatan Confederacy as in possession of a history, even a civil history, and he composed his own history around the desire for such an acknowledgment from others. But he was also making it clear that Virginia left in their hands was only ever in a state of potential cultivation and development. Their disputes, Beverley says, are few: "their labour ... is not so great, that they need quarrel for room, where the Land is so fertile, and where so much lyes uncultivated." In his *History of the Dividing Line*, decades later, Byrd would confirm that the Native Americans he encountered on his journey westward had "the same Natural Dignity" as any other people, for "we all know that very bright Talents may be lodg'd under a very dark Skin." What differences there were arose only from "Different Opportunities for Improvement."[43] Land is there, Beverley and Byrd confirm, for possession, and in setting up the representation of Native and settler populations as questions of acknowledging respective histories, both men were laying critical groundwork not only for Thomas Jefferson's own contribution to the genre, *Notes on the State of Virginia* in 1787, but for the importance of configurations of historical practice and capacity to two subsequent centuries of settler expansion and Indian removal, in no small part under Jefferson's direction.[44]

Ultimately, Robert Beverley's *History and Present State of Virginia* defined a provincial legal and political history that he and his peers hoped could protect their interests and position abroad and their immense social and economic power within the colony itself. That the first part of the fourth and final book begins with the heading "Of the Civil Polity and Government of Virginia" broadcasts Beverley's goal to depict Virginia as an independently developing extension of European and specifically English political order.[45] In describing the General Court and the legal order

[43] William Byrd, *The Dividing Line Histories of William Byrd II of Westover*, Kevin Joel Berland, ed. (Chapel Hill: University of North Carolina Press, 2013), p. 120; later in the text, attempting to describe Native American religious beliefs, Byrd suggests they have no anticipation of an afterlife and so no impetus to improvement of their lives or condition, and that their lack of cultivation should not be so surprising then, given that they "are contented with Nature, as they find her, and have no other Lights but what they receive from purblind Tradition," pp. 148–9.

[44] Indeed, Byrd's manuscripts of the histories were acquired by Thomas Jefferson and he later handed them over the American Philosophical Society; see Maude H. Woodfin, "Thomas Jefferson and William Byrd's Manuscript Histories of the Dividing Line," *The William and Mary Quarterly*, Vol. 1, No. 4 (October 1944), pp. 363–73.

[45] *Ibid*, p. 189.

of Virginia, Beverley again celebrated the sweeping jurisdictional authority of the Court. As the Court had always enjoyed authority in all sorts of legal disputes, "Civil and Ecclesiastical," deciding cases that came before it "by the Standard of Equity and Good Conscience," Virginia had managed to develop an autonomous legal system where "the tricking, and foppery of the Law" was "happily avoided."[46] The simplicity of the bases for legal decision-making allowed for desired maneuverability among a largely self-contained class of planter elites, who for the most part were without access to formal legal study in London. The lack of formal rules of procedure and explicitly defined jurisdictional authority allowed many elite Virginians throughout the colonial period to exercise control over decisions about property disputes and inheritance, protecting their social and economic power by retaining powerful places in the unsystematic legal infrastructure of the colony. The lack of all but the most necessary "Form and Nicety" from legal proceedings allowed for the kind of flexibility required for adaptation and development of English law to provincial contexts. Beverley repeatedly drew attention to the dangers of external impositions of "Form" on Virginia constitutionalism and law, particularly in the instances of governors mandating the adaptation of contemporaneous English common law principles and statutory law, or taking onto themselves the powers of equitable discretion appropriate to a Court of Chancery or other conciliar court. From Beverley's time to that of Jefferson's own legal practice and designs for revolutionary-era constitutional reform, contestations over the location of equitable judgment within constitutional orders would play a central role in wider disputers over the nature of imperial, colonial, and republican law and constitutionalism.

The personal manuscript notes of Beverley's ally William Byrd II further demonstrate the importance of jurisdictional confusion and conflict to imperial and colonial constitutional discourse, and more broadly how linked the political concerns of planters were with efforts to control narratives of civil history in the colony. In 1715, Byrd again traveled to England acting as an agent for the Virginia House of Burgesses, this time defending its effort to resist increases in royal control under the governorship of Alexander Spotswood. Even after he had returned to Virginia and a more sympathetic governor, William Gooch, was appointed in 1727, Byrd found himself concerned with disputes over the legal status of the

[46] *Ibid*, p. 204.

colony. In his notes, he copied down what he dismissed as the "performance" of Sir William Keith, former colonial governor of Pennsylvania, wherein Keith argued for greater imperial control of the commercial activity in North America, producing a historical narrative to ground his vision of a strengthened imperial state. Trade, Keith suggested, was essential to the power of the state, and the colonies were created solely for the purpose of extracting resources for the benefit of the mother country. This went along with legal and political understandings: "it is plain that none of the *English* Plantations in *America* can with any Reason or good Sense pretend to claim an absolute legislative Power within themselves; so that let their several Constitutions be founded on antient Charters, Royal Patents, Custom by Prescription, or what other legal Authority you please; yet still they cannot be possessed of any rightful Capacity to contradict... any Act of Parliament."[47] Keith described the legislative powers of the colonial assemblies as "improperly so called," and further suggested that colonial institutions lacked the strength and legitimacy to effectively safeguard the interests of the mother country, interests that had driven the creation of the colonies in the first place. He specifically attacked the pretension to chancery jurisdiction in the General Court as an absurdly premature localization of judicial power. As Byrd noted it down, Gooch responded in writing to the Privy Council, defending the history of the growth of Anglo-American civil institutions in Virginia and affirming that "the people of the Plantations conceive they are possessed of a Legislative Power, properly so called."[48]

Gooch went on to assert that questioning the legitimate authority of courts in colonial governments was historically unfounded, responding that, "however unintelligible the Civil Jurisdiction in the Plantations may be to some who are altogether unacquainted with American Affairs, the practice of these courts is exactly suited to the circumstances of the

[47] William Byrd, "Westover Manuscripts," (1692–1739), MS collections of the Virginia Historical Society, Mss10: no. 50, pp. 350–3. The offending piece was "A Short Discourse on the Present State of the Colonies in America, with Respect to the Interest of Great Britain," (1728); see Sir William Keith, *A Collection of Papers and other Tracts written occasionally on Various Subjects, to which is prefixed, by way of Preface, An Essay on the Nature of a Publick Spirit* (London: J. Mechell, 1740), p. 175. Keith went beyond what Mary Sarah Bilder calls the "repugnancy principle" that loosely governed legal relations between center and periphery for the colonies, such that colonial assemblies were relatively free to act so long as they did not directly contradict the laws of England or the spirit of the British Constitution; Mary Sarah Bilder, *The Transatlantic Constitution* (Cambridge, MA: Harvard University Press, 2004), pp. 1–3.

[48] William Gooch as quoted in Byrd, "Westover Manuscripts," p. 357.

Prospective Governments." Colonial legislatures had set up constitutional structures and court systems "as near as possible conformable to the Laws of England," and it was assumed that the protections of the common law were fundamental rights of British subjects in the colonies. Whereas Keith had attacked the independence of colonial courts from English judicial decisions, Gooch asserted that such independence was recognized by precedent, and that since the time of their settlement colonies had possessed the authority to craft laws fit for their particular circumstances, and establish courts, including Chancery courts, pursuant to the authority colonial governments possessed in the name of the Crown.[49]

In making such a defense, Gooch and Byrd were laying claim to the mixed foundations of colonial constitutionalism. They asserted that the assembly of the colony possessed a legislative sovereignty of its own, that a distinct legal system could and had developed in Virginia, which was neither repugnant to nor exactly the same as the English common law. But this claim was predicated upon the continuity of the liberty of English subjects and its protection under the British Constitution through the historical process of settlement. Provincial claims to legitimacy were rooted in both the authority of English constitutionalism and the relative independence of colonial constitutional structures. In inscribing the dispute in his personal papers, Byrd implicated self-possession in the political efforts to carve out collective legal self-possession for his provincial polity. Only within the context of the mixed and disputed legal status of the colony can we understand the connection between law and historical consciousness in Virginia. Defining Virginia as a polity involved locating and narrating the history of its government.

ORGANIZING LEGAL HISTORY

As Keith's attack on their legitimacy indicates, it would be difficult to overstate the importance of charters, patents, and customs to the project of building a historical identity for Virginia's political culture. In his later history of the colony, William Stith related that the "greatest and most considerable Assistances from authentick Manuscripts, Sir John Randolph's Collection of publick Papers, and the Capitol Records, have been of no little Use to me," and he described his dependence on "a very full and fair Manuscript of the London Company's Records, which was

[49] Byrd, "Westover Manuscripts," pp. 360–1.

communicated to me by the late worthy President of our Council, the Honorable William Byrd."[50] From the copied laws collected by Randolph, the court books and company records in the possession of William Byrd, and the records in the library of the Governor's Council in Williamsburg, Stith made what sense he could and applied the compilation to what he considered their proper use: "forming a good History." Against the narrative of Keith, who sought to draw the colonies within a larger economic history of the British imperial project, provincial historians such as Stith and Robert Beverley were compelled to focus their attention on the particular history being acted out in Virginia.[51] These colonial histories reinforced a civic identity that was balanced between the original sources of their own self-understanding and the limits of those sources in the colonial context.

Just as important as the formal works of history written in colonial Virginia were the variety of projects involved in printing the Laws of Virginia. Both the seventeenth-century planter William Fitzguh and Sir John Randolph had intended but never managed to complete a colonial collection of the laws, and so lawyers and legislators relied on editions printed in London well into the eighteenth century.[52] Any frequent occurrence to recently passed laws and local ordinances demanded handwritten fair copies, and a council member like Robert "King" Carter kept handwritten records of further legislative activity in his personal copy of the

[50] William Stith, *The History of the First Discovery and Settlement of Virginia* (Williamsburg: William Parks, 1747), preface. Through estate purchases made in 1775 and 1776, both of these manuscript collections come to the ownership of Thomas Jefferson, including the commonplace book, reports, and legal notes of Sir John Randolph; see the Thomas Jefferson Papers of the Library of Congress, Series 8: Virginia Records Manuscripts, 1606–1737; and on Randolph's personal papers, Series 7, "The Commonplace Book of Sir John Randolph," see Sowerby, *Catalogue of the Library of Thomas Jefferson*, Vol. 2, p. 224, #1796, #1798.

[51] See Sir William Keith, *The History of the British Plantations in America* (London: S. Richardson, 1738).

[52] The earliest attempt at a comprehensive edition after the Restoration was one complied by Francis Moryson and Henry Randolph, *The Lawes of Virginia, Now in Force* (London: E. Cotes, A. Seile, 1662), but the most common of these in the late seventeenth and early eighteenth centuries was the Purvis edition, *A Complete Collection of All the Laws of Virginia, Now in Force* (London: T.J., for J.P., c. 1684). A later collection of colonial laws was published in London after the Glorious Revolution, reflecting the eighteenth-century organization of the empire: *An Abridgement of the Laws in Force and in Use in Her Majesty's Plantations; (Viz.) Of Virginia, Jamaica, Barbados, Maryland, New-England, New-York, Carolina, etc.*, (London: John Nicholson, 1704); see Warren M. Billings, *Little Parliament: The Virginia General Assembly in the Seventeenth Century* (Richmond: Library of Virginia, 2004), ch. 11.

Laws of Virginia.[53] Up to and beyond the American Revolution more than three-quarters of a century later, these palimpsests of personal copies and their accompanying marginalia or inlaid manuscript material marked the transmission of provincial legal tradition and inheritance as they were passed from down through generations. In 1722, William Beverley, the son of Robert Beverley who died that same year, published *An Abridgment of the Publick Laws of Virginia in Force and Use*, printed in London, and brought out a second and expanded edition in 1728.[54] Not until 1733 did the transplanted Maryland printer William Parks get permission to print the laws in Virginia, leading to the seminal publication of John Mercer's *Abridgement of the Public Acts* by Parks in 1737, and the subsequent periodic publication of abridgments of the laws of Virginia, the Journal of the House of Burgesses, and the Acts of Assembly.

These volumes became staples of law libraries, and they served to reinforce the balance of the metropolitan and provincial components of

[53] *A Complete Collection of All the Laws of Virginia, Now in Force* (London: T.J., for J.P., c. 1684), personal copy of Robert "King" Carter (1664–1732), Special Collections, John J. Rockefeller, Jr. Library, Colonial Williamsburg. The back cover of the volume has a beautiful inscription identifying it as a gift to Robert Carter by John Carter, most likely his oldest half-brother who died in 1690, in Latin, dated December 30, 1691, shortly after Robert took a seat from Lancaster County in the House of Burgesses in spring of 1691, which would account for the shift in handwriting from the laws recorded through 1686 and the laws recorded beginning in 1691, resuming again in 1699 but ending there, when Robert Carter was appointed to the Governor's Council by Francis Nicholson. The text was very much a family possession that marked the continuity of the family's immense economic power and its substantial role in colonial governance; see Emory G. Evans, *A "Topping People": The Rise and Decline of Virginia's Old Political Elite, 1680–1790* (Charlottesville: University of Virginia Press, 2009).

[54] Robert Beverley, *An Abridgement of the Publick Laws of Virginia in Force and Use, June 10, 1720* (London: F. Fayram, J. Clarke, 2nd edn., 1728), to which Beverley had added a collection of Virginia court judgments and orders that established distinct precedent for the colony, claiming explicitly the historical fact and legal authority of colonial departures from English practice, and on no other issue was this more important than on the issue of slavery and the legal status of slaves before courts as both criminals and property; indeed, Beverley's precedents include instances of a judge issuing an order of mittimus for a slave accused of a crime, and a public order to kill on sight slaves who had escaped and were "out-lying." Both of these precedents demonstrated the necessity of Virginia's distinctive legal culture and the importance of provincial control of the collection and representation of law, and both instances were pursuant to the October 1705 Acts that defined slavery in explicitly racial terms, strengthened the legal protections of the institution, and defined slaves as inheritable property; see Beverley, *Abridgement*, pp. 170, 181–2; William Waller Hening, *The Statutes at Large, Being a Collection of the Laws of Virginia from the First Statute of the Legislature, in the Year 1619*, Vol. 3 (Philadelphia: Thomas Desilver, 1823), ch. XXIII, pp. 333–42, ch. XLIX, pp. 447–62; see Sowerby, *Catalogue of the Library of Thomas Jefferson*, Vol. 2, p. 264, #1870.

law and jurisprudence in Virginia.[55] In the Laws, which open with a preface of March 1661, after "the late unhappy Disturbance" and the eventual restoration of Charles II, the Assembly declares in the first pages its "adherence to those excellent and often refined Laws of England, to which we profess and acknowledge all Reverence and Obedience, and that the Laws made by us are intended as brief Memorials of that which the Capacity of our Courts is utterly unable to collect out of its vast Volumes, though sometime perhaps, for the Difference in our and their Condition, varying in small things."[56] As early as the middle of the seventeenth century, legislators in Virginia were aware of the secondary, inherited origins of their nevertheless particular constitutional history. The declaration of that awareness still prefaced every printed edition of their legislative activity in the eighteenth century. Laws and legal structures were memorials in every sense of the term: historical constructs made from the tools of an inherited legal history but which nevertheless were characterized by their own unique unfolding in Virginia.

The collection and display of these books, particularly law books, was an act of cultural authority. As the preface to the Acts suggests, outside of the Laws of Virginia and Acts of Assembly printed in Williamsburg, the vast majority of law treatises and reports were imported. They were, therefore, rare and expensive commodities. Very few colonials had the financial capacity to accumulate great libraries. Law professors such as George Wythe and leading attorneys such as John Randolph (Sir John Randolph's son and the King's Attorney in the colony) had to go to great lengths to secure the latest court reports and parliamentary records from London.[57] While local attorneys in the counties might have small libraries

55 See Bryson, *Census of Law Books in Colonial Virginia*, pp. 22–5. As A.G. Roeber has argued, printing had a profound impact on legal practice, for it provided for the regularization of legal interpretation in the county courts, centered cultural authority in Williamsburg, and assisted the in the phasing out of signed oaths and other local ritualistic court practices; see A.G. Roeber, "The Scrutiny of the Ill-Natured and Ignorant Vulgar': Lawyers and Print Culture in Virginia, 1716–1774," *Virginia Magazine of History and Biography*, Vol. 91, No. 4 (October 1983), pp. 387–417. Practicing attorney John Markland's poem, "Typographia," printed by Parks in 1730 as the first imprint in Virginia, glorified William Gooch for his service to the colony, and sang the praises of the epochal transition from manuscripts to printed texts.

56 *Acts of Assembly now in Force in the Colony of Virginia* (Williamsburg: William Rind, Alexander Purdie, and John Dixon, 1769), pp. 1–2.

57 *John Norton and Sons: Merchants of London and Virginia, Being the Papers from their Counting House for the Years 1750–1795*, ed. Frances Norton Mason (Richmond: The Dietz Press, 1987), entries for June 13, 1768, May 8, 1770, August 26, 1771, May 29, 1772.

of key texts, and a slightly wealthier, more connected man such as Patrick Henry might collect upwards of 128 titles by his death, about a quarter of them law books, the libraries of Mercer, Byrd, and eventually Jefferson would number in the several thousands, including hundreds of law books each.[58]

Private libraries were sites of self-constitution for public men, and an eccentric gentleman like William Byrd guarded access to his library carefully. The library of William Byrd at Westover was an entirely separate structure, standing as a separate domain from the domestic sphere of the home while keeping the planter in contact with the plantation itself. His various surviving diaries, some of which were written in code, recount numerous instances of retreating to the library for privacy. In one famous episode, he described his wife being upset with him for refusing to allow her to take books from the library, and in another instance he records retreating to the library to instill his armorial book plate: "I put arms into my books."[59] He sometimes slept there, he exercised there, and of course, he read there, for reading, especially in the area of the law, was inseparable from the power structures and cultural politics of elite colonial life. In this regard reading Coke was especially important: Byrd collected large amounts of Coke's work in his library, and continued to record in his diaries retreating to the library or the bedroom "to read some Coke upon Littleton" until the end of his life.

The two institutional libraries of colonial Virginia, the law and history books in the Governor's Council Library in the capitol building, and the ecclesiastical library of the College of William and Mary were each reserved for the select few to whom they were open, members of the council, the Governor himself, clerical leaders and a mostly aristocratic student body studying law and divinity.[60] Because access to law books was so limited in the colonies, legal education remained grounded in older, more fundamental texts of the law, most visibly in the writings of

[58] Kevin J. Hayes, ed. *The Library of William Byrd of Westover* (Madison: Madison House, 1997).

[59] William Byrd, *The Secret Diary of William Byrd of Westover, 1709–1712*, Louis B. Wright and Marion Tinling Wright, eds. (Richmond: The Dietz Press, 1941), p. 361; *Another Secret Diary of William Byrd of Westover, for the years 1739–1741*, Maude H. Woodfin, ed. (Richmond: The Dietz Press, 1942), p. 100.

[60] *A Catalogue of the Library of the State of Virginia* (Richmond: Samuel Shepard & Co., 1828), books in the colonial Council Library were probably among those marked "old" in the 1828 catalog. See John M. Jennings, *Library of the College of William and Mary in Virginia* (Charlottesville: University of Virginia Press, 1968).

Coke. This served to reinforce the connection between law and history. As an order of knowledge, law was a construction, rooted in practices. In the context of Virginia these practices were constantly caught in the inherent tensions of the provincial status of the colony, the social and economic security of its leaders, and their consequent need to uphold their own historical subjectivity while locating discourses and mechanisms by which to deny historical subjectivity to others. And yet, as a self-conscious historical construction, law and political authority carried the means of their own critique. Among the Virginia gentry of the eighteenth century, collecting, reading, and "commonplacing" on matters of law and politics formed primary methods by which they located themselves in historical time.

As a justice of the peace for Richmond Co., especially one without legal training, Landon Carter placed a great deal of value in having frequent recourse to the Laws of Virginia.[61] In the 1752 edition, published after the 1748 Revisal of the Laws, Carter inscribed the book as a gift to his son Robert, "my Son, this contains the Laws of your Country, and as no Gentleman should be ignorant of them, I am persuaded I shall not be in need of any arguments, to enforce my claim to you." The work of reading the law might be tedious, the elder Carter warned, but he hoped his son would gain "a Capacity to lend a hand toward their improvements." The inscription is symbolic of the meaning attached to reading and understanding the particularity of the laws, even for men who were not attorneys, of the importance of law configured literally in this case as carefully transmitted inheritance, and of the importance attached to forming a self for public life.

The front pages of another volume are full of notes from Landon Carter's efforts in that regard, and the notes are a fitting memorial to the balancing project involved in preserving a British-American constitutional identity. Referencing the formation of what would become the two-tiered General Assembly, Carter noted that the Governor's Council had originally been part of the House of Burgesses, but at some time had seen fit to separate itself in "imitation of the Upper house in England, and claimed a Negative," or executive veto, of legislative activity in the lower

[61] On Landon Carter and his books, see Jack P. Greene, *Landon Carter: An Inquiry into the Personal Values and Social Imperatives of the Eighteenth Century Virginia Gentry* (Charlottesville: University of Virginia Press, 1965); Rhys Isaac, *Landon Carter's Uneasy Kingdom: Revolution and Rebellion on a Virginia Plantation* (Oxford: Oxford University Press, 2005).

house. While some might prefer this as "more conformable to the English constitution," he went on, "we stand in no need of such imitation," for "I suppose the laws made before the alteration were at last as valid as now and it is only by his Majesty's Prerogative that we have assembly."[62] In his own preface to the law, Carter asserted the particular history of the constitution in Virginia, but did so within a framework of his place in the larger constitution of the British Empire. Significantly, Carter also anticipated that the claim to the location of legislative powers in the assemblies would be a conflict with the authority of Parliament and a question of the linkage between colonial and metropolitan legislative bodies, and that colonists would paradoxically need to rely on the power of the Crown as transmitted to the colonies through the original charters in making their claims.

Amid the outbreak of the imperial crisis, leading Virginians found themselves increasingly driven to probe the mixed character of their constitutional history. They began to organize their own provincial legal history as a separate one, but they continued doing so in a manner and language they took from their uniquely partial inheritance of English jurisprudence until very late in the crisis. The antiquarian Richard Bland, who Roger Atkinson described as having "something of ye look of musty old Parchen'ts w'ch he handleth and studieth much," argued in his pamphlets of the Stamp Act Crisis that the common law and full liberty of English subjects had continued through the act of settlement, a fact which at the same time guaranteed the right of colonists to internal governance of their own affairs.[63] This was standard, and yet Bland was also driven to speak of the threat to "our constitution" in the joining of ecclesiastical and civil powers he perceived would result if attempts to secure an Anglican bishop for the colonies were successful. By 1774, he was publishing pieces of his private manuscript collection in the *Virginia Gazette*, providing documentary, textual grounding to colonial arguments about the liberty they derived from the 1624 charter of the

[62] Landon Carter's copies of *The Laws of Virginia, Now in Force* (Williamsburg: William Rind, Alexander Purdie, and John Dixon, 1752), *Acts of Assembly Now in Force in the Colony of Virginia* (Williamsburg: William Rind, Alexander Purdie, and John Dixon, 1769), Sabine Hall Library, Special Collections: Rare Books, University of Virginia.

[63] Roger Atkinson to Samuel Pleasants, October 1, 1774, *Virginia Magazine of History and Biography*, Vol. 15 (1908), p. 356; Richard Bland, *The Colonel Dismounted* (Williamsburg: Joseph Royle, 1764), *Inquiry into the Rights of the British Colonies* (Williamsburg: Alexander Purdie, 1766).

colony.[64] His 1766 pamphlet, *Inquiry into the Rights of the British Colonies*, had grounded the basis of colonial Virginian resistance to the Stamp Act in the natural rights of settlers as long recognized by the English common law (indeed, as dating back at least to the Gothic liberties of the ancient constitution of the Anglo-Saxons, who themselves were a settler society). What Bland articulated was an increasingly wider American constitutional argument that the white subjects of the Crown in the British North American colonies carried with them the rights of Englishmen, and that as a consequence they had a right to the exercise of internal political representation in the legislative bodies of their colony, independent of Parliament.

JEFFERSON IN PRACTICE

It is only possible to fully understand the legal studies and arguments of Thomas Jefferson at the receiving end of this tradition of colonial legal humanism, and it is important to appreciate that tradition both as a European intellectual tradition and a provincial form of cultivating and expressing a particular, historically constituted civic identity. Indeed, for Jefferson that reception was uniquely problematic and so all the more relevant: the death of his father in 1757 and the loss of most of his and his father's book and papers to a fire in 1770 meant that Jefferson experienced the material transmission of identity as a broken process, and it is no wonder that amid a wider crisis of colonial governance he came to see civic identity and historical consciousness as broken with it. Jefferson's legal commonplace books and the arguments before the General Court that the reading in those books informed were the products of more than a century of practicing legal study and constructing legal history in colonial Virginia, but they also demonstrate where Jefferson began to depart from that tradition while immersed in its materials and the processes of their transmission.

The form of the commonplace book registered the understanding of the law as an immense artifice, as a historical achievement that was built up layer upon layer over time. Jacob Soll has called the practice of

[64] Richard Bland to Thomas Adams, August 1, 1771, Correspondence of Thomas Adams in the Adams Family Papers, Virginia Historical Society. Purdie and Dixon's *Virginia Gazette*, April 4, 1774, April 21, 1774, printed in Peter Force, ed., *Tracts and Other Papers, Relating to the Origin, Settlement, and Progress of the Colonies in North America, from the Discovery of the Country to the Year 1776, Collected by Peter Force* (Washington, DC: Peter Force, 1838), Vol. 2, No. 5–6, pp. 106–14.

collecting rhetorical commonplaces for formation and argument in law, politics, and ethics one of "material rhetoric," a kind of writing transparently constituted through the reassembling of other writings.[65] The commonplace book provided Jefferson with a plane of collecting, assembling, and taking apart of narratives of the law that allowed for careful consideration of its palimpsest character, practicing reading as a kind of writing, or rewriting.[66] The legal commonplace book of Thomas Jefferson exhibits a process of gradual unraveling of the governing confines of a strictly legal research and an explosion of reading into the historical building blocks of the legal edifice and eventually multiple histories of law, government, and politics, particularly regarding the origins of constituted authority in collective assemblies.[67] Jefferson's reading began with notes from case reports and major legal treatises, including the third and fourth parts of Coke's *Institutes*, alongside the King's Bench case reports of William Salkeld and Sir Thomas Raymond on norms of legal remedies and court procedures as well as principles of common law adjudication.

The central themes of the earlier part of the legal commonplace book were English legal principles governing property transmission and

[65] Jacob Soll, *Publishing the Prince: History, Reading, and the Birth of Political Criticism* (Ann Arbor: University of Michigan Press, 2005), p. 13; in a sense, Jefferson's method of commonplacing was more Erasmian than Lockean, and he owned a 1663 edition of the printed book of Latin commonplaces by Erasmus, the *Adagiorum D. Erasmi Roterodami Epitome*, see Sowerby, *Catalogue of the Library of Thomas Jefferson*, #1363; on the extension of this tradition in the early American legal context, see Daniel R. Conquillette and Neil Longley York, eds., *The Portrait of a Patriot: The Major Political and Legal Papers of Josiah Quincy Junior* (Boston: Colonial Society of Massachusetts, 2005) and *Portrait of a Patriot, Volume 2: The Law Commonplace Book* (Boston, Colonial Society of Massachusetts, 2007); Mary Sarah Bilder, "James Madison, Law-Student and Demi-Lawyer," *Law and History Review*, Vol. 28, No. 2 (May 2010), pp. 389–449.

[66] As Kirstie McClure suggests, "the practice of commonplacing encouraged the decomposition of printed texts into fragments and their reassemblage," Kirste M. McClure, "Between the Castigation of Texts and the Excess of Words: Political Theory in the Margins of Tradition," *Democracy and Vision: Sheldon Wolin and the Vissictititudes of the Political*, Areyh Botninick and William E. Connolly, eds. (Princeton: Princeton University Press, 2001), p. 199. On the importance of the commonplace book in early modern educational theory and practice, see Ann Moss, *Printed Commonplace Books and the Structuring of Renaissance Thought* (Oxford: Clarendon Press, 1996); Bradin Cormack and Carla Mazzio, *Book Use, Book Theory: 1500–1700* (Chicago: University of Chicago Library, 2005), pp. 70–3; Ann M. Blair, *Too Much to Know: Managing Scholarly Information before the Modern Age* (New Haven: Yale University Press, 2010).

[67] Probably begun in 1765, concurrent with the start of his legal education under George Wythe; see Douglas L. Wilson, "Jefferson's Early Notebooks," *The William and Mary Quarterly*, Vol. 42, No. 4 (1985), pp. 434–52.

disputes, and the application of English common law and the power of English courts in the American colonies. These were questions of direct relevance to Jefferson's legal practice as well as his broader thinking about the nature of legislative authority in the colony of Virginia. He recorded a line from the 1705 decision in *Smith* v. *Brown & Cooper*: "the laws of England do not extend to Virginia, which being a conquered country, their law is what the King pleases." Chief Justice Holt declared that a suit to recover debt for a slave transported through England had to be amended by the plaintiff to reflect that the slave was in Virginia rather than London at the time of sale. As the reporters transcribed, "as soon as a Negro comes into England, he becomes free: one may be a villein in England, but not a slave."[68] The brief entry is telling in a number of ways. It registers a large part of the socioeconomic context of slavery to the disjunction between the application of law in England and in its plantations abroad. It also signifies the emergence of Jefferson's awareness, confirmed by contemporary historical analysts of the British American situation such as the Abbé Raynal that the English common law applied in the legal practices of the colonies by the civil and common law logic of prescription, made authoritative only by established and continuous practice.[69]

Just as important as the imperial context was the development of a certain legal imagination in the colony that took root after the 1705 revision of the slave code making tenured possession of slaves more

[68] Thomas Jefferson, *Legal Commonplace Book*, Thomas Jefferson Papers, Series 5, Library of Congress Manuscripts Division, Washington, DC, #231; *Smith* v. *Brown & Cooper*, in William Salkeld, *Reports of Cases Adjudged in the Court of King's Bench, with some Special Cases in Chancery, Common Pleas, and Exchequer* (London: E. Nutt, R. Nutt, and R. Gosling, 1721), p. 666. On this and other decisions as precursors to Justice Mansfield's decision in *Somerset* v. *Stewart* of 1772, see Robert M. Cover, *Justice Accused: Antislavery and the Judicial Process* (New Haven: Yale University Press, 1975), p. 16.

[69] The application of common law constraints to property ownership and inheritance was a gradual, never fully completed product of the development of a relatively independent court structure in the colony, particularly after the restoration of the Stuart monarchy in 1661. As Jefferson's researches into the charters and legal origins of the colony would indicate within the decade, and as he would argue in his 1774 memo to the delegates of the Continental Congress (published without permission as "A Summary View of the Rights of British America"), land had been distributed to settlers by the Crown in the form of "allodial" holdings, or in absolute dominion, in the King's realm. See "The Sentiments of a Foreigner on the Disputes of Great Britain with America" (Philadelphia: Humphreys, 1775), translated, extracted, and circulated from Raynal's *L'Histoire philosophique et politique des éstablissements et commerce des Européens dans les deux Indes*, published in 1770.

secure by redefining slaves as real estate rather than chattel. The shift entailed a transference of the "feudal" laws of property holding and transmission described by Coke to the logic of maintaining a race-based slave regime in eighteenth-century Virginia. In his own collection of case reports from cases before the General Court of Virginia, Jefferson reported on an October 1768 case, *Blackwell* v. *Wilkinson*, in which the continuum from the early modern image of medieval English law to Virginia implied by this transference served as the basis for deciding specific issues relative to the problematic legal status of slaves.

The Court found for the defendant that slaves needed to be specifically annexed to the land to be subjects of entail. Both arguments from attorneys took as given the parallel between feudalism and slavery. This was despite the legal disjunctions not only between contemporary English practice and that of Virginia but between the feudal villein and the plantation slave. As a denizen of England, even as a peculiar kind of property, the villein had a legal personage before the eyes of the common law and enjoyed the protection of basic rights dating back to "time immemorial."[70] The slave in Virginia, by and large recognized as naturally possessing the basic qualities of personhood, all the same had no legal personage at all. Indeed, as the Virginia slave codes indicated, the accidental killing of a slave that occurred during punishment for resistance by a master or overseer would result in no punishment for the responsible party, "as if such accident had never happened."[71] That slaves had the right to appear in court in disputes with their masters before 1705 only further emphasizes the conceptual work involved in appropriating a timeless image of the continuity of law to remove slaves from the plane of legal and thereby historical subjectivity.

[70] Indeed, as Charles M. Gray has shown, chancery provided an increasing path of access to legal protection and action on the part of villains and copyholders as the authority of manorial custom declined relative to courts of common law from the fifteenth to the early seventeenth centuries, *Copy-Hold, Equity, and the Common Law* (Cambridge, MA: Harvard University Press, 1963).

[71] "An Act Concerning Slaves and Servants" (1705, XXXIV), in *A Collection of all the Acts of Assembly, now in force, in the colony of Virginia* (Williamsburg: William Parks, 1733), p. 226. On the distinction between natural and legal personage in colonial Virginian legal practice and its influence on the U.S. Constitution, see Malick W. Ghachem, "The Slave's Two Bodies: The Life of an American Legal Fiction," *The William and Mary Quarterly*, Vol. 60, No. 4 (2003), pp. 809–42; see also John T. Noonan, *Persons and Masks of the Law: Cardozo, Holmes, Jefferson, and Wythe as Makers of the Masks* (Berkeley and Los Angeles: University of California Press, 2002), pp. 29–65.

One of Jefferson's own cases provided a medium for him to begin probing not only the legal framework for Virginia's slave system but also the temporal continuity implied by the authority of any instituted legal framework. In an April 1770 case, *Howell* v. *Netherland*, Jefferson took a case on behalf of Samuel Howell, the grandchild of a white woman and a black man. Bound by the 1705 laws to serve until the age of thirty-one, his mother's owner had claimed the same right over the lives of the offspring. Jefferson sought their freedom with the overarching logic that "under the law of nature, all men are born free."[72] Pointing to the fact that the 1705 law formalizing a shift from patrimonial to matrimonial transmission of servitude was a pact between the legislature and church-wardens over ownership of descendants of slave relationships, and was anyway intended to "punish and deter [white] women from that confusion of species, which the legislature seems to have considered as an evil," Jefferson stipulated that as the servitude was conventional, a condition of compact rather than nature or conquest, the terms of the compact did not extend to the grandchildren of the slaves in 1705. The argument was ineffective at best; Jefferson was not allowed to finish his argument before the judges interrupted and decided the case for the opposing side. He could not have been surprised, for in his argument he had broached a number of fundamental components of the jurisprudence prevalent in eighteenth-century Virginia, engaging a language of natural jurisprudence and equity to admit the descendants of slaves to legal subjectivity, or in his argument, to the reach of laws and contracts, in this case relating to property in land and people. While over the course of his life Jefferson would become reluctant to express much less act on anti-slavery sentiment, this tendency to focus on the constant making and remaking of legal authority through time would become increasingly central to Jefferson's thought both in his career as a lawyer as well as a critic and draftsman of legal and constitutional text.

Like his legal commonplace book, Jefferson's collections of reports of cases that had occurred before the General Court of Virginia, some his own and others much earlier, when taken in sum, demonstrate an unfolding of legal reporting and research into more primarily historical and political accounts of law and legal authority. Laws concerning slavery and religion were the areas that most engaged Jefferson's legal reading and writing. In

[72] Thomas Jefferson, *Reports of Cases Determined in the General Court of Virginia, 1730–1740, 1768–1772* (Charlottesville, VA: Carr, 1829), p. 92.

an October 1771 case, *Godwin* v. *Lunan*, Jefferson reported on his own disagreement with Wythe over the nature of his advocacy for lay members suing under the ecclesiastical jurisdiction of the General Court for the dismissal or punishment of their priest.

Wythe and Jefferson both represented the plaintiffs, but Jefferson was skeptical of the power of the Court as an ecclesiastical court to decide on such matters, as "visitation and deprivation are no parts of the office of an ecclesiastical judge." On these grounds, Jefferson launched into a historical investigation, for his own use, "into the first establishment of Christian churches in Great Britain, to develop their several kinds and constitutions, to see who is entrusted with their care and visitation; and to apply the principles which this inquiry would evolve to the parochial churches of our own country."[73] Jefferson carried out an inquiry into the origins and division of church structures in England, making use of his extensive collection of books concerning ecclesiastical law and church history, elucidating the growth of different legal types of parish. Donatives originated from the situation of churches on the manors of feudal lords, to which the tenants of the land would tithe, and from them they would receive support for land, a building, and a cleric. With Blackstone, Jefferson delineated two further classifications of churches that grew out of donatives over time: presentatives, where the bishop-in-charge of the parish claimed a right of review over the appointment of a cleric to the parish on the land of a lord; and collatives, in which a parish stood on land no longer owned by a lord, and control of it thereby naturally resided with the local bishop. In donatives, the patron of the church, whomever or whatever that might be, retained rights of visitation and removal beyond the sphere of ecclesiastical power assigned to the bishops by the development of ecclesiastical courts alongside the common law.

The law that governed donative patronage, reasoned Jefferson, did not therefore rest in ecclesiastical law, but in the particular set of customs and practices on the manor that the patron (and through him his tenants) recognized, as protected by the foundations of the common law in *lex non scripta*. "When any ecclesiastical Judge doth usurp the temporal law, ... the interest or cause of the subject is drawn in *aliud examen* [from all review] (viz.) to be decided and determined by the ecclesiastical law; and this is truly said *contra coronam et dignitatem regiam*" [(against the

[73] *Ibid*, p. 97.

crown and the royal prerogative)].[74] Only with the immemorial custom of the bishop's right of visitation recognized in presentatives, and following upon that the jurisdiction of ecclesiastical courts, would the General Court in its sometime capacity as an ecclesiastical court have power over the fate of the cleric. "But our parishes pretend to no immemorial existence, for that would make them older than our government itself: they have been created by acts of Assembly long within memory, to be found by any one who will recur to our records," Jefferson concluded.[75]

For Jefferson, who was again arguing for the power to remove the priest, this removal was illegitimate if carried out under the jurisdiction of ecclesiastical law. Having launched into a historical essay on the origins of ecclesiastical law to undo its power over particular cases in Virginia, Jefferson reached a conclusion far outside the bounds that governed the responses of Wythe and Randolph, the Attorney General arguing for the defendant: "the truth is, the parish is erected, the church and its soil given, and also the endowment, by the legislature, or in other words, the people they represent. Now that is a civil, not an ecclesiastical body. The churches are therefore of lay foundation."[76] Absent laws particularly granting the parish and the parishioners exclusive authority over the cleric, patronage of the parish rested in the figure of the King; the parish itself, under Jefferson's settler and constituent understanding of the constitutional structure of the British Atlantic empire, sat in the King's dominion, and the laws were that of the local legislature. Needless to say, suggesting the secular, legal, and democratic origins of the church and its legal authority, and seeking to restore those origins to political practice in Anglican Virginia, was a radical interpretation, and it relied on the further practical assumption that widespread and critically engaged recourse to the fundamental laws of the land was not only acceptable but necessary for the maintenance of jurisdictional dispute settlement in a free polity.

Jefferson's reading and extraction patterns point us to the groundwork for a critical mode of historical practice carried out in full awareness of the stitched together character of legal knowledge constructed in the manner of continuity and tradition. As his reading began to include histories of English law, he turned particularly to those that challenged Coke's antedating of what had become known as feudal tenures in the

[74] *Ibid*, p. 102; see William Blackstone, *Commentaries on the Laws of England* (Oxford: Clarendon Press, 1766), Vol. 2, pp. 22–5.

[75] Jefferson, *Reports of Cases*, p. 103.

[76] *Ibid*, p. 105.

descent of property to the pre-Conquest period, namely the works of the seventeenth-century royalist Sir Henry Spelman, Matthew Hale's *History of the Common Law*, and John Dalrymple's *An Essay Towards a General History of Feudal Property in Great Britain*. This reflected Jefferson's sense that in fact the positing of the continuity of the ancient constitution from the Anglo-Saxon period was a myth, and demonstrably so.

His selections from more broadly framed legal treatises included Obadiah Hulme's *An Historical Essay on the English Constitution*, (published in 1771), and which was written to trace the concept of the "elective power of the people" to the Saxon period and consequently justify the power of Parliament in its representative capacity to tax the colonists. He also included Sir John Fortescue's fifteenth-century *De Laudibus Leges Angliae*, a theoretical account of the long history and superiority of the English common law relative to alternative jurisdictions within England and the legal traditions of other constitutions in Europe. From these sources, Jefferson extracted narratives of the constituent assembly practices in which customary legal frameworks gained widespread legitimacy, focusing on origins, but again, not in any attempt to legitimate subsequent institutional development and codification, but, in the context of outspoken, sometimes riotous political activity on the part of increasing numbers of subjects during the imperial crisis, to recover and actualize the action of originating law.[77]

Especially crucial here are the references from Hulme to the Anglo-Saxon *witen*, or the *witena gemot*, the posited institutional and theoretical basis for parliamentary sovereignty in the British Constitution, and "where their principal power was lodged, annually moveable, and entirely subject to the elective power of the people," while giving a "more fixed state to executive authority, ... confined within a certain sphere of action," and "prescribed by law."[78] Likewise, Fortescue's delineation of the origins of political rule in the "Embrio" of the people would come to inform Jefferson's legal and constitutional thought. From a manuscript compilation of Fortescue's writings, eighteenth-century lawyer John Fortescue-Aland published *The Difference between an Absolute and Limited Monarchy* in 1714, the preface to which served as the source of

[77] Michael A. McDonnell, "Class War? Class Struggles during the American Revolution in Virginia," *The William and Mary Quarterly*, Vol. 63, No. 2 (2006), pp. 305–44.

[78] Jefferson, *Legal Commonplace Book*, #803; Obadiah Hulme, *An Historical Essay on the English Constitution* (London; Edward and Charles Dilly, 1771). See also William Blackstone, *Commentaries on the Laws of England* (Oxford: Clarendon Press, 1769), Vol. 4, pp. 405–6.

a great number of the entries on Fortescue in the legal commonplace book. In the preface, Fortescue-Aland summarized Fortescue's historical work on the origins of the common law before King Alfred's compilation.[79] As Fortescue-Aland demonstrated, Fortescue had sought to prove that in its antiquity and its independent continuity, the common law of England was not only the equal but the superior of the European civil law inherited from Rome. For Fortescue, the foundations of this continuity lay in the participation of the population in the process of legitimating law and legal authority. Like the heart in a "body natural," Fortescue argued, "so in the Body Politic the intention of the people is the first living thing, having in it the blood, namely political provision for the interest of the people, which it transmits to the head and all the members of the body, by which the body is nourished and quickened."[80] This entailed a synchronic understanding of the temporality in which legislation and adjudication took place, for in any case where laws that did not "give full effect to the intention of the makers, they can speedily be revised, and yet not without the consent of the commons and nobles of the realm, in the manner in which they first originated."[81] The original process of lawmaking in an assembly was considered a constant presence in constitutional history, reenacted each time a law is made, either through representative institutions or the people themselves. Where Jefferson was coming to differ from Fortescue was in his refusal to see the historical moments of actually making law as solid threads in a longer continuum of legal development. Confronting a constitutional arrangement where legislative sovereignty had been, in the eyes of the colonists, forcibly removed to the locus of a non-representational, alien political institution, Jefferson's isolation of the constituent process of lawmaking at the historically informed theoretical origins of law and political society was part of a process of gathering past exemplary moments with which to think outside of inherited narratives of legal authority.

[79] John Fortescue-Aland, *The Difference between an Absolute and Limited Monarchy; As it more particularly regards the English Constitution. Being a Treatise written by Sir John Fortescue, Kt.* (London: William Bowyer, 2nd edition, 1719).

[80] Sir John Fortescue, *On the Laws and Governance of England*, Shelly Lockwood, ed. (Cambridge: Cambridge University Press, 1997), pp. 20–1. On Fortescue, his context, and his place in subsequent history, see Alan Cromartie, *The Constitutionalist Revolution: An Essay on the History of England, 1450–1642* (Cambridge: Cambridge University Press, 2006), pp. 1–32; Thomas Garden Barnes, *Shaping the Common Law: From Glanvill to Hale, 1188–1688* (Stanford: Stanford University Press, 2008), pp. 61–78.

[81] Fortescue, *On the Laws and Governance of England*, p. 28.

By far Jefferson's largest commonplace book, and perhaps consequently his least appreciated one, was his notebook on theory and practice in equity jurisprudence. It was around the exploration and use of the concept of equity in the history of legal thought and institutions that the radicalism of Jefferson's designs for a revolutionary constitution for Virginia would be built.[82] During the rise of chancery jurisdiction under the respective Tudor governments, equity had been considered the "King's conscience," and therefore the conscience or spirit of the law, a corrective to the rigidity of the common law. By the eighteenth century, many jurists decried the potential for judgment in equity cases to rest on little but the conscience of the particular judge. While chancery practice had played an important role in getting around the feudal constraints of common law rules regarding real property and inheritance, it was in part out of concern for the growing power of this alternative jurisdiction that Blackstone and Chief Justice Mansfield began defending the legitimacy of common law judges interpreting the law with the assistance of principles of equity as part of their projects for conservative law reform.[83] Indeed, for Blackstone, it was imperative to de-emphasize the distinctions between equity and common law, at some length discussing the strict rules by which equity jurisprudence was bound, and the liberality of interpretation that had always been a component of common law adjudication. Equity by itself could lead anywhere. As John Fortescue-Aland put it, "to have no rule to decide controversies, but the rule of Equity, is to begin the World again, and make of a choice of that Rule, which out of

[82] See Edward Dumbauld, "Thomas Jefferson's Equity Commonplace Book," *Washington and Lee Law Review*, Vol. 48 (1991), pp. 1257–83; Peter Charles Hoffer, *Law's Conscience: Equitable Constitutionalism in America* (Chapel Hill: University of North Carolina Press, 1990), pp. 6–79; Matthew Crow, "Thomas Jefferson and the Uses of Equity," *Law and History Review*, Vol. 33, No. 1 (February 2015), pp. 151–80.

[83] William Blackstone, *Commentaries on the Laws of England* (Oxford: Clarendon Press, 1768), Vol. 3, pp. 428–42; see Thomas Jefferson to Philip Mazzei, November 1785, in *The Papers of Thomas Jefferson*, ed. Julian P. Boyd (Princeton: Princeton University Press, 1954), Vol. 9, pp. 67–72; David Lieberman, *The Province of Legislation Determined: Legal Theory in Eighteenth Century Britain* (Cambridge: Cambridge University Press, 1989), ch. 3, 6–7. On earlier debates over developments in equity, see G.W. Keeton, *An Introduction to Equity* (London: Pitman, 1961); Michael Macnair, "Common Law and Statutory Imitations of Equitable Relief under the Later Stuarts," *Communities and Courts and Britain, 1150–1900*; Christopher Brooks and Michael Lobban, eds. (London: Hambledon, 1997), pp. 115–31; *The Concept of Equity: An Interdisciplinary Assessment*, Daniela Carpi ed. (Heidelberg: Winter, 2007); Bradin Cormack, *A Power to Do Justice: Jurisdiction, English Literature, and the Rise of the Common Law, 1509–1625* (Chicago: University of Chicago Press, 2007), ch. 2.

mere necessity was made use of in the Infancy of the State, and Indigency of Laws, and to set up this Rule, after Laws are established, to relieve hard Cases, and leave the Matter at large, is it not rather to unravel, by Unperceived Degrees, the fine and close Texture of the Law, which has been so many hundred years in the making?"[84]

Given Jefferson's ideological contempt for any supposed remnants of the Tudor or Stuart monarchs, and particularly given his later quite forceful critique of judicial power in confrontation with the Marshall Court, equity seems a bizarre place for Jefferson's interest. And yet, in the wording of Fortescue-Aland, we can see an intellectual project that would have caught Jefferson's eye: an opportunity to theorize the "unraveling" of the "Texture of the Law," woven carefully and tightly over so many centuries. By far the largest amount of entries in the equity commonplace book are from Scottish Jurist Lord Kames's *Principles of Equity*, and if taken with the passages from Kames's *Historical Law-Tracts* in the legal commonplace book, Kames on law and legal history emerges as one of the most cited and copied sources in Jefferson's reading life.[85] While Blackstone nervously sought to check the near legislative power of equity adjudication, Kames was busy using his position on Scotland's Court of Session to openly carry out legal reform from the bench, bringing about significant reform surrounding his two pet projects: the undoing of feudal restraints on landed property, and the reformation of the criminal law.[86] Both of these aims would be pillars of

[84] John Fortescue-Aland, preface to *The Difference between an Absolute and Limited Monarchy; As it more particularly regards the English Constitution. Being a Treatise written by Sir John Fortescue, Kt.* (London: William Bowyer, 2nd edition, 1719), p. xii.

[85] In a later letter to Peter Carr, Jefferson would allow that Kames might be "too metaphysical," and suggested that the jurist had composed an ideal theory, "what should be the system of equity," rather than an accurate description of the multilayered and distinctive equity jurisdictions, precedents, and practices in England and Scotland; see Jefferson to Peter Carr, June 22, 1792, John Catanzariti, ed. *The Papers of Thomas Jefferson* (Princeton: Princeton University Press, 1990), Vol. 24, p. 108. That such a theory appealed to Jefferson is clear; he organized his entries from Kames in the equity commonplace book according to and then copied the table of contents of the first edition of *Principles of Equity*; see Jefferson, [*Equity*] *Commonplace Book* (The Huntington Library, San Marino, California, BR13), pp. 108b–9a, between #1131–2; see Sowerby, *Catalogue of the Library of Thomas Jefferson*, Vol. 2, #1716–8, pp. 192–3.

[86] These were projects informing and informed by his historical work, "Of the Introduction of the Feudal Law into Scotland," in *Essays upon Several Subjects Concerning British Antiquities* (Edinburgh: A. Kincaid, 1757); "History of the Criminal Law," in *Historical Law-Tracts* (Edinburgh: A. Kincaid and J. Bell, 1758). See David Lieberman, "Property, Commerce, and the Common Law: Attitudes to Legal Change in the Eighteenth Century," *Early Modern Conceptions of Property*, John Brewer and Susan Staves, eds. (London: Routledge, 1994),

Jefferson's own proposals for a new constitution and law reform in the newly declared Commonwealth of Virginia.

The centerpiece of Jefferson's inspiration from Kames was not merely practical legal reform goals. It was the methodology and language of equitable interpretation that conditioned the possibility for thinking anew about what the law had been, what it was, and what it might be. Indeed, Kames's dictum, citing Bolingbroke, that one could not study the law without studying it historically, without comparing it to other systems of jurisprudence, and without understanding the social and governmental contexts in which law had developed, was perhaps the single most important idea shaping Jefferson's approach to learning in the area of the law.[87] Likewise, Kames's conceptualization of equity gave Jefferson language to think with in the crisis of legal legitimacy that characterized his experience of the outbreak of revolution in the colonies. The concept of equity was often fundamental to philosophical debates about the character of sovereignty, and was thereby the defining factor in locating within a vision of constitutional order the power to make and define the meaning of the law. Equity would prove to be a significant influence on Jefferson in his attempts to grapple with what a revolutionary, republican jurisprudence and constitutionalism would look like.

CONCLUSION

Jefferson continued his study of law and legal history beyond his brief legal career, which came to an abrupt end with the closure of the General Court in 1772 amid intensifying conflict between Parliament and colonial assemblies. No longer a practicing attorney, he put his reading to work as a member of the House of Burgesses, and of course, as a member of the Second Continental Congress where we would go on to be the principal author of the Declaration of Independence. He also concerned himself with the drafting of a new republican constitution for Virginia, and the collection and reformation of Virginia law. Recognized as a legal

pp. 144–58, and "The Legal Needs of a Commercial Society: The Jurisprudence of Lord Kames," *Wealth and Virtue: The Shaping of Political Economy in the Scottish Enlightenment*, Istvan Hont and Michael Ignatieff, eds. (Cambridge: Cambridge University Press, 1983), pp. 203–34; Michael Lobban, "The Ambition of Lord Kames' Equity," *Law and History: Current Legal Issues*, Vol. 6 (2003), pp. 97–121.

[87] Henry Home, Lord Kames, preface to *Historical Law-Tracts* (Edinburgh: A. Kincaid and J. Bell, 1758).

antiquarian and an authority on the subject, Jefferson would bring his cultivated erudition to bear on taking stock of legal development from the earliest years of the colony, thinking in conversation and sometimes in contest with others about the continuity of common law after independence, and so about the material representation and temporality of law in a republic.

In seeking to reform the laws and draft a new constitutional framework in which the laws could be used, Jefferson took on the task of implementing a republican constitutional culture. As he went about his designing, drafting, and new-modeling, he would carry two very important colonial legacies with him. One, he would have at his disposal an immense and unparalleled collection of Virginia's colonial records. What occurred to Jefferson during the American Revolution was that nothing about that momentous event would change the fact that law and constitutionalism were textually inscribed for him and his fellows, and that if not only political but constitutional power was to be made something public, the peculiar textuality appropriate to sharing in that power would need to be made public, too. Second, Jefferson would turn to both the jurisdiction and more broadly philosophical idea of equity, which held such a troubled and contested history in early modern English constitutional conflict and in competing visions of the legal structure of the British Empire in the Atlantic world. Law in a republican polity would need to confront this very un-republican history, and Jefferson would need to think through how it was that the necessary power of discretionary judgment in law could be made safe for republican legal and political life. In Jefferson's hands, both of these legacies could be distilled into a singular concern with reforming not only the law but the citizen in whose hands that law would be placed.

3

New-Modeling and Rewriting in Revolutionary Virginia

From 1776 to 1779, while George Washington had taken command of the Continental Army and was combatting British control in Boston and New York, and while Benjamin Franklin and John Adams led Congress and then the American diplomatic mission abroad, Jefferson was immersed in the archive of Virginia's colonial legal history. Jefferson served as a member of the committee appointed to revise the body of Virginia's laws, and this historical project entailed taking stock of the existing laws, asking whether or not those laws continued in force, and if so, on what terms, on whose authority, and how that body of law should be represented in a commonwealth. Recalling his work on the committee, Jefferson wrote to his colleague and former law professor George Wythe that his "researches" into colonial legal history had led him to discover the ruined state of the manuscript copies of the laws. Jefferson described combing the county clerk offices of the oldest counties along the James River looking for handwritten copies of legislative records that would have been given to counties by the General Assembly, expecting to find them buried in the offices of the clerks or "in the hands of careful and curious individuals." Confronted with negligence of Virginia's antiquarian legal culture, Jefferson vowed to collect all that he could so that someday "the public should advert to the magnitude of their loss in these precious monuments of our property, and our history," and that the public could take consolation that a few fragments had been "saved from the wreck," and which were worthy of "attention and preservation."[1] Writing in 1796, Jefferson was proposing

[1] Thomas Jefferson to George Wythe, January 16, 1796, John Catanzariti, ed. *The Papers of Thomas Jefferson* (Princeton: Princeton University Press, 2000), Vol. 28, p. 583.

not just another revisal but a printed edition of the laws Jefferson had collected in his private library to be distributed at the public expense and for public use. To understand the power of the connection between history, textuality, and legal authority for revolutionary constitutionalism, it is perhaps useful to begin with the simple if surprising image of Jefferson himself, slave-owning planter, aristocrat, soon to be governor and already author of the Declaration of Independence, digging through the trash heap of a tavern in Charles City Co., Virginia, looking for more fragments of legal history.

Uniquely among his fellow "founders," Jefferson continued largely until the end of his life to understand constitutions in the style characteristic of what Charles McIlwain identified as "ancient constitutionalism," as a historical assemblage of custom, practices, and statutes, rather than the "modern" sense of a single, fundamental text.[2] Contrary to the oft-depicted image of an almost inspirationally naïve political idealist, Jefferson was critically aware of the relationship between the design and practice of political institutions and the modes of historical understanding that underlay their authority. In his designs for limited public participation in councils, juries, and amendments to constitutional text, as well as in his drafting of reports on law reform like the bill for proportioning crimes and punishments, Jefferson experimented with the constitutional politics of law. Revolutionary constitutional texts were material conditions of republican politics that a revolutionary people would work and rework in time. Codification, and the sealing off of particular aspects of the life of the law from potential revision and contestation, was the chief target of Jefferson's constitutional criticism.

Jefferson's concerns for the textuality of law can be understood in the context of the importance of narratives of constitutional history to

[2] Charles Howard McIlwain, *Constitutionalism: Ancient and Modern* (Ithaca: Cornell University Press, 1947); see also James Tully, *Strange Multiplicity: Constitutionalism in an Age of Diversity* (Cambridge: Cambridge University Press, 1995). This framework captures the productive tension between the agency of historical subjectivity in assembling and disassembling and the given character of the material assembled and the contexts and histories within which that activity takes place, and that distinguishes Jefferson's attention to materiality and plasticity, to say nothing of the embodiment of historical subjectivity itself, from its iterations in more contemporary anti-foundationalist legal theory; see Roberto Mangabeira Unger, *False Necessity: Anti-Necessitarian Social Theory in the Service of Radical Democracy* (Cambridge: Cambridge University Press, 1987), *The Self Awakened: Pragmatism Unbound* (Cambridge, MA: Harvard University Press, 2007); Stanley Fish, *Doing What Comes Naturally: Change, Rhetoric, and the Practice of Theory in Literary and Legal Studies* (Durham: Duke University Press, 1989).

revolutionary political thought. Landon Carter, for his part, remained fearful of the outbreak of violence and what it meant for the claims to English liberty colonists had been making all along. Carter supported the American cause, but was disgraced by the style and arguments about English monarchy and law in Thomas Paine's *Common Sense*, deploring the threat to the "constitutional freedom" of the Americans and the "new and dangerous doctrines to the peace and happiness of every society" that he found in the pamphlet.[3] Carter succinctly registered the fracturing of the British-American "constitutional freedom" and the historical narrative that underwrote that freedom, remaining uncertain and anxious about it throughout the revolution. Upon hearing in April 1776 that movements were under way to form a new government with a written constitution, Carter despaired: "[I]f our form of Government is changed I hope some divine Inspiration will possess our rulers to establish the common Law of England amongst us. Otherwise, I cannot see what incouragement People of my age can have in America for improving our possessions since it is the Common Law of England alone that establishes the descent in our posterity."[4] Carter continued to think of security in liberty and property as grounded not simply in history but in the widespread acceptance of continuity of a particular history of law and social order in time.

Similar arguments for the maintenance of entail and primogeniture would be made by Carter Braxton, as "A Native of this Colony," in his pamphlet aimed at the state constitutional convention in 1776, *An Address to the Convention of the Colony and Ancient Dominion of Virginia on the Subject of Government, and Recommending a Particular Form to their Attention.*[5] It was not republican institutions per se that made the Carters nervous; it was the threat of losing the continuity of the common law and the security it provided to the inseparable link between property and identity. Civic identity for leading members of what constituted a kind of *ancien regime* in Virginia was tenuously reinforced by their continued capacity to narrate and thereby legitimate the stability of

[3] Jack P. Greene, ed. *The Diary of Landon Carter* (Charlottesville: University of Virginia Press, 1965), Volume II, February 14, 1776, p. 981, April 13, 1776, p. 1016.

[4] *The Diary of Landon Carter*, Volume II, April 13, 1776, p. 1017.

[5] Carter Braxton (1736–1797), "An Address to the Convention of the Colony and Ancient Dominion of Virginia on the Subject of Government in General, and Recommending a Particular Form to their Attention," *American Political Writing during the Founding Era, 1760–1805*, Charles S. Hyneman and Donald S. Lutz, eds. (Indianapolis: Liberty Fund, 1983), Vol. 1, pp. 28–339.

their property holdings across generations in a grand narrative of the continuity of an English customary constitution.[6] The constitutional and legal reform proposals that Jefferson developed grew out of his complex relationship to this civic identity and its material underpinnings.

Protecting power where it existed already did not preclude practical efforts at expanding landholding power by defending and extending the borders of Virginia itself. Jefferson used the early colonial documents to which he had access to defend Virginia land claims in the west, and attempted to provide legal basis for the sole right of representatives of the government to purchase recognized Native American land west of the Blue Ridge Mountains.[7] In 1773, George Mason, an early investor in the Ohio Company, combed over the historical documentation from Byrd's library in Stith's *History* to justify the power of the colonial government, as a representative of the Crown, to grant land tracts to individual claimants, "so that Mr. Stith, in his History of Virginia, (which is chiefly extracted from ancient Records), mentioning this right & Custom, had good reason for his remark; that 'this is the ancient, legal, & a most indubitable Method of granting Lands in Virginia.'"[8] Desire for land was an important part of the material project of collecting colonial documents and the broader legal culture of customary continuity as measured in these texts.

Additionally, while the Second Continental Congress approached and made its decision to declare independence, Jefferson, its newest member, was just as, if not more, concerned with the writing of a new state constitution for Virginia. Since 1774, when Lord Dunmore, then the royal governor of the colony, had dissolved the House of Burgesses and in so doing closed the courts of law in response to the growing

[6] See David Thomas Konig, "Virginia and the Imperial State: Law, Enlightenment, and 'the crooked cord of discretion'," *The British and Their Laws in the Eighteenth Century*, David Lemmings ed. (London: Boydell, 2005), pp. 206–29; on the concept of civic identity in the imperial, colonial, and postcolonial contexts, see Greg Dening, "Texts of Self," Mechal Sobel, "The Revolution in Selves: Black and White Inner Aliens," and Kenneth Lockridge, "Colonial Self-Fashioning: Paradoxes and Pathologies in the Construction of Genteel Identity in Eighteenth-Century America," *Through a Glass Darkly: Reflections on Personal Identity in Early America*, Ronald Hoffman, Mechal Sobel, and Fredrika J. Teute, eds. (Chapel Hill: University of North Carolina Press, 1997), pp. 157–62, 163–205, 274–339; Christopher Tomlins, *Freedom Bound: Law, Labor, and Ideology in Colonizing English America, 1580–1865* (Cambridge: Cambridge University Press, 2010), p. 14.

[7] Jefferson, "Vindication of Virginia's Claim Against the Proposed Colony of Vandalia," *The Papers of Thomas Jefferson*, Vol. 6, p. 656.

[8] George Mason, *The Papers of George Mason*, Robert A. Rutland, ed. (Chapel Hill: University of North Carolina Press, 1970) Vol. 1, pp. 166–7.

intensity of the imperial crisis, Virginia, like many of the other colonies, went without recognizable constitutional government for an extended period of time. It was not until Congress issued orders to all the colonies to form new state governments after the Crown had declared them illegitimate that political ground existed for constitutional conventions.[9] When George Mason wrote to George Washington in 1775, he enclosed a copy of the Fairfax County resolves and calling up of the militia, which were written in response to the threat of the "destruction of our antient Laws & Liberty," and were described by Mason as a plan for "embodying the people."[10] Firmly rooted in a British opposition language of ancient and popular constitutionalism and an early modern juridical discourse about where the making and defining of law occurred in the constitutional order, in their reflection of the real presence of public insurgencies, such articulations pointed to a shared experience of the unraveling of the narratives underlying the customary civic identity to which these men were accustomed.

It was in this wider context of historical unraveling and a turn toward historical exemplars of political action and constitutional organization that Jefferson began to connect the unique qualities of his own education with an equally unique understanding of law in a republican polity. Jefferson's mode of study provided him with critical tools for thinking about what revolutionary constitutionalism needed to look like for it to be both revolutionary and constitutional, and his study and his thinking about that study informed his designs for legal and constitutional reform. Jefferson crafted himself into a student of transmission, of narratives of transmission, and of the politics of those narratives, coming to understand legal and political authority as closely related, and the power to exercise judgment in both law and politics as constituted by the possession and representation of a history to legitimate that power. His republican constitution was less a text or an institutional order than a form of life, predicated upon establishing and cooperatively maintaining space where the constituting materials of civic history could

[9] On the ideologies of state constitution making, see Willi Paul Adams, *The First American Constitutions: Republican Ideology and the Making of the State Constitutions in the Revolutionary Era*, Rita and Robert Kimber, trans. (Chapel Hill: University of North Carolina Press, 1980). On the role of the concept of popular sovereignty, see Christian G. Fritz, *American Sovereigns: The People and America's Constitutional Tradition before the Civil War* (Cambridge: Cambridge University Press, 2008).

[10] Mason to George Washington, February 6, 1775, *Papers of George Mason*, Vol. 1, pp. 214–15.

be read, used, and in their use, reread, rewritten, and remade. From this historical understanding of constitutions, Thomas Jefferson drew radical implications.

Laws and institutions, inherited from the past, were as such rightfully subject to the interpretive powers of republican bodies of legal actors in the present and future. Jefferson's historically inflected approach to law was part of a wider historical, juridical orientation that guided much of his political thought and designs for the structure and practice of revolutionary republican practices and institutions. An experience of unraveling and fragmenting in the fixed lines of sovereignty and institutional authority gave Jefferson the intellectual equipment to consider the histories out of which his own identity and that of his polity had grown. The results of that consideration were twofold: on the one hand, there was a mode of constitutional practice that amounted to a kind of civic materialism, or at least a materialist account of legal and constitutional culture; and on the other hand, a correlating project of not only instituting a material, textual culture of republican constitutionalism but instituting a mode of historical subjectivity – the citizen as an idealized, self-governing subject with the cultivated capacity to make use of the manifold historical contexts in which they actively embedded themselves. It was around his efforts to secure the conditions and the boundaries of this particular subjectivity that the arch of Jefferson's intellectual and political life would turn.

LAW, EMPIRE, AND EQUITY

The most radical and creative element in Jefferson's revolutionary constitutionalism was a multifaceted exploration of judgment in both law and politics, and particularly in the problem of locating the power to judge safely in the constitution of a republican polity. Being subject to discretionary judgment was a hallmark of the colonial complaints against metropolitan understandings of their legal status within the empire. The veto of the Privy Council over colonial legislation and its power as a supreme court of appeal over colonial legal decisions was a potent symbol of the sovereign power of the Crown and Parliament over dependent governments in the colonies. This was in effect a conciliar jurisdiction exercised over certain types of imperial territories. By the logic laid out by Sir Edward Coke at the beginning of the seventeenth century, the existing legal orders of territories acquired by the conquest of a non-Christian people (like the aboriginal inhabitants of North America) were automatically abrogated, and the conqueror ruled themselves or through appointed judges according to "natural equity."[11] Equity here could be taken in the broadest possible sense, as relative conformity with and due consideration of the basic principles of justice. At the same time, over the course of the seventeenth and eighteenth centuries in England the jurisdiction of equity exercised by the High Court of Chancery, presided over by the Lord Chancellor, would develop into an established and regular part of the central courts in London. Equity, in this usage, was the peculiar body of rules, precedents, and procedures of chancery jurisdiction. As discussed in the previous chapter, colonial Virginia had seen its fair share of controversies over the proper place of this jurisdiction within its own legal structures, and over what the presence of that jurisdiction meant for the legal status of the colony within the empire. Equity was both a representation of sovereign power itself and a court or mode of proceeding that was often concerned with some of the most everyday aspects of property law in a commercial age and for a commercial nation. Jefferson would come to understand these dual historical lives of equity as inseparable.

What made them inseparable to Jefferson were two things. First, colonial disputes over the legitimacy and relative dependence of American laws and legal institutions revealed linkages between equitable consideration as part of private law and equity as a crucial part of attempts to theorize public law for the imperial constitution. If decisions in the Privy Council or Chancery, or for that matter in the Court of King's Bench, could abrogate or ignore colonial law, and if royal governors could preside over or directly appoint judges who presided over high courts in the colonies themselves, then these were in fact instances of Coke's "natural equity" as both sovereign constitutional power and as the particularity of conciliar jurisdiction, acting in the name of the Crown. Second, and this was the rub for Jefferson, what united all of the different definitions and contexts of equity of which it was possible to conceive in the early modern Anglo-American legal context was at the basic level a question of judgment. Where was this higher, potentially discretionary and arbitrary power to judge certain legal disputes according to conscience or accepted principles of justice and utility to be found? By what rules, if any, was this power bound? What would a

[11] Sir Edward Coke, "Calvin's Case, or the case of the Postnati" (1608), *Selected Writings of Sir Edward Coke, Volume 1: Reports* (Indianapolis: Liberty Fund, 2003), p. 207. On the use of the power of the royal prerogative by both the Court of King's Bench and the High Court of Chancery beginning in this period, see Paul M. Halliday, *Habeas Corpus: From England to Empire* (Cambridge, MA: Harvard University Press, 2010).

revolution predicated on the constituent power of the people mean for the legitimacy of judicial power in a new government? Jefferson's engagements with equity, and his proposals for revolutionary legal and constitutional reform amounted to a nervous and halting project of relocating the judicial power of equitable judgment and the particular instantiation of sovereignty it represented to assembled bodies of the citizenry at varying levels throughout the republican constitutional order. It was equity, specifically, and not simply the government, that needed to be put in the hands of the people. And the people, by these lights, would need to be prepared to handle the powers of interpretation and judgment that this vision, for lack of a better word, entailed.

To understand the uses to which Jefferson put equity and how important these uses were to the trajectory of his thought, it is important to understand the conceptual materials that were available to him. No single source was more significant for Jefferson's early study and his subsequent thinking than the legal writings of Henry Home, Lord Kames, a seminal figure in the transatlantic intellectual culture of the Scottish Enlightenment, and just as importantly, a judge of the Scottish Court of Session and the author of several works that prominently feature in Jefferson's commonplace books. In fact, if we take Jefferson's legal and equity commonplace books together, no single author is more prominent. From Kames' *Historical Law-Tracts*, and from a host of other sources, Jefferson absorbed histories of ancient constitutions, and the course of his legal commonplace book traces an expansive reading from precedents in English common law treatises and case reports to narratives of legal change and development. But at 2,008 entries of theory and precedent from Scottish and English chancery courts, the equity commonplace book contains more than twice the entries of his legal commonplace book, which has received far more attention from scholars.[12] From Kames'

[12] While Jefferson's literary and legal commonplace books have long been studied as keys to the development of his thought, but with a few notable exceptions, scholars have often ignored Jefferson's equity commonplace book, composed for the most part concurrently with the others from the middle of the 1760s to the cusp of the early 1770s; on the equity commonplace book, see Edward Dumbauld, "Thomas Jefferson's Equity Commonplace Book," *Washington and Lee Law Review* 48 (1991), pp. 1257–83. On the role of equity cases for Jefferson's legal career, see Peter Charles Hoffer, *Law's Conscience: Equitable Constitutionalism in America* (Chapel Hill: University of North Carolina Press, 1990). On Jefferson's commonplace books and their dating, see Douglas L. Wilson, "Thomas Jefferson's Early Notebooks," *William and Mary Quarterly* Vol. 42, No. 4 (October 1985), pp. 433–52; Kevin J. Hayes, *The Road to Monticello: The Life and Mind of Thomas Jefferson* (Oxford: Oxford University Press, 2008).

Principles of Equity, Jefferson made extensive recordings of the jurist's thoughts on the nature of equity jurisprudence.[13] The sheer volume of textual evidence of Jefferson's interest in equity reveals the importance of it to Jefferson's thought, and to the importance of chancery jurisdiction as both an idea and a set of practices to the legal and intellectual history of early modern Britain and its oceanic empire.

From his perch at the Scottish Court of Session, a civil court that exercised both common law and equity jurisdiction by its own discretion, Kames was in a unique position to theorize equity both as legal procedure and as a significant part of legal development over time. This was an important tool in the hands of a judge who understood law in the light of current Scottish social theory and philosophical history. Kames actively embraced the corrective power of equity, using his position to advance his wider goals of undoing the constraints of primogeniture and entail on land tenures and advancing reformation of the criminal law.[14] In these projects, Kames understood himself to be acting in a history of

[13] Indeed, both Douglas Wilson and Kevin Hayes highlight the importance of the theoretical treatment of equity in the first part of Kames' *Principles of Equity* and as recorded in Jefferson's equity commonplace book (#1077–1131), but it is equally important to point that the other sources all point to a practical use of established rules of precedent in chancery case law; as Dumbauld illustrates, Jefferson's limited interpolations in the text testify to that; see *Eyton* v. *Eyton*, *Champernoon* v. *Grubbs*, *Foster* v. *Foster* (#395, #398) in the extensive entries from Thomas Vernon, *Cases Argued and Adjudged in the High Court of Chancery* (Dublin: J. Watts, 1726), (#22–618, #1812); Dumbauld, "Thomas Jefferson's Equity Commonplace Book," pp. 1267–9; see also John Tracy Atkyns, *Reports of Cases Argued and Determined in the High Court of Chancery in the Time of Lord Chancellor Hardwicke* (London: H. Woodfall and W. Strahan, 1765), Vol. 1, (#2000–2017). Hardwicke's jurisprudence as recorded in these and other reports would have been particularly important as it established and asserted against critics of an independent jurisdiction of equity that in point of fact equity as a branch of jurisprudence had developed its own system of maxims; see David Lieberman, *The Province of Legislation Determined: Legal Theory in Eighteenth Century Britain* (Cambridge: Cambridge University Press, 1989), pp. 76–8, 81–3.

[14] Kames, "Of the Introduction of the Feudal Law into Scotland," *Essays upon Several Subjects Concerning British Antiquities* (Edinburgh: A. Kincaid, 1757); preface, "History of the Criminal Law," *Historical Law-Tracts* (Edinburgh: A. Kincaid and J. Bell, 1758); see David Lieberman, "Property, Commerce, and the Common Law: Attitudes to Legal Change in the Eighteenth Century," *Early Modern Conceptions of Property*, John Brewer and Susan Staves, eds. (London: Routledge, 1994), pp. 144–58, and "The Legal Needs of a Commercial Society: The Jurisprudence of Lord Kames," *Wealth and Virtue: The Shaping of Political Economy in the Scottish Enlightenment*, Istvan Hont and Michael Ignatieff eds. (Cambridge: Cambridge University Press, 1983), pp. 203–34; Michael Lobban, "The Ambition of Lord Kames' Equity," *Law and History: Current Legal Issues* 6 (2003), pp. 97–121.

legal change in which the jurisdiction of equity had played and needed to continue to play a very important role in both England and Scotland. Like so many of his peers, he understood himself as a practitioner of philosophical history and its applications to law and politics. For Kames, law was not simply reflective of social processes and progress, but was a driver of that progress. In a preliminary discourse attached to the second edition of *Principles of Equity*, "An Investigation of the Moral Laws of Society," Kames made the philosophical background and immediate historical context to his jurisprudence explicit. "Men were made for society," Kames declared, "and one great blessing of that state is a candid intercourse of hearts in conversation, in communication of sentiments, of opinions, of desires, and of wishes; and to admit any falsehood or deceit into such intercourse, would poison the most refined pleasures of life."[15] In line with the social promises of the cultivated sensibility appropriate to an emerging commercial society outlined by Scottish theorists like Adam Smith, Kames situated human behavior in a naturally social and communicative context, and he understood the promise of Scottish development after the Act of Union in 1707 as in part an opportunity to fulfill this fundamentally social nature of human beings. Commerce, for Kames, was a vehicle for achieving the most noble ends of humanity, and equity was a crucial mechanism in that vehicle's operation, steering around the rigid corners of normal law and finding open space in which to manoeuver toward needed reforms. Law carried out in light of the developing moral sense of people inhabiting societies increasingly predicated on interlocking relationships of exchange would depend not on the private morality of individuals, but on the moral framework of the wider scope of humanity: the moral sense, according to Kames, required not the degree of "vigilance and attention" available to each man, but that of "the common nature of the species." Equity comprehended nothing less than the species-being of humanity.

Such intellectual ambitions were in accordance with not only the historical and philosophical project of the Scottish Enlightenment but the actual practice of chancery jurisdiction. Historically, the judge or judges exercising such jurisdiction preceded to judgment through an examination of the consciences of litigants, aiming to base the judgment on consideration of the intentions and knowledge of circumstances on the

[15] Henry Home, Lord Kames, *Principles of Equity*, Michael Lobban, ed. (Indianapolis: Liberty Fund, 2014), p. xxi.

part of each party to the case at the time of the event in dispute.[16] Such consideration of conscience was necessary to what Kames was not hesitant in calling the discipline necessary for well-ordered collective life in a refined and civilized nation. For Kames, equity stood at that balancing point of two principles, that of justice and that of utility, by which he meant social utility, and it was necessary for courts of equity to be increasingly active in the present because the adjudication of cases where these principles were at stake were themselves increasing in frequency. Commercial society demanded a branch of jurisprudence that policed and enforced basic maxims of benevolence as well as honesty and trustworthiness, virtues hardly instantiated or necessarily required, it was thought, by the normal operation of the law. As Jefferson recorded in his commonplace book from Kames, "equity, in its proper sense, comprehends every matter of law that by the common law is left without remedy... Thus mutual duties among individuals multiply by variety of connections; and in the progress of society, benevolence becomes a matter of conscience in a thousand cases, formerly disregarded."[17] White at first the jurisdiction of equity moved reservedly, Kames suggested that it had grown in confidence and so in importance, rigor, and regularity, and by such processes had been "imperceptibly moulded into a system." Like the long and continuous temporality of the common law, equity itself had developed into a mature jurisprudence, informed by "custom and reflection," and able to enforce "benevolence where the law of nature makes it our duty," even going so far in its pursuit of the principles of justice and utility to "correct or mitigate the rigour, and what in a proper sense may be termed the *injustice* of the common law."[18] At the Scottish Court of Session, equity was now a vital and perennial part of adjudicating a vast array of civil issues from inheritance to contract and commercial law, and its union in the same seat as the basic common law jurisdiction of the court, for Kames, was precisely what allowed for the necessary role of equity jurisprudence.

[16] On early modern equity procedure and its impact on jurisprudence in the United States, see Stephen N. Subrin, "How Equity Conquered the Common Law: The Federal Rules of Civil Procedure in Historical Perspective," *University of Pennsylvania Law Review*, Vol. 135, No. 4 (April 1987), pp. 909–1002; and Amalia D. Kessler, "Our Inquisitorial Tradition: Equity Procedure, Due Process, and the Search for an Alternative to the Adversarial," *Cornell Law Review*, Vol. 90 No. 5 (July, 2005), pp. 1181–276.

[17] Thomas Jefferson, [*Equity*] *Commonplace Book* (The Huntington Library, San Marino, California, BR13), #1077; Kames, *Principles of Equity*, pp. 20–1.

[18] Kames, *ibid*, pp. 22–3, 24–5.

Despite the growth in both Scotland and England of a system of precedents in chancery, precisely what the boundaries of equitable consideration were in eighteenth-century legal theory was still very much in question, in both Scotland and England. As Kames explained in his brief discussion of the history of chancery, since the successive chancellorships Lord Ellesmere and Francis Bacon, when conciliar courts including the Chancery emerged as direct institutional rivals to the high common law courts, the High Court of Chancery had developed a system of rules and precedents of its own that existed in parallel with the other central courts. With the rise of parliamentary sovereignty after the Glorious Revolution, formal chancery jurisdiction was no longer the feared tool of royal prerogative that it had been for much of the seventeenth century. Even so, the jurisdictional limits of equitable consideration were still a subject of debate. Coke himself, acting to blunt the growing power of a separate jurisdictional authority, had defined equity as the reason and spirit of the law, and as such a legitimate framework of consideration for a common law judge. In his *Commentaries on the Laws of England*, Blackstone would go on to echo that sentiment, noting the uniqueness of England's formal jurisdictional separation of equity and common law. Such a distinction, Blackstone noted, "is not at present known, or seems to have been known, in any other county at any other time."[19] Indeed, Blackstone continued, the late medieval commentators all discuss equity, but not as a separate court. Rather, equity provided an appeal for redress from regular judgment to the King, assisted by the Privy Council. The office of the Lord Chancellor, according to Blackstone, exercised this mitigating power from as early as the rule of Edward I, and this jurisdiction increased over time as it took on increasing consideration of disputes relating to uses of land. Still, equity was as much a matter of constitutional politics as it was of a developing jurisprudence. As Blackstone noted, the High Court of Chancery was not widely recognized as exercising a distinct and definable jurisdiction with its own maturing doctrine and practices until the chancellorship of Heneage Finch, 1st Earl of Nottingham, beginning in 1673. Over the course of the eighteenth century, the process begun by Lord Nottingham had expanded dramatically, making the court of equity a court, in Blackstone's words, "of the highest judicial significance."[20]

[19] William Blackstone, *Commentaries on the Laws of England* (Oxford: Clarendon Press, 1768), Vol. 3, p. 49; see Dennis R. Klinck, *Conscience, Equity, and the Court of Chancery in Early Modern England* (Farnham: Ashgate, 2010).

[20] Blackstone, *Commentaries on the Laws of England*, Vol. 3, p. 49.

By the time of Blackstone's writing, not only was the High Court of Chancery a developed and separate jurisdiction; it was in fact a growing component of how the judicial power of common law judges was understood. Blackstone defined equity more broadly than simply the power of chancery courts, as "in its true and genuine meaning, the soul and spirit of the law: positive law is construed, and rational law is made by it."[21] Citing Kames' *Principles of Equity*, Blackstone argued it was unnecessary to construe equity as correcting the literalist rigor of the common law, for both equity and common law as exercised in his day were bound by custom and statute, and both needed to interpret the law, a basic fact that required even a common law judge to have recourse to equitable construal of the law. Blackstone wrote just as William Murray, Lord Mansfield ascended to be Chief Justice of the Court of King's Bench after a distinguished career that had included substantial time before the High Court of Chancery, and began to notably exercise and defend the legitimacy of equitable discretion's rightful place in the highest common law court of the land.[22] While commentators decried the potential for arbitrary decisions and the lack of judicial restraint, Kames, Blackstone, and Mansfield each in their own contexts pointed to the elaboration of doctrine in equity jurisprudence and went about theorizing and practicing the widespread use of that jurisprudential framework. Indeed, the second edition of the *Principles of Equity* included a dedicatory epistle to Mansfield, himself a Scot, and who had commended the publication of the work in correspondence with Kames and expressed admiration for the wisdom and power of the Scottish Court of Session where, it seemed, the powers of equity and common law were united, and in an age of increasing business for the courts, the idea was that those powers ought to be.

[21] Blackstone, *ibid*, p. 429.

[22] Blackstone, *Commentaries on the Laws of England*, Vol. 3, pp. 428–42; Jefferson would later pick up this theme in his defense of chancery courts; see Jefferson to Philip Mazzei, November 28, 1785, in *The Papers of Thomas Jefferson*, pp. 67–72; Lieberman, *The Province of Legislation Determined: Legal Theory in Eighteenth Century Britain*, ch. 3, 6–7. On earlier debates over developments in equity, see G.W. Keeton, *An Introduction to Equity* (London: Pitman, 1961); Michael Macnair, "Common Law and Statutory Imitations of Equitable Relief under the Later Stuarts," *Communities and Courts and Britain, 115–1900*, Christopher Brooks and Michael Lobban, eds. (London: Hambledon, 1997), pp. 115–31, *The Concept of Equity: An Interdisciplinary Assessment*, Daniela Carpi ed. (Heidelberg: Winter, 2007); Bradin Cormack, *A Power to Do Justice: Jurisdiction, English Literature, and the Rise of the Common Law, 1509–1625* (Chicago: University of Chicago Press, 2007), ch. 2.

In Blackstone's systematic framework of legal theory and jurisdictional authority, and in Mansfield's jurisprudence from the bench, particularly as it regarded the institution of slavery, the perils and potentials of equitable consideration and the application of philosophical principles of natural justice to common law adjudication were made clear to many interested parties inhabiting the British Atlantic world of the mid-to late eighteenth century. An acute episode of uncertainty in the legal status of Anglo settlers in the thirteen British North American colonies occurred in the famous case of *Somerset* v. *Stewart* in 1772, where Mansfield ruled on the case of James Somerset, a slave brought to England by his American master only to escape and later be captured and re-enslaved. Slavery, Mansfield wrote, was everywhere a product of positive law and repugnant to nature. No such positive law existing in England, there was no legal protection of human property, and so Somerset was set free. As has been widely noted, *Somerset* not only put into question the safety of transporting slave property throughout the empire (an already contentious issue for planters) but in his ruling Mansfield anchored the decision to recognize Somerset's freedom in an appeal to natural law.[23] In the eyes of colonists, Mansfield thus exhibited the liberality of judiciary discretion that was widely believed to characterize his tenure as the Chief Justice of the Court of King's Bench (a perception that reflected, in part, the development of the theoretical legitimacy of equitable consideration throughout the English court system).[24] The real significance of *Somerset* lay just as much in what it said about the constitutional politics of the empire as

[23] David Waldstreicher, *Slavery's Constitution: From Revolution to Ratification* (New York: Hill and Wang, 2009); George William Van Cleve, *A Slaveholder's Union: Slavery, Constitution, and Politics in the Early American Republic* (Chicago: University of Chicago Press, 2010), pp. 1–58; Jack Greene draws particular attention to the Debt Recovery Act of 1732, whereby Parliament allowed creditors to consider property in land and thereby in slaves as legitimate targets of repossession, and Lord Dunmore's Proclamation of 1775, which offered emancipation to Virginian slaves who joined British efforts to subdue colonial resistance; Greene, *The Constitutional Origins of the American Revolution* (Cambridge: Cambridge University Press, 2010).

[24] Lieberman, *The Province of Legislation Determined: Legal Theory in Eighteenth Century Britain*; Michael Lobban, *The Common Law and English Jurisprudence, 1760–1850* (Oxford: Oxford University Press, 1991), pp. 71–121; James Oldham, *English Common Law in the Age of Mansfield* (Chapel Hill: University of North Carolina Press, 2004); Wilfrid Prest, *William Blackstone: Law and Letters in the Eighteenth Century* (Oxford: Oxford University Press, 2008); John H. Langbein, "Blackstone on Judging," and John V. Orth, "Blackstone's Rules on the Construction of Statutes," *Blackstone and His Commentaries*, Wilfrid Prest, ed. (London: Hart, 2009), pp. 65–77, 79–90; Norman S. Poser, *Lord Mansfield: Justice in the Age of Reason* (Montreal and Kingston: McGill-Queen's University Press, 2013).

did about the security of property in slaves (indeed, those issues were inseparable in the first place). Mansfield stated that the real question of the case was "whether any dominion, authority, or coercion can be exercised in this country, on a slave according to the American laws?"[25] That is to say, the question was whether the decision he might reach was bound to any extent by the Virginia laws protecting the institution of slavery and the individual property rights of slave owners, and his answer was a resounding no. This reflected the status of the colonies as, in Blackstone's wording, "distinct (though dependent) dominions" and as conquered territory within the constitutional structure of the empire. In the eyes of agitated colonial legal elites, this meant a territory whose inhabitants were subject to a centralized judgment seemingly unrestrained by a system of customary, historically legitimated rules that were supposed to provide colonists with criteria for claiming the possession of an English and provincial legal history and so the protections of English law.[26]

In delineating distinct legal statuses of imperial territory, Blackstone was simplifying the tripartite distinctions laid out by Coke in *Calvin's Case*. Whereas Coke had described three types of territory – settled, conquered, and inherited, the latter denoting James VI of Scotland's inheritance of the English crown in 1603 – Blackstone outlined two essential ways of acquiring territory recognized in English law: settlement and conquest. "For it is held," Blackstone stated, "that if an uninhabited country be discovered and planted by English subjects, all the English laws are immediately there in force. For as the law is the birthright of every subject, so wherever they go they carry their laws with them."[27] In this framework, deduced from Coke's own use of the Roman law distinction between the *ius gentium* and the *ius civilis*, occupancy established possession and historical, geographical continuity of law if the settlers

[25] Mansfield, *Somerset v. Stewart* (1772), Melvin I. Urofsky and Paul Finkelman, eds., *Documents in American Legal and Constitutional History: Volume 1: From the Founding to 1896*, 2nd Edition (Oxford: Oxford University Press, 2002), pp. 44–5. As a young attorney, Jefferson had to a certain extent anticipated the argument in his failed attempt to free the grandchildren of a mulatto slave woman bound by the 1705 slave laws to serve until the age of thirty-one, and her owner had claimed the same right over the lives of the offspring. Jefferson sought their freedom with the overarching logic that "under the law of nature, all men are born free." See Jefferson, *Howell* v. *Netherland* (April, 1770), *Reports of Cases Determined in the General Court of Virginia, from 1730 to 1740 and 1766 to 1772* (Charlottesville: F. Carr & Co., 1829), pp. 90–6.

[26] Blackstone, *Commentaries on the Laws of England*, Vol. 1, p. 105.

[27] *Ibid*, pp. 104–5.

found the land "desart and uncultivated." On the other hand, in a conquered or ceded territory, Blackstone continued, "that already have laws of their own, the king may indeed alter or change those laws," but until he does, the laws remain in force, unless they are laws "against God, as in the case of an infidel Country."[28] It was to prove a point of great significance to the leaders of colonial resistance just a few years later that Blackstone began the next paragraph of his discussion with the following observation: "Our American Plantations are principally of this latter sort, being obtained in the last century either by right of conquest and driving out the natives (with what natural justice I shall not at present enquire) or by treaties. And therefore the common law of England, as such, has no allowance or authority there..."[29] The colonies were subject to the authority of Parliament, although specific acts were not binding unless the colonies were mentioned in the legislation, and just as significantly, the colonies possessed a legal system of their own, for which the highest court of appeal was the king in council. Blackstone's framework, building as did off of Coke's finding that in territory acquired by conquest of a non-Christian people, the conqueror ruled only according to "natural equity," directly contradicted the colonial understanding of the place of the colonies in the legal structure of the empire.[30] It was very much a slap in the face to the carefully constructed civic identities of colonial elites, particularly the Virginians, whose property in land and human beings along with the laws that secured that property were found to be subject to the discretionary judicial power inherent in the consolidated imperial state of the late eighteenth century.

From the outset of the imperial crisis, colonists asserted on Cokean and Lockean grounds that they had settled an uncultivated and so effectively empty land, and necessarily therefore enjoyed the rights of Englishmen. What they met in the form of Blackstone's exposition of the theory of

[28] *Ibid*, p. 105.

[29] *Ibid*; on that significance, see Mary Sarah Bilder, *The Transatlantic Constitution* (Cambridge, MA: Harvard University Press, 2004); Black, "The Constitution of Empire: The Case for the Colonists;" Daniel J. Hulsebosch, *Constituting Empire: New York and the Transformation of Constitutionalism in the Atlantic World, 1664–1830* (Chapel Hill: University of North Carolina Press, 2005).

[30] Coke, "Calvin's Case, or the case of the *Postnati*," p. 207. The further stipulation Coke makes that common law rules of descent restrict the legality of royal action to change the laws of a historically conquered and inherited infidel territory by requiring the consent of Parliament by the eighteenth century become absorbed into the regular constitution of imperial governance; it was Parliament by Blackstone's time that was in a position to carry out such action in the first place.

conquest and the Declaratory Act of 1766 was the assertion that the juridical space of the North American continent was conquered territory, and therefore the acting sovereign, Parliament, was not bound by English customary constitutionalism in its governance of the colonists and Native Americans alike.[31] As Aziz Rana has demonstrated, the fact that the colonists found themselves occupying a shared legal status with Native Americans, and that as a result of the Quebec Act, French Canadians in newly acquired British territory retained an apparently greater constitutional self-governance than their fellow subjects to the south made the legal terms of the debates taking place leading up to 1776 a crisis in American legal identity.[32] Formerly confident "transplanted Englishmen" found themselves living with a host of others, against whom they had always measured their civilization, in the borderlands of law, in the realm of equity. Resistance to the implications of Blackstone's formulation developed over the course of the imperial crisis from an assertion of the continuity of the English liberty through the colonizing process as evidenced by the original charters and subsequent presumed enjoyment, to arguments that challenged parliamentary supremacy over the empire, acknowledging the distinct and dependent status of the colonies as well as the sovereignty of the crown, but refuting Parliament's right to legislate on matters of internal taxation and police. It ultimately fell to Jefferson to carry forward the argument that the King had lost his legitimate rule over the colonies in failing to check the overreaching power of Parliament and his Council. In constitutional terms, this meant that the Americans had declined to acknowledge the king in parliament and the king in council as the institutions with which the colonies were actually contending.

Jefferson's revolutionary legal and constitutional thinking is best understood as a creative response to the constitutional politics of the

[31] For while God had given the "world to men in common," that did not mean that the world was meant to remain "common and uncultivated" so that just possession of the world belonged to the "Industrious and Rational" for the purposes of ownership and cultivation; John Locke, Second Treatise on Government, in *Two Treatises of Government*, Peter Laslett, ed. (Cambridge: Cambridge University Press, 1970), p. 291; Barbara Arneil, *John Locke and America: The Defense of English Colonialism* (Oxford: Oxford University Press, 1996); Tully, "The *Two Treatises* and Aboriginal Rights," *An Approach to Political Philosophy: Locke in Contexts* (Cambridge: Cambridge University Press, 1993), pp. 137–76; Craig Yirush, *Settlers, Liberty, and Empire: The Roots of Early American Political Theory, 1675–1775* (Cambridge: Cambridge University Press, 2011).

[32] Aziz Rana, *The Two Faces of American Freedom* (Cambridge, MA: Harvard University Press, 2010).

imperial crisis. Creative, because in the manner and terms in which Jefferson gradually articulated that response he was unique among his peers, even eccentric. As Eric Nelson points out, it would be a mistake to take Jefferson's arguments in his 1774 pamphlet, *A Summary View of the Rights of British America*, or for that matter those presented in any draft of the Declaration of Independence as representative of colonial or revolutionary political thought.[33] But Jefferson's marginality illuminated the nature of the debates going on around him in at least three interesting and important ways. First, Jefferson understood the nature of the imperial crisis not simply as a constitutional debate, or even simply a jurisdictional one, but as a kind of jurisprudential problem that concerned the criteria and location of the power of equitable judgment within any constitutional order. Seizing on the consolidation of the distinct power of equitable consideration in the high common law courts, and in an imperial context in the sovereign power of parliamentary and council oversight, Jefferson developed over the course of his legal study an archaeological hermeneutic of disentanglement of the authoritative history of legal transmission presented in the systematic framework of Blackstone's *Commentaries*.[34] Jefferson's interest in Anglo-Saxon materials and the moments of construction and transition in the subsequent history of English law and legal learning grew from his attempt to think about an alternative history full of cracks and fissures that responded to a present moment of fracturing in the historical edifice that had grounded the construction of civic identity in the colonies. Secondly, Jefferson appreciated more than most that an effective retort to the implications of conquest theory required another alternative history, one that established the settler credentials of the colonists and legitimated the settler colonial project of purchasing or otherwise negating Native title. Jefferson's *Summary View* advanced a radical argument that based legitimate government in the historically repeated activity of consenting on the part of settler populations, the members of which possessed the ultimate power of deciding legal and constitutional legitimacy and meaning. This was not in keeping with the substance of contemporary concerns in Philadelphia for fixing the limits of Parliament's imperial authority in the colonies, but it registered the fundamental importance of the project

[33] Eric Nelson, *The Royalist Revolution: Monarchy and the American Revolution* (Cambridge, MA: Harvard University Press, 2014).

[34] Daniel J. Boorstin, *The Mysterious Science of the Law: An Essay on Blackstone's Commentaries* (Chicago: University of Chicago Press, 1996).

of identifying and securing the propertied and ultimately racial boundaries of settler liberty, and the settler subject who enjoyed it.

Finally, even more eccentrically, Jefferson would go on to explore the formulation of a constitutional design that fused the jurisprudential and intellectual aspects of his concern for the practice of legal study and interpretation with the civic aspects of the challenges of implementing a revolutionary republican constitutional settlement, and with it a republican textuality. A creative use and relocation of equity lay at the center of Jefferson's constitutionalism, but he certainly had sources at hand that had previously explored equity as a multifaceted idea. Coke had described equity as the "assemblage" of practices and assumptions on which judges drew in applying principles of natural right to particular cases. The sixteenth-century jurist William West, in a book that Jefferson owned, wrote of equity as the crucial jurisprudential site of the critical practice of "symboleography," a term that West used to refer to the rules governing the authoritative and appropriate organization, transmission, and writing of legal text.[35] In these contexts, precisely because equity jurists ventured beyond the letter to the spirit of the law and its history, rules of procedure and interpretation were all the more important, as both Kames and Blackstone insisted in their agreement that chancery jurisdiction in both Scotland and England was characterized by a regular and established if evolving set of rules and precedents. At the same time, the open recognition of such rules as at once constitutive of and products of a purposefully unfixed tradition of legal theorizing and adjudication, when taken with the anxieties of equity jurisdiction that characterized political discourse on the topic, reveal a set of tensions in the historically consolidated image of law configured by the legal theory of the day in the gradual assumption of equitable jurisdiction within the overall edifice of the legal and constitutional order.

Discussing the laws pertaining to private wrongs and injuries against the property interests of the crown (in some cases an issue of chancery jurisdiction), Blackstone would ask, "but who, that is acquainted with the difficulty of new-modelling any branch of our statute laws," confronting the tensions and contradictions inherent in a legal order built on such an overlapping system of differing jurisdictions, "will conceive it feasible to

[35] William West, *The Second Part of Symboleography, Newly Corrected and Amended* (London: Miles Flesher and Robert Young, 1642); see Peter Goodrich, *Languages of Law: Logics of Memory and Nomadic Masks* (London: Weidenfeld and Nicholson, 1990).

alter any fundamental point of the common law, with all its appendages and consequents, and set up another rule in it's stead?"[36] The growth of courts of equity allowed for a regular process of correcting the application of the common law in particular cases to meet the demands of "remedial justice," Blackstone reasoned, as "the more liberal and enterprising judges" had seen fit to accomplish legitimately and gradually over the previous centuries. Blackstone represented the structure not only of the common law but of the British constitution as an old and continually updated building:

> We inhabit an old Gothic castle, erected in the days of chivalry, but fitted up for a modern inhabitant. The moated ramparts, the embattled towers, and the trophied halls, are magnificent and venerable, but useless. The inferior apartments, now converted into rooms of convenience, are cheerful and commodious, though their approaches are winding and difficult.[37]

As he set out on a project that he was quite clear was one of "new-modeling," it is imperative to note how keenly tuned in to the jurisprudential aspects of the constitutional controversy of the imperial crisis Jefferson actually was. Equity, taken as both a particular jurisdiction and a broader framework for understanding the dependence of colonial law on appeals to the higher discretionary power of Parliament, the parliamentary courts, the king in council and ultimately the crown itself played a fundamental role in Blackstone's configuring of the edifice of law. It was, in fact, the cement that held the edifice together and allowed for the representation of its history as authoritative and continuous. As their understanding of the place in the edifice fell apart, colonists in the various newly declared states would turn to the project of

[36] Blackstone, *Commentaries on the Laws of England*, Vol. 3, p. 267.

[37] *Ibid*, p. 268; see Carol Matthews, "A 'Model of the Old House:' Architecture in Blackstone's Life and *Commentaries*," *Blackstone and His Commentaries*, Prest, ed. (London: Hart, 2009), pp. 15–34. In this context, Jefferson's lifelong fascination with ancient architecture, both British and Roman, in Britain and in continental Europe, might be understood as an extended formulation of an alternative architectural model for the republic, as seen most explicitly in his early sketch for a round church as a proposal for a chapel at the College of William and Mary, or his design of the state capitol of Virginia, and the design of the University of Virginia and his home, Monticello; see Frederick Doveton Nichols, *Thomas Jefferson's Architectural Drawings* (Charlottesville: Thomas Jefferson Memorial Foundation, 1961); Karl Lehman, *Thomas Jefferson: American Humanist* (Charlottesville: University of Virginia Press, 1985); Fiske Kimball, *The Capitol of Virginia: A Landmark of American Architecture* (Richmond: Library of Virginia, 2002); Hugh Howard, *Thomas Jefferson's Architecture: The Built Legacy of our Third President* (New York: Rizzoli, 2003).

building a new house, and Jefferson perceived more than any other thinker of the time that the fact that Americans were turning to the building blocks of the house they had just left because they had nothing else to build with necessarily brought up challenging questions as to what it meant to be using inherited materials in the context of a revolution. Who, then, decided what to use, and what were the rules of that use, if any? It was very telling that Jefferson, perhaps taking a cue from Kames' own fascination with ancient British law and society, described the extant copies of the laws of Virginia that would be the objects of revolutionary legal reform not only as monuments of the history and property of Virginians but as ruins. His constitutionalism took stock of this historical, or more appropriately, historiographical situation as an opportunity to institute a culture where the responsibilities for exercising equitable use of the assembled historical materials that inscribed the polity could be safely put in the hands of assembled bodies of the people.

That equity was a critical part of Jefferson's republican and even democratic vision for constitutionalism is apparent not only from the sheer immensity of his engagement with it as a student but also in the shaping of some of his most crucial political texts surrounding the emergence of the independence movement in the 1770s. The *Summary View*, after all, was a final appeal to the King's conscience, "a humble and dutiful address presented to his majesty," in the midst of a situation that would require the surrender of "not only the principles of common sense, but the common feelings of human nature." And, Jefferson noted, this was after the failure of legal and constitutional arguments grounded in the applicability of the common law rights of Englishmen to colonial subjects.[38] Jefferson's pamphlet, his directions and advice for the Virginia delegates to the first Continental Congress, and published without permission in 1774, accomplished a radical critique of the imperial constitutional structure in the form of a narrative of the constituent freedom enjoyed by the settlers and their posterity to establish, disestablish, and reestablish what constitutional structures they chose, "government," as Jefferson put it, "erected for their use, and consequently subject to their superintendence."[39] Harmony and common sentiment, the mutuality appropriate to a shared British Atlantic identity, could only be maintained within a broad institutional arrangement where public liberty

[38] Jefferson, "A Summary View of the Rights of British America," *The Papers of Thomas Jefferson*, Julian P. Boyd, ed. (Princeton: Princeton University Press, 1951), Vol. 1, p. 121.
[39] *Ibid.*

was cultivated and enjoyed in multiple visible, direct, and local polities. Such an expression of the essential if fragile order of "common feelings" was firmly attached to the historically inflected juridical issues at stake in the narrative of settlement and constitutional multiplicity put forth in the course of Jefferson's argument. The conscience of the King was the final arbiter of legal and constitutional debate in an imperial constitution where the Crown ruled and appointed judges who decided on the basis of natural equity.

Likewise, the Declaration of Independence was a careful response to the condition of being subject to the distant judgment associated not only with the power of the Privy Council and the legislative authority of Parliament but with the "Mansfieldian Moment" in English jurisprudence.[40] Such judgment was based on criteria and took place within institutional structures that the judged had not had a hand in making, and the argumentative logic of Jefferson's text makes a critical move that indicates a reworking and relocation of equity itself. The people, in taking action to dissolve constituted legal bonds that had become harmful to the spirit in which they were originally made with appeal to natural justice, inherited not so much the overall political sovereignty of the Crown as the responsibility for constitutional judgment invested in offices of conciliar adjudication.[41] Jefferson's revolutionary constitutionalism can be understood as an attempt to institute in practice the people's inheritance of the burden of equitable judgment. The people assume the powers and responsibilities to make a judgment on their own, when, "in the course of human events," such action seems necessary. Jefferson sought to make this kind of activity a legitimate and essential part of politics. The Declaration of Independence made recourse to natural right and natural rights, laying forth a list of grievances prefaced by a claim to the rights of the people to renegotiate or dissolve legal bonds that had become injurious to

[40] Waldstreicher, *Slavery's Constitution*, p. 41.

[41] Declaration of Independence, http://avalon.law.yale.edu/18th_century/declare.asp, April 29, 2012; the public philosophy of the Declaration and the legal tradition of equity touch bases in their foregrounding of the issue of the grounds on which judgment to take political or legal action: Gary Wills was absolutely right to suggest the importance of the Scottish Enlightenment to Jefferson's thought here, but we can identify greater influence of different aspects of Scottish thought, especially the overall work of Kames and the later, more historically configured moral sense philosophies of Adam Smith and David Hume; see Jay Fliegelman, *Declaring Independence: Jefferson, Natural Language, and the Culture of Performance* (Stanford: Stanford University Press, 1993); Peter Onuf and Ari Helo, "Jefferson, Morality, and the Problem of Slavery," *The Mind of Thomas Jefferson* (Charllotesville: University of Virginia Press, 2006), pp. 236–70.

the ends for which those bonds were made in the first place. No doubt, the Declaration, like the founding era itself, bears the markers of "multiple traditions" of legal and political thought, including the translation of Locke's "life, liberty, and estate," into "life, liberty, and the pursuit of happiness."[42] But the form of the innovative argument Jefferson sought to make becomes clearer when seen in light of his conceptual borrowing across the boundaries of public and private law and the practice of legal argumentation appropriate to the corrective use of principles of equity, applied to covenants and contracts between peoples.[43] While proclaiming independence, both Jefferson's drafts and the final published product directly tapped into early modern legal and political theory concerned with the extent to which a constituted public had legitimate power to exercise judgment in law and politics, particularly on the constitutional level. That in Jefferson's formulation the people themselves are in the interpretive place held by the Chancellor rather than the King is a sign of the radical constitutional theory being imagined, one predicated on the reemergence of the people in their capacity as critical actors in the making and defining of law.[44]

NEW-MODELING AND THE COMMON LAW MIND

Jefferson's constitutional proposals during the revolutionary period flowed from this central concern to experiment in the democratization of judgment, and the feasibility of such an experiment for Jefferson rested on his own sense of intellectual practice and its civic implications, on a fusion of early modern legal humanism with the demands of revolutionary republican politics. Jefferson crafted models for institutional design

[42] Locke, "Second Treatise on Government,"; Thomas Jefferson, "Autobiography," in *Writings* (New York: Library of America, 1984), p. 19

[43] See Alan Gibson, *Interpreting the Founding* (Lawrence: Kansas University Press, 2006), ch. 6. On the "liberal" interpretation in its confrontation with the "republican synthesis," in reference to the Declaration, see Carl Becker, *The Declaration of Independence: A Study in the History of Political Ideas* (New York: Vintage, 1922); James T. Kloppenberg, "The Virtues of Liberalism: Christianity, Republicanism, and Ethics in Early American Political Discourse," *Journal of American History*, Vol. 74, No. 1 (1987), pp. 9–33.

[44] On popular pressures in elite politics during the Revolution in Virginia, see Michael A. McDonnell, *The Politics of War: Race, Class, and Conflict in Revolutionary Virginia* (Chapel Hill: University of North Carolina Press, 2007). On the cultural assumption of "popular constitutionalism" in the common law and American Revolution, see Larry D. Kramer, *The People Themselves: Popular Constitutionalism and Judicial Review* (Oxford: Oxford University Press, 2004).

that relied on assemblies of the people at crucial junctures as instantiations of their "superintendence." In crafting such a model, Jefferson built on four particular aspects of his wider civic, humanist understanding of constitutionalism: the involvement of popular assemblies in constitutional change, a dramatic expansion of juries throughout all levels of the legal structure of the new state, a guarantee of the basic material, economic basis of independent settler proprietorship and a concordant understanding of the right of the public to secure and maintain that basis in property ownership, by direction action through the state or through repossession if necessary, and finally, most significantly, an understanding of the citizen required for such a constitution to last as a self-owning and self-governing, cultivated subject, one that was himself constituted (and it was indeed him) by a particular relationship to the authoritative texts that inscribed the polity and its laws. Jefferson's constitutional draft, his own legal reform proposals, and his wider elaboration of his peculiarly republican constitutionalism in correspondence and his *Notes on the State of Virginia* all called for extensions of the degree an acknowledgment of material, textual practice had always been and needed to continue to be an essential component of constitutional politics.

Jefferson understood the American Revolution not as a clean departure or break from customary temporality of inherited constitutional history, but as a kind of fragmentation of that history, an instance of fractured constitutional time. In Jefferson's constitutional draft proposal of 1776, which was ultimately passed over in favor of that of George Mason, the cracked-open temporality of the revolutionary moment was built into the text itself. The result of this framing of current historical experience on Jefferson's part was an understanding of the legal materials that he had studied and collected and from which a provincial customary history had been assembled as fragments, scattered ruins that now appeared in a different light and were available for different use. An extended preface in the first and third of three drafts Jefferson composed in the summer and fall of 1776 paralleled the legal argument against the crown that would surface in the text of the Declaration, but in the case of the constitutional text, the criticism led directly into the design and practice of new institutional structure. Declaring the illegitimacy of the royal governance in the colonies, Jefferson carried out a textual dethroning of the King's rule, offering an extended legal indictment of the negative power exercised in the name of the King over colonial law and legal decisions.

Also anticipating the Declaration, he criticized the Crown for its incitement of the rebellions of slaves and Native Americans in the west, "prompting our negroes to rise in arms among us; those very negroes whom by an inhuman use of his negative he hath (*from time to time*) refused us permission to exclude by law," and encouraging the warfare of the "merciless Indian savages."[45] These indictments register the conjoined significance of civic identity and security, responding at once to the perceived failure of the English government to recognize English colonists as bearing the full rights and liberties of Englishmen and to the jarring threat to the security of life and property posed by imperial willingness to encourage other subjects to ally themselves against the colonial cause, evidenced by Lord Dunmore's proclamation of 1775. This was only part of the evidence Jefferson needed to feel comfortable asserting that the end of monarchial rule might not be enough, that it would "become further necessary to re-establish such ancient principles as are friendly to the rights of the people and to declare certain others which may cooperate with and fortify the same in the future." He then proceeded to outline a model of state government in the name of "the authority of the people."[46] In his draft proposal, Jefferson characterized the revolutionary moment not as beginning over again but as a kind of project of historical recovery, as the return to freer use of previously wrapped up and circumscribed histories of law and politics.

Jefferson's proposal was not altogether more radical in its basic structure than many of the other proposals on the table, and was in some ways less so. Carter Braxton's proposal to essentially codify the colonial constitution and affirm the continuity of English common law was deemed unpalatable by most. John Adams' pamphlet, *Thoughts on Government*, written partly in response to Thomas Paine's *Common Sense*, struck a moderating tone. Embracing the fracturing of British American constitutionalism, Paine had written that the Crown not only had to be removed from the head of the King but "demolished, and scattered among the people whose right it is."[47] The revolutionary constitution of Pennsylvania announced the fundamental principle of the public's

[45] Jefferson, "Jefferson's Third Draft," *Papers of Thomas Jefferson*, Vol. 1, p. 357.

[46] Mason's draft included the 1776 Virginia Declaration of Rights in the form of a Bill of Rights, although in most respects like Jefferson's draft, it was comparatively moderate; unlike Jefferson's draft, it did not guarantee white males property, and it did not provide for the degree of public power represented in juries and constitutional amendment councils; Jefferson, Draft Constitution for Virginia, 1776, "Jefferson's Third Draft," *Papers of Thomas Jefferson*, Vol. 1, p. 357.

[47] Thomas Paine, *Common Sense*, Isaac Kramnick, ed. (New York: Penguin Classics, 1986), p. 98.

ultimate, active authority to judge their representatives as well as the adequacy of constitutional structures themselves.[48] Adams also hoped to stave off the possibility of other states besides Pennsylvania adopting unicameral, largely democratic legislatures in their state constitutions, and his pamphlet was passed by George Wythe to Richard Henry Lee, who published it. The most influential of the proposals, George Mason's, paralleled Jefferson and Adams in setting up a bicameral legislature with a governor, stipulating property qualifications for voting, although unlike Jefferson's, making the upper house popularly elected. Mason's framework, with some edits, provided the basis for the constitutional committee's recommendations to the General Assembly and the eventual adopted text, which included large parts of Jefferson's extensive preamble.

The principal differences between Jefferson and Mason's, however, centered on core assumptions of the relationship between law and politics, and on the responsibility of the state to provide for the means of substantive economic independence as required for exercising the franchise. As far as accessing a development of Jefferson's legal and constitutional thought, there are a couple of things that stand out in the draft constitution of 1776: the maintenance of a profoundly British constitutional understanding of the relationship between judges and the legislature, for judges in the General Court and the proposed High Court of Chancery would sit and have voice (although not suffrage) in the Senate, and members of a proposed Privy Council would exercise the privilege to sit in, speak, and vote in the upper house. Combined with a dramatic expansion of the use and power of juries, this made for a closer relationship between law and republican constitutionalism in Jefferson's proposal, a relationship Jefferson would develop, even insist on, throughout his life. There was an astonishingly weak executive, an "administrator," who would be elected along with a deputy annually by the lower house of the legislative assembly; and a liberalization of property qualifications for voting, including all male (white) persons who owned land, a quarter of an acre in town or twenty-five acres in the country. Uniquely, Jefferson wanted to commit the state to ensuring the franchise of very adult white male, enforcing the colonial promise held out to indentured English settlers, providing that "every person . . . shall be entitled to an appropriation of 50 acres or to so much as shall make up what he owns or

48 Constitution of Pennsylvania, September 28, 1776, http://avalon.law.yale.edu/18th_century/pa08.asp, April 29, 2012.

has owned 50 acres in full and absolute dominion."[49] Finally, Jefferson tried to expand the importance of juries in state-level courts, expanding trial by jury to "all causes, whether of Chancery, Common, Ecclesiastical or Marine law," placing juries in the fact-finding and, if deemed necessary, interpretive office of the Lord Chancellor.

He went on to suggest a provision for banning the importation of slaves into the state, a plan of statewide public education, a ban on standing armies except in time of war, a guarantee of the right to keep arms on one's property, a relatively generous naturalization process, the total freedom of religious conscience, a replacement of common law inheritance principles of primogeniture and entail with Kentish *gavelkind*, excepting "that females shall have equal rights with males."[50] For Jefferson, male citizenship and property were inseparable, to the extent of a right to private property for settlers of "unappropriated" land. From its

[49] *Ibid*, pp. 362–3.

[50] As William Blackstone argued and Jefferson knew well, *gavelkind* was a species of land tenure that, according to Selden and Blackstone, had prevailed throughout England before the Norman conquest, and still did in Kent, home of Canterbury and so the historical seat and power center of the Church of England. As Christopher Curtis shows, in his legal commonplace book's turn to treatises on the history of property Jefferson included William Somner's *A Treatise of Gavelkind, Both Name and Thing*, which confirmed the continuity of distinct tenures through the Norman Conquest; Curtis, *Jefferson's Freeholders and the Politics of Ownership in the Old Dominion* (Cambridge: Cambridge University Press, 2012), pp. 58–9. Gavelkind was not, it is important to note, allodial, as Jefferson had described the land colonists possessed in his *Summary View of the Rights of British America*, but it was a form of "free and common socage" that allowed for partible inheritance and alienation of all or parts of the land, and so was not controlled by common law principles of primogeniture and entail; see Blackstone, *Commentaries on the Laws of England*, Vol. 2, pp. 81, 84–5. Interestingly, Jefferson proposed including women in inheritance and full legal possession of property, but did not in any way allow for further legal or political emancipation, which speaks strongly to the uncertainties of legal and political subjectivity opened up by the revolution and the hedges on openings to full legal personhood that constituted an important part of revolutionary politics; indeed, it is important not to overstate the radicalism of Jefferson's proposal: women's property would have still belonged to their husband upon marriage (making marriage generally a more profitable enterprise for the man; Jefferson himself married Martha Wayles Skelton in 1772, and in 1773 inherited the entirety of her father's estate, including his slaves and his extensive debts). It seems clear that in many cases women by necessity were already exercising varying degrees of control over personal and family property in eighteenth-century Virginia; see Linda L. Sturtz, "As Though I My Self Was Pr[e]sent: Virginia Women with Power of Attorney," and John G. Kolp and Terri L. Snyder, "Women and the Political Culture of Eighteenth Century Virginia: Gender, Property Law, and Voting Rights," *The Many Legalities of Early America*, Christopher L. Tomlins and Bruce H. Mann, eds. (Chapel Hill: University of North Carolina Press, 2001), pp. 250–71, 272–91.

beginning, it is important to note, Jefferson's career-long constitutional thought was predicated, implicitly here and explicitly later, on the purchase and, if need be, legal cancelation of Native title in the name of the freehold property rights of settlers. At the same time, undeniably, Jefferson's draft assumes a neoclassically republican understanding of what it means to establish and maintain a free state, anchored in the rights and liberties of the arms-bearing male citizen, himself grounded in the security and economic independence of freely holding property. Jefferson's proposals for ending the slave trade, along with his provisions for property, the laws of inheritance, the extension of the jury system, and the sitting of judges in the upper legislative chamber, were left out. Both Mason's draft and the eventual constitution as adopted explicitly insist on the full institutional separation of the three branches of government.

Jefferson concluded his draft by outlining the means of amending the constitution. "None of these fundamental laws and principles of government shall be repealed or altered, but by the personal consent of the people on summons to meet in their respective counties on one and the same day," and given a two-thirds majority of the people present, "such repeal or alteration shall take its place among these fundamentals and stand on the same footing with them, in lieu of the article repealed or altered."[51] Jefferson imagined a summoning of active members of the polity to collectively go over proposed drafts of amendments to the constitution. This vision depended on the creation of a citizenry capable of exercising judgment in such a context, as well as an assumption about the desired availability of constitutional text as something that was written, read, debated, and then reread and rewritten within the envelope of a constituted local, collective, and political setting.

The provisions for religious liberty, the immediate end of the slave trade, expanding the power and use of juries, and the socialized distribution or property were proposals unique to Jefferson's constitutional draft, and were decisive factors in its defeat. But the project of restoring "such ancient principles as are friendly to the rights of the people," in Jefferson's eyes, entailed a grander series of reforms than he or Mason or anyone else had yet proposed, reforms that he had the opportunity to propose when selected as a member of the special committee appointed by the General Assembly, at Jefferson's urging, for the revisal of the Virginia legal code in October 1776, which included Edmund Pendleton, George Wythe,

[51] Jefferson, "Draft Constitution for Virginia-Fair Copy," p. 345

George Mason, and Thomas Ludwell Lee.[52] Their goal as stated by the assembly was to collect and read over the entire body of law that had prevailed in the colony, including applicable English laws as well as laws passed in Virginia, and to make a report of what should be kept and what should not, and on how the authority of that body of laws should be represented and understood.

Well known for his deep reading and study of Virginian as well as English legal history, Jefferson was assigned the review of the application of the common law and statutory law through to the founding of the colony. Lee and Mason removed themselves on account of not feeling qualified, Pendleton took subsequent Virginia law, and Wythe took subsequent British law. According to Jefferson's autobiography, written much later, as he had been assigned the English origins of common law rules of descent and the criminal law, he sought the guidance and permission of the committee to develop bills of total reform in these as well as other areas of the law. Out of the final report submitted by the committee, which amounted to 90 pages of 126 individual bills reforming, eliminating, or condensing previous legal material and an even more substantial abbreviation, Jefferson later isolated four fundamental components of the revisal report that he deemed particularly important for "forming a system by which every fibre would be eradicated of antient or future aristocracy; and a foundation laid for a government truly republican."[53] These included the abolition of entail, or common law rules of descent written to preserve the integrity of elite landed estates over time; the similar abolition of the law of primogeniture; the freedom of religion and the disestablishment of the Anglican Church in Virginia; the consequent outfitting of the College of William and Mary as a public university, with the chair of divinity being converted into a chair of "law and police," a seat occupied first by Wythe; and finally, the introduction of trial by jury into the chancery courts, the separation and independence of which was further provided for in the report of the revisers in 1779.[54] Out

[52] See Dumas Malone, *Jefferson the Virginian* (University of Virginia Press), pp. 251–85; Edward Dumbauld, *Thomas Jefferson and the Law* (Norman: University of Oklahoma Press, 1978), ch. 7; David N. Mayer, *The Constitutional Thought of Thomas Jefferson* (Charlottesville: University of Virginia Press, 1994).

[53] Jefferson, "Autobiography," *Writings*, p. 44.

[54] The use the word "police" here is highly significant in the context of early modern political theory; the police power of the modern state was understood as the core of its regulatory authority, and its transference to and maintenance by the states was equally a central tenet of republican revolutionary constitutionalism; for Jefferson, the power of

of these, only the abolitions of entail and primogeniture were successful at the outset, and these with great controversy and heated debate, and without further legislation that Jefferson saw as crucial to implementing and maintaining even these proposed reforms. The total disestablishment bill failed and was not passed until 1786, and the idea for juries in equity cases failed outright. Jefferson's other pet project, a moderate reform of the criminal law, also met overwhelming resistance.

When the special committee was appointed to take stock of the laws of Virginia and propose reform bills to the General Assembly, Jefferson later recalled, the members debated whether to propose reform bills or produce a new *Institutes* along the lines of that of Justinian, the more reformist members inclined to the former, fearing the fixed status a foundational text of fundamental law would come to play in subsequent legal and constitutional disputes. As Jefferson wrote in the query on laws in the *Notes on the State of Virginia*, "it was thought dangerous to reduce it to a text."[55] This would seem to be in the same spirit of the closing lines of Jefferson's original draft constitutional proposal, that "the laws heretofore in force in this colony shall remain in force, except so far as they are altered by the foregoing fundamental laws, or so far as they may be hereafter altered by acts of Legislature."[56] In other words, for all of the leaping into the new and flight from history we traditionally associate with Jefferson, and perhaps with the American Revolution more generally, in his mind, a polity reconstituted as a revolutionary republic required not an absolute new beginning, but the adoption of a new framework for using inherited materials that had been handed down in the form of an authoritative tradition that had come apart on the shoals of the imperial crisis. For Jefferson and his comrades, the past of the law and the legal security of property were inescapably transmitted and embodied in texts. Jefferson thought the publicly funded printing of these laws and subsequent legislative activity, such as the report of the committee on law reform, was an essential component of enabling his particular understanding of what was needed for republican constitutionalism. The experience of civic participation in a republican constitution would need to be a specifically textual one, for the assembled

"superintendence" needed to be further devolved to public tribunals. On republican constitutionalism and the concept of the police as public supervisory power in Jeffersonian thought, see Christopher Tomlins, *Law, Labor, and Ideology in the Early American Republic* (Cambridge: Cambridge University Press, 1993), pp. 43–59, 81–9.

55 Jefferson, *Notes on the State of Virginia*, Frank Shuffleton, ed. (New York: Penguin, 1999), p. 144.

56 Jefferson, "Jefferson's Third Draft," *Papers of Thomas Jefferson*, p. 364.

people needed to be able to get their hands on at least a degree of power, and power was made and unmade in writing. Jefferson's constitutionalism proceeded as an experiment in the civic pliability of constitutional text.

MODELING CONSTITUTIONAL TEXT

The constitution of Jefferson's imagining could be accurately described as a kind of collective commonplace book, a repository of recorded law and history available for use.[57] This vision in turn was dependent on an understanding of the constituted citizen as a subject of multiple histories, natural and civil. For such an understanding Jefferson drew from his reading of Montesquieu's *The Spirit of the Laws*, where laws were described as the necessary relationships that arise from the nature of things, understood here not simply as the eternal divine and natural laws of God and the universe, but as the systems of complex relationships that had developed historically in human society.

Jefferson devoted extended attention to Montesquieu in his legal commonplace book, particularly to the analysis of the adaptation of appropriate laws given the principles at work in the diverse constitutions of different types of polity.[58] In complex modern societies, constitutions were mixtures of monarchial, aristocratic, and republican or democratic elements. The condition of being in civil society and subject to systems of civil law did not isolate citizens and their governments from broader contexts of natural history, most notably geographical distribution, climate, and their effects on the population. The first and most extended extractions and commentaries from Montesquieu come from

[57] On the importance of commonplace books in early modern humanist intellectual culture, see Peter Burke, *The Renaissance Sense of the Past* (London: Edward Arnold, 1969); on Renaissance legal humanism, see Quentin Skinner, *Foundations of Modern Political Thought: The Renaissance* (Cambridge: Cambridge University Press, 1978); Donald R. Kelley, *The Human Measure: Social Thought and the Western Legal Tradition* (Cambridge, MA: Harvard University Press, 1990); J.G.A. Pocock, "The Origins of the Study of the Past," *Political Thought and History: Theory and Method* (Cambridge: Cambridge University Press, 2009), pp. 145–86; on commonplace books, see Ann Moss, *Printed Commonplace Books and the Structuring of Renaissance Thought* (Oxford: Clarendon Press, 1996); Bradin Cormack and Carla Mazzio, *Book Use, Book Theory: 1500–1700* (Chicago: University of Chicago Library, 2005), pp. 70–3.

[58] Jefferson, *Legal Commonplace Book*, #775–805, on Montesquieu and the subject of multiple laws, see Sheldon Wolin, *The Presence of the Past: Essays on the State and the Constitution* (Baltimore: Johns Hopkins University Press, 1989), p. 104; see also Andrew Lewis, "Montesquieu Between Law and History," *Law and History: Current Legal Issues* Vol. 6 (2003), pp. 83–95.

the beginning of the crucial Book V, where Montesquieu discusses the task of the legislator in different types of polities. Democracy, he reasoned, required the love of equality, which to be reinforced by a love of frugality and the legal encouragement of relative equality. "Love of *equality* and love of *frugality* are strongly aroused by equality and frugality themselves, when one lives in a society in which both are established by the laws." Thus "legislators of ancient times, like Lycurgus and Romulus, divided the lands equally. This could only happen at the founding of a new republic," for if "if the legislator who makes such a division does not give laws to maintain it, his is only a transitory constitution; inequality will enter at the point not protected by the laws, and the republic will be lost."[59] Jefferson summarized in his commonplace book:

> He considers political virtue, or the *amor patriae*, as the energetic principle of a democratic republic . . ., and shows that every government should provide that its energetic principle should be the object of the education of its youth. . ., that its laws also should be relative to the same principle, in a democracy, equality and frugality should be promoted by the laws, as they nurse the *amor patriae*. To do this, a census is advisable, discriminating the people according to their possessions; after which, particular laws may equalize them in some degree by laying burthens on the richer classes, & encouraging the poorer ones.[60]

Jefferson's extractions from Montesquieu, particularly sections dealing with a range of classical exemplars on the relationship between property distribution and political power, cumulatively form the basis for his proposals for ending entail and primogeniture in Virginia.[61] These proposals, Jefferson believed, were essential for his project of having "a foundation laid for a government truly republican." In his autobiography, Jefferson observed that the transmission of large estates across generations had resulted in the establishment of a permanent aristocratic order that controlled all levels of government and from which the ministers of the Crown in the colonial period had selected members of the Governor's Council and General Court without exception. The legal encouragement of the breaking up of these estates through equal division would not be a "deprivation of natural right, but rather an enlargement of it," for ending primogeniture, along with discouraging

59 Montesquieu, *The Spirit of the Laws*, Anne M. Cohler, Basia Carolyn Miller, and Harold Samuel Stone, eds. trans. (Cambridge: Cambridge University Press, 1989), pp. 44–5.
60 Jefferson, *Legal Commonplace Book*, #777–8.
61 See Eric Nelson, *The Greek Tradition in Republican Thought* (Cambridge: Cambridge University Press, 2004), pp. 200–9.

unhealthy accumulation through land law and taxes, would eventually place the sons and grandsons of the gentry "by natural generation on the level of their fellow citizens." Thus the abolition of entail would guard against the establishment of a permanent body of select families, and the abolition of primogeniture and "equal partition of inheritances" would remove "the feudal and unnatural distinctions which made one member of every family rich, and all the rest poor, substituting equal partition, the best of all Agrarian laws."[62] A democratic republic would require ensuring at the outset an equitable, if not precisely equal, distribution of property to ensure the access of the broader citizenry to participation in politics and collective self-governance.

For Montesquieu, and for Jefferson, the citizen was the subject of multiple strands of what Jefferson would go on to call "history, natural and civil." A political analysis and constitutionalism aware of such historical multiplicity would need to be exercised through methods of study that could enable the analyst to see and take stock of the multifaceted spatial and temporal field in view. "He had been a great reader," Jefferson wrote of Montesquieu to William Duane in 1810, "and had commonplaced everything he read. At length he wished to undertake some work into which he could bring his whole Commonplace book in a digested form. He fixed on the subject of his Spirit of laws, and wrote the book."[63] Jefferson placed great value on the assembled, commonplace character of the text Montesquieu composed, and a similar spirit would govern Jefferson's composition of his own work, the *Notes on the State of Virginia*. As will become clear, Jefferson's particular treatment of humanist intellectual practice and reading as crucial components of constitutionalism would persist throughout his career, and his shifting valuations of textual practice on the part of the citizenry, as reflected in his shifting valuations of Montesquieu's work, would prove to play a critical role in the transformation of constitutionalism from the late eighteenth to the early nineteenth centuries.

In Jefferson's case, it was not simply ideas about law and sovereignty that came into question: the written, composed, textual character of law had ceased to appear whole. Indeed, Jefferson's unique attention to the materiality of law and legal knowledge as writing was an essential aspect of the development of his revolutionary constitutional criticism

62 Jefferson, "Autobiography," in *Writings*, pp. 32, 44.

63 Jefferson to William Duane, August 10, 1810, *Papers of Thomas Jefferson: Retirement Series*, J. Jefferson Looney, ed. (Princeton: Princeton University Press, 2010), Vol. 3, p. 6.

and method, growing as it did out of his concern for the representation of historical and conceptual authority in the presentation of text in the form of the book. In the fourth volume of his commentaries, Blackstone hailed the composition of the Laws of King Alfred out of the disparate assemblage of local laws: Alfred's codification had been "a most great and necessary work," aiming at no less than to "new-model the constitution; to rebuild it on a plan that should endure for ages; and, out of its old discordant materials, which were heaped upon each other in a vast and rude irregularity, to form one unified and one connected whole."[64] Whatever undesirable elements had been woven into the texture of the law by periodic conquests and abrupt revolutions, the feudal constraints introduced by the Norman Conquest, for example, were so "interwoven in the body of our legal polity, that they cannot now be taken out without a manifest injury to the substance."[65] Jefferson's own representation of constitutions as assemblages of law and history was a direct response to Blackstone's structuring of English legal history. For Jefferson, the edifice was in ruins, and what was left to work with were fragments of histories only tenuously and problematically attached to their traditional transmission across time and space. His widely noted interest in ancient Britain and the Anglo-Saxons in particular (another settler society) grew out of this constitutional project of recollection.

Undoubtedly, enthusiastic narratives of Anglo-Saxon origins were themselves building blocks of Whig historiography and a developing racial narrative of English liberty, and certainly Jefferson participated in, made use of, and developed these narratives for his own purposes. The rooting of the argument of the *Summary View of the Rights of British America* in the history of "our Saxon ancestors" speaks plainly enough to the inextricably racialized character of the civic identity being constructed there, as well as to its use in establishing a historical theory of settler liberty and exclusive rights of possession. Throughout his life, Jefferson valued and even recommended the adoption of Anglo-Saxon language study in curricula. Likewise, Jefferson embraced the poems of Ossian, a fictional ancient Scottish authorial identity constructed by Scottish poet James MacPherson, and included extensive entries in his literary commonplace book, continuing to recommend and enjoy them long after he became aware of their true origin.[66] In his proposal for the seal of

[64] Blackstone, *Commentaries*, Vol. 4, pp. 403–4. [65] *Ibid*, p. 410–11.

[66] *Jefferson's Literary Commonplace Book*, Douglas L. Wilson, ed. (Princeton: Princeton University Press, 1989), pp. 143–51; see note, pp. 171–3.

Virginia, Jefferson went so far as to suggest representations of Hengist and Horsa, the Saxon chiefs who began the conquest of Britain. What appears to have interested Jefferson about these periods so much was their represented character as founding, legitimating moments of law and its subsequent history. In his drafting of constitutional and legal text, as in his attentiveness to the representation of history in writing, what concerned Jefferson most was what was gained and what was lost at the moment when not yet foundational constitutional experience became inscribed for posterity in the form of a singular codified text.

Like Blackstone in his historical summation of the laws of England, Jefferson took up as an exemplar the ninth-century codification of English laws under the efforts of Alfred the Great, but he did so not, as was typical of the period, as a primordial origin point beyond which historical memory could not venture with much legitimacy, but as a constituent building block of the history of the British Constitution as presented by Blackstone and others, and therefore something like a fragment. Indeed, in his correspondence with Edmund Pendleton and in his autobiography, when Jefferson spoke of restoration with regards to the ancient constitution, he referred to the eighth rather than the ninth century, to the collective historical experience behind the composition of the Laws of King Alfred, its being taken up as a legitimating document of subsequent constitutional authority, and the narrative of unbroken descent that legitimated this authoritative vision of legal history.[67] This moment of British constitutionalism struck Jefferson precisely when he confronted a fracturing and open moment for the constitutionalism of his own polity, the every identity and existence of which was unthinkable without transmitted histories of English law and empire, and yet at the same time found itself in a moment where those histories had ceased to be authoritative.

A key way in which Jefferson sought to spread his particular concerns for the study of law and history was in his enthusiastic guidance of young men in their reading material and habits. In a letter to an inquiring student sent sometime in the early 1770s, Jefferson advised a student on commonplace books of law, urging him to make use of Coke and the earlier legal treatises of Bracton and Glanville "when tracing the history of particular portions of the law," warning against relying on more recent texts, such as the surveys of Matthew Bacon and Blackstone, which had been produced more out of a need to organize into a unified body the "voluminous"

[67] Thomas Jefferson to Edmund Pendleton, August 13, 1776, in *The Papers of Thomas Jefferson*, Vol. 1, p. 492.

development of law in the eighteenth century than to provide a history.[68] Likewise, in the 1803 preface to his edition of Blackstone's *Commentaries*, Jefferson's friend and ally, St. George Tucker, echoed Coke's description of legal study in his critique of Blackstone: "with the appearance of the Commentaries, the Laws of England, from a rude chaos, instantly assumed the semblance of a regular system ... The crude and immethodical hours of Sir Edward Coke were laid aside, and that rich mine of learning, his Commentary upon Littleton, was thought to be no longer worthy of the labor requisite for extracting its precious ore."[69] Perhaps a bit ironically, the intellectual culture of law constructed by this rarified image of Cokean learning allowed elite Virginians to think through the problems of instituting new, republican constitutional cultures, because the customarily pliable quality of textuality and the materiality of law appropriate to that mode of learning allowed them to frame the legitimacy of legal transformation and reformation, even of legal revolution.

When read with this context in mind, previous aspects of Jefferson's early constitutional thought that have been dismissed as misplaced idealism or as sloppy thinking can begin to be understood as products of this experience and astute theorization of fracturing in constitutional time. The proposal for the reform of the criminal law, for example, was written with the main text of the law running down the center of the page while marginalia consisting of historical footnotes that referenced ancient precedents and developments in both civil and common law as well as political theory decorated all sides of the page, with citations to Bracton, Coke, and Beccaria's *On Crimes and Punishments*. The composition of the bill mirrored the medieval glossator's method of commentary that was employed by Coke in his tract on Littleton. Jefferson understood himself as a commentator, a glossator, but he transferred the textual form of the commentary into the writing of a proposed law. The text of the crime bill Jefferson composed, while drawing on the form of Coke's writing, and in particular on the "commonplace book" that was Coke's tract on Littleton, departed dramatically from anything else in the report on law reform and from any other legal or constitutional

[68] Thomas Jefferson to Bernard Moore, date unknown, later enclosed to John Minor, August 30, 1814, in *Writings*, pp. 1558–9. See Julia S. Waterman, "Jefferson and Blackstone's Commentaries," *Illinois Law Review* Vol. 27, (1932–3), pp. 629–59.

[69] St. George Tucker, preface to *Blackstone's Commentaries on the Laws of England* (Philadelphia, 1803).

proposals in the period. In marked contradistinction to the desire on the part of other members of the committee to produce a new code, a codified and singularly authoritative text, Jefferson's draft resists even the possibility of codification in the material display of its own constructed character. The text of the crime bill is a small piece that reflects a larger Jeffersonian project involving the restoration of constituent components to the realm of representation on the face of the page, and thereby to usage. By putting glosses and extended footnotes onto the text of the draft, Jefferson was extending the logic of his critical reading and commonplace book methods directly to work in the drafting of legislation.

Having become keenly aware of the cultural and ultimately juridical significance of method and issues of textual representation and interpretation as a student and lawyer, Jefferson knew that there could be a politics to playing with order, margins, and footnotes. Moreover, he was becoming increasingly concerned to theorize ways of ensuring the possibility of new readings, rewritings, and new usage in constitutional politics beyond the moment of founding. Reporting on the existing laws as he found them, Jefferson's method was to offer extended histories of the political, contingent origins of rules and legal practice. Sure enough, the crime bill preserves a surprising amount of corporal punishments for major theft and sexual crimes, as well as capital punishment for murder and treason alone.[70] Later in life, Jefferson himself expressed disappointment in the bill, explaining that it had been his desire to completely abolish capital punishment and the *lex talionis*, but that the guidelines provided for the committee, for his task in particular, as well as the politics of the time, did not allow for such reforms. Inspired by the historically developed legal theories of Lord Kames and Cesare Beccaria, which tied legal change to wider shifts in the social and political conditions of society and the resulting changes in moral sentiment, Jefferson provided for this history in the marginal footnotes.[71] What that

[70] See Markus D. Dubber, "An Extraordinarily Beautiful Document:' Jefferson's Bill for Proportioning Crimes and Punishments and the Challenge of Republican Punishment," *Modern Histories of Crime and Punishment*, Markus D. Dubber and Lindsay Farmer eds. (Stanford: Stanford University Press, 2007), pp. 115–50.

[71] Jefferson, "Report of the Committee for the Revisal of the Laws, Bill No. 64," *Papers of Thomas Jefferson*, pp. 492–507; see Kathryn Preyer, "Crime, the Criminal Law, and Reform in Post-Revolutionary Virginia," and "Two Enlightened Reformers of the Criminal Law: Thomas Jefferson of Virginia and Peter Leopold, Grand Duke of Tuscany," *Blackstone in America: Selected Essays of Kathryn Preyer*, Mary Sarah Bilder, Maeva Marcus, R. Kent Newmeyer, eds. (Cambridge: Cambridge University Press, 2009), pp. 147–84, 252–76; Jefferson, *Legal Commonplace Book*, #806–831. Beccaria's

meant was that when the legislator, the judge, and the citizen read the law, they would encounter not simply a table of gradation matching crimes and punishments, but the multitude of theories and histories of law and the challenge of punishment to the law that both informed and could be used to criticize or undermine the law presented. This was law written to help ensure it would not be written in stone. Jefferson copied the text into a small vellum-bound commonplace book, and while he submitted the text with its additions to the committee, the printed edition approved by the legislature carried only the main text of Jefferson's draft, without the historical footnotes.[72] This could have only served to reinforce the particularity of Jefferson's practiced manuscript and palimpsest-oriented intellectual life in the age of print.

Jefferson's proposed bill for the total disestablishment of the Anglican Church in Virginia, another cornerstone of his project, was, like the crime bill, a product of an immense reading in the history of the institutions and concepts at hand. His collected papers include several pages of notes on the history of the church in Virginia, on assembly acts concerning religion in the colony, on Parliamentary acts concerning religion in the colony, and repeated efforts to expand civil liberties for Dissenters in the colony. Among these pages are also extensive notes on the history of episcopacy and the origins of ecclesiastical juridical authority, the definition of heresy according to ancient and English ecclesiastical jurisprudence, as well as on treatments of religion by John Locke and Anthony Ashley Cooper, the Third Earl of Shaftesbury. His reading in the latter demonstrated his participation in an enlightenment project of redefining traditional religion as a matter of specifically individual opinion.[73] Jefferson included language that proclaimed religion to be just that in the text of the bill for religious freedom itself.

Even more significant for his constitutional project, however, was the historicization of doctrine and the power to punish attached to it that Jefferson recorded in his reading of the history of councils and theological disputes within the history of the Church. He noted in general that one of the justifications of ecclesiastical jurisdiction in England had been the

historically oriented philosophical project of law reform, alongside that of Kames, had significant influence on Jefferson; Cesare Beccaria, *On Crimes and Punishments*, Richard Bellamy, ed. Richard Davies, trans. (Cambridge: Cambridge University Press, 1995).

72 Editorial note, *Papers of Thomas Jefferson*, Boyd, ed. Vol. 2, pp. 504–7; Sowerby, *Catalogue of the Library of Thomas Jefferson*, Vol. 2, #1797.

73 J.G.A. Pocock, "Perceptions of Modernity in Early Modern Historical Thinking," *Intellectual History Review* Vol. 17, No. 1 (2007), pp. 55–63.

likeness of the figure of the bishop to that of the monarch. This linkage between sovereignty and religion was crucial for the development of a Jeffersonian critique of Christianity. He wryly noted that it would be more appropriate for them to be governed by a presbytery than a bishop, and that while the clergy had been too blind to notice, bishops were always "mere tools of the crown." His reading, thinking, and writing going hand in hand, he continued by noting that the spirit of presbytery "is known to be so congenial with friendly liberty, that the patriots after the restoration finding that the humour of the people was running too strongly to exalt the prerogative of the crown, promoted the dissenting interest as a check and balance, and thus produced the Toleration act."[74] Toleration, as it had been for Locke, was about more than the individual freedom of worship and religious belief, or opinion. It was about deepening and expanding a civic and humanist constitutional and political culture of discourse, supplanting a hierarchical model of government reinforced by the image of its divine sanction.[75]

Jefferson's radical ecclesiology fit in with the gradual development of his radical constitutionalism. Just as his reading in the common law tradition compelled him to appreciate the historicity of legal authority, he practiced a similar kind of reduction to the constituent origins of ecclesiastical authority. Jefferson thought through religion and the rights of religious conscience by thinking about institutions, practices, and their history. From John Milton's *Areopagitica*, Jefferson extracted St. Peter's use of the word *clergy* to denote the laity as well as the priests. As Jefferson notes, Origen, the third-century layman, heretic, and a glosser of the Christian scriptures paralleled in his age only by Jerome, and whose *Hexapla* Jefferson would later purchase and undoubtedly use for his own edition of the New Testament, had run into trouble when he began to expound the scriptures publicly. But laymen, Jefferson records, were anciently permitted to teach, and the Council of Nicea had relied on "the assistance of many learned lay brethren."[76] What bears noticing here is that Jefferson's continuing critique of ecclesiastical power, and

[74] Jefferson, "Notes on Episcopacy," *Papers of Thomas Jefferson*, Vol. 1, p. 552.

[75] See James Tully, *An Approach to Political Philosophy: Locke in Contexts* (Cambridge: Cambridge University Press, 1993), ch. 6.

[76] "Notes on Episcopacy," *Papers of Thomas Jefferson*, Vol. 1, p. 552; Jefferson here draws on the Protestant ecclesiastical histories of Johann Lorenz Mosheim and Conyers Middleton, both of whom extensively narrated the lack of a juridical distinction between the clergy and laity in the democratic governance of the early Church; see Jefferson, "Notes on Heresy," *ibid*, pp. 553–5.

even Christianity itself, was grounded in a reading of the past that saw the history of theology and religion not simply as a history of opinion, but as a history of discourse, politics, and institutions. Jefferson read and contextualized the history of doctrine and its authority as issues that arose out of society and its various ways of associating and organizing itself. This amounted to a radical usage of the conventionalist spirit appropriate to the common law thinking Jefferson had found in Coke, and we can see his reading and notes for the disestablishment of the Anglican church here as continuing from his arguments about the lay origins of the church in the colonial court case of *Godwin* v. *Lunan*.[77] Ecclesiastical history provided Jefferson with an extended framework for thinking about the goals of his wider constitutional project as a recovery and instantiation of the political power of the laity.

In continuing to fill his legal commonplace book after his legal education and career, Jefferson included an extended essay on the history of the law and the historicity of its intertwinement with religious authority, an essay that he later edited slightly and bound with his volume of case reports. The essay, "Whether Christianity Is a Part of the Common Law," began with an English example in which a similar question arose as to what extent the common law was bound to respect an ecclesiastical jurisdiction. The defendant, Bishop of Lincoln, asserted that common law courts were bound to defer to his rights over a parish as recognized by ecclesiastical law because Christianity was a part of the common law. The reporter of the case interpreted the law-French of the argument that the necessary place of Christianity in the common law was made clear in *ancien scripture*, as "holy scripture," "*covient a nous a donner credence*" [requiring us to give our assent].[78] But Jefferson hit upon the error in this transcription from the argument, for this phrase "can only mean the ancient laws of the church," for while it was true that the ecclesiastical law drew its authority from its recognition by the common law, the common law did not thereby grant legal authority to the scriptures or

[77] See above; indeed, the proposal for dealing with the Glebe lands, or landed property of the Church, after disestablishment called for the property to remain with the Church but as the common property of the lay members of each parish; see "A Bill for Saving the Property of the Church Heretofore by Law Established," *Papers of Thomas Jefferson*, Vol. 2, pp. 553–5.

[78] Thomas Jefferson, "Whether Christianity Is a Part of the Common Law?," appendix to *Reports of Cases*, p. 137. See also Jefferson, *Legal Commonplace Book*, #873, later included in letter of Thomas Jefferson to Thomas Cooper, February 10, 1814, Papers of Thomas Jefferson: Retirement Series, Vol. 7, pp. 190–1.

admit of its grounding in sacred authority. Littleton and Bracton, Jefferson reasoned, recognized no such place of Christianity in the common law, for if the power of ecclesiastical law grew out of the common law, judges of common law courts comprehending both courts ecclesiastical and of admiralty, then ecclesiastical law itself was "not founded on the Law of God, but subject to the modification of the law-giver."[79] If the law is subject to augmentation, it is a product and an affair of the temporal word and human hands, not the imposition of God, nor that of ecclesiastical power constituted in God's name.

Asserting the supremacy of the common law over other branches of English jurisprudence, Jefferson then undermined the powerful image of the common law that this project required by stringing together the transmission of the above error in common law authorities. The assumption that Christianity is part of the common law had become a commonplace by the seventeenth and eighteenth centuries: "Thus we find a string of authorities, when, examined to the beginning, all hanging on the same hook; a perverted expression," Jefferson wrote, "or on nothing."[80] He then went on to discuss the earlier ages of the law, the definition of the common law as *lex non scripta*, but agrees with Hale's *History of the Common Law* that while the common law ends at the Magna Carta where statute law begins, nevertheless the evidence for the substance of the common law exists in records insofar as it is transmitted through the opinions of judges and cases, "for all these laws have their several monuments in writing, whereby they are transferred from one age to another, and without which they would soon lose all kind of certainty."[81] The problem, for Jefferson, in reference to the immutable authority claimed by religious institutions, was that "our judges have piously avoided lifting the veil under which it was shrouded." Having used the antiquarian scholarship of the earlier law reporters and David Houard's *Traites sur les coutumes Anglo-Normandes* (1776) to illustrate the absence of the legal recognition of Christian authority in the early Anglo-Saxon period, he noted that editions of the Laws of King Alfred were subsequently copied with a preface of four chapters of Exodus and two verses from the Acts of Apostles. The summation of the essay called particular attention to the "fabrication" processes by which the divergent aspects of

[79] Jefferson, "Whether Christianity Is a Part of the Common Law?," p. 138.
[80] *Ibid*, p. 138; see Sir Matthew Hale, *The History of the Common Law of England*, Charles M. Gray, ed. (Chicago: University of Chicago Press, 1971), ch. 1–2.
[81] Jefferson, "Whether Christianity Is a Part of the Common Law?," p. 139.

constitutional history are stitched together to form a totalizing, singular image of authority in the composition of the texts that transmit the legal knowledge underpinning that very authority. Again, critical attention to the processes of transmission was a guiding principle of Jefferson's own sense of intellectual practice, and in his vision for republican constitutionalism he experimented with ways of crafting what began as a hermeneutic principle into a mode of constitutionalism, or as a peculiarly historical and textual, civic form of life.

Nowhere in Jefferson's constitutional thought is his multivalent restorative mode of reading more apparent than in his valuation of the importance of juries, and in particular his proposed expansions of juries throughout the legal system. In the context of centuries of debates over the rise and power of chancery jurisdiction, Jefferson's proposal to provide for juries in these cases can be seen as institutionalizing, inscribing in the fabric of the law, precisely the kind of unraveling and open interpretation of cases that critics of equity feared. Symbolically, the proposal augmented the tradition of the King's conscience with the discretion of an expanded definition of the people actively present at the trial, and provided a deliberative check to the power of the single judge. The proposal died a soft death, as juries were allowed only by the consent of both parties and the judge (and as Jefferson explained, no party would start off a civil case by suggesting the incompetence of the bench).[82] In a letter expounding on the significance of juries, Jefferson included Leveller and British radical tracts: Hawles' *Englishman's Right*, John Jones' commentary on Hawles, *Juror's Judges of Law and Fact*, the *Security of Englishmen's Lives* by Henry Care, and *Juries Justified* by William Walwyn.[83] He continued, exaggerating considerably, that "we think in America that it is necessary to introduce the people into every department of government as far as they are capable of exercising it." While Jefferson admits that the people are probably not capable themselves of being the executive, or the legislature, or for that matter the judge, and he retains a distinction between the law-finding powers of the judge and the fact-finding powers of the jury, he further stipulates the power of the jury to overcome this division of labor should it find the judgment the product of any "bias." Indeed, he continues, "were I called upon to decide had best

[82] "Report of the Committee for the Revisal of the Laws, Bill No. 90," in *Papers of Thomas Jefferson*, Vol. 2, pp. 566–9; Jefferson, "Autobiography," pp. 33, 45.

[83] Jefferson to the Abbé Arnoux, July 19, 1789, *Papers of Thomas Jefferson*, Vol. 15, pp. 282–3.

be omitted in the Legislative or the Judiciary department, I would say it is better to leave them out of the Legislative. The execution of the laws is more important than the making of them. However, it is best to have the people in all the three departments where that is possible."[84]

Jefferson did not go as far as others in extending jury powers. But as Shannon Stimson argues, Jefferson saw juries as one among many avenues for a wider, political and educational relationship between law and the citizenry, to be distinguished from a strictly legal vision that would circumscribe this relationship to participation in a jury.[85] Ideally, for Jefferson, it was in juries and other assemblies that at least a good deal of the power of equitable interpretation of the law would be practiced and retained. Indeed, given the initial importance of equity as interpretive and civic practice to Jefferson's broader thinking on law and constitutionalism, it seems appropriate to see in his constitutionalism not only a desire to keep alive the textuality of manuscripts in an age of print, but in doing so to establish a materialist constitutional culture of equitable use.

CONCLUSION: EQUITABLE USE

The political failure of much of Jefferson's vision for a new constitutional order and in particular the central of role of equity within that order did not go unremarked by either Jefferson or his mentor George Wythe, who took up the post as the judge of a newly formed High Court of Chancery for Virginia. The court lacked the final appellate power and the strong jury that Jefferson had imagined when proposing it, and in 1795, a disgruntled George Wythe published his own edition of decisions from the court. Wythe's volume rebuked fellow justices in the court system for their lack of erudition and grounding in the distinctive principles and procedures of both common law and chancery jurisdictions. His own copy of the volume, which like many of his books eventually found their way into Jefferson's possession, includes Wythe's handwritten appendix to the series of references he had made to classical literature and rhetoric in his own remarks, including several to the legal arguments of Demosthenes and to Sophocles' *Antigone*.[86] Like much of their correspondence, their respective legal

84 *Ibid.*

85 Shannon C. Stimson, *The American Revolution in the Law: Anglo-American Jurisprudence Before John Marshall* (Princeton: Princeton University Press, 1990).

86 Wythe quoted from a contemporary translation Antigone's rebuke of Creon's authority: "...unwritten laws divine / Immutable, eternal, not like these / Of yesterday, but made e'er time began," *The Tragedies of Sophocles, from the Greek* (London: R. Francklin, 1759),

arguments as attorneys, and Thomas Jefferson's own commonplace books, Wythe's extensive commentaries claimed participation in an early modern legal and intellectual culture. Wythe and Jefferson both took their opportunities to castigate the legal order of the state's constitutional settlement and ongoing constitutional politics. In doing so both were explicitly concerned with their own status as learned authorities, and in Jefferson's case, he did not take his critique of Virginia's legal order as insufficiently republican to be at odds with his critique of that order for giving insufficient power to the jurisdiction of equity.

Debates over the legitimacy and location of equitable consideration centered around a dialectic of the universally authoritative formality of rules and the case-by-case dynamism of usage and judgment. In a letter to Philip Mazzei of 1785, Jefferson explained in agreement with the narrative of Kames that a distinctive jurisdiction of equity had arisen in England "when commerce began to make progress, when the transfer of property came into daily use, when the modifications of these transfers were infinitely diversified," and when "with the improvement of other faculties that of the moral sense became also improved."[87] A regular jurisdiction of equity developed in the face of what David Lieberman has called the legal needs of a commercial society, and institutions arose that distributed powers of adjudication in new conditions and new cases away from the ecclesiastical monopoly on mostly Roman legal learning and into an established court system.[88] In the developmental historical

Thomas Francklin, trans., George Wythe, *Decisions of Cases in Virginia by the High Court of Chancery* (Richmond: Thomas Nicholson, 1795), p. 130n; Wythe's inclusion of the more extensive original Greek passage in his personal appendix is in his and later Jefferson's copy of the volume in the Special Collections of the Library of the University of Virginia. The quotation comes in the middle of an extensive footnote to a 1793 case between Carter Page and Edmund Pendleton, representatives of Archibald Cary and his British creditors, respectively. Wythe found for the creditors on the grounds of natural law, dismissing the claim that the Treaty of Paris made pre-revolutionary contracts and debts null and void, and arguing in an extended footnote that by the logic of the argument of the plaintiff all manner of persons could be excused from their obligation to constituted legal authority: "women, infants, and many others, deprived of suffrage, cannot, either by themselves or their representatives, be truly said to yield their assent to any law," Wythe, *Decisions*, 130n; see *Page* v. *Pendleton*, Wythe, *Decisions*, pp. 127–32. It becomes easy to see here how problematic the natural law and rights discourse of the revolution and its potential opening of legal personhood was to many elite legal actors, and how concerned those actors would be to construe that discourse so that it could be controlled.

87 Jefferson to Philip Mazzei, November 28, 1785, *Papers of Thomas Jefferson*, Vol. 9, p. 68.

88 Lieberman, "The Legal Needs of a Commercial Society: The Jurisprudence of Lord Kames, *Wealth and Virtue*, pp. 203–34.

narratives sketched by Scottish moral philosophers, changes in the moral sensibility of members of society and therefore of society itself allowed for and depended on entrusting the carrying out of justice to the cultivated and improved faculty of judgment.

The achievement of equity in a particular case was the product of the complex development of the capacity of human beings in specific social environments over time.[89] No positive law or jurisdiction could ever be fully aligned with natural law, but equity allowed for bringing the human ordering of cases and actions into an instance of proximity to natural justice. As Adam Smith suggested, the inclination to theorize a natural jurisprudence, or a general system of laws underlying the particular laws of all nations, was itself a product of recent history, and such a theoretical inquiry was to be carried out through the study of human nature as it had interacted with the world in time, in the varieties of practices and institutions that different societies had created, maintained, and adapted.[90] Jefferson took equity a step further in his projects of exploring institutional arrangements that nurtured the abilities of citizen participants to exercise judgment, to inherit the responsibility for applying jurisprudence to the operation of the laws. This was to, in effect, double down on the importance of judgment, of the capacity of citizens for the exercise of self-possession and propriety in their political usages of law and even language itself.[91]

89 See Adam Smith, *The Theory of Moral Sentiments*, Ryan Patrick Hanley, ed. (New York: Penguin, 2010), pp. 100–12; John Robertson, "The Scottish Enlightenment at the Limits of the Civic Tradition," Nicholas Phillipson, "Adam Smith as Civic Moralist"; J.G.A. Pocock, "Cambridge Paradigms and Scotch Philosophers: A Study of the Relations Between the Civic Humanist and the Civil Jurisprudential Interpretation of Eighteenth Century Social Thought," *Wealth and Virtue*, pp. 137–202, 235–52; Graham Burchell, "Peculiar Interests: Civil Society and the Governing 'The System of Natural Liberty," Burchell, Colin Gordon, and Peter Miller, eds. *The Foucault Effect: Studies in Governmentatlity* (Chicago: University of Chicago Press, 1991), pp. 119–50; Emma Rothschild, *Economic Sentiments: Adam Smith, Condorcet, and the Enlightenment* (Cambridge, MA: Harvard University Press, 2001), pp. 7–12, 88–115.

90 Adam Smith, *The Theory of Moral Sentiments*, pp. 386–404.

91 On the increased importance of propriety in usage where particular language has been unmoored from its metaphysical bearings, see John Locke, *An Essay Concerning Human Understanding*, Peter H. Nidditch, ed. (Oxford: Oxford University Press, 1975), pp. 476–9; Hannah Dawson, *Locke, Language, and Early Modern Philosophy* (Cambridge: Cambridge University Press, 2007); see also Mark Glat, "John Locke's Historical Sense," *Review of Politics* Vol. 43, No. 1 (January, 1981), pp. 3–21. On the concept of propriety in Locke, Montesquieu, Smith, J.S. Mill and T.H. Green, see Duncan Kelley, *The Propriety of Liberty: Persons, Passions, and Judgment in Modern Political Thought* (Princeton: Princeton University Press, 2011).

The key to success in this project was equipping the citizenry not only with critical educational tools but with a textual inheritance that remained open for perpetual submission to new use. This was why Jefferson felt comfortable suggesting to Mazzei that state legislatures should take the developed precedents of equity courts and "reduce these rules to a text, and transplant them into the department of the common law," keeping the common law responsive to change from an external, more open conduit of rule formation while maintaining a distinction between equity and common law jurisdictions.[92] It was the unification of the open quality of equitable judgment and the power of common law judges that Jefferson saw as the danger in the jurisprudences of Blackstone and Mansfield. The whole legal system became subject to the central and arbitrary rule when we "relieve the judges of the rigour of text law, and permit them, with pretorian discretion, to wander into it's equity," as had been the fate of every nation "where the fixed, and the discretionary law had been committed into the same hands."[93] Discretionary law, or equitable judgment, when practiced in construing the common law, made itself sovereign and uncontestable. If there is a constancy to Jefferson's revolutionary-era constitutionalism, as well as his later embrace of the idea of council democracy in the form of ward republics, it is the firm belief that public liberty cannot survive being subject to a singular and potentially arbitrary will or judgment. Rather, public liberty required a fragmenting and diffusion of sovereign judgment across multiple spaces of both legal and political deliberative activity.[94]

Equity was undoubtedly a flexible at best and uncertain but useful concept in early modern legal and political thought. As such, it lent itself to use in a variety of contexts that ranged from the mundane to the extra-constitutional, and it is important to appreciate not only the centrality of equity as a political and constitutional idea in the early modern context but its attractive applicability within a multitude of subcontexts. Indeed, equity was at the very least a way of thinking about the presence of broader constitutional issues in the everyday operation of legal practice, as well as the reality of legal, political, and intellectual practice for

[92] Jefferson to Mazzei, November 28, 1785, *Papers of Thomas Jefferson*, Vol. 9, p. 70.

[93] Jefferson, *ibid*, p. 71.

[94] Stimson, *The American Revolution in the Law: Anglo-American Jurisprudence before John Marshall*, pp. 94–105; see also Daniel D. Blinka, "Jefferson and Juries: The Problem of Law, Reason, and Politics in the New Republic," *American Journal of Legal History* Vol. 47, No. 1 (January 2005), pp. 35–103; Alison LaCroix, *The Ideological Origins of American Federalism* (Cambridge, MA: Harvard University Press, 2010).

philosophical reflection on the foundation of sovereignty and the exercise of high constitutional politics. But for Jefferson, equity was something even more: a way of reading and representing the law's civic status, and that particular use of equity not only played a central role in his thinking; it was also tied directly to his understanding of modes of possible political life. For Jefferson, equity was more than an avenue of legal practice, although it certainly was that, and it was more than a legal philosophy, although it certainly was that, too. Equity for Jefferson was a hermeneutic tool for thinking about what law and constitutionalism could look like in a revolutionary republican polity, and the fact that he used the tool for other things than many of its previous makers and users had intended illuminates a peculiar quality of Jefferson's thinking. The historically inflected natural jurisprudence appropriate to broad considerations of equity allowed Jefferson to imagine the founding of a new legal subjectivity, one centered on participation in necessarily ongoing projects of legal transformation.

In his subsequent career as an actively engaged participant theorist in politics and constitutionalism, Jefferson turned his attention to the cultivation of this citizen and the constitutional culture in which this particular mode of legal and historical subjectivity that Jefferson had constructed would be enabled. In his 1776 draft of a constitution for Virginia, Jefferson had discussed an elaborate amendment process, writing that "none of these fundamental laws and principles of government shall be repealed or altered, but by the personal consent of the people on summons to meet in their respective counties on one and the same day" to vote in small bodies on the repeals or alterations to the text of the constitution.[95] Similarly, Jefferson would write to Madison from Paris that among his disappointments in the federal Constitution was the lack of the text having been "duly weighed & canvassed by the people."[96] Resting constitutional politics on the capacity of the citizenry for exercising judgment required, of course, a heavy investment in the "education of the common people." In Jefferson's mind, one of the most egregious failures of the first state constitutional convention in 1776, and the second one in 1783, was the failure to adopt his plans for a codified right to basic economic security and free access to public education, which he proposed

[95] Jefferson, "Jefferson's Third Draft," *Papers of Thomas Jefferson*, Vol. 1, p. 364.

[96] Jefferson to James Madison, December 20, 1787, *Papers of Thomas Jefferson*, Vol. 12, p. 441.

"to be chiefly historical." History would enable students "to judge of the future; it will avail them of the experience of other times and other nations; it will qualify them as judges of the actions and designs of men." If it was true that "every government degenerates when trusted to the rulers of the people alone," and that therefore "the people themselves are its only safe depositories," then this required embedding law and politics in an institutional setting of an actively engaged populace armed with a conceptual museum for their own thinking and actions.[97] The last part of Jefferson's recommendations for further law reform not adopted by General Assembly was for a public library and gallery, "laying out a certain sum annually in books, paintings, and statutes" to further allow for solid material bases of shaping and practicing judgment, of using books and other media of transmitting historical memory to "impress" the minds of the young, to create citizens possessed of the capacity to exercise constitutional judgment.[98]

In its emphasis on the conditions and criteria for judgment, the language of equity framed Jefferson's efforts to think about the design of institutions. His efforts to multiply the spaces within a polity where the burdens of judgment were taken up and to diffuse power across "several bodies of magistracy" and a "plurality of hands," necessitated thinking about the practices that would be appropriate to collective life in such institutions.[99] Jefferson's theory demanded a particular kind of reader, one capable of seeing the tradition and structure of constituted legal authority as assembled, as a kind of collective commonplace book of the polity. Such a reader was to be created and sustained through a particular kind of textuality. Jefferson criticized the very idea of the new state constitution as fundamental law, arguing that legislators, meeting in ordinary session, had been seduced by the idea of themselves as

[97] Jefferson, *Notes on the State of Virginia*, Frank Shuffleton, ed. (New York: Penguin, 1999), p. 155.

[98] *Ibid*, p. 275; James Tully has read the educational and epistemological writings of John Locke in the context of different modes of implementing a particular kind of subjectivity, and to use Tully's analysis, we can see Jefferson following in Locke's footsteps, particularly in his concern to "impress" on the minds of the young, even while Jefferson persists in maintaining a particularly civic humanist bent on the education of the subject in a juridical polity, a subject measured in his capacity for critically engaged, historical, civic judgment against the assumed incapacity, or at least unequal capacity, of others, or in Jefferson's case specifically, African American slaves; see Tully, *An Approach to Political Philosophy: John Locke in Contexts*, ch. 6–8.

[99] Jefferson, *Notes on the State of Virginia*, pp. 149, 129–30.

founders of a new state and authors of a new code. Nothing, Jefferson wrote in the pages of his *Notes on The State of Virginia*, could be "perpetual and unalterable." He rejected what he understood to be the theory behind written fundamental law: "to get rid of the magic supposed to be in the word *constitution*, let us translate it into its definition as given by those who think it above the power the of the law, '...We, the ordinary legislature, establish an act *above the power of the ordinary legislature*."[100] The authors of such an imagined fundamental and unchanging constitution, Jefferson wrote, "had been seduced in their judgment by the example of an ancient republic, whose constitution and circumstances were fundamentally different." For Jefferson, the way to avoid "tumults" and upheavals that would result in the undoing of the republic, the trusting of sovereignty to one figure out of temporary emergency, was to place rule in a "plurality of hands." This meant literally putting laws and proposed changes to them in the hands of assemblies as part of ongoing processes of writing and rewriting.

Jefferson persistently maintained a criticism of constitutional text and thought that had been constructed expressly for the purpose of putting itself beyond its status as an object always susceptible to the dynamism of continued use. Equity, understood as a framework within which to challenge, correct, disrupt, or ameliorate the normal and traditional grounds for usage, can thus be said to have had an enormous impact on Jefferson's thinking. "The earth belongs in usufruct to the living," he famously informed James Madison.[101] This assumption was spread across Jefferson's career. And constitutions, for Jefferson, were not the only thing that needed to be submitted to democratic processes of reconsideration in every generation. His draft of a constitution for Virginia in 1776 called for the distribution of land to every adult white male in the state.[102] When property rights had accumulated or been construed to leave people without property, Jefferson also wrote to Madison, it was plain to him that the right of property had been allowed to run afoul of natural right, and in such a circumstance the people had the right to appropriate adequate property. "Legislators," he

[100] *Ibid*, p. 130.

[101] Jefferson to James Madison, September 6, 1789, *Papers of Thomas Jefferson*, Vol. 15, p. 392; on Jefferson's intellectual debts to the British doctor Richard Gem and their correspondence on generational liberty, see editorial note and correspondence, Jefferson, *ibid*, pp. 384–99, Herbert E. Sloan, *Principle and Interest: Thomas Jefferson and the Problem of Debt* (Oxford: Oxford University Press, 1995).

[102] Jefferson, "Jefferson's Third Draft," p. 362.

wrote, "could not invent too many devices for subdividing property."[103] A healthy republic required an equitable economic basis, and so property, like law, should be subject to rearrangement, reconsideration, and redistribution.

The participatory textuality Jefferson had pulled from reflection on his own habits of thought and study rested on a particular understanding of legal subjectivity, of a historically aware and engaged citizen, self-possessed and self-governing, and with the cultivated capacity to exercise a dynamic relationship to the materials of the histories, legal and otherwise, in which they found themselves embedded. This controlled self-situating was crucial for the maintenance and possession of one's histories, and just as importantly, how those histories could be represented to or narrated, governed, and adjudicated by others. It was thus to these others and their respective histories that Jefferson turned.

[103] Jefferson continued: "The descent of property therefore to all the children, or to all the brothers and sisters, or other relations in equal degree, is a politic measure and a practicable one. Another means of silently lessening the inequality of property is to exempt all from taxation below a certain point, and to tax the higher portions or property in geometrical progression as they rise. Whenever there are in any country uncultivated lands and unemployed poor, it is clear that the laws of property have been so far extended as to violate natural right. The earth is given as a common stock for man to labor and live on. If for the encouragement of industry we allow it to be appropriated, we must take care that other employment be provided to those excluded from the appropriation. If we do not, the fundamental right to labor the earth returns to the unemployed," Jefferson to Madison, October 28, 1785, *Papers of Thomas Jefferson*, Vol. 8, p. 682; see Katz, "Thomas Jefferson and the Right to Property in Revolutionary America," *Journal of Law and Economics*, Vol. 10, No. 3 (1976), pp. 467–88, and "Republicanism and the Law of Inheritance in the American Revolutionary Era," *Michigan Law Review*, Vol. 76, No. 1 (1977–1978), pp. 1–29; Jennifer Nedelsky, *Private Property and the Limits of American Constitutionalism* (Chicago: University of Chicago Press, 1990); David Schultz, "Political Theory and Legal History: Conflicting Depictions of Property in the American Political Founding," *The American Journal of Legal History*, Vol. 37, No. 4 (October 1993), pp. 464–95; Gregory S. Alexander, *Commodity and Propriety: Competing Visions of Property in American Legal Thought, 1776–1970* (Chicago: University of Chicago Press, 1997); Eric Nelson, *The Greek Tradition in Republican Thought* (Cambridge: Cambridge University Press, 2004), pp. 200–9.

4

Labor, Language, and the Legal Subject of the *Notes on the State of Virginia*

The presence of slaves in the economy, daily life, and legal culture of Virginia brought Jefferson's consideration of historical subjectivity face to face with the problem of imagining a political community of pluralistic and historically constructed subjects. The condition of plurality was the very center of Jefferson's writing of his *Notes on the State of Virginia*, but the work of the text itself needs to be understood in a variety of contexts. Jefferson's constitutional criticism was meant in part to respond to his own harsh experience of the political realities facing revolutionary republics. Frustrated and even to a certain extent temporarily displaced as a founding authority figure, Jefferson used the opportunity to engage in an exploration of the possibility of nothing less than another founding. The writing of the *Notes* provided Jefferson with space and time to explore the implications of his developing constitutional theory and his politically charged constitutional criticism.

The text that Jefferson produced bears the signs of its practical construction in the service of exhibiting and constituting a new form of civic life. The book is less a focused work than an assemblage of notes in which Jefferson employs the conceptual equipment of a vast array of eighteenth-century strands of thought, making use of and in turn seeking to contribute to discussions of law, empire, constitutionalism, economics, and natural history prevalent in the Atlantic republic of letters. The *Notes* served as a template to reconstruct and resituate the subject of republican political life in a plurality of contexts, through "considerations of policy, of morals, of history natural and civil."[1] That the writing stems from Jefferson's doubts, fears, and insecurities concerning the durability of revolutionary republicanism is clear from the often critical and sometimes fearful tones of the text, and that Jefferson came to think of the text itself as potentially problematic is just as clear. Jefferson wrote to Madison that he did not think of himself as an author with respect to the *Notes* as much as a compiler or recorder, and he refused publication outside of private circulation among friends for five years after the initial composition of the text.[2] Even so, the text is of a piece with Jefferson's unique place in the intellectual practice of the "planter enlightenment."[3]

While the book blends narratives of civil and natural history to the point where the two become nearly indistinguishable, imaginatively embedding subjectivity in a thick material context consisting of trees and fossils as much as laws and institutions, the logic of the text and its composition is consistently jurisprudential. No doubt, the book provided Jefferson with what Leo Marx aptly calls a "naturalistic basis for utopian reverie," but the conceptual tools of exploration were drawn from Jefferson's revolutionary-era legal and constitutional projects.[4] In responding to the queries of the French diplomatic official François Marbois, Jefferson reorganized the order of the chapters from the original questionnaire, which had begun with laws, charters, constitution, and demographics. He began instead with a wide survey of natural history, which turned into civil history, and then moved on to details of agricultural

[1] Jefferson, *Notes on the State of Virginia*, Frank Shufftleton, ed. (New York: Penguin, 1999), p. 169.

[2] Jefferson to James Madison, May 11, 1785, *Papers of Thomas Jefferson*, Vol. 8, pp. 147–8.

[3] On the epistemologies of natural history and collecting in Atlantic imperial contexts, see Myra Jehlen, *American Incarnation: The Individual, the Nation, and the Continent* (Cambridge, MA: Harvard University Press, 1986); Christopher Looby, "The Constitution of Nature: Taxonomy as Politics in Jefferson, Peale, and Bartram," *Early American Literature*, Vol. 22, No. 3 (1987), pp. 252–73; Ralph Bauer, *The Cultural Geography of Colonial American Literatures* (Cambridge: Cambridge University Press, 2003); Timothy Sweet, "Jefferson, Science, and the Enlightenment," *The Cambridge Companion to Thomas Jefferson*, Frank Shuffleton, ed. (Cambridge: Cambridge University Press, 2009), pp. 101–3; Andrew Lewis, *A Democracy of Facts: Natural History in the Early Republic* (Philadelphia: University of Pennsylvania Press, 2011); and on the particularity of "planter enlightenment," see Christian P. Iannini, *Fatal Revolutions: Natural History, West Indian Slavery, and the Routes of American Literature* (Chapel Hill: University of North Carolina Press, 2012).

[4] Leo Marx, *The Machine in the Garden: Technology and the Pastoral Ideal in America* (Oxford: Oxford University Press, 1964), p. 120.

production, population, and economy. Scholars have often taken this to demonstrate Jefferson's rationalization and naturalization of the politics and history discussed later in the text, but to assume that Jefferson is merely seeking to ground society in natural law or provide a natural model for political life is to miss the layered temporality of his blending of natural and civil history.[5] The materials of natural and civil history were equally constitutive of the context in which the subjects of Jefferson's practical theorizing found themselves embedded. In his use of the language of a historicized natural jurisprudence and the data of natural history, and in combining both with legal and political history, Jefferson was playing with the boundaries of these disparate discourses, making connections and seeing each particular query in the context of the others. He laid out a geographical, demographic, and historical survey of Virginia and used that survey as a jumpring-off point for criticizing the constitutional culture of the state on the grounds of its in many ways dangerous inattentiveness to the human subjects and possible modes of subjectivity alive in the commonwealth.

In the discursive context of the Atlantic republic of letters and the circulating theories of American degeneracy, most notably in the work of the Comte de Buffon and the Abbé Raynal, Jefferson's very particular

[5] See Hannah Spahn, *Thomas Jefferson, Time, and History* (Charlottesville: University of Virginia Press, 2011); Eva Sheppard Wolf, "Natural Politics: Jefferson, Elections, and the People," in Boles and Hall, eds. *Seeing Jefferson Anew: In His Time and Ours* (Charlottesville: University of Virginia Press, 2010); Maurizio Valsania, *The Limits of Optimism: Thomas Jefferson's Dualistic Enlightenment* (Charlottesville: University of Virginia Press, 2011), *Nature's Man: Thomas Jefferson's Philosophical Anthropology* (Charlottesville: University of Virginia Press, 2013). Robert Ferguson has uniquely appreciated and argued for the fundamental importance of jurisprudence to Jefferson's thought and to the writing of the *Notes on the State of Virginia* in particular, but even for Ferguson the concept of nature available to Jefferson from early modern thought is a kind of structural model for human society rather than a substantive and influential aspect of human thought and action in civil as well as natural history; Ferguson, "Mysterious Obligation: Jefferson's Notes on the State of Virginia," *American Literature* Vol. 52, No. 3 (November 1980), pp. 381–406. On the complexities and interrelatedness of natural and civil in addition to legal history in eighteenth-century thought, see Mark Salber Phillips, *Society and Sentiment: Genres of Historical Writing in Britain, 1740–1820* (Princeton: Princeton University Press, 2000), and *On Historical Distance* (New Haven: Yale University Press, 2013); Peter Reill, *The German Enlightenment and the Rise of Historicism* (Berkeley and Los Angeles: University of California Press, 1975), and *Vitalizing Nature in the Enlightenment* (Berkeley and Los Angeles: University of California Press, 2005); Karen O'Brien, *Narratives of Enlightenment: Cosmopolitan History from Voltaire to Gibbon* (Cambridge: Cambridge University Press, 1997); J.G.A. Pocock, *Barbarism and Religion, Volume IV: Barbarians, Savages, and Empires* (Cambridge: Cambridge University Press, 2005).

attitude toward history, natural and civil, went hand in hand with a uniquely vitalist and historical concept of nature. The human subjects of Jefferson's imagining were situated in a richly layered confluence of contextual materials, and what was at stake in defending not only American natural history but the civil history made in and with it was the jurisprudential and geopolitical status of work and labor done with those materials. Facing west, Jefferson described the scene of Virginia's Blue Ridge Mountains as leaving the observer with an undoubted feeling that "this earth has been created in time," that nature, in other words, had a history, and that it was history not only intertwined with the history of human societies but, like that history, contained evidence of a complex and eventful past in the remnants and ruins in which human beings lived.[6]

Experiencing the great monuments of natural history, like the "natural bridge" in central Virginia, "you involuntarily fall on your hands and feet . . . it is impossible," Jefferson wrote, "for the emotions arising from the sublime, to be felt beyond what they are here."[7] This subjective feeling of being overpowered by nature is recurrent: lines of limestone out of parallel with the surface of the earth were always, Jefferson observed, "attended with signs of convulsion." The presence of fossilized seashells in the mountains could possibly be evidence of "some great convulsion of nature."[8] But there is a deeper significance to the active and dynamic historicity ascribed to nature and our knowledge of it in the *Notes*. "Convulsion' is how Jefferson will go on to describe not only revolutions in nature but in society, too, including both white populist resistance to government or economic inequality and the potential rebellion of black slaves. What was at stake was the very capacity for a secure and self-governing yet inescapably embodied self amid the flux and convulsions of time. The Jeffersonian project, in due course, would become one of governing the inherent instability of those conditions, of disciplining context and its use.

As we have seen, the central problem confronting the Jeffersonian project was the security of its subject, the historically aware, textually active, self-governing, self-owning, judicious citizen, and it is the place of this problem at the center of the *Notes on the State of Virginia* more than any specific discussion of law and constitutionalism that configures the text as a recognizably jurisprudential and juridical one. What Jefferson confronts in the *Notes* is the possibility that the revolutionary mode of subjectivity would come to include a host of others, who

[6] Jefferson, *Notes on the State of Virginia*, p. 21. [7] *Ibid*, p. 26. [8] *Ibid*, pp. 32, 33.

after all shared with Jefferson the same environmentally situated and so perhaps the same potentially dynamically, contextually activated form of life. In the writing of the *Notes on the State of Virginia*, Jefferson began to discipline his own theoretical practice, circumscribing the historical subjectivities of others, namely African Americans and Native Americans, by introducing grounds for skepticism of their respective possession of a particular kind of legal history and so their capacities for a particular kind of civic relationship to the materials of those histories.[9] The result is a reconstitution of racial difference, and as important as the racial logics of the *Notes* are to the book and to the trajectory of Jefferson's thought, it is the binding of revolutionary legal subjectivity and praxis by the qualities of self-possession, the mastery of self and others, that drive the argumentative structures of the text.

The racial science Jefferson developed cannot be fully understood without appreciating this rootedness in the textual, historical practices appropriate to the peculiar anti-foundationalism that made Jefferson's legal and constitutional thought so radical in the first place. In turn, Jefferson's description of limited Native capacities for the productively dynamic use of the materials of their histories, including custom, language, and most of all, land, would prove to be the cornerstone of his reconceptualization of transmission and communicability as symbolic exchange in the context of commerce and liberal empire. Property in land was a crucial aspect of the idealized human subject of what would come to be called Jeffersonian democracy, consisting as it did of a particularly

[9] Pamela Regis, *Describing Early America: Bartram, Jefferson, Crevecoeur, and the Influence of Natural History* (Philadelphia: University of Pennsylvania Press, 1999); Lee Quinby, *Freedom, Foucault, and the Subject of America* (Boston: Northeastern University Press, 1991); Mitchell Breitwieser, "Jefferson's Prospect," *Prospects*, Vol. 10 (1985), pp. 315–52; Andrew Burstein, *The Inner Jefferson: Portrait of a Grieving Optimist* (Charlottesville: University of Virginia Press, 1995); Thomas Hallock, *From the Fallen Tree: Frontier Narratives, Environmental Politics, and the Roots of a National Pastoral* (Chapel Hill: University of North Carolina Press, 2006); Dana D. Nelson, *National Manhood: Capitalist Citizenship and the Imagined Fraternity of White Men* (Durham: Duke University Press, 1998), and "Consolidating National Masculinity: Scientific Discourse and Race in the Post-Revolutionary United States," *Possible Pasts: Becoming Colonial In Early America*, Robert Blair St. George, ed. (Ithaca: Cornell University Press, 2000), pp. 201–15; David Kazanjian, *The Colonizing Trick: National Culture and Imperial Citizenship in Early America* (Minneapolis: University of Minnesota Press, 2003), pp. 89–124; Betsy Erkkila, *Mixed Bloods and Other Crosses: Rethinking American Literature from the Revolution to the Civil War* (Philadelphia: University of Pennsylvania Press, 2004), ch. 2; John Michael, *Identity and the Failure of America: From Thomas Jefferson to the War on Terror* (Minneapolis: University of Minnesota Press, 2008).

rigid conjunction of natural with civil history, of the raw material of the natural environment with the labor of the citizen and the human practice of making and using law.

Jefferson's thinking fleshes out the thought of the philosopher Stanley Cavell, who argues that "it is internal to a convention that it be open to change in *convention*, in the convening of those subject to it, in whose behavior it lives."[10] Jefferson's theorization of law and language had as its goal the keeping of conventions in touch with the history of their making and transmission, or with the memory and activity of convening. This foregrounded the question of the capacity of the citizen to exercise self-command and self-governance while engaged in convention, in reflective, deliberative, and collective action. And it raised the question, as Cavell and others have recognized, of who does the convening, or who gets to convene, or more accurately, who will be acknowledged in the space opened up for convening? Society, culture, language, politics, and law were all arenas where British Americans by Jefferson's lights convened and took hold of their distant inheritances and explored putting them to new use, refusing to restrict the potentiality of usage to what was felt to be the commanding force of inheritance. That Jefferson established this radical space of collective exploration as extending to language itself played a crucial role in Jefferson's later efforts to theorize boundaries that would keep apparently separate histories of experience, language, and usage from becoming too intertwined. Practices of linguistic and cultural recognition, or even acknowledgment, were rooted in wider material contexts of labor, power, and possession.

USAGE, PROPRIETY, AND HISTORY

Jefferson's attention to historical subjectivity as measured by the use of labor, land, and language indicate the conceptual tools with which it was possible to constitute a republican polity predicated on the proprietary use and ordered circulation of bodies, words, and things. Language in its history and present use proved to be an essential aspect of Jefferson's imagining and measuring of citizenship. In the conjectural histories of eighteenth-century social theory, law and language emerged together at the theoretically posited origins of social institutions, and so for Jefferson capacity for use and judgment was inseparable from linguistic capacity

[10] Stanley Cavell, *The Claim of Reason: Wittgenstein, Skepticism, Morality, and Tragedy* (Oxford: Oxford University Press, 1979), p. 120.

and development. Republican education was of course a very important part of Jefferson's constitutional project, and for Jefferson cultivating the young men of the state for political life entailed not only reading in ancient and modern history but practice in ancient and modern language. "There is a certain period of life," Jefferson wrote, "say from eight to fifteen or sixteen years of age, when the mind, like the body, is not firm enough for laborious and close operations." In this period, "memory is then most susceptible to impressions; and the learning of languages being chiefly a work of memory, it seems precisely fitted to this period." Indeed, Jefferson continued, "if this period be suffered to pass in idleness, the mind becomes lethargic and impotent, as would the body it inhabits if unexercised during the same time. The sympathy between body and mind during their rise, progress, and decline, is too strict and obvious to endanger our being mistaken while we reason from the one to the other."[11] Jefferson imagined civic capacity as the product of disciplined self-cultivation.

"Nature hath implanted in our breasts a love of others, a sense of duty to them, a moral instinct, in short, which prompts us irresistibly to feel and to succor their distresses," he wrote to Thomas Law in 1814, part of a life-long history on Jefferson's part of instructive correspondence with young men in their studies and preparation for careers in law and politics.[12] "Whenever you are to do a thing, ... ask yourself how you would act were all the world looking at you, and act accordingly," he wrote to his nephew Peter Carr in 1785. "Encourage all your virtuous dispositions," he continued, for just as physical exercise made the body stronger, so habit of virtue would strengthen the natural inclination to right action. To put it bluntly, "a strong body makes the mind strong."[13] Forming the human material of the republic was a critical aspect of founding the republic well. As was the case with his legal education, Jefferson practiced and went on to preach a strenuous daily regimen of tightly organized outdoor and studious activities from walking and horsemanship to wide-ranging reading and quiet reflection.

Accessing relative collective capacities for language use and attending to the proprietary and judicious use of language itself was foundational

[11] Jefferson, *Notes on the State of Virginia*, p. 154

[12] Jefferson to Thomas Law, June 13, 1814, *Papers of Thomas Jefferson: Retirement Series*, J. Jefferson Looney, ed. (Princeton: Princeton University Press, 2010), Vol. 7, p. 414.

[13] Jefferson to Peter Carr, August 19, 1785, *Papers of Thomas Jefferson*, Vol. 8, p. 407.

to the Scottish Enlightenment moral philosophy and the peculiarly historicized strand of natural jurisprudence out of which that moral philosophy grew. In attending to language use and to the broader principle of utility, Jefferson was using a particular vocabulary of moral sense and propriety. "Men living in different countries, under different circumstances, different habits and regimens, may have different utilities," Jefferson wrote to Thomas Law. Because of "the general existence of a moral instinct," that instinct worked, developed, and adapted differently in different cultures, and judgment in matters of law and ethics had to be understood as relative to the environments in which people acted. Indeed, civil history and collective memory were the conduits through which one's sense of nature and natural law grew and influenced our judgments and actions in time. Jefferson's efforts to theorize the mode of subjectivity appropriate to republicanism, and the institutional setting appropriate to cultivating that way of life, turned around questions of how to understand and support the appropriate stream of natural impulses.

Individual behavior, in this framework, was never isolated, or even particularly individual. In his work of 1672, *De jure naturae et gentium*, Samuel Pufendorf criticized the previous natural law theories of Hugo Grotius and Thomas Hobbes as impossibly atomistic, and he rearticulated the theoretically posited state of nature as one of historically posited natural sociability, and thereby rearticulated natural law as the ethics of exchanging words and things in inescapably (if varied) social contexts. The human subject of ethics imagined in the modern natural jurisprudence of Pufendorf was thus embedded in a web of corresponding or at times conflicting natural and communal rights and responsibilities. Just so, naturally social human beings living together in society were subject to a variety of different routes of influence on their behavior – a historical fact that made the maintenance of sociability dependent on the self-government of the individual over themselves, their bodies, and their relations with others. As human beings had been directed by nature to social life, what natural law required of human beings in their specific social contexts was to be social, "to cultivate and preserve sociality."[14] As contemporaries, subsequent students, and modern scholars have observed, the natural

[14] Samuel Pufendorf, *De jure naturae et gentium libri octo* (Amsterdam: Andreas Hoogenhuysen, 1688), p. 309; *On the Duty of Man and Citizen According to Natural Law*, Tully, ed. Silverthorne, trans. (Cambridge: Cambridge University Press, 1991), p. 35.

duty to be sociable could only be applied in specific, social, historical contexts.[15] An increasingly historically inflected natural jurisprudence made possible a unique historical sensibility that would be developed by Scottish philosophical historians and French *philosophes* as the challenges and promises of practicing sociability confronted a fractious Atlantic and indeed global world of commercial empires.

For Pufendorf as well as for John Locke, the historical fact of life in commercializing and denominationally pluralistic societies placed the weight of the dictates of natural law on the dimensions of the relational and symbolic, and in particular on the ethics of using communicable signs. In juridical writings of Pufendorf, the epistemological writings of Locke, and later in the moral theory of Adam Smith, great emphasis gets placed on the right or "proprietary" use of language, and the concern in each is to prohibit, or at least marginalize, use of language in speech and writing that could threaten the historically developing natural order of societies increasingly predicated on exchange.[16] By the middle of the eighteenth century, theories of Atlantic empire and the emergent European state system had made these concerns just as important for international as for civil law. Exchange of goods, ideas, and sentiments, for Adam Smith as well as for the multiple authors of Raynal's *Histoire des deux Indes*, carried the promise of diminishing a

[15] See T.J. Hocstrasser, *Natural Law Theories in the Early Enlightenment* (Cambridge: Cambridge University Press, 2000); Ian Hunter, *Rival Enlightenments: Civil and Metaphysical Philosophy in Early Modern Germany* (Cambridge: Cambridge University Press, 2001); on the development of a distinctively "modern" natural jurisprudence in the early modern period, see Richard Tuck, *Natural Rights Theories: Their Origin and Development* (Cambridge: Cambridge University Press, 1979); Knud Haakonssen, *The Science of a Legislator: The Natural Jurisprudence of David Hume and Adam Smith* (Cambridge: Cambridge University Press, 1981) and *Natural Law and Moral Philosophy from Grotius to the Scottish Enlightenment* (Cambridge: Cambridge University Press, 1996); Richard Tuck, "The 'Modern' Theory of Natural Law," and Istvan Hont, "The Language of Sociability and Commerce: Samuel Pufendorf and the Theoretical Foundations of Four Stages Theory," *The Languages of Political Theory in Early Modern Europe*, Pagden, ed. (Cambridge: Cambridge University Press, 1987), pp. 99–119, 253–76.

[16] John Locke, *An Essay Concerning Human Understanding*, Nidditch, ed. (Oxford: Oxford University Press, 1975), pp. 290, 476–9; Hannah Dawson, *Locke, Language, and Early Modern Philosophy* (Cambridge: Cambridge University Press, 2007); Fonna Forman-Barzilai, *Adam Smith and the Circles of Sympathy: Cosmopolitanism and Moral Theory* (Cambridge: Cambridge University Press, 2010); Ryan Patrick Hanley, *Adam Smith and the Character of Virtue* (Cambridge: Cambridge University Press, 2009); Nicholas Phillipson, *Adam Smith: An Enlightened Life* (New Haven: Yale University Press, 2010).

world of expansive territorial empires and instituting in its place an international culture of sociable interdependence.[17]

The governance of the passions in both individual and social moral development was a central concern of enlightened social theories, and well before these vocabularies of moral sense, utility, and propriety were taken up by Jefferson, their previous formulators were concerned with language as a critical indicator of other areas of social inquiry. In a conceptual conjunction that would prove crucial for eighteenth-century Anglophone thought and for Jefferson in particular, John Locke configured both internal and external constraints on the conduct of individuals as historically developed and mutually reinforcing. In his two most significant works, the *Essay Concerning Human Understanding*, and the *Second Treatise on Government*, both published in 1689, Locke theorized self-governed conduct in civil society as in accord with natural law when in line with both the divine and politically prudent imperative to make good and judicious use of the materials with which people established and maintained a commonwealth. In other words, in peaceful and lawful commonwealths there were rules of conduct that governed subjectivity through disciplining the boundaries of appropriate use. "God, who hath given the World to Men in common," Locke wrote in the *Second Treatise*, "hath also given them reason to make use of it to the best advantage of Life, and convenience."[18] Locke continued, "He gave it to the use of the Industrious and the Rational, not to the Fancy or Covetousness of the Quarrelsom and Contentious."[19] Use for life was acknowledged as labor that cultivated the land and so established private property, and the ethos of industrious and rational (not quarrelsome and contentious) use likewise

[17] Denis Diderot, *Political Writings*, Mason and Wokler, eds. trans. (Cambridge: Cambridge University Press, 1992), pp. 205–7; Anthony Pagden, *Lords of all the World: Ideologies of Empire in Spain, Britain, and France, c. 1500-c. 1800* (New Haven: Yale University Press, 1998); Istvan Hont, *The Jealousy of Trade: International Competition and the Nation-State in Historical Perspective* (Cambridge, MA: Belknap, Harvard University Press, 2005); Pocock, Barbarism and Religion, Volume IV; Emma Rothschild, *Economic Sentiments: Adam Smith, Condorcet, and the Enlightenment* (Cambridge, MA: Harvard University Press, 2001); Foucault, *Security, Territory, and Population: Lectures at the College de France*, Senellart, ed. Burchell, trans. (New York: Palgrave Macmillan, 2007); Paul Cheney, *Revolutionary Commerce: Globalization and the French Monarchy* (Cambridge, MA: Harvard University Press, 2010).

[18] John Locke, *Two Treatises of Government*, Peter Laslett, ed. (Cambridge: Cambridge University Press, 1960), p. 286.

[19] *Ibid*, p. 291.

informed the rational use of language in making compacts, laws, and money to protect and represent that property.

Language, then, was quite literally foundational to the establishment and maintenance of law and political community. And for Locke, language as one encountered it in reality was a historical construct, and it was only in appreciating the complex and intermixed histories that constituted language that one could hope to avoid slipping into a contentious indeterminacy. Language fit standards of utility, relative to the society in which it developed, and was therefore constitutive of the developed capacity to understand and judge of experience. Names of substances and schemes of classification, even in the natural world, were for Locke a product of accumulated human activity. Naming and classifying "depend on such Collections of Ideas, as Men have made; and not on the Real Nature of Things: since 'tis not impossible that in propriety of Speech, that might be a Sun to one, which is a Star to another."[20] The use of language consisted in the collection and recollection of words and the making and further use of complex ideas that were the result of the cumulative and collective experience that constitute a people's linguistic history. While Locke distinguished between two uses of language: civil or common use and philosophical use, he worried that what counted as propriety could come into dispute even among philosophers.[21] The rule of propriety, or attentiveness to the civil history within which one was acting, was thus all the more important.

Proprietary use of language played an equally important role in the thought of Adam Smith, for whom the pacifying potential of commercial society depended on the civil exchange of ideas, sentiments, as well as goods, of words and things. "Political disquisitions, if just, reasonable, and practicable, are of all the works of speculation the most useful. Even the weakest and the worst of them are not altogether without their utility," Smith wrote in *The Theory of Moral Sentiments*, published in 1759, and which Jefferson recommended in his letter to Thomas Skipwith in 1771. "They serve at least," Smith continued, "to animate the public

[20] *Ibid*, p. 439.

[21] Locke, *ibid*, p. 476; See Hannah Dawson, *Locke, Language, and Early Modern Philosophy* (Cambridge: Cambridge University Press, 2007); see also Mark Glat, "John Locke's Historical Sense," *Review of Politics*, Vol. 43, No. 1 (January 1981), pp. 3–21; Duncan Kelley, *The Propriety of Liberty: Persons, Passions, and Judgment in Modern Political Thought* (Princeton: Princeton University Press, 2011); Sean Silver, *The Mind is a Collection: Case Studies in Eighteenth Century Thought* (Philadelphia: University of Pennsylvania Press, 2015).

passions of men, and rouse them to seek out the means of promoting the happiness of the society."[22] The quality of political disquisition, for Smith as for Locke, was to be measured by its usefulness in particular social and political contexts, and that was inseparable from the author of the disquisition's own use of the material provided in those contexts for the art of discussing politics.

Questions of social interaction were questions of the peculiar qualities of the human subjects of those interactions. "The characters of men, as well as the contrivances of art, or the institutions of civil government, may be fitted either to promote or to disturb the happiness both of the individual and the society," Smith suggested. "The prudent, the equitable, the active, resolute, and sober character promises prosperity and satisfaction, both to the person himself and to every one connected with him," but, "the rash, the insolent, effeminate, and voluptuous, on the contrary, forebodes ruin to the individual, and misfortune to all those who have anything to do with him."[23] Different societies will have different customs and fashions, and so what counted as useful and fitting to the demands of utility would be different, but the imperative of propriety in exercising reason and self-command in the service of self and others would be essential in any society or even in any particular case, particularly in a post-absolutist, post-mercantilist, and global and commercial age.

Jefferson's own construction of these issues in the *Notes* owes a great deal to this lineage, but it just as important to note at what points he departed from it or at least used its conceptual vocabulary differently. The dynamism and relative contingency of use in law and language was paramount in Jefferson's thought. Given the importance of law to shaping past, current, and future imaginable subjectivities in Jefferson's thinking, it also matters for our overall picture of the trajectory of his thinking to see him extending his historical and critical enterprise from laws and constitutions to language itself. As with law and landed property, Jefferson came to language and found use, so to speak, going all the way down. His enthusiasm for the French practice of "neology," or the development of new words, which continued throughout his life, registers Jefferson's concern with restoring to common awareness the potential for new directions inherent in usage. The goal of language, Jefferson told John Waldo upon receiving the latter's *Rudiments of English Grammar* in

[22] Adam Smith, *The Theory of Moral Sentiments*, Ryan Patrick Hanley, ed. (New York: Penguin, 2010), p. 217.

[23] *Ibid*, p. 218.

1813, is to be "ductile and copious." As Jefferson wrote, "I have been pleased to see that in all cases you appeal to usage, as the arbiter of language; and justly consider that as giving law to grammar, and not grammar to usage."[24]

Rules of grammar were established by the contingencies and utilities of common usage over time, rather than directing or governing common usage. "I am a friend to neology," he wrote to John Adams in 1820:

> Dictionaries are but the depositories of words already legitimated by usage. Society is the workshop in which new ones are elaborated. When an individual uses a new word, if illformed it is rejected in society, if wellformed, adopted, and, after due time, laid up in the depository of dictionaries. And if, in the process of sound neologization, our transatlantic brethren shall not choose to join us, we may furnish, after the Ionians, a second example of a colonial dialect improving on it's primitive.[25]

The role of the dictionary here parallels how Jefferson thought about law and constitutions: as belonging in usufruct to the living, to those who in Locke's framing made "use for life," and as material that shaped concepts while providing for endless processes of experiment and renewal. Again, that is not to say that dictionaries are merely compendiums of dead words; on the contrary, they are the record of past usage and therefore the jumping-off points for thinking about our concepts and the words we use to communicate them. Jefferson further emphasizes and develops the postcolonial context of American language, or the degree to which American culture possesses a secondary relationship to its British origins. As was the case with law, American language operated through the productive usage of these inherited parts.

In his essay "Thoughts on English Prosody," composed after his return from Paris in 1789, Jefferson conducted a survey of English poetry, searching for a historical explanation of the generation of rules of verse, rhyme, and pronunciation. A system of rules for teaching accent and grammar in Latin might have proven useful, but in English, Jefferson suggested, rules and exceptions formed to the extent that they "would reach every word in the language" and would prove "too great a charge on the memory for use either in reading or conversation." In a similar spirit as his critique of legal codification, Jefferson assumed that an

[24] Jefferson to John Waldo, August 16, 1813, *Papers of Thomas Jefferson: Retirement Series*, J. Jefferson Looney, ed. Vol. 6, p. 402.

[25] Jefferson to John Adams, August 15, 1820, *The Adams-Jefferson Correspondence*, Lester J. Cappon, ed. (Chapel Hill: University of North Carolina Press, 1959), p. 67.

attempt to systematize the imperfections and contingencies of the history of English would simply lead to a mistaken sense of authority and actually multiply error over time. "It is usage which has established the accent of every word, or rather I might say it has been caprice or chance, for nothing can be more arbitrary or less consistent."[26] Only discursive practice and intermittent consultation could help a foreigner learn English pronunciation. Jefferson saw language as not only a convention but as an activity, such that even rules for usage and processes of transmission over time could be seen to have a changing history.

When Jefferson dealt with issues of language, he explored what Ludwig Wittgenstein called "forms of life," practices and institutions corresponding to particular orders of representation.[27] In radicalizing custom and convention, Jefferson upped the ante on historical subjectivity, intensifying the degree to which imagined modes of civic life could restrict inclusion in that life, and placing his configuration of the embodied lives of others at the center of his constitutional project.

THE JEFFERSONIAN SUBJECT

In his seminal account of natural history in *The Order of Things*, Michel Foucault argued that for natural history to emerge as an authoritative discourse in the eighteenth century, history had to become natural, but it is clear from a close look at Jefferson's intellectual practice in writing the *Notes* that he was working in a conceptual world where nature had become historical. Eighteenth-century thinkers had access to a variety of ways of conceptualizing natural history, human and civil history, and the possible ways of conceptualizing the relationships or differences between these categories. Jefferson was no exception. Indeed, his engagement with discourses of natural history circulating in the Atlantic republic of letters

[26] Jefferson, "Thoughts on English Prosody," *Writings*, Merrill D. Peterson, ed. (New York: Library of America, 1984), p. 607.

[27] "And to imagine a language means to imagine a form of life," Ludwig Wittgenstein, *Philosophical Investigations*, Revised Fourth Edition, P.M.S. Hacker, Joachim Schulte, ed., G.E.M. Anscombe, Hacker, Schulte, trans. (Oxford: Wiley-Blackwell, 2009), §19; on the historical and philosophical overlap of linguistic and jurisprudential theories of custom and use, particularly in Wittgenstein and the common law tradition, see James Tully, *Strange Multiplicity: Constitutionalism in an Age of Diversity* (Cambridge: Cambridge University Press, 1995), pp. 102–16, and "Wittgenstein and Political Philosophy: Understanding Practices of Critical Reflection," in *The Grammar of Politics: Wittgenstein and Political Philosophy*, Cressida J. Heyes, ed. (Ithaca: Cornell University Press, 2003), pp. 26–8.

in the eighteenth century was not merely a product of his interest in science. It was both a theory and a performance of creole historical subjectivity, and it was a defense of the American Revolution and the promise of the new nation to a European audience of potential creditors, trading partners, and allies that required a defense of something like an American history, and specifically of the materials with which that history had been and continued to be made.

While Jefferson's turn to natural history is in clear conversation with the theory of American degeneracy articulated in the works of Buffon and Raynal, the question of the possible historical and civic identities in the British North American colonies and later in the revolutionary republican states was a widespread concern in Atlantic intellectual networks. The French aristocrat and émigré to the colony of New York, Hector St. John de Crevecoeur, fled the colonies during the outbreak of revolutionary conflict and carried with him the manuscript of his *Letters from an American Farmer*. Published in France in 1782, just as Jefferson was composing the initial draft of the *Notes*, the text of the *Letters* consists of the correspondence of a traveling agriculturalist, James, documenting the progress of European settlement. As Ralph Bauer and Christian Iannini suggest, the status of James as a creole witness speaking for the enlightened European author allows the text to perform and construct categories of subjectivity, or particular forms of life, at the same time that these categories are called into question, their instabilities and contradictions documented and observed like the fauna of natural history.[28] "What is this American, this new man,?" James asks, and in his answer he takes stock of the American as a product of the conjoined forces of civil and natural history. "Everything has tended to regenerate them," James writes of the established farmers of New England, "new laws, a new mode of living, a new social system. Here they are become men: in Europe they were as so many useless plants, but by "the power of transplantation, like all other plants they have taken root and flourished" in America.[29] The at once independent and communal form of life was clearly something that by the experience of transplanting had shaped new subjects: "he is an American," James continues, "who, leaving behind all his ancient

[28] Ralph Bauer, *The Cultural Geography of Colonial American Literatures* (Cambridge: Cambridge University Press, 2003); Christian P. Iannini, *Fatal Revolutions: Natural History, West Indian Slavery, and the Routes of American Literature* (Chapel Hill: University of North Carolina Press, 2012).

[29] J. Hector St. John de Crevecoeur, *Letters from an American Farmer, and Other Essays*, Dennis D. Moore, ed. (Cambridge, MA: Harvard University Press, 2013), p. 30.

prejudices and manners, receives new ones from the new mode of life he has embraced, the new government he obeys, and the new rank he holds."[30] That this new laboring and independent man both receives influence from his new context and in his work and settlement acts on that context is key. The gendered and racialized settler subject of the *Letters* actively situates himself in time and place. His form of life translates into a new and dynamic relationship with the materials of the environment, natural and civil.

Appropriate to this intellectual context, Jefferson begins the *Notes* with a defense of the contexts in which the history of American usage has proceeded, and this beginning involves him with the work of the French naturalist George Louis LeClerc, Comte de Buffon. While natural history was a central and self-sustaining discourse of Atlantic intellectual practice by the late eighteenth century, it is impossible to separate Jefferson's use of it in the *Notes* from geopolitical and specifically jurisprudential concerns about the historical and so legal status of American societies. Like Montesquieu, Buffon gave Jefferson a framework within which to think about human life in the context of the blending of natural and civil history. Buffon's *Histoire Naturelle* concerned itself with "the history of Nature at large," and in our examination of that history above and below the surface of the earth, Buffon suggested, "we find matter in every form, dry and humid, warm and cold, solid and brittle, blended in a chaos of confusion, which can be compared to nothing but a heap of rubbish, or the ruins of the world."[31] Since Thomas Burnet's *Sacred Theory of the Earth*, published in 1681, it had become commonplace to describe both the manifold imperfections of the earth's surface and the fossil evidence of past life as ruins that provoked in the attentive observer a sense nature having an equally turbulent history as that of human society, and that the two were inseparable.

What order could be seen in the direct experience and widespread, undeniable historical evidence of chaos and contingency was the question that motivated Buffon's work, and this project had direct and obvious ramifications for the science of society. "These ruins, however," Buffon continued, "we inhabit with perfect security .... With regard to us, everything has the appearance of order: the earth, formerly a chaos,"

[30] *Ibid*, p. 31.

[31] George Louis LeClerc, Comte de Buffon, *Natural History: General and Particular, by the Count de Buffon, Translated into English*, William Smellie, trans. (London: William Strahan and Thomas Cadell, 1781), Vol. 1, pp. 2, 5.

is now a "delightful habitation."[32] Even so, Buffon cautions, it would be a mistake to overlook the ruins human beings inhabit: "we shall soon perceive the utility, even the necessity of this arrangement. With a little attention, we shall perhaps discover an order of which we had no conception, and general relations that cannot be apprehended by a slight examination."[33] Like his contemporaries the French Physiocrats, Buffon was self-consciously attempting to take Montesquieu's inquiry into the necessary relations of things beyond the daunting scope of plurality and "perhaps" toward the literal unearthing and careful reconstruction of an underlying order through established and authoritative knowledge-building practices.

Such a hope carried with it elements that were at once imperial and utopian, and a significant part of Jefferson's response will be to contest the place of Americans in an emergent global order predicated on historically observed and developed natural law. Such contestation was necessary for Jefferson because the theory of the historical degeneracy of American nature had real implications for the philosophical evaluation of American economic potential. Evidence of the past existence of great quadrupeds such as the American mastodon, evidence that Jefferson would go on to share with Buffon and expect an acknowledgment of error from the naturalist, for Buffon himself only reinforced the scope and scale of degeneracy in the Americas, and in the British North American territories in particular. Many other species might have undergone such transformations or disappeared altogether, and it was then a question of why, "either from degeneration or improvement, occasioned by the great vicissitudes of the earth and waters" or, perhaps, from "the neglect of the cultivation of Nature" and "the continued influence of favorable or hostile climates?"[34] American species might have possibly been identifiable with their European counterparts, but that was clearly no longer the case. Natural and human history, in the sense of both the influence of climate and natural events as well as contingencies of societal development such as the failure to cultivate, had left American nature unable to sustain dynamic history. "Nature," Buffon allowed, "is in a perpetual state of fluctuation," and he continued, "but it is enough for man to seize her in his own image, and to look backward and forward, in order to discover her former condition, and what future appearances she may probably assume."[35] Finding the gendered labor of cultivation and use

[32] *Ibid*, p. 5. [33] *Ibid*, p. 6. [34] *Ibid*, Vol. 5, p. 150. [35] *Ibid*, p. 151.

in American history insufficiently conquering and so of insufficiently productive fertility, for Buffon, whether collective life worthy of recognition not only had appeared but could appear in this context was very much an open question.

As was with the case with his *Summary View of the Rights of British America*, a large part of Jefferson's project in the *Notes* is to establish that not only sufficient but rather impressive conquering has and will continue to take place. This compelled Jefferson to defend the natural historical context in which his evidence was situated. He was especially concerned to argue that American fauna could be compared favorably to European cousins, and might consist of entirely new and distinct species whose existence would demand reconsideration of the classificatory scheme of the European naturalists themselves. Jefferson insisted that American natural history could produce something new. In his notes from Mark Catesby's *The Natural History of Carolina, Florida, and the Bahama Islands*, made in preparation for the writing of the *Notes*, Jefferson listed examples of Virginian specimens not included in the work of Catesby and Buffon, and suggested that the hare observed in America may be "a new species altogether," distinct from the European hare or rabbit.[36] In his manuscript notes and in the later printed editions of the *Notes*, Jefferson reserved his iteration of the Algonquin name *whabus* for the American hare, establishing home-grown classifications for home-grown fauna and for an elite European audience, using the Native language for the sake of a self-consciously creole knowledge and identity.

Making full use of the vast expanse of untamed nature in America and the discovery of giant fossils such as those of the mastodon, Jefferson dismissed the degeneration thesis and described what he imagined to be a more cosmopolitan natural history. "The truth is," he wrote, "that a Pigmy and a Patagonian, a Mouse and a Mammoth, derive their dimensions from the same nutritive juices. The difference of increment depends on circumstances unsearchable to beings with our capacities."[37] All of

[36] "Catesby's description of undescribed birds and animals of Virginia," Massachusetts Historical Society, *Thomas Jefferson Papers*, pp. 2–4 (www.masshist.org/thomasjeffersonpapers/doc-viewer.php?item_id=1800&mode=nav), accessed July 31, 2013; Jefferson, *Notes on the State of Virginia*, pp. 2–53, 57–8.

[37] Jefferson, *Notes on the State of Virginia*, p. 48; on Jefferson and the controversies over the degeneration thesis, see Paul Semonin, *American Monster: How the Nation's First Prehistoric Creature Became a Symbol of National Idnentity* (New York: New York University Press, 2000); Lee Alan Dugatkin, *Mr. Jefferson and the Giant Moose: Natural History in Early America* (Chicago: University of Chicago Press, 2009); Keith Thompson,

existence derived its being from the same "nutritive juices," and toiled under the same sun. Jefferson saw a universal nature operating elaborately on the vital fluids and mechanisms of the human and animal body, in almost precisely the same way he saw nature acting as a force on the moral sense of men. Quoting Buffon at length on the moral, physical, and sexual inferiorities of natives in North and South America, Jefferson dismissed such claims as absurd, counting tales of fundamental human difference as akin to those of Aesop. "This belief" in the universality of human beings, he wrote, "is founded on what I have seen of man, red, white, and black, and what has been written of him by authors, enlightened themselves, and writing amidst an enlightened people."[38] Again, Jefferson established an equality of intellectual exchange between his own observations of North American peoples and the work of European naturalists. Jefferson's was an understanding of nature that was at once vitalist and historical at the same time it was universal. The transatlantic debate over American degeneracy came down to a question of whether "nature has enlisted herself as a Cis or Trans-Atlantic partisan?" It was a part of Jefferson's project to say that not only was the question but the debate a truly transatlantic phenomenon. Defending a transatlantic basis of natural material to work with was crucial to the goal of writing and defending a "cis-Atlantic" history.

Cis-Atlantic, because the goal of the writing was not only to critique contemporary constitutional practice but to present the style and erudition of that critique as one among many pieces of evidence for the dynamic potentiality of the materials with which Americans would continue to form and reform their histories. The question of slavery comes up in the queries on law and constitutionalism, respectively, and in those chapters Jefferson set about narrating the legal history of slavery in Virginia as a way of reifying the legal subjectivities and civic capacities of enslaved and free African Americans. In doing so Jefferson acknowledged that slaves mix their labor with the same nutritive juices, land, and

Jefferson's Shadow: The Story of His Science (New Haven: Yale University Press, 2012); on the controversy more generally, see Antonello Gerbi, *The Dispute of the New World: The History of a Polemic, 1750–1900*, Moyle, trans. (Pittsburgh, 1973); Anthony Pagden, *European Encounters in the New World: From Renaissance to Romanticism* (New Haven: Yale University Press, 1993); Stewart J. Brown, ed. *William Robertson and the Expansion of Empire* (Cambridge: Cambridge University Press, 1997); E.C. Spary, *Utopia's Garden: French Natural History from the Old Regime to the Revolution* (Chicago: University of Chicago Press, 2000).

[38] Jefferson, *Notes on the State of Virginia*, pp. 62–3.

overall natural history as their white yeoman and planter counterparts. Jefferson situated his construction of race in natural history across the board. The situating of Native Americans and African Americans in natural history follows directly upon an extended embedment of white Virginians in a context of that same natural history. The fundamental distinction made in Jefferson's racial theorizing is not between subjects of natural history and subjects of civil history, but between subjects of natural history and those who, lacking appropriate and sufficient historical capacity, have made themselves civilly incapacitated. Emphasizing capacity, Jefferson was able to give scientific gloss to the distinctions that he made not simply by distinguishing races as natural categories, but by making a more cutting distinction between respective capacities for use, between the use of the living and the civilly dead.

Because slaves share in the natural history in which white Virginians and even masters like Jefferson find themselves, they also share a legal history, and how different peoples share these histories was more important to Jefferson than the fact of their having them. What mattered for Jefferson was that slaves had and continued to exist under a condition of dependence and submission, remaining out of the realm of economic and political independence and therefore incapable of balancing the flow of natural passions in their thoughts, words, and actions with propriety. "Slaves," he wrote, describing the legal status of slavery in Virginia, "pass by descent and dower as lands do .... Slaves, as well as lands, were entailable during the monarchy: but, by an act of the first republican assembly, all donees in tail, present and future, were vested with the absolute dominion of the entailed subject."[39] Jefferson had of course pushed several republican reforms through the rewriting of the constitution of Virginia, including the abolition of the practice of entail, where landed property was guaranteed through the custom of primogeniture to pass to the first son, to a system of fee simple, where property was held absolutely in the hand of the property owner and its fate was entirely in his hands.[40] While this legal revolution could have at least short-term democratic results for potential white land owners, it had negative consequences for slaves:

[39] *Ibid*, p. 141.

[40] Holly Brewer, "Entailing Aristocracy in Colonial Virginia: 'Ancient Feudal Restraints' and Revolutionary Reform," *William and Mary Quarterly*, Vol. 54, No. 2 (April 1997), pp. 307–46; see also Christopher Michael Curtis, *Jefferson's Freeholders and the Politics of Ownership in the Old Dominion* (Cambridge: Cambridge University Press, 2012).

the minimal checks guaranteeing location were wiped away and slaves became less serfs in a kind of race-based neo-feudal regime and much more like commodities, making them "distributable among the next of kin, as other movables."[41] They were subject to "absolute dominion," mere "movables," living in a state of total domination by and dependence on the people who owned them. The entailed subjects, in this telling, were legally cut lose from even the barest continuity, subject to a history not of their own making and the textual and bodily materials of which were not in their possession.

"I advance," he wrote, "as a suspicion only, that the blacks, whether originally a distinct race, or made distinct by time and circumstances, are inferior to the whites in the endowments of body and mind," although, he claimed, such an opinion must be "hazarded with great diffidence." For, as Jefferson continued, "though for a century and a half we have had under our eyes the races of red and black men, they have never yet been viewed by us as subjects of natural history."[42] We have been viewing ourselves as subjects of natural history, but not these others in our company. Jefferson's project extends and intensifies the gaze of historical knowledge production and the measuring of peoples according to their places in a schema of conjectural history, but that extension and intensification transforms the project into one not about the philosophy of history but about the subject or subjects of the histories under examination. The thesis of natural racial inequality, hazarded as a suspicion only in the discursive world of natural historical knowledge, emerges in the *Notes* as a product of the refutation of the degeneracy thesis, and most crucially, it allows Jefferson not only to draw clean distinctions between peoples inhabiting shared contexts but to actually make it possible to sidestep all possible examples of human equality as effectively irrelevant to the question of whether collective historical experience was sufficiently available to acknowledge people as citizens. The question became not so much one of materials but of possessing those materials and the resulting abilities to use them. The project then turned to a rigid set of circumscriptions of these divergent capacities.

John Noonan has argued that Jefferson together with his teacher and collaborator George Wythe worked very hard to re-cloak the law in a robe of majesty in the wake of declaring independence, providing necessary authority to a new order and especially to that order's retention of

[41] Jefferson, *Notes on the State of Virginia*, p. 144. [42] *Ibid*, pp. 150–1.

laws protecting the institution of slavery.[43] But as discussed in the previous chapter, Jefferson spilled a great deal of ink in and beyond the *Notes* uncloaking the foundational authority of legal text, and this is the crux of the issue. The question for Jefferson is whether or not African Americans have the cultivated capacity to live with law that has been uncloaked, to be included among the plurality of hands in which the state rests. His task in Query XIV was to put his negative answer to that question on empirical footing. He zeroed in not on morals but on histories and relations to histories, on memories and the capacity to actively reform or break out of given models of thought and action. His comparisons of black poets such as Phylis Wheatley and Ignatius Sancho with the record of classical Roman poetry written by European slaves served Jefferson as evidence of underlying, natural racial inferiority, but it is important to note that the argument Jefferson constructed worked to put the question of naturalness aside. Evidence of racial equality could still be dismissed as exceptional, or as circumstantial, and that was a consequence of Jefferson's turn to collective capacity as determinant.[44] The racial logic of the text is not simply to put race and racial hierarchy on certain scientific footing, but to make questions over natural ability academic and peripheral to the actual question at hand, which concerns the civic implications of the observed distinctions.

Jefferson asked, "Why not retain and incorporate the blacks into the state, and thus save the expense of importing white settlers to replace them?" And he has an answer: "Deep rooted prejudices entertained by the whites, ten thousand recollections" on the part of slaves of their experience in slavery and the "real distinctions which nature has made" in history "will divide us into parties, and produce convulsions which will probably never end but in the extermination of one or the other race. To these objections, which are political, may be added others, which are physical and moral."[45] This is not the only instance where Jefferson used

[43] John T. Noonan, Jr. *Persons and Masks of the Law: Cardozo, Holmes, Jefferson, and Wythe as Makers of the Masks* (Berkeley and Los Angeles: University of California Press, 1976).

[44] Jefferson's contempt for the poems of Phylis Wheatley, labeled as "beneath the dignity of criticism," flows from a configuration of her work as merely the unenlightened product of slavish religious devotion and as the equally slavish example of elementary and routinized neoclassical form; *Notes*, p. 147; David Waldstreicher, "The Wheatleyan Moment," *Early American Studies*, Vol. 9, No. 3 (Fall 2011), pp. 522–51; Eric Slauter, *The State as a Work of Art: The Cultural Origins of the Constitution* (Chicago: University of Chicago Press, 2009), pp. 179–203.

[45] Jefferson, *Notes on the State of Virginia*, p. 145.

language not merely of violence or disorder but extermination, of disappearance and expatiation, and it is clear from that language that what Jefferson was contemplating went beyond the fear of bloodshed and disruption to the terrifying image of being erased from remembered history. The burden that the concept of recollection carries in this framework is, to say the least, immense. The frightful idea of those who recollect and thereby narrate and so judge differently in politics was the fearfully constructed opposite of Jefferson's theory of the citizen as a historically activated wielder of the histories in their possession, but that possible recollection and judgment was also for him a force, a "convulsion" of nature that was not only disruptive but destructive of particularly ordered histories of use, collection, and possession.

Jefferson's brief but revealing moves beyond the performance of disinterested knowledge production intensify rather than contradict the careful construction of racial difference going on in the text. The stakes might be raised, but it was still the cultivated capacity to actively and critically, reflectively inherit, and so the lack of cultivated ability to appear in civic, social space designed for the project of individual and collective self-government that distinguished the white settler farmer from his African American and Native American counterparts. The African in America, Jefferson surmised, free or enslaved, lived out an existence that "appears to participate more of sensation than reflection," and "thought above the level of plain narration" appeared not at all, whereas the citizen must above all else be reflective upon a history that is not just narrated but grasped and shaped. The "eternal monotony" of expression, "that immovable veil of black," and at bottom their very inexpressiveness in Jefferson's formulation rendered them naturally unsociable and so incapable of civic, social, governable exchange of words and things, and so it was that their bodies remain part of that exchange.[46]

Even the slaves find the whites more beautiful, Jefferson asserted, "as uniformly as is the preference of the Oranootan for the black women over those of his own species. The circumstance of superior beauty, is thought worthy of attention in the propagation of our horses, dogs, and other domestic animals; why not in that of man?" Their skin sweats more, he

[46] Jefferson, *Notes on the State of Virginia*, pp. 145–6; on the role of speech and public appearance as essential aspects of defining citizenship and slavery in revolutionary thought, see Hannah Arendt, *On Revolution* (New York: Penguin Books, 1963), ch. 2; Jay Fliegelman, *Declaring Independence: Jefferson, Natural Language, and the Culture of Performance* (Stanford: Stanford University Press, 1993).

continued, "giving them a strong and disagreeable odour," and as a result their bodies were found to be more tolerant of heat and less of cold than white bodies. "They seem to require less sleep," as evidenced by the collective "amusements" Jefferson must have heard from his study and bedroom late at night, and while they might be "at least as brave, and more adventuresome," this might come simply "from a want of forethought." Their love for one another consisted more in simple desire "than a tender delicate mixture of sentiment and sensation. Their griefs are transient," he asserted, painful tragedies being "sooner forgotten with them." Although Jefferson was drawing out distinctions he described as "physical and moral," it is important to note that African Americans in the Jeffersonian vision actively participate in histories of morality, even if the collective experiences that make up those histories are distinct, but not in histories of thought and barely of remembrance, and so not of law and politics.

Comparing the races of master and slave for their faculties of memory, reason, and imagination, "in memory they are equal to whites," he stated, but in reason "much inferior," and in imagination "dull, tasteless, and anomalous."[47] It was not their capacity for memory so much as the substance of that memory and their capacity to do things with it that Jefferson emphasized. In Jeffersonian terms, there was simply no possibility of such a people participating in the art of recollection. The security of the Jeffersonian project came to rest squarely not just on a property regime or sense of racial superiority, although these were certainly present and inseparable from Jefferson's thought and from each other, but on a relegation of the recollections of others to a place outside of recognizable legal and political subjectivity. One way or another, a culture of recollection as bound by the mastery of self and others must also be a culture of forgetting.

There is a question in the text of whether nature or collective experience is responsible for these distinctions, and so for its modern readers as to whether race or property was the prime mover in Jeffersonian ideology, and the truth is that the two cannot be separated. Confronting the stereotype of slaves as natural thieves, Jefferson turned to context and collective historical experience, and specifically the experience of being owned as by definition not self-possessive and as such inherently incapacitating. "The man, in whose favor no laws of property exist, probably feels

[47] Jefferson, *Notes on the State of Virginia*, p. 146.

himself less bound to respect those made in favor of others," Jefferson observed.[48] This is a judgment of equity: thievery might be illegal, but the rights of property are for Jefferson relative and conditional, and the case of subversive slaves was at least in this case no exception. Like the white settlers who live by their right to the common stock of the earth, the slaves of Jefferson's imagining are cognizant of the limits of the rights of property. This did not, however, stop Jefferson from speculating on their natural inferiority. That opinion was hazarded because the distinctions between nature and nurture in the context of natural history were at best blurry, and more likely meaningless. What squared Jefferson's ability to draw racial distinctions with philosophical confidence was property, and the near identity he established for himself between mode of possession and mode of life. It is only the lack of ownership of the plot of nature and the body with which one labors, for Jefferson, that distinguishes the condition of the slave from that of the idealized settler-farmer. The configuration of black bodies, faces, and physical and intellectual capacities rested on the critique of these bodies as not self-possessed. Property was the crucial mediating factor that allowed the sensing subject of these histories, natural and civil, to be a subject of these histories, a user of the material of these histories, rather than be subject to them.

The "convulsions" possible in the history Jefferson surveyed were potential threats to property and to the constituted space of self-reflexive and judicious participation in law and politics that possession made possible. From the end of the revolution, Jefferson wrote, "we shall be going down hill," for "it will not then be necessary to resort every moment to the people for support."[49] Lacking constant practice in sharing the responsibilities of political power, the people will be forgotten, but even more importantly "they will forget themselves, but in the sole faculty of making money, and will never think of uniting to effect [sic] a due respect for their rights." The situation will continue, Jefferson warns, until "our rights shall revive or expire in a convulsion."[50] Like the natural history surveyed in the opening queries, civil history included its share of ruins and other evidence of "convulsions," and the feeling of the weight of that history in Jefferson's mind

[48] *Ibid*, p. 149. [49] Jefferson, *Notes on the State of Virginia*, p. 167.

[50] *Ibid*; the quotation comes at the conclusion of Query XVII on religion and religious liberty, but Jefferson is clearly not referring solely to rights of conscience, as the concern for resorting to the people and the fear of their slippage into solipsism illustrates.

gets redistributed in the *Notes* onto the shoulders of the theoretically posited ideal citizen of the republic.[51]

No potential sudden or sublime event aroused Jefferson's fears more than the possibility of a slave revolt, the most potent example of an unmediated upheaval and the gravest threat to the conditions of self-government as theorized in the *Notes*. What prompted Jefferson into a famous if brief meditation on what Walter Benjamin calls "divine violence"[52] was the question of whether "the liberties of a nation" can be "thought secure" when the idea that those liberties are God-given and universal are removed from the minds of the people who are fortunate enough to enjoy them: "I tremble for my Country when I reflect that God is just: that his justice cannot sleep forever."[53] It was the threat to the white subject's bodily security and cultivated self-governance so carefully constructed over the course of the *Notes* that was at stake here for Jefferson. "It is impossible to be temperate and to pursue this subject through the various considerations of policy, of morals, of history natural and civil," Jefferson wrote, describing his own project in the *Notes* perfectly. His premonition of a racial revolution from below concludes Query XVIII on customs and manners, where Jefferson began by discussing the threat of the habit of owning slaves on the morals of the owners themselves. The presence of slaves and slavery in the new republic was dangerous, in this framework, first and foremost to the ethical and political aptitudes of its citizens.

Appropriately, the immediately following Query XIX on manufacturing and political economy offered the theoretical counter-image to the divinely sanctioned rupture of rebelling slaves. "Those who labour in the earth are the chosen people of God," Jefferson proclaimed, banking the health of the body politic on those "not looking up to heaven" but "to their own soil and industry," for "corruption of morals

[51] On the genealogy of racial concepts and in particularly on the ideas of African inferiority and the slavery itself available to Jefferson, see Winthrop D. Jordan, *White Over Black: American Attitudes toward the Negro, 1550–1812* (Chapel Hill: University of North Carolina Press, 1968); David Brion Davis, *The Problem of Slavery in Western Culture* (Ithaca: Cornell University Press, 1966), and *The Problem of Slavery in the Age of Revolutions, 1770–1823* (Ithaca: Cornell University Press, 1975), pp. 169–84; Christian P. Iannini, *Fatal Revolutions: Natural History, West Indian Slavery, and the Routes of American Literature* (Chapel Hill: University of North Carolina Press, 2012), ch. 5.

[52] Walter Benjamin, "Critique of Violence," *Selected Writings, Volume 1: 1913–1926*, Marcus Bulluck and Michael Jennings, eds. Edmund Jephcott, trans. (Cambridge, MA: Harvard University Press, 1996), pp. 236–52.

[53] Jefferson, *Notes on the State of Virginia*, p. 169.

in the mass of cultivators" was unheard of in history.[54] What distinguished the construction of the sweating, laboring body of the black slave as represented in the *Notes* from that of the white laboring farmer, which is the crucial distinction being at times implicitly and at times explicitly drawn throughout the text, can be and ultimately is boiled down to this wording: "their own."[55] The question with which Jefferson began his extended treatment of the presence of African Americans in Virginia, "why not retain and incorporate the blacks into the state," gets answered over the course of Query XIV on the laws and Query XVIII on manners and customs by doubting their capacity for legal and political

[54] *Ibid*, pp. 170–1; on the ambivalence about manufacturing in Jeffersonian political economy, see Drew R. McCoy, *An Elusive Republic: Political Economy in Jeffersonian America* (Chapel Hill: University of North Carolina Press, 1980).

[55] The argument here differs slightly from that advanced by Peter Onuf and Ari Helo, who suggest that Jefferson's use of the historical and jurisprudential language of the Scottish Enlightenment to think about race characterized enslaved African Americans as morally unprepared for political life. But Jefferson does not posit any innate or developed moral inferiority as such, and in fact his discussion of slaves having the acknowledged right to take and to rebel is little different from his equitable calculation with regard to free whites in the same situation (see Jefferson to Madison, October 28, 1785, *ibid*); it is essential to grasp the critical linkage between *ownership* and the capacity for legal and political as opposed to moral subjectivity in accessing the origins of Jefferson's racial thinking; Peter Onuf and Ari Helo, "Jefferson, Morality, and the Problem of Slavery," *The Mind of Thomas Jefferson* (Charllotesville: University of Virginia Press, 2006), pp. 236–70; Ari Helo, *Thomas Jefferson's Ethics and the Politics of Human Progress: The Morality of a Slaveholder* (Cambridge: Cambridge University Press, 2014). That being said, it is equally essential not to overstate the significance of Jefferson's rhetorical commitments to abolitionism: as Peter Onuf points out, Jefferson understood emancipation of the captive nation of enslaved Africans as possible only as the precondition for colonization and national self-determination; see Onuf, "To Declare Them a Free and Independent People," *Jefferson's Empire: The Language of American Nationhood* (Charlottesville: University of Virginia Press, 2000), pp. 147–88. But as the text of the *Notes* makes clear, the identity of race and nation that would prove to be such a core building block of the nationalist imperial ideologies of Jeffersonian and Jacksonian democracy at full strength took ideological work to construct, and that identification was hardly something that could be taken for granted in the political and intellectual debates surrounding slavery in the new nation or in the framework of European vocabularies of natural jurisprudence with which Jefferson was thinking (indeed, the focus on Virginia indicates that the language and assumption of nationhood and national identity was still in the works at the time of Jefferson's writing of the *Notes*, which took place at the moment of a transformation from the legal plurality of early modern empires to the theorized uniformity of imperial nation states, see Pagden, *Lords of all the World*). The task in the *Notes* was not just to assert the identity of race and nation, but to construct it as a way of foreclosing the implicitly acknowledged and publicly debated possibilities of African American citizenship and civic capacity; see Robin Blackburn, *The American Crucible: Slavery, Emancipation, and Human Rights* (London: Verso, 2013); Davis, *The Problem of Slavery in the Age of Emancipation* (New York: Knopf, 2014).

subjectivity, a capacity carefully constructed as something that needs to be cultivated and so proceeds from self-possession and self-government. Slaves work and labor in Jefferson's language, but they never cultivate.

In a famous passage of Crevecoeur's *Letters from an American Farmer*, James narrates his travels through South Carolina, and in his encounter with the dying body of a punished runaway, he sets up a stark contrast between the beleaguered body of the slave and the industriously fruitful body of the independent farmer. James comes across a slave in a cage hanging from a tree: "I shudder to recollect that the birds had already picked out his eyes; his cheekbones were bare; his arms had been attacked in several places; and his body seemed covered with a multitude of wounds. From the edges of the hollow sockets and from the lacerations with which he was disfigured, the blood slowly dropped and tinged the ground beneath."[56] Covered with insects, bruises, and open wounds, the slave's body as depicted is utterly subject to the forces of nature. The slave has been deprived even of the ability to move, and life itself is on the verge of surrender. Locke had argued in the *Second Treatise* that it was a violation of natural law to sell one's self into slavery, life being a gift given in trust by God and the only thing in one's possession that was not the product of human work and so subject to higher claims on its use than the will of the temporary owner.[57] In the representation of the slave body in *Letters from an American Farmer*, the mockery that slavery makes of natural law is clear as James contemplates a merciful killing of the slave, whose life and death are totally in the hands of another.

In the face of the "living specter" of the slave, who in his "uncouth dialect" begs for water, James recounts that "humanity herself would have balanced whether to lessen such reliefless distress or mercifully with one blow to end this dreadful scene of agonizing torture." What James narrates here is not only the injustice of slavery through a depiction of its reduction of human life to necessity but the consequences of that reduction for the observer in increasingly anxious possession of their own subjectivity. The blood stains the soil, the image is one that the observer even shudders to recollect, "humanity herself" would be at pains to reach a balanced, equitable judgment about what to do, and the scene of the suffering is just as important to bring to an end as the suffering itself. "I found myself," James writes in the middle of the passage, "suddenly arrested by the power of fright and terror; my nerves were convulsed;

[56] Crevecoeur, *Letters from an American Farmer*, p. 129.
[57] Locke, *Two Treatises of Government*, pp. 284–5.

I trembled, I stood motionless, involuntarily contemplating the fate of this Negro in all its dismal latitude."[58] Involuntary contemplation is surely the sign that the free subject of enlightened observation has been caught up in the natural necessity of the slave's world. The conjunction of troubled recollection and the force of convulsion stages a confrontation between the subjectivities of the free and enslaved, a confrontation that exploded in the pages of Thomas Jefferson's *Notes on the State of Virginia*. This conjunction of the apparent threat of the presence of enslaved black bodies to the self-command of the independent subject and the particular embedment of the slave in natural history for Crevecoeur and even more so for Jefferson crystalized the work that the configuration of subjectivities does in the *Notes*. Jefferson's physiognomic account of slaves proceeded under the pressure of retaining a form of self-government that was tied to the mastery of self and others.

That account matters today because of how the lived and imagined relationship between master and slave shapes the intellectual history of recognition and difference. In an extended discussion of Wittgenstein's concept of aspect dawning and its relevance for the problem of acknowledging others, Stanley Cavell writes that "the idea of the allegory of words," is a treatment of the fear that one's sensations as expressed to one's self and others in the form of words are at once not recognized as uniquely one's own and at the same time not understood because not recognized as common, as precisely not uniquely one's own. The idea here "is that human expressions, the human figure, to be grasped, must be *read*. To know another mind is to interpret a physiognomy ... I have to read the physiognomy, and see the creature according to my reading, and treat it according to my seeing."[59] At once responding to and echoing Hegel's *Phenomenology of Spirit*, Cavell takes up the problem of acknowledging another as cohabiting the same realm of expected justice, a problem rooted historically in the relationship between master and slave and their respective modes of self-consciousness.[60] By these lights, Jefferson's reading of the bodies and faces of his slaves proceeded from his thinking about language, law, and history. It was historical subjectivity and the lived effects of particular civil and natural histories that he saw, and it is with such criteria that he judged of their capacities.

[58] Crevecoeur, *Letters from an American Farmer*, p. 129.
[59] Cavell, *The Claim of Reason*, p. 356.
[60] Cavell, *The Claim of Reason*, p. 363; see Georg Wilhelm Friedrich Hegel, *The Phenomenology of Mind*, J.B. Ballie, trans. (New York: Harper Collins, 1967), pp. 228–40.

At stake here is the question of what Hannah Arendt calls "the right to have rights," and it is a question that has particular usefulness for any understanding of how it is possible for authors of declarations of universal rights to abide by and in fact reinforce violent exclusions of people and peoples from acknowledged enjoyment of those rights.[61] This possibility is inseparable from a history of the practices of regarding self and others: what the master has over his slaves is of course legal ownership, Cavell writes, but at least in the master's own imagining it is also something more: "power over his experience in relation to them." The master "may acknowledge everything about them ... with the sole exception of their existence in the realm of justice," and from that position he expects "nothing about him" in return except "acknowledgment of his mastery." The security of this position, however, rests solely on the assumption that the slaves lack access to the fragility of the master's self-possession. Should they ever exercise their power "to acknowledge him," in fact "to see his experience as he sees it, then he would see himself through their eyes," and then "they would know that they had seen themselves through his, and he would number his days."[62] It is quite possible in sum to read the arguments about race and slavery in the *Notes* (to say nothing of Jefferson's famously terrified later correspondence on the topic) as an extended and at times expressly unsuccessful effort to avoid this moment of acknowledgment.

To take full advantage of Cavell's discussion of the power of acknowledgment, two things need to be noted.[63] First, while he was not comfortable doing it, Jefferson brought his inquiry as it proceeded through the writing of the *Notes* to a point where he saw the existence of slaves in the realm of justice as obvious, even perhaps self-evident. The question then was not the existence of slaves in the realm of justice, but their existence in the realm of law, of laws and institutions. Their sharing in the realm of divine and natural law (and even their possible privileged place in it) did not translate into legal personhood or citizenship here, and that is because of Jefferson's introduction and use of the concept of civic capacity, and his bonding of that concept to histories of cultivating self-governance

[61] Hannah Arendt, *The Origins of Totalitarianism* (New York: Harcourt, 1951), p. 296.

[62] Cavell, *The Claim of Reason*, p. 377.

[63] On the work of James Tully and Stanley Cavell's relevance to problems of cultural or racial difference and the promise and limits of the politics of acknowledgment, see Patchen Markell, *Bound by Recognition* (Princeton: Princeton University Press, 2003); Aletta J. Norvall, *Aversive Democracy: Inheritance and Originality in the Democratic Tradition* (Cambridge: Cambridge University Press, 2007).

through self-possession. Secondly, there is a difficult lesson to be learned from the first point, and that is that there is no rule of history that says that the politics of acknowledgment and the critically respective spirit that nurtures it must in any case lead to greater actually existing justice. Jefferson's treatment of Native American language and historical practice in the *Notes* and beyond should make it clear that acknowledging cultural and historical distinctiveness can be perfectly safe for the project of empire if the legal, institutional, and communicative data and tools of study are predicated not only on conditions and assumptions of ownership, mastery, and possession but on a more dangerous – because more subtle – discourse of cultural adequacy and civic capacity.

In his situation of human beings as "subjects of natural history," and in the historical and physiognomic lines that he drew between these subjects, Jefferson pictured the convulsion of justice manifest in the slave revolt as an event in natural history, all the more stunning and terrifying because not tempered by the habits of propriety or reflection, carried out by people with no supposed access to constituted histories of use and no materials with which to represent their histories to themselves and others. This image of the life of the slave subject to nature and without the capacity for self-governing recollection is a myth around which Jefferson reconstitutes racial inequality, even as that myth morphs into its apparent opposite in the form of the sudden revolt. In the pages of the *Notes*, Jefferson came to confront the very real possibility of disruption to the conditions of civic and material remembrance and so to the security of the Jeffersonian subject. Jefferson's study of Native American language as a kind of archive of historical practice went forward from its beginning in the *Notes* under the pressure of securing that subject at any cost.

LANGUAGE, HISTORY, AND EMPIRE

The importance of Native Americans in the development of Jefferson's thinking cannot be overstated. In the *Notes*, Jefferson foregrounded the question of Native historical development, and he went on to understand Native languages as the principal criteria for providing answers to that question. As is the case with the rest of the material in the *Notes*, Jefferson proceeded in his treatment of Native Americans in Queries VI and IX under pressure to contest the degeneracy thesis as articulated by Buffon. The image of the Native American Jefferson constructed in the *Notes* and in his collaboration with the Historical and Literary and Committee at the American Philosophical Society bore a double burden as both indicative of American potential and as a particular, contingent historical example of the failure to quite literally capitalize on that potential.

To understand Jefferson's reworking of his own practice and theorization of that practice, it is essential to understand his circumscription of Native American linguistic and so historical subjectivity, and to appreciate how intertwined the treatment of Native American historical practice was with the changing theoretical venture of his own. The scholarship on Jefferson's purposive depictions of and relations with Native Americans is rich, but it has tended to treat Jefferson's collecting of Native artifacts and linguistic data in relative isolation from other areas of his thinking, particularly his legal and historical thinking, two areas that, as I have tried to show, can hardly be separated themselves. The conceptual tools Jefferson used to study and circumscribe Native historical practice and subjectivity grew out of his own particular attentions to the legally constructed historical subjectivities of revolutionary constitutionalism. It cannot be assumed that Jefferson simply applied inherited Enlightenment narratives of social development to Natives, locating them on the continuum of conjectural history and finding them underdeveloped, and conveniently so for the sake of settler access to western land.[64] There is of course a general truth there, but such a picture misses not only the fundamental importance of the jurisprudential categories Jefferson brought to bear on his treatment of Native American historical practices and language in particular but the degree to which Jefferson's thought changed over the course of his life, and changed in response not only to varying political contexts but specifically to the challenge that the presence of Native Americans posed to his project.

For Buffon, once again Jefferson's interlocutor, Native Americans were simply savages, and their uncomplicated and unsophisticated lives were indicative of nothing more or less than the negative influence of the degenerating natural history they inhabited. Whereas accounts of great Mexican and South American civilizations testified to civilizational potential prior to histories of declension and conquest in the present, North

[64] Anthony F.C. Wallace, *Jefferson and the Indians: The Tragic Fate of the First Americans* (Cambridge, MA: Belknap, Harvard University Press, 1999); Peter Thompson, "Judicious Neology": The Imperative of Paternalism in Thomas Jefferson's Linguistic Studies," *Early American Studies*, Vol. 1, No. 2 (Fall 2003), pp. 187–224; Thomas Hallock, "*Notes on the State of Virginia and the Jeffersonian West*," and Gordon M. Sayre, "Jefferson and Native Americans: Policy and Archive," *The Cambridge Companion to Thomas Jefferson*, Frank Shuffleton, ed. (Cambridge: Cambridge University Press, 2009), pp. 47–60, 61–72.

America and its native inhabitants offered no such evidence to Buffon. "A people who live without the restraint of fixed laws, or of a regular government, can only be considered as a tumultuous assemblage of barbarous and independent individuals," Buffon wrote, explicitly in the vocabulary of early modern legal humanism and civil history, "who obey no laws but those of passion and caprice, and who, having no common interest, are incapable of pursuing any standard of manners, which supposes general views that have obtained the sanction both of time and a majority of numbers."[65] The capacity for complex associational life required cultivation, but even that cultivation required conditions of historical continuity, awareness of that continuity, and sufficient population to maintain that continuity across time and space. Not possessing law and legal histories, according to Buffon Native Americans lacked the necessary constitutive relations to themselves and their surroundings from which further history could be made. Their languages were simple, continued Buffon, and hardly indicative of abstract reasoning and reflection beyond the satisfaction of basic wants. By Buffon's lights, Native North American inferiority was clear to the enlightened observer in light of the poverty of their historical consciousness and practice.

The savage of the North American continent for Buffon was the creature of a decrepit nature. To behold the lone Native American warrior was to see a man "weak and small in the organs of generation, with "neither hair nor beard nor ardor for his female." He might be faster than his European counterpart because more accustomed to running, but he was "less strong in body; he is also less sensitive and yet more fearful and cowardly; he has no vivacity, no emotion; the activity of his body is less an exercise, a voluntary movement, than it is a necessary action caused by need..."[66] While they lacked ardor for their females and family structures were supposedly weak, "they have no community, no commonwealth, no social state. Bodily love makes up their morality; their heart is icy, their society cold, and their rule harsh. They look upon their wives as laborers, as beasts whom they without consideration load with the burdens from their hunting," and whom the men force to labor beyond the limits of their strength. This meant there were few children, which only compounded the lack of social development and advancement beyond the barbarous sexual mores and backward gender roles of the tragic past. Crucially, for Buffon, this situation was a consequence of the turgid

[65] Buffon, *Natural History*, Vol. 3, p. 171. [66] *Ibid*, Vol. 5, p. 130.

natural environment of North America, with little of the vital force and "germs" necessary for development.[67] But it was also the case that the failure to cultivate compounded and locked in the original problem, so that the manifold failures Buffon narrated were not simply facts of natural history but conditions of an inability to master nature and to cultivate an appropriately productive relationship between civil and natural history. It was quite possible, even for Buffon, to imagine that "some centuries hence," after nature had been subdued and cultivated, British North America could be the most fertile and productive land on earth.

Buffon's depiction of Native Americans is similar to how Jefferson would go on to discuss slaves, as passively experiencing the condition of their being subject to the forces of nature, as creatures. Jefferson set out largely to defend Native Americans from Buffon's relegation of them to the status of savages, all the while moving the conceptual space of enlightened critique of Native historical practice onto different grounds. Why he chose to do so can be understood in terms of his larger departure from Buffon: a divergent understanding of what Jefferson calls in this context the "oeconomy of nature." Contrary to Buffon's suggestion that, despite evidence of their historical existence, it was certain that the American mastodon was extinct, Jefferson held out the possibility of a living specimen in the west: "such is the oeconomy of nature, that no instance can be produced of her having any one race of her animals to become extinct; of her having formed any link in her great work so weak as to be broken."[68] What was at stake for Jefferson was the context in which the subjects of natural history inhabiting the North American continent could be situated. It was very important for Jefferson to insist that whatever the great Buffon had made of the natural history of the rest of the world, in North America the germs of nature had not yet come to ruin; in fact, the seeds of fruitful germination had not yet been planted. Against what he saw as Buffon's transatlantic natural history of nature as an apparently cis-Atlantic partisan, Jefferson posited a transatlantic and historical nature that could be particularly powerful in the specific cis-Atlantic context of American settlement.[69]

Very little of the picture painted by Buffon of Native Americans rang true for Jefferson, who was enough of a student of British North American colonial history to know that such a history of settlement had not proceeded in violent fits and starts because settlers had encountered cowardly

[67] *Ibid*, pp. 130–1. [68] Jefferson, *Notes on the State of Virginia*, p. 55.
[69] *Ibid*, pp. 68–9.

wanderers upon their arrival. Indeed, in his study and portrayal of Native life, Jefferson was at pains to walk a fine line between the depiction of Indians in North and South America as naked savages and the considerable evidence amassed by early modern European ethnographers that the original inhabitants of the Americas were in full possession not only of a self-consciously natural but a civil history. As J.G.A. Pocock and Anthony Pagden have demonstrated, much of the historical work addressing the Americas in early modern European thought situated Native Americans at various points along a continuum running from savagery to barbarism, or perhaps even an ancient level of civilization.[70] While both were terms of classical origin and neoclassical implication, the state of savagery denoted primordial dwellers of the woods, living without recognizable modes of property or judicature and whose speech exhibited historical proximity to a theoretically posited transparent language of completely natural expression. Barbarism by contrast was generally a state of social development where a particular group had laws, customs, manners, and a distinct linguistic identity but had lost the ability to alter these aspects of their history. The lines between savagery and barbarism were blurry, and Jefferson frequently had recourse to both, but by and large he dismissed Buffon's depiction of Native Americans in North America as savages in favor of an understanding of them as barbarous, and he did so in the midst of switching the framework for narrating Native degeneracy as a question not of nature but a question of historically developed capacity to use that nature sufficiently, and so participate actively in history, natural and civil.

Tellingly, where Jefferson agreed with Buffon was on the apparent confusion of gender roles observed in many Native societies, and like Buffon, Jefferson found the lack of normatively gendered divisions of labor to be a key factor in explaining their failure to cultivate and germinate at sufficient levels. "The women are submitted to unjust drudgery," Jefferson asserted confidently. "This I believe to be the case with every barbarous people. With such, force is law. The stronger sex therefore imposes on the weaker," he continued, defining Indian domestic life as a domain of force. In a remarkable passage, Jefferson used the work of Native women as an example of the emancipatory power of settler civilization. "It is civilization alone that replaces women in the enjoyment of their natural equality. That first teaches us to subdue the selfish

[70] Anthony Pagden, *The Fall of Natural Man: The American Indian and the Origins of Comparative Ethnology* (Cambridge: Cambridge University Press, 1982); Pocock, *Barbarism and Religion, Volume IV*.

passions, and to respect those rights in others which we value in ourselves. Were we in equal barbarism, our females would be equal drudges."[71] Confusion and even disgust at divergent gender roles in various Native American societies had been a veritable trope of colonial discourse since the historical moment of contact. Observations of matrilineal or even in some cases matriarchal social practices had played a crucial role in the construction of a historical narrative that represented the zone of contact between Natives and British settlers as one of the confrontation between barbarism and the civilizing force of conquest. And to this Jefferson was no exception, but he goes further here and in his other discussions of Native life than previous colonizing discourses had in describing the perceived failures of indigenous family structures not as a moral problem per se but as a historical and economic one. At the very least, if Jefferson could be said to have a moral critique of gender norms in his under-construction image of Native society, it was a critique tied not to moralistic or religious values on their own terms, but to the ethics appropriate for the project of settler cultivation.

Contested gender roles in the larger context of republican revolution and settler liberty also disturbed the security of the Jeffersonian subject, to say nothing of Jefferson himself. While his legal reform proposals for Virginia had suggested the equal right of women to inherit and own property, Jefferson's plans for land provision would quite literally codify the domestic place of women's labor and social role. Indeed, the control of female political subjectivity went hand in hand with the need to secure the stability of patriarchal management of the household and so the material conditions for the exercise of civic virtue in politics. Observing the engagement of women in social and political life in pre-revolutionary Paris, Jefferson informed his correspondent Anne Willing Bingham that for such women and the men they interact with "the days of life are consumed, one by one, without an object beyond the present moment; ever flying from the ennui of that, yet carrying it with us; eternally in pursuit of happiness, which keeps eternally before us."[72] The explosion of possible interactions contrasted directly with the undisturbed and stable domestic scenes of America, Jefferson assured her, where the maintenance

[71] Jefferson, *Notes on the State of Virginia*, 64–5; on Jefferson's gendered critique and its role in thinking about historical progression and national expansion, see Brian Steele, *Thomas Jefferson and American Nationhood* (Cambridge: Cambridge University Press, 2012).

[72] Jefferson to Anne Willing Bingham, February 7, 1787, *Papers of Thomas Jefferson*, Vol. 11, p. 123.

of gendered divisions of labor provided the material conditions for actually fulfilling the promise of the Declaration of Independence, a text to which Jefferson was coming to ascribe increasing world-historical significance as republicanism asserted itself in Europe. "You too have had your political fever," he later writes. "But our good ladies, I trust, have been too wise to wrinkle their foreheads with politics. They are contended to soothe and calm the minds of their husbands returning ruffled from political debate," he continues, having as they do, he suggests, "the good sense to value domestic happiness above all other, and the art to cultivate it beyond all others."[73] The labor of women in Jefferson's project is cultivation, too, but the cultivation of domestic as opposed to public happiness, and the imperative of the domestic only intensified as the image of republican politics as the collective pursuit of happiness became increasingly untenable amid the conflict and violence of early national politics in the United States and a politically electrified Paris on the eve of revolution.

The gendered division of household and political life, mastery, and inequality in the management of the *oikos* for the sake of civic equality in the forum of the *polis*, is as old as politics itself. More directly, Jefferson's own ability to participate in the political life of his time was directly dependent on the management of Monticello as a site of domestic production, and while his garden and farm books attest to the assiduousness of his efforts in that regard, as we now know beyond any reasonable doubt, his own sense of domestic tranquility was tied to his sexual mastery of human property in the form of his later lifelong relationship with Sally Hemings and the ownership of their offspring. Seen in this light of the inherently gendered quality of the art of possessing one's self and others, Jefferson's critique of insufficient domestic mastery on the part of Native men laid the groundwork for his critique of their insufficient cultivation of the land, confirming and ratcheting up the degree to which settler conquest and civilizing work could be characterized as historically progressive and liberating for willing Native beneficiaries. It also stood at odds with another aspect of the image of Native American life Jefferson was constructing in the *Notes*. Among such barbarous peoples as these, Jefferson wrote, "force is law."[74] Insufficient cultivation was ultimately synonymous with insufficient use of not only land but of all the materials out of which subjectivity was constructed and practiced, of bodies, words,

[73] Jefferson to Bingham, May 11, 1788, *Papers of Thomas Jefferson*, Vol. 13, p. 151.
[74] Jefferson,*Notes on the State of Virginia*, p. 64.

and things. The cultivated capacity for political liberty and legitimate collective sovereignty was predicated on the discipline of a particular mode of use.[75] But Jefferson also depicts Native Americans as enjoying a unique form of collective liberty and contrasts that way of life with the legal culture of the new nation. Their practice of living in spread-out, small societies, Jefferson suggested, resulted from their "never having submitted themselves to any laws, any coercive power, any shadow of government. Their only controuls are their manners, and that moral sense of right and wrong, which, like the sense of taste and feeling, in every man makes a part of his nature."[76] In proceeding to narrate Native Americans in a history of manners, customs, and laws, Jefferson was setting the stage for situating them and his study of them at the confluence of several divergent but interrelated strands of enlightened historiography that informed his own rubric for the measurement of historical practice and capacity.

The discussion of Native Americans in the *Notes* allowed Jefferson to advance his particular understanding of legal subjectivity as constructed by the conjunction of histories of labor, language, and law, as histories of particular modes of use, and specifically of using the historical materials of land and goods, words in speech and text, and the customs and records of a people's civil history. And so in the *Notes* Jefferson proceeds to configure the poverty of Native American use as evidenced by the poverty of their history, a history that could be gleaned only from their language. "Before we condemn the Indians of this continent as wanting genius, we must consider that letters have been introduced among them," Jefferson

[75] Of course, as discussed previously, in respective early modern European jurisprudential theories of empire, productive use of land was the critical evaluative tool that granted legal legitimacy to European conquest. This was the case even as early modern Spanish theorists in particular debated the legality of their conquest, and did so in the face of their own increasing if contested awareness of the complexities of the American societies they encountered. Specifically, the work of linguists such as José de Acosta (1539–1600) for Spain and Joseph-François Lafitau (1681–1746) for French interactions with the Iroquois and other groups in North America helped establish a noteworthy ambivalence in the history of legal and political thought about Atlantic empire – noteworthy not because it was radically challenging to respective imperial projects, but because the intellectual possibility of the coexistence of both awareness and dismissal of Native American civilizations as such constituted an overlap of use as a linguistic and economic concept that made evaluating the life of their usage a critical component of modern forms of empire; Pagden, *The Fall of Natural Man*; Andrew Fitzmaurice, *Sovereignty, Property, and Empire, 1500–2000* (Cambridge: Cambridge University Press, 2014).

[76] Jefferson, *Notes on the State of Virginia*, p. 98.

responds to Buffon, following and confirming many of the naturalist's own crude observations of the bodies of Native Americans but refusing to find the life of the Natives naturally or culturally degraded. Allowing for the "circumstances of their situation," Jefferson had suggested, "we shall probably find that they are formed in mind as well as in body on the same module as the "Homo sapiens Europaeus."[77] We lack written evidence of their participation in histories of creative and critical thought, Jefferson intones, but their lack of writing should not be confused for a lack of mental capacity in and of itself: "The principles of their society forbidding all compulsion, they are to be led to duty and to enterprise by personal influence and persuasion. Hence eloquence in council, bravery and address in war, become the foundations of all consequence with them. To these requirements all their faculties are directed."[78] The history Native Americans had been making were histories driven and represented by rhetoric, and in particular by the rhetorical demands on speech in the contexts of intertribal conflict and internal tribal debate.

The protest of the Mingo warrior called Logan to the colonial governor Lord Dunmore against settler raids on Native villages in 1774, and with it Logan's justification for retaliatory violence was evidence enough to Jefferson of Native dexterity in the art of persuasion. The oration of Logan was matched only in European history by those of Demosthenes and Cicero, Jefferson asserted, with whom he wrote he was comfortable comparing Logan's eloquence favorably.[79] Acknowledging even the recent history of settler violence in western Virginia and the Ohio River Valley, Jefferson quoted Logan's opening salvo before directly moving to his observation that letters had not been introduced among them, which begins the conclusion of his extended response to Buffon and Raynal in Query VI and leaves his discussion of Native life and language to its own specific chapter in Query XI. As many previous critics have noted, Jefferson's admiration of Logan's eloquence is janus-faced at best, as his treatment romanticized Native expression as representative of their being lost to the developmental forces of modern history, effectively condemning the concrete historical existence of Native American presence as revealed even by their artful use of spoken language to a quickly receding past.[80] Nevertheless, characterizing Jefferson's treatment of Native rhetoric and linguistic history as

[77] *Ibid*, p. 68. [78] *Ibid*, p. 66. [79] *Ibid*, p. 67, appendix IV, pp. 233–64.

[80] Andrew F. Wallace, *Jefferson and the Indians*; Sandra M. Gustafson, *Eloquence is Power: Oratory and Performance in Early America* (Chapel Hill: University of North Carolina Press, 2000).

simply an Enlightenment or Romantic configuration of noble savagery would be a mistake.[81] His comparison of Logan with the pillars of Greek and Roman rhetoric, his discussion of Native American language and history later in the *Notes*, and his correspondence with historical linguists at the American Philosophical Society on the project of collecting Native American languages reveal that Jefferson was at the very least aware of different ways of situating Native Americans as a group in history, including a particularly neoclassical idiom for framing Native possession of not only a natural and linguistic but through language a substantively legal and so civil, political history.

Using classical models for reconstructing and representing Native American life was common in discourses of Enlightenment historiography and natural history, particularly when these discourses intersected. As Martin Thom and J.G.A. Pocock have shown in different contexts, the dichotomy between civilization and barbarism in classical and in particular Tacitean historiography was central to how eighteenth-century thinkers situated themselves and their knowledge of Native Americans in history.[82] This was particularly true of how many eighteenth-century thinkers understood Native American civic life and the linguistic and specifically rhetorical capacities appropriate to republican deliberation in ancient civilization, whether in the ancient city's forum or the tribal or village council. Cadwallader Colden's colonial history of the Iroquois Confederacy, *A History of the Five Indian Nations*, made the classical framework for understanding Native societies explicit. Colden, an imperial official and minister to the Confederacy, observed that "the people of the Five Nations are much given to speech-making, ever the natural consequence of a perfect Republican Government: where no single person has the power to compel, the arts of persuasion alone must prevail." And he continues, "their best speakers distinguish themselves in their public Councils and Treaties with other nations, and thereby gain the Esteem and Applause of their Countrymen."[83] The Indian that Colden described was

[81] Indeed, the concept itself is hardly indicative of the role distinctive images of natural man, the savage, or indigenous people played in early modern social theory; see Ter Ellingson, *The Myth of the Noble Savage* (Berkeley and Los Angeles: University of California Press, 2001).

[82] Martin Thom, *Republics, Nations, and Tribes* (London: Verso, 1995); Pocock, *Barbarism and Religion, Volume IV*.

[83] Cadwallader Colden, *The History of the Five Indian Nations of Canada* (London: T. Osborne, 1747), p. 14; the passage is later directly quoted by Peter S. Du Ponceau in his own historical and linguistic notebooks, Du Ponceau, *Philological Notebooks*, Papers

a citizen, a crafter and user of rhetoric in a public discourse, a man of action. To be sure, Colden, later a vigorous defender of the royal prerogative in the colonies and a loyalist, dying in 1776, was not a natural admirer of "perfect republican government." Nevertheless, Colden was clearly impressed with the arts of persuasion among the Iroquois, and in his use of neoclassical historical categories for reconstructing Native history, he was hardly alone. In his manuscript notes on the Creek Indians, William Bartram would go on to paint an image of a specifically civic and republican society, describing the cleared space at the center of villages as "the Public Square, or Areopagus," and their winter council house as nothing other than a "Great Rotunda."[84] Bartram refuted any depiction of the natural savage; the Creek and Choctaw peoples are possessed of polities, of confederacies and empires, of "laws, usages, and customs" that regulate a complex understanding of both individual and collective property holding, possessed, in short, of histories that could be understood, even if imperfectly, both on their own terms and in a wider legal, political, and imperial history of European and American peoples.

The classical eloquence that modern writers so admired and that even in modern eyes had remained unsurpassed proved to be an essential component of the larger project of philosophical history. As David Hume wrote in his essay, "On Eloquence," in a "time of temperate and calm speakers," who would or could follow the example of Demosthenes and make use of an *apostrophe*, or endure "such a bold and poetical figure," as Cicero's impassioned description of the crucifixion of a Roman citizen? "In ancient times," Hume wrote of Greece and Rome, "the municipal laws, in every state, were but few and simple, and the decision of causes, was, in a great measure, left to the equity and common sense of the judges." Modern complex societies and the growth of an administrative state made even the suggestion that an eloquent man who had not spent his whole life mastering the law could possibly participate in court advocacy or adjudication simply, in Hume's word, "ridiculous." Hume was therefore prepared to admit that while it was not the only cause of the mediocrity of modern eloquence, "the multiplicity and intricacy of the

of Peter Stephen Du Ponceau, Manuscripts Collection, Library of the American Philosophical Society, Philadelphia, Vol. 2, pp. 48–50; see John M. Dixon, *The Enlightenment of Cadwallader Colden: Empire, Science, and Intellectual Culture in British New York* (Ithaca: Cornell University Press, 2016).

84 William Bartram, *Travels and Other Writings*, Thomas P. Slaughter, ed. (New York: Library of America, 1996), pp. 533, 537.

laws, is a discouragement to eloquence in modern times."[85] Jefferson of course had well noted and bemoaned the increase in the volume of statutes in eighteenth-century Britain and the corresponding changes in the production of legal learning and knowledge toward rational organization and calls for codification. His depiction of Native Americans as living without constituted legal histories and thereby as thoroughly practiced in the rhetorical skills necessary for effective participation in council certainly contrasts with the overburdened legal structure of the modern state, and to a certain extent, favorably so. But the particularly civic form of life that centered Jefferson's theorizing throughout the *Notes* demanded a particularly textual material culture for its context, and so the kind of historical nakedness he ascribes to Native life and thought contrasts to with the dynamic historicity of revolutionary republicanism in Jefferson's configuration.

Oral communication, after all, was only one of the skill sets of Jeffersonian subjectivity, and a subsidiary one at that: not least owing to his own difficulty with public speech, Jefferson remained skeptical throughout his life of impassioned eloquence and its ability to distort or disrupt practices of deliberative judgment. Text grounded Jefferson and his vision of legal and political life, and with their lack of written histories and laws, Native Americans were found to be lacking in the cultural tools necessary for anything more than a fleeting and momentary historical and political subjectivity. What "equity" they were capable of exhibiting in their own form of life was in this framework just as fleeting and momentary, lacking materials with which it could be maintained in continuous projects of being made and remade. To understand the significance of Jefferson's projection here, it is important to understand how it grew out of wider conversations in the United States and in the Atlantic world about Native American language and what studies of language could be made to inform enlightened minds about human histories, about law, and about the human mind.

Discussions of the history and philosophy of language as part of a boarder inquiry into the history of the human mind found a home at the American Philosophical Society in Philadelphia, and in particular at its Historical and Literary Committee, begun in 1784 and led by French-American linguist Peter Stephen Du Ponceau, who served as the Committee's corresponding secretary. In 1791, Jefferson circulated a blank sheet

85 David Hume, *Essays: Literary, Moral, and Philosophical*, Eugene F. Miller, ed. (Indianapolis: Liberty Fund, 1985), pp. 102, 103.

of English words to be used as a form for taking Indian vocabularies and reporting them back to Philadelphia. Jefferson and the Committee gave the forms to anyone with whom they were in contact and knew would also have access to diverse Native groups around the country, including to Lewis and Clark for the expedition of 1803. Du Ponceau, a student of Chinese and Hebrew as well as Native American and European languages, transported to the United States the French philosophical project of *Ideologie*, associated not only with developments in the study of language but in its attempt at a rational science of mind and communication, with developments in psychology and political economy. The ideologists could trace their project to the work of Etienne Bonnot de Condillac, whose *Essay on the Origin of Human Knowledge* of 1746 was a cornerstone of later Enlightenment thought throughout the Atlantic republic of letters.

Written as a commentary on Locke's *Essay Concerning Human Understanding*, Condillac's work furthered the conjectural history of language and thought posited by Locke's empirical project, explaining the development of language as mental equipment that arose out of the interaction of the embodied human mind with its contexts. We have, Condillac wrote, "no ideas that have not been acquired: the first come directly from the senses, the others from experience and increase in proportion to the capacity for reflection."[86] For Condillac, our experience of the world provides us with a table of material sensations available to the mind. Reflection allows the sensing human subject to arrange and rearrange the material on the table, material that is made conceptual and available for being reflected upon through the senses. Language serves a constitutive role as a mediating agent, and makes reflection possible by allowing us to give names to the assembled stuff of our individual and historically collective experience. In reflecting we take stock of our experience as collected and recollected in language. Condillac theorized the human subjects of his inquiry as diversely embedded historical beings, differently situated in respectively divergent contexts. They enjoyed a varied wealth of materials with which to constitute their language,

[86] Etienne Bonnot de Condillac, *Essay on the Origin of Human Knowledge*, Hans Aarsleff, trans. (Cambridge: Cambridge University Press, 2001), p. 12; on the philosophy of language in early modern European thought and in particular on the genealogy of the ideological school and its impact, see Aarsleff, *From Locke to Saussure: Essays on the Study of Language and Intellectual History* (Minneapolis: University of Minnesota Press, 1982); Sophia Rosenfeld, *A Revolution in Language: The Problem of Signs in Eighteenth Century France* (Stanford: Stanford University Press, 2001).

thoughts, and customs and consequently displayed an equally varying complexity of reflections on their constitutive histories. The study of language was a useful tool to those who found themselves in a position to govern and legislate; indeed, it was an archive of the respective histories and the capacities for further action and development in those histories of the peoples of the world.

That is not to say, however, that the project of collecting linguistic history concentrated in Philadelphia was a uniform or unidirectional one. In fact, it was hardly a single project. Disparate visions, styles, and modes of intellectual practice combined with different personal ambitions and circumstances made for different goals and projects. Contributors to the collection included Jefferson, the naturalist Constantine Rafinesque, the philosopher and travel writer Constantin de Volney, botanist and first recipient of Jefferson's simple vocabulary list André Michaux, missionary John Heckewelder, Swiss émigré, political economist, and Jefferson's Secretary of the Treasury Albert Gallatin, planter and later Indian agent Benjamin Hawkins, paleontologist Caspar Wistar, and Du Ponceau himself. To take just one example, Rafinesque, who unsuccessfully sought patronage from Jefferson in the form of an appointment to the faculty of the University of Virginia, kept up a personal correspondence with Jefferson and founded a literary and scientific journal he called *Western Minerva, or American Annals of Knowledge and Literature*. The journal, which was published for just one extensive volume in 1821, combined collected literary pieces, almanac information, and a significant amount of the findings of the Historical and Literary Committee. In correspondence and in the journal, Rafinesque trumpeted the work of the Committee and its associates, anthologizing the work of Heckewelder and others as strong evidence pointing to the existence of a natural and civil history of ancient, pre-contact North America.[87]

Rafinesque was at pains to represent the North American continent as having an ancient past, and to convince Jefferson in particular of the fact that Native Americans possessed a living tradition of organized history in the form of an oral and material culture, a fact that Jefferson, Gallatin, and other members of the committee were at best ambivalent about acknowledging. If anything united the various members of the Native

[87] To Thomas Jefferson from Constantine Samuel Rafinesque, "Three Letters on American Antiquities," August 1, 1820, August 7, 1820, and August 10, 1820, Founders Online, National Archives (http://founders.archives.gov/documents/Jefferson/98-01-02–1430, ver. 2014-05-09).

language project, it was their certainty in the urgency of their effort, confident as they were in the inevitability of the living objects of their study disappearing from view. As Wistar wrote to Heckewelder in 1816, "a fair view of the mind and natural disposition of the savage, and its difference from that of civilized man, would be an acceptable present to the world." The urgent goal, Du Ponceau wrote, was to furnish "additional facts for theorists" of the philosophy of language.[88] However much they differed on questions of the historical reality of what Rafinesque and others called American antiquities, contributors to the Historical and Literary Committee's collections agreed that the disappearance of whatever had existed of Native American history and more importantly historical self-consciousness was certain, necessary, and inevitable.

Soon, it was feared, entire languages, to say little of their users, could disappear. Just as "a knowledge of their several languages would be the most certain evidence of their derivation which could be produced," and indeed such knowledge being "the best proof of the affinity of nations which can ever be referred to," Jefferson wrote in the *Notes*, "it is to be lamented, very much to be lamented, that we have suffered so many of the Indian tribes already to extinguish, without our having previously collected and deposited in the records of literature, the general rudiments at least of the languages they spoke."[89] Du Ponceau and Heckewelder were also convinced of the inevitability of Native American decline and the necessity of getting a clearer picture of their history for the sake of European and American knowledge production before such a project became impossible. Resigned to the effective disappearance of the American Indian, in the aftermath of Jefferson's civilizing policy, the Louisiana Purchase, the Indian Wars and the War of 1812, Heckewelder added to his report to the Historical and Literary Committee a mournful aside that he hoped the product of his efforts to collect their languages and write their history could serve as a "small frail monument to their memory."[90] Native history, captured in the assembled archive of their languages, would become wrapped up as one chapter among many in the project

[88] Caspar Wistar to John Heckewelder, January 9, 1816, *Transactions of the Historical and Literary Committee of the American Philosophical Society* (Philadelphia: Abraham Small, 1819), Vol. 1, p. 359; Peter Stephen Du Ponceau to Heckewelder, July 13, 1816, *ibid*, pp. 384–5.

[89] Jefferson, *Notes on the State of Virginia*, p. 107.

[90] Heckewelder, "An Account of the History, Manners, and Customs of the Indian Native Who Once Inhabited Pennsylvania and the Neighboring States," *Transactions of the Historical and Literary Committee of the American Philosophical Society*, p. 25.

of constructing an American historical self-understanding, one predicated on the invisibilities even of its component parts.

It is nevertheless important to understand some of the philosophical distinctions inherent in differing modes of intellectual practice, and different ways of situating the history of Native historical practice and consciousness in particular. As the publications of the *Transactions* and of the collections of Rafinesque demonstrated, Heckewelder was especially concerned to establish grounds for acknowledging a living sense of continuity and tradition among the Lenni-Lenape people, part of the Delaware nation. His travels among the Lenape, a small tribe that had been subject to the power of the Iroquois Confederacy, convinced him of their possession of a history: the Lenape with whom he spoke were quite explicit that they had suffered a "denial of common justice" at the hands of whites and more powerful tribes alike, and the memory of injustice was a "part of the tradition or history which they preserve for posterity."[91] Native Americans transmitted collective memory to their posterity "by a regular chain of tradition."[92] The chiefs of the tribes with whom he lived, Heckewelder reported, took pains to preserve their interactions and treaties with other tribes. While they had no written laws, they "have usages founded on the most strict principles of equity and justice."[93] As noted by commentators like Colden and Bartram in the previous century, a peculiar form of life equipped these peoples with a historical sense of collective identity and justice that was articulated in the continued life of a discussed and remembered oral tradition. Even so, Heckewelder concluded his report to the Historical and Literary Committee by urging a policy of peace between tribes and between Native Americans generally and the United States, hoping that "they might be brought to a state of civilization, and become Christians," and that "this work will be accomplished by a wise and benevolent government."[94] The slightly more gentle paternalism of Heckewelder and Du Ponceau's linguistic studies was different in tone but not in its fundamental assumptions from Jefferson's more aggressively expansionist imperative.

A contributor to the project of collecting Native American vocabularies from the early stages, and Secretary of the Treasury to Jefferson and Madison, Albert Gallatin published his own work, *A Table of Indian Languages of the United States* in 1826 and *Synopsis of the Indian Tribes of North America* in 1836. While findings and arguments

[91] *Ibid*, p. 9. [92] *Ibid*, p. 10. [93] *Ibid*, p. 328. [94] *Ibid*, p. 345.

depended heavily on the earlier work of Jefferson, Du Ponceau, and Heckewelder, and his work also had wide impact in American ethnology, Gallatin made a telling shift that picked up and carried on a particular aspect of the Jefferson's depictions of Native Americans in an impoverished state of historical existence and awareness. Gallatin conjectured that what evidence existed of a past "semi-civilization" in the American west among the remains of the mound-builders of the Ohio River Valley could only be explained by the benevolent interference of visitors from abroad, possibly from Asia. It would be impossible to imagine a "retrograde step" in historical development absent evidence of some unrecorded conquest or natural disaster, and so the failure of the remaining peoples to accept or build on these achievements had to be explained through their barbarity, through their self-imposed incapacity for dynamic social growth and productive land use.[95] Whatever the causes of Native American backwardness, for Gallatin, it was unlikely that a few "persuasive figures" could peacefully guide them to civilization. The survival of Native Americans, which rested comfortably for Gallatin on their ceasing to be an "impediment" to expansion and further implementation of an agricultural commercial republic, depended on the promise of a more forceful and direct intervention into Native history. Either they would find themselves consenting to the imposing will of a conquering sovereign legislator, or they would perish. Building on the by then strong ideological footing of Jeffersonian and Jacksonian expansion policy, Gallatin was developing a conceptual scheme that by 1836 had been a long time in the making.

CONCLUSION

Du Ponceau himself had instructed Heckewelder and others that the principal promise of their work was to uncover and display a diversity of ways of combining ideas with word usage of which the European mind was unfamiliar. He wrote in his opening of the first volume of the transactions of the Historical and Literary Committee that he was willing to advance an understanding of Native American language as "polysynthetic," or as characterized by multiple layers of combinations

[95] Albert Gallatin, "A Synopsis of the Indian Tribes of North America," *Transactions of the American Antiquarian Society* (Cambridge, MA: Folsom, Wells, and Thurston, 1836), Vol. 2, pp. 143–4.

of basic word units.[96] In this, Du Ponceau argued, Native Americans were much closer to the classical Greek and Latin languages than to modern European languages, and he was fully aware of the widely held belief that the one aspect where the moderns had failed to surpass the ancients was in the arena of language and the art of its eloquent and effective use. For Du Ponceau, Native American language proved itself to be complex, diverse, and innovative, and he dismissed the theory of Adam Smith's essay on the origin of language, which suggested that peoples of savage nations had failed to develop the capacity to distinguish between the general and the specific.[97] Such a theory proved untenable given the evidence gathered by the Historical and Literary Committee, Du Ponceau declared. What their collections showed, according to Du Ponceau, was that unlike modern European languages, which developed through changes in inflection and pronunciation, Native American languages relied on a seemingly unending process of combining basic word units to represent diverse combinations of ideas. In the "customs, manners, and usages" to which an inquiry into Native American language offered a window, Du Ponceau found a record representing an albeit minimal level of capacity for reflective and productive use that was almost entirely dismissed by Jefferson.

Du Ponceau interpreted the history of usage through the inherited lens of the early modern emphasis on civil and intellectual history as the manifold development of and deployment of commonplaces. It was no accident that while he was sure of the Asiatic origins of the Native American population, it was what he found to be the structural similarities with Greek and Latin that most excited him. Nor was it an accident that he saw fit to record his initial inquiries with regard to Native American language in a commonplace book; indeed, in the blank pages of what started out as a personal legal docket book. He and Jefferson were antiquarians and historians of their respective states, and noted scholars of the law in addition to being talented attorneys. For both men, their own configurations of Native American language and history

[96] Du Ponceau, "Report of the Corresponding Secretary," *Transactions*, pp. xxvii, xxix.

[97] Adam Smith, "Considerations Concerning the First Formation of Languages," *The Theory of Moral Sentiments*, see pp. 407–9 (the essay was originally published in 1761, and included in the third edition of *The Theory of Moral Sentiments* in 1767); see Matthew Lauzon, *Signs of Light: French and British Theories of Linguistic Communication, 1648–1789* (Ithaca: Cornell University Press, 2010); Sean P. Harvey, *Native Tongues: Colonialism and Race from Encounter to the Reservation* (Cambridge, MA: Harvard University Press, 2015).

were linked to different visions of the organization of law and history for the new republic, and these were in turn linked to different visions for the legal basis and procedure for the extension of American sovereignty over the west. Du Ponceau, the European civil lawyer and committed, if eccentric, constitutional nationalist, who argued for the organic continuity of English common law in the new nation, stood in contrast to what Jefferson and others thought of as the jurisprudential imperatives of settler liberty and possession.

For his part, Jefferson had configured the ideal subject at the center of his project as a particular kind of user of the materials found in their environments. The goal of his legal and constitutional thought was to nurture a subject with the cultivated capacity actively situate themselves in multiple contexts and use the materials of those contexts dynamically in maintaining a republican polity. And if Jefferson's early theorizing was intended to make such a subject possible, his project in the *Notes* and in his turn to a national political career that would take him to the presidency was to secure that subject. At its core, as the text of the *Notes* makes clear, this was a rigidly racialized and gendered project, as well as a profoundly anxious and insecure one. What Jefferson confronted was not an ideal plane of Jeffersonian users, but a varied and incalculably pluralistic world of multiple lines of histories of usages, intersecting and colliding in equally unpredictable and ultimately ungovernable ways. The security of the usufruct of the living would come to depend on a political project of the circumscription and indeed the government of use.

5

Governing the Usufruct of the Living

When Thomas Jefferson returned to the United States from serving as minister to France in 1789, he took up his post as Secretary of State in the Washington administration and soon came to oppose much of what he found going on there. Against Alexander Hamilton's reports on the credit of the federal government and the long-term plans to contract a national debt, establish a national bank, compel use of federally issued paper currency among the citizenry at large, and encourage industrial development, Jefferson posed a vision of an agrarian commercial republic of specie currency whose factories would be in Europe, whose private and public debts would be paid off, and where concentrations of both economic and political power would be plural and diffuse across an expansive and expanding territory. Against Hamilton's attempts to align the United States with Great Britain in foreign affairs while emulating its political economy at home, Jefferson argued that revolutionary-era treaties with France were binding between the two nations regardless of the execution of Louis XVI, and that the vast potential of American agricultural production could give the United States sufficient leverage in Atlantic geopolitics to safely avoid alliance with Britain.[1] And in the

[1] On the practice of emulation in the development of political economy, see Sophus A. Reinhert, *Translating Empire: Emulation and the Origins of Political Economy* (Cambridge, MA: Harvard University Press, 2011); Drew R. McCoy, *The Elusive Republic: Political Economy in Jeffersonian America* (Chapel Hill: University of North Carolina Press, 1980); on the idea of the historical power of commerce to transform society, see J.G.A. Pocock, *The Machiavellian Moment: Florentine Political Thought and the Atlantic Republican Tradition* (Princeton: Princeton University Press, 1975, 2003), pp. 506–83; Lance Banning, *The Jeffersonian Persuasion: Evolution of a Party Ideology* (Ithaca:

animating spirit of the political culture of Jeffersonian democracy, against attempts to secure a political culture of deference and constituted sovereignty in the new federal government and the office of the presidency, Jefferson followed Democratic-Republican societies and allied writers and publishers in cultivating an oppositional stance characterized by the purposive imaging of populist sympathies and republican simplicity.[2]

Jefferson and Madison reacted to what they saw as a dangerous attempt to walk back one of the most basic ideas of the American Revolution, that sovereignty in a free state needed to be divided rather than concentrated. Indeed, the argument that High Federalism amounted to monarchy, monocracy, or consolidation, repeatedly made by Jefferson, Madison, and their allies in correspondence, pamphlets, and most famously in the Virginia and Kentucky Resolutions of 1798, testifies to the idea that what was at stake for republican opposition in the 1790s was a defense of a particular understanding of federalism.[3] Jefferson and Madison both took advantage political pressures and opportunities made by more popular, local, and radical political movements manifest in the spread of the Democratic-Republican societies in both rural and urban areas, and in the Whiskey Rebellion of 1794.[4] Jefferson and Madison

Cornell University Press, 1980); Joyce Appleby, *Capitalism and a New Social Order: The Republican Vision of the 1790s* (New York: New York University Press, 1984); *Liberalism and Republicanism in the Historical Imagination* (Cambridge, MA: Harvard University Press, 1992); Cathy D. Matson and Peter S. Onuf, *A Union of Interests: Political and Economic Thought in Revolutionary America* (Lawrence: University of Kansas Press, 1989); Gordon S. Wood, *Empire of Liberty: A History of the Early American Republic, 1789–1815* (Oxford: Oxford University Press, 2008); *The Reports of Alexander Hamilton*, Jacob E. Cooke, ed. (New York: Harper, 1964).

2 Andrew W. Robertson, *The Language of Democracy: Political Rhetoric in the United States and Great Britain* (Charlottesville: University of Virginia Press, 1994); Joanne B. Freeman, *Affairs of Honor: National Politics in the New Republic* (New Haven: Yale University Press, 1999); Jeffrey L. Pasley, *The Tyranny of Printers: Newspaper Politics in the Early American Republic* (Charlottesville: University of Virginia Press, 2002); Pasley Robertson, and David Waldstreicher, eds., *Beyond the Founders: New Approaches to the Political History of the Early American Republic* (Chapel Hill: University of North Carolina Press, 2003).

3 See Peter Onuf, *Jefferson's Empire: The Language of American Nationhood* (Charlottesville: University of Virginia Press, 2000); Brian Steele, *Thomas Jefferson and American Nationhood* (Cambridge: Cambridge University Press, 2012); on Madison's editing of his own notes from the constitutional convention to be more amenable to the republican opposition, see Mary Sarah Bilder, *Madison's Hand: Revising the Constitutional Convention* (Cambridge, MA: Harvard University Press, 2015).

4 Alfred F. Young, *The Democratic Republicans of New York: The Origins, 1763–1797* (Chapel Hill: University of North Carolina Press, 1967); Thomas P. Slaughter, *The Whiskey Rebellion: Frontier Epilogue to the American Revolution* (Oxford: Oxford

were themselves both slave owners, they represented men of similar means, and their attempt to secure their own propertied independence involved the rigid gendering and racialization of civic identity, constant, even desperate vigilance in the maintenance of checks on federal power, and the projection of a settler liberty predicated on the cancellation of Native American title to western land.[5]

The political project of Jeffersonian democracy emerged confronting differing interests and visions within its own camp and in rhetorical combat with the High Federalism of the 1790s and early years of Jefferson's presidency. Reacting against skepticism of the new constitution, and the global spectacle of the French Revolution and the prospect of transatlantic radicalism, Federalist leaders crafted their own politics of history, historiography, of reading and text. In his *Defense of the Constitutions of the Governments of the United States*, published in response to French criticism of the ordered bicameralism of American state and federal constitutionalism, John Adams sought to "lay before the public a specimen of that kind of reading and reasoning which produced the American constitutions."[6] Offering an extended constitutional history, ancient and

University Press, 1985); Richard J. Twomey, "Jacobins and Jeffersonians: Anglo-American Radical Ideology, 1790–1810," *The Origins of Anglo-American Radicalism*, Margaret C. Jacob and James R. Jacob, eds. (Atlantic Highlands and London: Humanities Press International, 1991), pp. 313–28; David Waldstreicher, *In the Midst of Perpetual Fetes: The Making of American Nationalism, 1776–1820* (Chapel Hill: University of North Carolina Press, 1997); Saul Cornell, *The Other Founders: Anti-Federalism and the Dissenting Tradition in America, 1788–1828* (Chapel Hill: University of North Carolina Press, 1998); Andrew Shankman, *Crucible of American Democracy: The Struggle to Fuse Egalitarianism and Capitalism in Jeffersonian Pennsylvania* (Lawrence: University of Kansas Press, 2004); Sean Wilentz, *The Rise of American Democracy: From Jefferson to Lincoln* (New York: Norton, 2005); Terry Bouton, *Taming Democracy: "The People," The Founders, and the Troubled Ending of the American Revolution* (Oxford: Oxford University Press, 2007); Matthew Rainbow Hale, "On Their Tiptoes: Political Time and Newspapers during Advent of the Radicalized French Revolution," *Journal of the Early Republic*, Vol. 29 (Summer 2009), pp. 191–218.

[5] Robin L. Einhorn, *American Taxation, American Slavery* (Chicago: University of Chicago Press, 2006); Caroll Smith-Rosenberg, *This Violent Empire: The Birth of an American National Identity* (Chapel Hill: University of North Carolina Press, 2010); George William Van Cleve, *A Slaveholder's Union: Slavery, Politics, and the Constitution in the Early American Republic* (Chicago: University of Chicago Press, 2010); Barbara Young Welke, *Law and the Borders of Belonging in the Long Nineteenth Century United States* (Cambridge: Cambridge University Press, 2010); Padraig Riley, *Slavery and the Democratic Conscience: Political Life in Jeffersonian America* (Philadelphia: University of Pennsylvania Press, 2015).

[6] John Adams, *A Defense of the Constitutions of Government of the United States of America, Against the Attack of M. Turgot in his Letter to Dr. Price* (Philadelphia: Budd and Bartram, 1797), Vol. 1, p. xv.

modern, Adams argued that American leaders had distilled the lessons of classical and more recent political history directly into political practice, designing institutions that reflected political and philosophical capacities not usually credited to Americans theorists by their European counterparts. Americans, Adams suggested, had observed the dangers of unifying sovereignty in any one component of the government, in the executive, legislative, judicial, or in the people themselves. Power and political judgment had been set apart from the ungovernable circulation of common sense, popular will, and public opinion.

Adams understood Jean-Jacques Rousseau's concept of the general will and French revolutionary republicanism more generally as an attempt to reinstitute ancient liberty and the confusion of the divine or absolute with the finite and historical that had allegedly plagued ancient republics. In contrast, he asserted an ordering of distinct spaces of different modes of reading and reflecting for politics and political judgment. The formation of a politicized populace through the instruments of print culture and social interaction and exchange would be one of those spaces to be sure, but it would not the only or even the driving one in any republic that hoped to last. Jefferson and Madison, too, each in their respective ways, cared deeply for the broadly conceived federalist project of breaking up concentrated political power. In their responses to the increasingly partisan political situation in which they found themselves, both Jefferson and Madison turned to the circulation of words and things in the print culture of a commercial republic as a retort to Federalist politics. Their challenge was to articulate an alternative theory of national governance, and that is exactly what they did.

To clear space for the land that would guarantee the independence of the proprietary citizen, but before articulating a legal basis for expansion, Jefferson and Madison had to articulate a logic by which a single polity spread out over vast territory could retain its coherence and its governability. Just so, what Jefferson, Madison, and their cohort of Republican leaders began to accept and argue for, largely through their translation and attempt at emulation of French social theory and political economy, was an understanding of an expanded republic held together by the conjoined bonds of commercial exchange and the diffusion of a national print culture, the organs of which were already proving to be powerful instruments of politics.[7] Crucially, the argument that they made was not

[7] The existence of a national print culture in the late eighteenth and early nineteenth centuries has been called into serious question by Trish Loughran; see *The Republic in Print: Print Culture in the Age of U.S. Nation Building, 1770–1870* (New York: Columbia

that such an arrangement would limit government, but that such an arrangement would be a more effective and efficient kind of government. As a result, the richly textured concept of liberty that had gone into the making of Jefferson's own revolutionary and even radical constitutionalism was emptied and transformed. In Jefferson's theoretical formulation, the activities of exchange overran the activities of republican political life, and the distribution and consumption of newspapers supplanted civic participation in the writing and rewriting of the text of the law. The origins of the enterprising and modernizing "empire of liberty" lay in particular historical configurations of early modern intellectual practice, and likewise the origins of much of the Jeffersonian language of a free press and deliberative democracy lay in an active forgetting of the concepts of legal and political practice that had given the very expression of that language its substance and vitality.

This argument dovetails with critical accounts of the emergence of liberal economic and political philosophy, liberalism, and liberal governmentality as elaborated in the work of Michel Foucault.[8] On a different register, it is important to note that this is not simply a story about the transition from republicanism to liberalism. Political thought shifted frequently in the face of real political challenges and the implications for law and government of territorial expansion. Jefferson and Madison, despite their substantive differences, could not fully imagine and implement what Jefferson called the "empire of liberty" without the blending of a settler

University Press, 2009); what I call attention to here is the importance of the idea of a national print culture to the political thinking of the time in addition to the impact of the idea and experience of print culture on the conditions for the theory and practice of political life and territorial governance, and I take that to be a salutatory implication of the original argument of Michael Warner, *Letters of the Republic: Publication and the Public Sphere in Eighteenth Century America* (Cambridge, MA: Harvard University Press, 1980); on the significance of print culture in the material conditions for nationalist imagining and capitalist social organization, the classic argument is of course Benedict Anderson, *Imagined Communities: Reflections on the Origin and Spread of Nationalism, Revised Edition* (London: Verso, 2006).

[8] See Michel Focuault, *Security, Territory, and Population: Lectures at the Collége de France, 1977–1978*, Graham Burchell, trans. Michel Senellart, ed. (New York: Palgrave Macmillan, 2007), and *The Birth of Biopolitics: Lectures at the Collège de France, 1978–1979*, Michael Sennelart, ed. Graham Burchell, trans. (New York: Palgrave Macmillan, 2008); Mary Poovey, *A History of the Modern Fact: Problems of Knowledge in the Sciences of Wealth and Society* (Chicago: University of Chicago Press, 1998); *Genres of the Credit Economy: Mediating Value in Eighteenth and Nineteenth Century Britain* (Chicago: University of Chicago Press, 2007); and Giorgio Agamben, *The Kingdom and the Glory: For a Theological Genealogy of Economy and Government*, Lorenzo Chiesa, trans. (Stanford: Stanford University Press, 2011), pp. 245–87.

concept of liberty, the project of cancelling Native title to western land, the articulation of a linear, uniform, and developmental idea of history, and perhaps most significantly, the idea that a flattened plane of commercial exchange and newspaper circulation allowed political thinking and constitutionalism to shed inherited wisdom on the limits of territorial sovereignty and expansion for republican governments. Transformations in theories of politics were as based in changing accounts of the circulation of words and things as they were in changing accounts of institutions.

These shifts in thinking and their implication for how Jefferson imagined the building of republican law and politics played a crucial role in the legal implementation of empire over the North American continent. Jefferson's turn to translating French political economy and social theory, apparent in his translation of Cosntantin-François de Volney's *Ruins of Empires* and most significantly and explicitly in Destutt de Tracy's *Commentary and Review of the Montesquieu's Spirit of the Laws* and the *Treatise on Political Economy*, played a crucial role in these shifts in thought. These changes in how Jefferson thought about the material and medial culture of political life in an expanded republic were in turn fundamental to the articulation and implementation of expansion policy and the cancelation of Native title. Seeking to break the cycle of translating and emulating the keys to the accumulation of wealth and power on the part of Atlantic imperial states, Jefferson turned to an alternative discourse for translation, and made a more powerful kind of empire conceptually possible. The contingencies of *translatio studii* were an essential part of the historical processes of *translatio imperii.*

For Jefferson, one part of the growing Republican critique of Federalist policy was a concern to maintain powers of police at local and state levels of governance. In 1811, after the rise of Napoleon, Jefferson would write to his collaborator Destutt de Tracy that such a consolidation of power in the central government, especially in the executive, was barely imaginable in the United States, where provincial assemblies and the diffusion of sovereignty across space checked centralization. In France, Jefferson wrote, "no provincial organizations existed to which the people might rally under authority of the laws, the seats of the directory were virtually vacant, and a small force sufficed to turn the legislature out of their chamber, & to salute its leader Chief of the nation."[9] A system of local

[9] Jefferson to Destutt de Tracy, January 26, 1811, *The Papers of Thomas Jefferson, Retirement Series*, J. Jefferson Looney, ed. (Princeton: Princeton University Press, 2007), Vol. 3, p. 338.

avenues for political participation and a revisionary constitutional culture were essential to representing and actualizing popular sovereignty, and channeling public supervision of the state. Jefferson could speak from experience. He would later testify in articulating the basis of his plan for ward republics in Virginia that such local political spaces were not only desirable on theoretical grounds but were in fact politically expedient, for he himself had felt the very grounds of the nation tremble under the widespread opposition in New England to the Embargo Act of 1807. In his drafting of the Kentucky resolution of 1798, Jefferson had gone beyond even Madison's doctrine of imposition and argued that states in some cases had a right and responsibility to nullify what they saw as unconstitutional federal legislation.

For Jefferson, what had been and continued to be at stake was the creation of civic spaces where deliberative citizens exercised the freedom to make use of the materials of their legal and constitutional history. What gradually supplanted this understanding was a circumscription of use in the service of a uniform territory tied together by commercial exchange. The exchange of goods and sentiments through commerce and the circulation of print reordered the textual and temporal contexts within which subjectivity was practiced, and the imaginary consent and the projection of historical inevitability constructed by that circulation were fundamental building blocks of the ideology of expansion. Indeed, in constructing a commercial and liberal justification for conquest, Jefferson and Madison arrived at a new ideology of empire.[10] It was this vision that allowed Jefferson and Madison to be so comfortable in asserting the political theory of an expansive republic and in defending their understanding of federalism. As we will see in the case of the Jefferson administration's attempt to reorder the legal structure of the New Orleans territory, and in Jefferson's own involvement in the political and legal complications of that attempt, the logic of this shift in

[10] For understanding the social and intellectual implications of print, I am heavily indebted here and elsewhere to Walter J. Ong, *Orality and Literacy: The Technologizing of the Word* (London: Routledge, 1982). On the historical dialectic of conquest and commerce as part of the ideology of *doux commerce*, see Anthony Pagden, *Ideologies of Empire: Britain, France, and Spain c. 1500–1800* (New Haven: Yale University Press, 1995); on liberalism as an ideology of nineteenth-century colonialism, see Uday Singh Mehta, *Liberalism and Empire: A Study in Nineteenth Century British Liberal Thought* (Chicago: University of Chicago Press, 1999); Jennifer Pitts, *A Turn to Empire: The Rise of Imperial Liberalism in Britain and France* (Princeton: Princeton University Press, 2005); Domenico Losurdo, *Liberalism: A Counter-History* (London: Verso, 2011).

thought lent itself to the projection of a uniform legal order over a territory of precisely the kind of jurisdictional multiplicity of which Jefferson himself had been such an admiring and attentive theorist. If Jefferson and Madison turned to political economy and their theory of commercial reciprocity in order to protect their understanding of republicanism at home and to guard the political and economic sovereignty of the United States abroad, to assert the nation's capacity to make law and historical direction for itself, their empire proved quite capable of organizing itself around the project of giving law and assigning history to others. For Jefferson, this amounted to a shift from the theory and practice of adaptive usage to the proscription and indeed the government of use.

This shift took place amid wider transformations in political thought from the legal multiplicity of early modern empires to the uniformity of the modern nation-state, and from jurisprudence to political economy as the organizing logic of social theory. Jefferson's fusion of theories of empire that had characterized Spanish and English justifications of conquest in the Americas was crucial here, arriving at a commercial argument for removal of Native title that blended the concerns of the theorists of Salamanca for the natural laws of trade and communication among peoples with the Lockean emphasis on appropriative cultivation. Jefferson obviously did not affect these transformations in thought on his own, but neither did he serve only as the passive register of inherited ideas or of historical transformation and development. His thinking, and his thinking about thinking, helped make the subject of revolutionary politics safe for commercial expansion and republican empire.

PROPERTY, CONSTITUTIONALISM, AND REPRESENTATION

"The earth," Jefferson famously wrote to Madison in 1789, "belongs in usufruct to the living."[11] A pithy statement that has always been easy to dismiss, it was in fact reflective of Jefferson's extensive thinking about the concepts of use, usufruct, and utility. Use, of course, was a fundamental concept of the English common law and wider legal humanist traditions in which Jefferson had immersed himself as a young law student, for whom the law and its history were nothing other than the

[11] Jefferson to James Madison, September 6, 1789, *The Papers of Thomas Jefferson*, (Princeton: Princeton University Press, 1953) Vol. 15, p. 392.

assemblage of accumulated usage over time.[12] Jefferson articulated the terms of the constitutional conflict that ultimately led to the American Revolution as nothing less than a request on the part of British American settlers to have the particular provincial uses they had made of themselves, their possessions, and their histories acknowledged by those whom they saw as their equals in a confederated empire of self-governing communities, and in the end this became a defense of the collective liberty to define the terms of that use itself. Settlers, Jefferson wrote in his 1774 pamphlet *The Summary View of the Rights of British America*, had set up their own polities upon settlement, and so the King was "no more than the chief officer of the people, appointed by the laws, and circumscribed with definite powers, to assist in working the great machine of government, erected for their use, and consequently subject to their superintendence."[13]

Amid the theoretical radicalism of salon intellectual life in which he participated as minister to France, Jefferson extended his critique of law and legal institutions that were subtracted from practices of historical reevaluation and use, and from spaces wherein such deliberative practices could take place. It will be useful here to briefly revisit Jefferson's correspondence with Madison. Property, like language and even law itself, was subject to having its laws reconsidered and remade for the possibility of new use. As he wrote to Madison in 1785:

> I am conscious that an equal division of property is impracticable, but the consequences of this enormous inequality producing so much misery to the bulk of mankind, legislators cannot invent too many devices for subdividing property, only taking care to let their subdivisions go hand in hand with the natural affections of the human mind. The descent of property of every kind therefore to all children, or to all the brothers and sisters, or other relations in equal degree, is a politic measure and a practicable one. Another means of silently lessening the inequality of property is to exempt all from taxation below a certain point, and to tax the higher portions or property in geometrical progression as they rise. Whenever there are in any country uncultivated lands and unemployed poor, it is clear that the laws of property have been so far extended as to violate natural right. The earth is given as a common stock for man to labor and live in. If for the encouragement of industry we allow it to be appropriated, we must take care that

[12] Pocock, *The Ancient Constitution and the Feudal Law: A Study of English Historical Thought in the Seventeenth Century, a Reissue with Retrospect* (Cambridge: Cambridge University Press, 1987).

[13] Jefferson, "Summary View of the Rights of British America," *The Papers of Thomas Jefferson*, Vol. 1, p. 121.

other employment be provided to those excluded from the appropriation. If we do not, the fundamental right to labor the earth returns to the unemployed.[14]

Jefferson recommends to a friendly but suspicious Madison that if legislators are going to avoid having property become a question of directly political contestation, where the conflict between property and the people could become so central and even violent that it would be a threat to the polity, then laws will need to be adjusted to provide for the maintenance of a roughly egalitarian holding of landed property, or if need be the dispossessed will justly look to other means of self-possessing provision. Much like Jefferson's later celebrations of the Shays Rebellion in correspondence with Madison and Abigail Adams, or in his tremendous fear of the very real possibility of a slave rebellion in the *Notes on the State of Virginia*, the tone and spirit of the note is at least as much one of Machiavellian caution as it is of revolution, even of a kind of Baconian reason of state: if a revolution happens against us we probably deserve it, so we should take care to ensure the stability and security of the state by effecting a relatively equal distribution of means and possession among a white proprietary class (note that "sisters," while not admitted to full legal personality in any of Jefferson's provisions, here are acknowledged as equally legitimate holders of the property of their mothers and fathers). "The small landholders," Jefferson continues, "are the most precious part of a state."[15] Just so, the maintenance of the free and republican state meant the protection and encouragement of this precious, self-possessed and self-governing citizen whose rights as a proprietary and independent settler if unacknowledged would again take the form of the right of revolution.

That the guiding principle for the legislator in Jefferson's formulation consists not simply in natural rights or a prudent respect for the lessons of history but instead in the "natural affections of the human mind" puts his thought in direct conversation with Scottish and French Enlightenment discourses of historical development, civil society, and the significance of opinion. "Nothing appears more surprising to those, who consider human affairs with a philosophical eye," David Hume famously wrote, "than the easiness with which the many are governed by the few." Upon inquiry, Hume declares in his essay "On the First Principles of

[14] Jefferson to Madison, October 28, 1785, *The Papers of Thomas Jefferson*, Vol. 8, p. 682.

[15] *Ibid*; in his 1776 draft of his proposal for the Virginia constitution, Jefferson included provision for putting property and inheritance law under Gavelkind with the exception of guaranteeing the equal property rights of women; Jefferson, Third Draft of Proposal for the Virginia Constitution, *The Papers of Thomas Jefferson*, Vol. 1, p. 363.

Government," published in 1742, we will find "as FORCE is always on the side of the governed, the governors have nothing to support them but opinion. It is therefore on opinion only that government is founded, and this maxim extends to the most despotic and most military governments, as well as to the most free and popular."[16]

For Hume, for Adam Smith, for Marie-Jean-Antoine-Nicolas de Caritat, marquis de Condorcet, and for Thomas Jefferson, modern societies would come to find themselves in the midst of revolutions in government wrought by and through changes in sentiments and opinion.[17] A growing and deeply historical awareness that the fates of governments and empires could be driven less by prudent statecraft than by the potentially ungovernable waves of shifts in intellectual history and public opinion often nurtured a spectrum of contradictory attitudes among leading theorists of the day. This spectrum could range from severe doubts and even cynicism about the wisdom of government policies interfering with domestic and international commerce to profound ambivalence about commercial activity itself, and from hopeful policy prescriptions to Condorcet's projection of the possibility of the perfection of humanity in his *Equisse d'un tableau historique des progrès de l'espirit humain* of 1795, the year after his death in a French revolutionary prison.[18] Jefferson was unique perhaps in his ability to express all of these attitudes over the course of his career in politics, even in some cases at roughly the same time. What tied these disparate turns in thought together and brought them into conversation with one another was an assumption that moral philosophy and political economy were inseparable, and that the promise of commerce for the achievement of a peaceful future rested not just with heads of state but with the broad cultivation of capacities for affective participation in modern civil and commercial life among the

[16] David Hume, "On the First Principles of Government," *Essays Moral, Political, and Literary*, Revised Edition, Eugene F. Miller, ed. (Indianapolis: Liberty Fund, 1987), p. 32; on coordination in Hume's thought generally and his *History of England* in particular, see Andrew Sabl, *Hume's Politics: Coordination and Crisis in the History of England* (Princeton: Princeton University Press, 2012).

[17] On the power of emotion and sentiment in the formation of politicized public opinion, and fear of that power as it was confronted by the political thought of the American Revolution, see Nicole Eustace, *Passion is the Gale: Emotion, Power, and the Coming of the American Revolution* (Chapel Hill: University of North Carolina Press, 2008); Sarah Knott, *Sensibility in the American Revolution* (Chapel Hill: University of North Carolina Press, 2009).

[18] See Condorcet, "The Sketch [of an Historical Account of the Progress of the Human Mind]," *Political Writings*, Steven Lukes and Nadia Urbinati, eds. (Cambridge: Cambridge University Press, 2012), pp. 1–147.

population at large. Just as Hume and Smith turned a great deal of their attention to the customarily developed rules of individual belief, moral behavior, and the artful and prudent communication of differing beliefs and opinions, so Condorcet followed these Scottish influences and those of his teacher, the Physiocrat Anne-Robert-Jacques Turgot, in envisioning a plan for universal national education that would cultivate desirable and constructive abilities, and in proposing a modern political and electoral system that would drive, direct, and take stock of developments in an increasingly well-informed and judicious public opinion.[19] At the center of the emergent discourse of political economy across the mid- and late eighteenth-century republic of letters was the question of the socially and historically situated subjectivity appropriate to that world.

These conjoined projects were attempts to practice and inculcate what Emma Rothschild has called a "disposition of enlightenment," the ability to live in and with "multiple contexts," and most of all, "a discursive, disputatious, theorizing way of life."[20] Principally, this meant fostering

[19] In the liberation of religious conscience from legal regulation, the establishment of universal systems of public education, and the increase of power and authority in provincial assemblies, both saw the promise for cultivating the "disposition of enlightenment" on a wide scale. While Jefferson, in theory, was more of a democratic constitutionalist than Condorcet, the latter saw no space in the new world of advanced civilization for slavery, for territorial conquest, or for the failure to recognize women as equals. Indeed, Jefferson began to translate Condorcet's essay on the condition of African slaves in the French colony of Saint-Domingue, an essay that saw any perceived lack of civilization among slave populations in the colonies as entirely an effect of the conditions to which they had been subject. On the reform projects of Condorcet, see "On the Influence of the American Revolution on Europe," "Essay on the Constitution and Functions of the Provincial Assemblies (postscript)," "On the Admission of Women to the Rights of Citizenship," and "The Nature and Purpose of Public Instruction," in Keith Michael Baker, ed. *Selected Writings of Condorcet* (Indianapolis: Bobbs-Merrill, 1976), pp. 33–87, 97–142; Thomas Jefferson "Jefferson's Notes From Condorcet on Slavery," *Papers of Thomas Jefferson*, Vol. 14, pp. 494–8; Emma Rothschild, *Economic Sentiments: Adam Smith, Condorcet, and Enlightenment* (Cambridge, MA: Harvard University Press, 2001), pp. 48–9. See also David Williams, *Condorcet and Modernity* (Cambridge: Cambridge University Press, 2004). On Jefferson's relation (or lack thereof) to Condorcet's social science, see Arnold B. Urken, "The Condorcet-Jefferson Connection and the Origins of Social Choice Theory," *Public Choice*, Vol. 72, No. 2/3 (1991), pp. 213–36, and Iain McLean and Arnold B. Urken, "Did Jefferson or Madison Understand Condorcet's Theory of Social Choice?" *Public Choice*, Vol. 73, No. 4 (June 1992), pp. 445–57. Jefferson would later translate Destutt de Tracy's skepticism of Condorcet's electoral project as an abstraction from actual, institutionally situated political life in Tracy's *Treatise on Political Economy*, Thomas Jefferson, trans. Jeremy Jennings, ed. (Indianapolis: Liberty Fund, 2011), p. 46.

[20] Emma Rothschild, *Economic Sentiments: Adam Smith, Condorcet, and the Enlightenment* (Cambridge, MA: Harvard University Press, 2001), pp. 48–9.

private persons who could also be conscious members of a complex, developed polity and participate in the formation of collective judgment on matters of social and political importance, who could be believers, citizens, workers, thinkers, and consumers, and live productively and sensibly in all of these various contexts. "I consider man as formed for society, and endowed by nature with those dispositions which fit him for society," Jefferson wrote in 1799. "I believe also, with Condorcet," he continued, "that his mind is perfectible to a degree of which we cannot as yet form any conception."[21] And yet despite the undeniable optimism for the future that he was capable of finding and expressing, it would be difficult to understand Jefferson's turn to the discourse of political economy as that of the organizing principles of society without appreciating the rather peculiar manner in which he arrived at that turn: through a unique focus on the material and textual forms of the relations of law, politics, and commerce in which members of society lived and grew as citizens. At least initially, even as he and his fellows embarked on careers in a newly constituted national political scene, Jefferson continued working with an understanding of the text of the law as the material in and through which a discursive, disputations, and theorizing citizenry constituted and governed itself.

The significance of texts and textuality to Jefferson's configuring of the republican citizen, the long reach of legal humanism in the trajectory of his thinking, and his concern for the historical construction of national identity are apparent in his rather eccentric approach to the symbolic valuation of money. The ductile malleability of denomination observed by Jefferson in the history of currencies in western Europe and the Americas provides a critical vantage point from which to see the tensions in his thinking about the human subject of commercial society unfolding as he preoccupied himself with the problems of the politics of nation-building. Building on his discussion of the state and federal currencies in the United States in his contemporaneous composition of the *Notes on the State of Virginia*, in a report later included as an appendix to the book, Jefferson laid out the principles of familiarity, ease of use in purchasing, and ease of calculation to guide the establishment of a single money unit

[21] Jefferson to William Green Munford, June 18, 1799, *The Papers of Thomas Jefferson*, Vol. 31, p. 127; on the importance of the conjunction of political economy and public opinion in the early republic, see Mark Schmeller, "The Political Economy of Opinion: Public Credit and Concepts of Public Opinion in the Age of Federalism," *Journal of the Early Republic*, Vol. 29. No. 1 (Spring 2009), pp. 35–61.

for the new nation. Working from the basic assumption of the intrinsic value of coin rooted in its backing by the respective weighted values of gold and silver in domestic markets, Jefferson urged averaging the statutory weights of the relative value of silver to gold among what he hoped would be the nation's future major trading partners, France and Spain, in order to foster favorable conditions of exchange. "The proportion between the values of gold and silver is a mercantile problem altogether," Jefferson suggested, but as the newly appointed minister to France, charged with opening markets to American whale oil and agricultural surplus, he was keenly aware of the importance of problems that would have otherwise struck the self-styled independent and self-contained Virginia planter as the concern of shopkeepers and traders.[22] That being said, the ease Jefferson assumes in surveying the range of options for not only the minting and denomination but the value of currency is striking, and telling of the fact that Jefferson was working with assumptions and arguments that were not widely shared. At the center of policy debates in the new federal government, Jefferson nevertheless remained what Mary Poovey calls a "money amateur," operating with conceptual categories and practices that were marginal to mainstream economic discourse to say the least. Indeed, Jefferson's insistence on seeing money as historical representation, as a kind of writing, was at odds with the prevailing processes bringing about naturalization of money as a mechanism within theoretically imminent and self-organizing systems of exchange.[23] Jefferson continued to be concerned with keeping the historical reality of practices of representation in view.

[22] Jefferson, "Notes on Coinage," The Papers of Thomas Jefferson, Vol. 7, p. 180; see pp. 175–88; Jefferson was responding to the proposals of Robert Morris to Congress advocating, among other things, basing the system of money of account and legal tender as much as possible on the British one for the convenience of its familiarity and use in Anglo-American trade, and laid out the possibility of a paper currency to grease the wheels of domestic commerce, an idea that was then and later anathema to Jefferson; see Robert Morris to the President of Congress, Office of Finance, January 15, 1782, *Papers of Thomas Jefferson*, Vol. 7, pp. 160–9; see Jefferson's correspondence with Morris and further on the subject, particularly in Jefferson's assistance on adopting the dollar and a decimal system for the relative values of the new coinage and for the system of weights and measures, *ibid*, pp. 189–202.

[23] Mary Poovey, *Genres of the Credit Economy: Mediating Value in Eighteenth and Nineteenth Century Britain* (Chicago: University of Chicago Press, 2008); see also March Shell, *Money, Language, and Thought: Literary and Philosophic Economies from the Medieval to the Modern Era* (Berkeley and Los Angeles: University of California Press, 1982); Christine Desan, *Making Money: Coin, Currency, and the Coming of Capitalism* (Oxford: Oxford University Press, 2015).

In manuscript notes folded into his personal copy of the 1787 edition of the *Notes*, very likely in conjunction with his authorship of the 1790 *Report on Weights and Measures* for Congress, Jefferson added an extended discussion of the history of the influence of Greek and Roman currency on British and colonial American coinage. Part of Jefferson's larger goal to place the standards of weight and measure and with them the valuation of coinage on a simple decimal system, his *Report* was also a reflection of its author's concerns for the histories represented in the choices he and others were making about the symbolic mediums of commercial exchange, and for the politics of those histories. By and large, the goal of the report was to advocate reforming practices already in use to make uniform standards of measurement, particularly of length, capacity or volume, and weight, the latter of which would have a direct effect on currency. "The first settlers of these states having come chiefly from England," Jefferson admited in the ambitious second and final draft of the report, "brought with them the measures and weights of that country. These alone are generally established among us, either by law or usage, and these therefore are alone to be retained and fixed."[24] But in a move that we should by now recognize as typical, Jefferson also noted that this history of use and establishment was more complex than a narrative of simple transition and adoption would have allowed.

Jefferson drew particular attention to the avoirdupois, noting what he found to be evidence of its ancient and continued use in Britain and the colonies, respectively, and further noting in drafts that not only would keeping it in general use be a matter of popular familiarity and convenience, but it would tie French and American commerce together more easily. And so in weights and coinage as in law and language Jefferson understood the political choices being made about the mathematical language of science and commerce as precisely that, as choices debated, legislated, and recast in time. Jefferson's notes made the connection between republican law and republican money explicit: in states where the dollar was valued at six shillings, he suggested, "the coincidence of their currency with that of the Greek and Roman monies is so singular as to be worthy of notice and to found a suspicion that this object may have had some influence in fixing our monies at this particular point, when the value of

[24] Jefferson, "Report on Weights and Measures," (1790), *Papers of Thomas Jefferson*, Vol. 16, p. 654; see Jefferson to Robert Patterson, November 10, 1811, *Papers of Thomas Jefferson, Retirement Series*, Vol. 4, pp. 222–30.

Greek and Roman learning was more justly estimated than at this day."[25] A classical historical framework and imagery here does the familiar ideological work of historicizing cultural attachment to a singular colonial-imperial history as authoritative or binding, recasting that history as one of creole settlers shedding or changing old uses and adopting new ones, in light of other histories of adoption and settlement.

Working from early modern British antiquarian scholarship on the values of Roman coins, Jefferson suggested that the gradual combinations and parallel uses of avoirdupois and tory measurements made them easily decimalized and so preferable for use in the establishment of the dollar as a basic money unit. "A more natural, accurate, and curious reconciliation of the two systems of Greece and Rome which happened to be found in use could not have been imagined; and the extension of the connection, from weights and measures, to coins, as is done so integrally by our *Lawful* currency... has completed the system."[26] The important thing to note here is Jefferson's insistence on the legislated and so historically contingent and pluralistic quality of even the denomination and value of currency, nearly a century after the triumph of the asserted natural laws of money and markets.[27] Flaunting that century of wisdom on the foolishness of regular legislative intervention in adjusting or changing currency, Jefferson

[25] The manuscript notes are in Jefferson's personal copy of the 1787 edition of the *Notes on the State of Virginia*, Special Collections Library, University of Virginia, and are printed in the explanatory and textual notes to Jefferson, *Notes on the State of Virginia*, Frank Shuffleton, ed. (New York: Penguin, 1999), pp. 322–4; Jefferson cites Edward Brerewood, Basil Kennett, and Robert Ainsworth in his notes; see Shuffleton, "Explanatory and Textual Notes," in *Notes on the State of Virginia*; John J. McCusker, *Money and Exchange in Europe and America, 1600–1775: A Handbook* (Chapel Hill: University of North Carolina Press, 1978); McCusker and Russell R. Menard, *The Economy of British North America, 1607–1789* (Chapel Hill: University of North Carolina Press, 1985); Niall Ferguson, *The Ascent of Money: A Financial History of the World* (New York: Penguin, 2008). Coinage had been a chief concern of Jefferson's in and before the writing of the *Notes*, as early as his work in the Second Continental Congress and on legal reform in Virginia; see Jefferson, "Notes for the Report on the Value of Gold and Silver Coins," September 2, 1776, and "Bill for Altering the Rates of Copper Coin in Virginia," November 7, 1776, pp. 511–18, 597.

[26] Jefferson, *Notes on the State of Virginia*, explanatory and textual notes, p. 324.

[27] Locke articulated the natural law of money in the wake of the publication of his *Two Treatises on Civil Government* and in the debates leading up to and surrounding the coinage controversy in 1696; John Locke, *Some Considerations on the Consequences of the Lowering of Interest and Raising the Value of Money* (London, 1691), and *Further Considerations on Raising the Value of Money* (London, 1695); Peter Laslett, "John Locke, the Great Recoinage, and the Origins of the Board of Trade," *William and Mary Quarterly*, Vol. 14 (1957), pp. 378–85; Joyce Appleby, *Economic Thought and Ideology in Seventeenth Century England* (Princeton: Princeton University Press, 1978); Carl

proceeded on the assumption that monetary value and the measurement system that supported it was like just about anything else subject to the deliberative practices of law and political life. The very media of associational and economic activity were not taken for granted nor assumed to be obeying unchanging natural laws but were in fact understood to be created, developed, and embedded in a civic and historical context of law.

Disappointed with the unwillingness of members of Congress to entertain an overhaul of the system of weights, measures, and coinage used for domestic and international trade, Jefferson cautioned that in the future "the citizens of the U.S. may be induced to undertake a thorough reformation of their whole system of measures, weights, and coins, reducing every branch to the same decimal ratio already established in their coins, and thus bringing the calculation of the principal affairs of life within the arithmetic of every man who can multiply and divide plain numbers," and even then further changes would be necessary.[28] Ideally, weights, measures, and coinage like law and language would be acknowledged and remembered as subject to future reconsideration. In a culture of republican political life, common use and the principles of encouraging and safeguarding it would guide the activities of an enlightened legislator. The operative assumption here is what Jedediah Purdy has identified as a legally constructed and constructivist one, and it proceeded in Jefferson's thinking quite directly from a profound and widely applied skepticism of attributions of meaning and value that were subtracted or enclosed from collective practices of consideration and revision in time.[29] A practical hermeneutics of common use, and a project of enabling a subject with the capacity for active participation in these practices would continue to guide much of Jefferson's thinking about national political life, particularly in his criticism of the spread of relations of credit and debt and for him the frightful prospect of a paper currency. But as he elaborated his own project in consort with ideological allies and in strident debate with the political culture, jurisprudence, and political economy of High Federalism, he would himself go a long way in changing the terms of that project, ultimately undermining it for the sake of its very coming to fruition.

Winnerland, *Casualties of Credit: The English Financial Revolution, 1620–1720* (Cambridge, MA: Harvard University Press, 2011).

[28] Jefferson, "Report on Weights and Measures," p. 663.

[29] Jedediah Purdy, *The Meaning of Property: Freedom, Community, and the Legal Imagination* (New Haven: Yale University Press, 2010).

COMMERCE AND EMPIRE

For Jefferson, domestic concentrations of wealth and power in the form of banks dictating policy to governments and the influx of foreign cash encouraged by the spread of private relations of credit and debt threatened both the republican government and indeed the sovereignty of the United States. By such means could both powerful private interests and foreign powers be in a position to give law to a purportedly self-governing people, a situation that would only be exacerbated by what in Jefferson's perspective would be the crippling effect of public debt maintained in the service of financial capitalism and the fiscal-military state. In correspondence with his son-in-law John Wayles Eppes in 1813, Jefferson argued against the holding of long-term public debt and the growing dependence of the national economy on the circulation and use of bank-issued notes whose value changed with the whims of bankers, shareholders, and the market, repeating his claim that the earth belongs to the living, that the usufruct of it passes to the next generation, and that in matters of debt as in matters of constitutionalism, no generation has any more right to bind another to its decisions than one nation has the right to direct another.[30] These were not mere speculations. For Jefferson, if the

[30] Jefferson to John Wayles Eppes, June 24, 1813, September 11, 1813, November 6, 1813, *The Papers of Thomas Jefferson, Retirement Series*, Vol. 6, pp. 220–6, 490–9, 578–94; the conjunction of national self-determination and individual self-ownership and so self-governance is explicit: "There have existed nations, & civilized & learned nations who have thought that a father had a right to sell his child as a slave, in perpetuity; that he could alienate his body & industry conjointly, and a fortiori his industry separately; and consume it's fruits himself. A nation asserting this Saticide right might well suppose they could burthen with public as well as private debt, their '*nati natorum, et qui nascentur ab illis*,' [the line is from Virgil's Aeneid: 'the children of their children, and those who will be born to them'] but we, in this age, and in this country especially, are advanced beyond these notions of natural law. We acknowledge that our children are born free; that their freedom is the gift of nature, and not of him who begot them; that tho' under our care during infancy, and therefore of necessity under a duly tempered authority, that care is confided to us to be exercised for the preservation & good of the child only; and his labours during youth are given as a retribution for the charges of infancy, as he was never the property of his father, so, when adult, he is *sui juris*, entitled himself to the use of his own limbs, and the fruits of his own exertions. So far we are advanced, without mind enough it seems, to take the whole step. We believe, or act as if we believed, and altho' an individual father cannot alienate the labor of his son, the aggregate body of fathers may alienate the labors of all their sons, & of their posterity, in the aggregate, and oblige them to pay for all the enterprises, just or unjust, profitable or ruinous, into which our vices, our passions, and our personal interests may lead us," Jefferson to John Wayles Eppes, September 11, 1813, *ibid*, p. 492. On Jefferson, debt, and the idea of generational

United States continued on its current path of being Britain's "unfortunate copyist" in matters of political economy, it would quickly be subject to the convulsive tendencies of speculation and driven into further conflict with European powers over the global balance of trade.[31]

By 1813, four years into his retirement from the Presidency and in the midst of war with Britain, Jefferson had good reason to take up his pen in correspondence on the subjects of banks and money. By then, his own ideological allies James Madison, Trench Coxe, and Albert Gallatin, the Secretary of the Treasury, were in agreement that letting the first national bank expire in 1811 and the failure to encourage manufacturing had proved a colossal roadblock in the federal government's ability to raise and move capital, and so to make war. For Jefferson, the Republican uptake of some of the basic assumptions of Federalist politics played into a classically republican narrative of corruption – the concentration of private and public capital would increase the power of the federal government and the ability of private interests to shape how that power was used, and it was not unreasonable in this framework to expect the creation of a standing army and a tax and tariff structure strong enough to support its maintenance and inevitably, its more frequent use. But by this time Jefferson, Madison, and Gallatin were at the tail end of more than two decades of attempting to articulate and implement a system of political economy that could safeguard American political and economic independence abroad while maintaining a republican government over what after the Louisiana Purchase in 1803 was an increasingly expansive territory at home. By Jefferson's retirement, the project of submitting the territory of the North American continent to the mechanisms and demands of what was with increasing urgency asserted to be self-governing, self-organizing, and self-perpetuating commercial society was well on its way.[32] And this project was one in which Jefferson had played a leading role.

Even so, it is undeniable that especially at the outset of his mature career in national politics, Jefferson felt a deep ambivalence about commerce and the entrapments of finance and credit that developed in

sovereignty, see Herbert E. Sloan, *Principle and Interest: Thomas Jefferson and the Problem of Debt* (Charlottesville: University of Virginia Press, 1995).

[31] Jefferson to John Wayles Eppes, September 1, 1813, *ibid*, p. 494.

[32] On the conjunction of the course of the War of 1812 and the course of the war with a commercial and liberal political culture at home with a vigorously asserted militarism, see Steven Watts, *The Republic Reborn: War and the Making of Liberal America, 1790–1820* (Baltimore: Johns Hopkins University Press, 1987).

its wake. He would write to John Jay from Paris in 1785 to address the question of whether encouragement of domestic manufacturing should become national policy. "We have now lands enough to employ an infinite number of people in their cultivation," Jefferson wrote, for "cultivators of the earth are the most valuable citizens." When the time came where land supply could no longer provide for infinite plots of small scale agriculture, Jefferson observed he would rather have citizens turn to the sea for employment than manufacturing labor. The dependence on wages from owners that characterized the plight of the "class of artificers" is what made that class the potential "instruments by which the liberties of a country are generally overturned."[33] Keeping the people employed in agriculture for as long as possible would be the best policy for the young republic, and it would allow the United States to be in a position to punish European powers for abuses against American sea trade with the threat of an embargo, cutting off Britain, France, or Spain from American produce.

Jefferson would write that same year: "Were I to indulge my own theory, I should wish them [American citizens] to practice neither commerce nor navigation, but to stand with respect to Europe precisely on the footing of China. We should thus avoid wars, and all our citizens would be husbandmen."[34] America would thus avoid for as long as possible the fluid and inter-subjective world of commercial exchange and credit in favor of, in theory, a totally self-contained and self-possessive practice of political economy. "But this is theory only," Jefferson continued:

> Our people have a decided taste for navigation and commerce. They take this from their mother country: & their servants are in duty bound to calculate all their measures on this datum: we wish to do it by throwing open all the doors of commerce & knocking off its shackles. But as this cannot be done for others, unless they will do it for us, & there is no great probability that Europe will do this, I suppose we shall be obliged to adopt a system which may shackle them in our ports as they us in theirs.[35]

It was precisely along these lines that in his second term as President Jefferson pursued his widely unpopular embargo of British goods and commerce in American ports, predicated as that policy was on a theory of

[33] Jefferson to John Jay, August 23, 1785, *The Papers of Thomas Jefferson*, Vol. 8, p. 426.

[34] Jefferson to G.K. von Hogendorp, October 13, 1785, *The Papers of Thomas Jefferson*, Vol. 8, p. 633.

[35] *Ibid*, p. 633.

commercial reciprocity.[36] The virtue and productive power of American agriculture could be used to demand international respect for its place "among the powers of the earth," in the words of the Declaration of Independence. But it was well known to Jefferson that public virtue and the spread of commercial relations within and between polities hardly went hand in hand. Despite his expressed belief that commerce, if allowed to follow its own historically developed natural rules, could reduce and ultimately eliminate the need for contests of Atlantic imperial rivalry and the standing armies necessary to fight them, Jefferson in fact possessed a deep ambivalence about commercial activity at the same time that he began to employ a language of historical inevitability about its triumph.

Not only did commerce threaten the economic independence of the farmer, and with that independence the civic health of the republic, but for all of its promise it risked the explosion in Hume's terms of the "jealousy of trade," the unwarranted but powerful and widely held belief that the wealth of other states was a direct threat to the wealth of one's own. "Nature, by giving a diversity of geniuses, climates, and soils, to different nations, has secured their mutual intercourse and commerce, as long as they all remain industrious and civilized," Hume asserted.[37] While commerce in theory pacified customs and deflated overzealous national sentiment, bringing about increasing interdependence, in its potential for the creation of large amounts of taxable flowing wealth, commerce could put even the most interdependent nations in conflicts of economic interest. Aside from the massive debt incurred by states seeking to protect their colonial possessions and commercial interests abroad, on both the domestic and international fronts the growing interdependence of commerce threatened local sovereignties by compelling dependence on an abstract

[36] Indeed, as Drew McCoy points out, Jefferson thought that the embargo would prove an opportunity to the greatly increased adoption of household manufacturing among the population at large, leading to what McCoy calls a hoped-for domestication of the industrial revolution, McCoy, *The Elusive Republic: Political Economy in Jeffersonian America*, pp. 227–30.

[37] David Hume, "The Jealousy of Trade," *Economic Writings*, Eugene Rotwein, ed. (Madison: University of Wisconsin Press, 1970), p. 79; Istvan Hont, *The Jealousy of Trade: International Competition and the Nation-State in Historical Perspective* (Cambridge, MA: Harvard University Press, 2005). On the embargo and the ideological origins of Jefferson's commercial policies as President, see Burton Spivak, *Jefferson's English Crisis: Commerce, Embargo, and the Republican Revolution* (Charlottesville: University of Virginia Press, 1979); Robert W. Tucker, and David C. Hendrickson, *Empire of Liberty: The Statecraft of Thomas Jefferson* (Oxford: Oxford University Press, 1990); Doron S. Ben-Atar, *The Origins of Jeffersonian Commercial Policy and Diplomacy* (New York: Palgrave-Macmillan, 1993).

and extra-national marketplace.[38] Such dependence made not only the fruits of the land but the land itself pieces of moveable, marketable, and creditable property, a daunting prospect for Jefferson's envisioned republic of self-sufficient, fee-simple land holders. Hoping to keep the United States out of the dangerous cycle of jealousy, emulation, and conflict identified by Hume, Jefferson turned to the translation of emergent French social theory critical of state intervention in the economy and positing the potential of commerce to render silent the jealous and contentious tendencies of modern states.

There was however a central ideological tension in the Jeffersonian vision of the republic, and that tension presented itself in how Jefferson himself received French historical philosophy and political economy. The tension arose from the shared commitment to the ideal of diffuse, fragmented sovereignties of multiple polities on the one hand and the extension of governance over an expanded space on the other, and it seems to have been the principal goal of Jefferson's thinking about commerce to either keep this tension at bay or to ignore it altogether. That tension was apparent in Jefferson's partial translation of Volney, begun in 1791, wherein the disparate and contentious peoples of the world gather at the feet of a group of philosophers and ask the men to decide on the questions and disagreements among the nations. Embodying what was increasingly a trope of continental Enlightenment thought, that religious difference (and not only religious intolerance) was at the root of human conflict, particularly in the previous centuries of religious wars that had plagued early modern Europe, the philosophers in Volney's projection are obliged to take up the task of codifying a natural law culled from their study of the rise and fall of empires that would in turn be binding on all of the nations of the world.[39] The tale enacts a fantasy of universal consent to the activities of enlightened legislators whose jurisdiction is the earth, a powerful fantasy indeed to self-styled enlightened legislators confronted

[38] As Adam Smith would observe in *The Wealth of Nations*, in contrast to ancient republics and the hopes of their modern admirers, modern states were driven to increasingly large expenditures on defense, and to such an extent that preparation for, to say nothing of prosecution of, war constituted the bulk of an inevitably large public debt in all of the commercial powers; see Smith, *An Inquiry into the Nature and Causes of the Wealth of Nations*, Edwin Cannan, ed. (Chicago: University of Chicago Press, 1976), Vol. 2, pp. 218–30.

[39] On Volney's contribution to national and racial historicisms, see Edward W. Said, *Orientalism* (New York: Vintage, 1979); Martin Thom, *Republics, Nations, and Tribes* (London: Verso, 1995).

with the condition of human plurality. In a separate essay on "The Law of Nature," translated and published with the English translation of *Les Ruines* in 1802, commerce served as the mechanism by which this universal code would be measured and enforced. Justice, in this framework, means recognizing and honoring the equality of all men in their rights of possession and exchange.

In labor and in equal exchanges of its fruits, in Volney's imagery, men would meet their need for "fraternal sentiments and reciprocal wants," and from this they will draw the "preservative and beneficent character of paternity."[40] The construction of a gendered and possessive subject of law and commerce is clear, and its attraction to Jefferson and his vision of an expansive republic of settler freeholders enacting the natural laws of sociable exchange is easily imaginable. That in a globalized age of commerce it was more necessary than ever to reform the law and structures of state power and international relations to reflect the "order of nature" asserted by Volney was another growing theme of enlightened narratives of government and society, as present in the earlier French Physiocratic positing of a natural order as it was in Adam Smith's positing of a "system of natural liberty."[41] Gradually coming to assume the possibility of a spontaneous and natural order that could be known and reflected with precision in the structure and activity of government was foundational to the emergence of a discourse of political economy comfortable with the minimization of formal state power over the market. Undoubtedly, the Physiocratic theory of encouraging agrarian commerce and the liberalization of international trade outlined by François Quesnay and Du Pont de Nemours influenced Jefferson's thinking, even if that influence was tempered by concerns elaborated in Smith's work for the potentially despotic power of the French state and in light of a fundamentally Scottish project of squaring commercial society with a civic if not

40 C.F. Volney, "The Law of Nature," *Volney's Ruins: Or, Meditation on the Revolutions of Empires*, Jefferson and Joel Barlow, trans. (New York: G. Vale, 1853), pp. 212–13.

41 Smith, *The Wealth of Nations*, Vol. 2, p. 208; Karl Polanyi, *The Great Transformation: The Political and Economic Origins of Our Time* (Boston: Beacon, 1944); Graham Burchell, "*Peculiar Interests: Civil Society and Governing 'the System of Natural Liberty,'*" Burchell, Colin Gordon, and Peter Miller, eds. (Chicago: University of Chicago Press, 1991); John Shovlin, *The Political Economy of Virtue: Luxury, Patriotism, and the Origins of the French Revolution* (Ithaca: Cornell University Press, 2006); Michael Sonenscher, *Before the Deluge: Public Debt, Inequality, and the Intellectual Origins of the French Revolution* (Princeton: Princeton University Press, 2007); Paul Cheney, *Revolutionary Commerce: Globalization and the French Monarchy* (Cambridge, MA: Harvard University Press, 2010); Hont, *Jealousy of Trade*.

completely or radically republican inheritance of political liberty.[42] But the ideological framework necessary for the attachment of the peaceful promises of *doux commerce* to a project of continental conquest, and without ambivalence or self-apparent contradiction, was not yet fully in place. For that, Jefferson would need further revisions of inherited political theory on the principles and limits of republics, and he would find and build on those revisions in consort and conversation with political allies at home and correspondents abroad.

Jefferson and Madison's republicanism as it was articulated over the course of the 1790s exhibited a belief that law, governance, and national attachment can be successfully extended across wide territory through the ties of interest and agricultural commerce.[43] That is not to say that they were champions of unfettered market forces. Their position as Virginia slaveholders gave them ample sensitivity to the dangers of personal as well as regional indebtedness and economic dependence on the energy of industrial and fiscal capital. More nobly, both passionately objected to Hamilton's policy of repaying revolutionary war bonds to current holders at face value. Many of the soldiers and merchants who supported the revolutionary cause had been paid in bonds by the Continental Congress, and in the ensuing economic slump had sold the bonds to monetary speculators and investors for fractions of their worth out of desperation.[44] Honoring the contracts of the bonds, now in the hands of speculators, was for both Jefferson and Madison a miscarriage of justice. Both possessed a genuine skepticism, even fear, of the rise of financial capitalism, what such forces could do to a republic, and the blurring of personal and public interest in the central state structure necessary to foster and support that vision of a national economy. For Jefferson in particular, the

[42] Hirschman, *The Passions and the Interests*; Donald Winch, *Adam Smith's Politics: An Essay in Historiographic Revision* (Cambridge: Cambridge University Press, 1978), and *Riches and Poverty: An Intellectual History of Political Economy in Britain, 1750–1834* (Cambridge: Cambridge University Press, 1996); Nicholas Philipson, *Adam Smith: An Enlightened Life* (New Haven: Yale University Press, 2010).

[43] This is not to say that Jefferson and Madison needed to significantly reinterpret human behavior as naturally self-interested; they, along with many other theorists, would have taken interest as part of human nature for granted and long before the triumph of modern arguments in favor of commerce and capitalism, and that taking account of interest was hardly to make an unqualified argument for either; see Albert O. Hirschman, *The Passions and the Interests: Political Arguments for Capitalism before Its Triumph* (Princeton: Princeton University Press, 1977); Pierre Force, *Self-Interest before Adam Smith: A Genealogy of Economic Science* (Cambridge: Cambridge University Press, 2003).

[44] See Laura Jensen, *Patriots, Settlers, and the Origins of American Social Policy* (Cambridge: Cambridge University Press, 2003).

privatization of the power to determine the value of paper was a dangerous consequence of a society tied together by relations of exchange increasingly characterized by credit and debt.

That being said, it remained the case that Jefferson lessened his ambivalence about commerce and even manufacturing over the course of his mature years in national politics. Part of that transition has to do with the nature of his task as the minister to France, where he had been instructed to establish European markets for American goods, most notably whale oil, and more broadly to ensure a free commercial relationship between France and America that could sidestep British mercantile policies at work in the Atlantic. His reading of the French economists and their vision of the Atlantic as a free trade zone gave Jefferson and his political allies in the 1790's a relatively coherent ideological framework within which to combat what they saw as surrender to British dominance in the arena of Atlantic commerce. Against a recognizably modern concept of the state as a distinct controlling agent, increasing and consolidating national strength by linking it to economic development through a sanctioned system of credit, debt, and profit, the Jeffersonian Republicans expressed a vision of diffusing the state across space.[45] Such a provision provided for a doctrine of the "freedom of the seas" directed against the hated Jay Treaty and its concessions to British economic and naval power, as well as a domestic doctrine of providing free space for agricultural commerce rooted in small farming and upon which European markets would come to depend more and more.

What underlay the Jeffersonian Republican vision was a faith that the ties established by commerce, between and within nations, would ultimately subvert the felt need for a consolidated fiscal-military state.[46] It was in this sense that the hoped-for triumph of commerce grew out of the civic republicanism that characterized so much of Jefferson's revolutionary

[45] See McCoy, *The Elusive Republic: Political Economy in Jeffersonian America*.

[46] The capital necessary to fund the powers and activities of such state was by its very definition unproductive, as Albert Gallatin articulated in his 1796 pamphlet, *A Sketch of the Finances of the United States*: "Almost all of the expenses of government, but especially that species which most usually engenders public debt, viz., the expenses of war, are a destruction of the capital employed to defray them. The labor of the men employed in the public service, had it been applied in the pursuits of private industry, would not only have supported them but probably afforded them some reward beyond mere sustenance, and therefore would have produced an excess beyond their consumption, an addition to the national wealth, an increase in the capital of the community," *Selected Writings of Albert Gallatin*, E. James Ferguson, ed. (Indianapolis and New York: Bobbs-Merrill, 1967), pp. 32–3.

constitutional criticism. That the ties of exchange were in this understanding at war with the consolidation of state and fiscal interest starts to become evident in some of the earliest efforts of Madison and Jefferson to theorize republicanism both before and after the approval of the U.S. Constitution. On the revolt of indebted farmers lead by Daniel Shays in 1786, Jefferson wrote to Edward Carrington that "the basis of our government being the opinion of the people, the very first object should be to keep that right; and if it were left to me to decide whether we should have a government without newspapers, or newspapers without government, I should not hesitate a moment to prefer the latter." Preventing such rebellions was a matter of giving the people "full information of their affairs" through the medium of the public papers, and to "contrive that those papers should penetrate the whole mass of the people."[47]

Jefferson thought that newspapers could provide the means by which a spread out people formed public opinion and participated in the critical reading component of citizenship. Insofar as "every man should receive those papers & be capable of reading them," Jefferson suggested the capacity for the freedom of public deliberation and exchange of ideas could be more effective governance than government itself. The circulation of print spread opinions, and in spreading them, it disciplined them. The fraught and contested treatment of the relation between the law and the public here is entirely absent. This marked shift on Jefferson's part to locating the legitimacy of the government in public opinion as expressed and informed by the circulation of newspapers was reflective of a wider shift in thought.

COMMERCE AND TRANSLATION

A society governed less by laws and a state then by the free-flowing medium of opinion fit perfectly with Jefferson's constructed image of the Native American, particularly as it had been expressed in his *Notes on the State of Virginia*. "I am convinced that those societies (as the Indians)," Jefferson wrote to Madison, "which live without government enjoy in their general mass an infinitely greater degree of happiness than those who live under the European governments." Among the former, Jefferson reasoned, "public opinion is in the place of law," whereas in the latter society had been divided into two classes, "wolves and sheep." In

[47] Jefferson to Edward Carrington, January 16, 1787, *The Papers of Thomas Jefferson*, Vol. 11, p. 49.

any society where the people were "inattentive to public affairs," and lacked avenues for substantive participation in politics, all bodies of the government became wolves, enablers if not leaders of the "general prey of the rich on the poor."[48] Just as in the supposedly naturally virtuous Indian societies, a lack of separation between government and people compelled all to be engaged members of the councils, in an American republic a mass of newspaper readers would prove capable of both individual and collective self-government. It was precisely the image of Native Americans as blessedly stateless that made it possible for Jefferson to posit the ease and inevitability of their consensual annexation into an empire governed by the mechanisms of exchange and circulation. Jefferson wrote that there were basically three types of societies: those without government (again, "as among our Indians,"), those where "everyone has a just influence" to a greater or lesser degree, and those governed by force. "It is a problem," Jefferson wrote, "not clear in my mind, that the 1st condition is not the best. But I believe it to be inconsistent with any degree of population."[49] By force of numbers, American republicanism would have to take up where the Native Americans of Jefferson's imagination left off: the point of the switch in social development of from hunter-gatherers to cultivating and proprietary agriculturalists.

For his part, James Madison wove a careful line between his co-authorship of the Federalist papers with John Jay and Alexander Hamilton and his later ideological alliance with his fellow Virginian. In Federalist 10, Madison had developed his classic statement of federalist principle, that in point of fact republican government could be strengthened by its expansion over large territory because the diffusion of governmental bodies would likewise diffuse the ability of any one faction to achieve unchecked supremacy. And in Federalist 14 Madison had argued that those who insist on the territorial limits of republics confuse democracy, where the people themselves meet in council, with republicanism, where the people's representatives deliberate on the people's behalf.[50] The theoretical apparatus for the constitution of

[48] Jefferson to James Madison, January 30, 1787, Vol. 11, pp. 92–3. [49] *Ibid*, p. 93.

[50] James Madison, Federalist 10, 14, *The Federalist* (New York: Heritage Press, 1945), pp. 48–62, 82–8. The question of the consistency of Madison's constitutional thought has been called the "James Madison Problem" by scholars, although most agree that there were changes within a roughly coherent set of concerns for the proper balance of state and federal power, and that Madison was naturally reacting to fundamental changes and challenges in political culture and public policy; see Drew R. McCoy, *The Last of the Fathers: James Madison and the Republican Legacy* (Cambridge: Cambridge University

republican empire was at least partially in place long before Jeffersonian Republicans would be in a position to fully constitute that empire, and commerce was an essential component in the elaboration of the theory.

In his essay "Consolidation," printed in the *National Gazette* on November 21, 1791, Madison sought to steer a middle course between the Anti-Federalist objections to the Constitution along lines of the internal sovereignty of states on the one hand and the new Federalism of Hamilton. Let the former, he wrote, guard against anything which "might lead to a gradual consolidation of the states into one government," and let the latter try to "consolidate the affairs of the states into one harmonious interest." Strong in the faith that interest could replace government as the foundation of national unity, Madison hoped that the nation could maintain the jurisdictional multiplicity of state and federal powers, erecting over the whole "one paramount Empire of reason, benevolence, and brotherly affection."[51] Less than a month later, in his essay "Public Opinion," printed in the *National Gazette* on December 19, 1791, Madison admitted that territorial expanse made it "less easy" for the real opinions of the public to be ascertained, but that problem could be mitigated by the calculation of social and national bonds being maintained over long distance through other means.

> Whatever facilitates a general intercourse of sentiments, as good roads, domestic commerce, a free press, and particularly a *circulation of newspapers through the entire body of the people*, and *Representatives going from, and returning among every part of them*, is equivalent to a contraction of territorial limits, and is favorable to liberty, where these may be too extensive.[52]

Where territory had grown beyond bounds traditionally associated with the healthy republic, the "intercourse of sentiments" made possible by commerce, newspapers, and the travel of representatives maintained liberty in society. It is important to note that within this imagining, it is historical technological limits alone that establish the proper limits of territorial expansion. What can presently be achieved by way of effective

Press, 1989); Ralph Ketcham, *James Madison: A Biography* (Charlottesville: University of Virginia Press, 1990); Lance Banning, *The Sacred Fire of Liberty: James Madison and the Founding of the Federal Republic* (Ithaca: Cornell University Press, 1995); Gordon S. Wood, "Is There a James Madison Problem?" *Revolutionary Characters: What Made the Founders Different* (New York: Penguin, 2006), pp. 141–72; Andrew Burstein and Nancy Isenberg, *Madison and Jefferson* (New York: Random House, 2010); Mary Sarah Bilder, *Madison's Hand: Revising the Constitutional Convention* (Cambridge, MA: Harvard University Press, 2015).

[51] Madison, *Writings*, pp. 499–500.

[52] Madison, *Writings*, p. 501.

communication of interests and sentiments sets natural limits to how far a republic could extend itself. The safe enjoyment of liberty in a commercial republic, the "empire of reason," would follow shortly upon the natural increase of the population and the capacity for that population to transport ideas and people across increasingly uniform space.[53] Commerce and technological progress could make expansion okay. As Jefferson would write to James Madison shortly after the latter became President, contemplating the annexation of Canada, America could then have an "empire of liberty" that was unparalleled in history: "I am persuaded no constitution was ever before so well calculated as ours for extensive empire & self-government."[54] A confederation of agrarian republics knit together by a national marketplace perfectly balanced the twin demands of expansion and republicanism.

The theory of an expansive republic put forward by Jefferson and Madison relied on the concept of commerce, and in this it required a refutation of the theory, present most notably in Montesquieu's *Spirit of the Laws*, that the virtue that sustained local democracy and its inclusion

[53] For Richard Matthews, the key to Madison's political thought is precisely this desire for an empire of calculable and economic rationality that instills constitutional framework appropriate for aggressive capitalism; see Richard K. Matthews, *If Men Were Angels: James Madison and the Heartless Empire of Reason* (Lawrence: University of Kansas, 1996). Stephen Elkin argues that the trajectory of American political and economic development outstripped Madison's original thinking even while that thinking contributed substantially to that trajectory; Stephen L. Elkin, *Reconstructing the Commercial Republic: Constitutional Thought After Madison* (Chicago: University of Chicago Press, 2006). Colleen Sheehan points to the shared intellectual inheritance Jefferson and Madison found in their reading of French social theory, particularly that of the economists and their students like Turgot, Condorcet, Gabriel Bonnot de Mably, the Marquis de Mirabeau, and Jacques Necker, and Sheehan draws particular attention to the importance of the idea of public opinion for these thinkers and for Madison; see Jefferson to Madison, September 1, 1785, *The Papers of Thomas Jefferson*, Vol. 8, pp. 460–4; Keith Michael Baker, *Inventing the French Revolution* (Cambridge: Cambridge University Press, 1990); Johnson Kent Wright, *A Classical Republican in Eighteenth Century France: The Political Thought of Mably* (Stanford: Stanford University Press, 1997). Sheehan draws attention to the importance of this train of thought for Madison's own thinking, but minimizes the degree to which Madison is at least as concerned to be arguing with more democratic visions of republican politics in the 1790s, including from Jefferson, and likewise minimizes the degree to which the empire of reason was indeed an empire. Madison is arguing for not just an extended republic but an expansive and expanding one, and the argument about commerce and public opinion was meant to make this project possible; see Colleen A. Sheehan, *James Madison and the Spirit of Republican Self-Government* (Cambridge: Cambridge University Press, 2009).

[54] Jefferson to Madison, April 27, 1809, *The Papers of Thomas Jefferson: Retirement Series*, Vol. 1, p. 169.

in the constitutional structure of ancient republics could only be maintained in the context of relatively small polities.[55] The reason for this was simple: the magistrate of a province had to be at once a civil and a military officer, who has a result held in his hands the combined powers of executive, legislator, and judge over the conquered territory. Despite the fact that it was precisely military men like George Rogers Clark and William Henry Harrison that served as government officers and governors in the western territories, the answer Jefferson and Madison provided to this dilemma, as we have seen, was confederation tied together by commerce, but, in theory, not to the point of total dependence of any economic region or class upon any other. Jefferson convinced himself that commercial activity could become the basis of an extensive national community without resorting to force and without surrendering the locality of republican political experience in confederated state and local governments.

One of the most important projects in which Jefferson tried to think through and publicize the unique capacities of Americans to be citizens of an at once virtuous and expansive republic was his translation and urging of the publication of Destutt de Tracy's *Commentary and Review of Montesquieu's Spirit of the Laws*.[56] William Duane, a reliable

[55] Montesquieu, *The Sprit of the Laws*, Anne M. Cohler, Basia Carolyn Miller, and Harold Samuel Stone, eds. trans. (Cambridge: Cambridge University Press, 1989), pp. 143–4.

[56] As Peter Onuf has shown, Jefferson was attracted to Tracy's work for rendering the assumptions of classical republican politics irrelevant in an age of globalized commerce, and criticizing Montesquieu's admiration for the British state and constitutional monarchy. But Jefferson's thought changed significantly in response to changing contexts, and to assume that Jefferson's interest in Tracy is somehow representative of his thought in general is to take for granted the authority of the discursive intervention that both men are making in their respective contexts. Both Tracy and Jefferson worked hard to make certain kinds of ideas about politics seem untenable or absurd for the sake of projecting commerce and commercial empire across expansive social space. In turning to Tracy, Jefferson was reworking his earlier commitment to a more radical vision of politics and property rights, and it is important to appreciate the historical significance of such processes of conceptual reworking in the history of thought; see Nicholas Onuf and Peter Onuf, *Nations, Markets, and War: Modern History and the American Civil War* (Charlottesville: University of Virginia Press, 2006), pp. 225–39, "Ancients, Moderns, and the Progress of Mankind: Thomas Jefferson's Classical World," Onuf and Nicholas P. Cole, eds. *Thomas Jefferson, the Classical World, and Early America* (Charlottesville: University of Virginia Press, 2013), pp. 35–55; see Pocock, "Cambridge Paradigms and Scotch Philosophers: Between the Civic Humanist and Civil Jurisprudential Interpretations of Eighteenth Century Social Thought," *Wealth and Virtue: The Shaping of Political Economy in the Scottish Enlightenment*, Istvan Hont and Michael Ignatieff, eds. (Cambridge: Cambridge University Press, 1983), pp. 235–52; see Jason Frank, *Constituent*

Jeffersonian publisher, printed Jefferson's English translation of the work in Philadelphia in 1811. While it is impossible to say what out of the entire work Jefferson might have endorsed, Tracy's criticisms match arguments put forward by Jefferson and Madison at a few crucial points. The sample Jefferson sent Joel Barlow in 1810 as encouragement to go forward with a publication of the entire work had included Tracy's commentary on Book 2, where Montesquieu had delineated the three fundamental types of government (republican, monarchical, and despotic). Tracy urged a jettisoning of the tripartite analytical framework with a simpler dualistic one: there were "national" governments where all citizens had equal rights before the law, and there were "special" governments, where some, whether kings, despots, or aristocrats, had certain rights not shared by all.[57] Montesquieu, in this framework, had been far too hasty in assuming that the virtues to be observed in the history of the ancient republics were no longer viable in an age of commerce. The basic virtues of good citizenship were more than apparent, for both Tracy and Jefferson, in the example of the United States, and the privileges, fears, corruptions, and mysteries of aristocratic or despotic power could be seen even in the most economically advanced nations, namely Britain.

As Jefferson and Madison had elaborated, the key to maintaining the power of public opinion in any form of constitutional government, democratic or monarchial, was providing for sufficient means of the exchange of goods and ideas outside of the tribunals of direct democracy. "Representative democracy," Tracy argued, was "democracy rendered practicable for a long time and over a great extent of territory," and in that sense it was "a new invention," unknown even as late as the writing of *The Spirit of the Laws*, originally published in 1748. Representative democracy, according to Tracy, "was almost impossible to put into practice

Moments: Enacting the People in Postrevolutionary America (Durham: Duke University Press, 2010); Joanna Innes and Mark Philp, *Re-Imagining Democracy in the Age of Revolutions: America, France, Britain, Ireland 1750–1850* (Oxford: Oxford University Press, 2013); Philp, *Reforming Ideas in Britain: Politics in the Shadow of the French Revolution* (Cambridge: Cambridge University Press, 2014).

57 Destutt de Tracy, *Commentary and Review of Montesquieu's Spirit of the Laws*, Thomas Jefferson, trans. (Philadelphia: William Duane, 1811), p. 12; see also Jefferson to William Duane, August 12, 1810, *Papers of Thomas Jefferson: Retirement Series*, Vol. 3, pp. 3–25, Montesquieu, *ibid*, p. 12; on the importance of the concept of the nation as a single entity and as an organizing principle of Jefferson's political thought, see Brian Steele, *Thomas Jefferson and American Nationhood* (Cambridge: Cambridge University Press, 2012).

before the invention of printing," which facilitated communication between constituents and representatives, and through its mediation of political language minimized the risk of "sudden storms" brought about by "the force of an impassioned and popular eloquence."[58] The expansive and commercial republic, made possible through the establishment of a widespread public print culture, was an answer to the classic and seemingly intractable problems of political philosophy.[59] Newspapers, in regulating and making somewhat uniform the medium of crafting and transmitting public opinion, kept government under the supervision of public opinion and effectively helped govern the directions public opinion could take.

Knowing, reading, and translating Tracy compelled Jefferson to be increasingly enthusiastic about both expansion and commerce. Tracy appreciated that a polity united primarily by commerce and print culture was a new phenomenon, and one that was changing what one could count as true in politics and political economy. Commerce was not only the "foundation and basis of society," Tracy wrote in Book 20, where Montesquieu treated the law in its relation to commerce historically up to the present, but "it is in effect the fabric itself; for society is nothing more than a continual exchange of mutual succours, which occasion the concurrence of the powers of all for the more effectual gratification of the wants of each." Given this fact, it was "therefore ridiculous to doubt of commerce being a good," doubts which Jefferson, as we have seen, maintained during his career in national politics.[60] And yet, we can observe a gradual fading of these doubts over the course of that career, and by the time he was in early retirement, he was, as a student of Tracy, a fairly committed convert to the political economy of the *Ideologues*.[61]

Embracing commerce, even agricultural commerce, was not in this case the most dramatic reversal of Jefferson's earlier thinking. Jefferson had written to Madison in 1785 that when there were uncultivated lands and unemployed poor, the right of property had violated natural right, that "legislators could not invent too many devices for subdividing property," and that another means of lessening inequality was to exempt holdings below a certain point and "tax the higher proportions of property in

[58] Tracy, *Commentary and Review of Montesquieu's Spirit of the Laws*, p. 19.

[59] Joyce Appleby, *Liberalism and Republicanism in the Historical Imagination* (Cambridge, MA: Harvard University Press, 1992).

[60] Tracy, *Commentary and Review of Montesquieu's Spirit of the Laws*, pp. 205–6.

[61] See Thomas E. Kaiser, "Politics and Political Economy in the Thought of the Ideologues," *History of Political Economy*, Vol. 12, No. 2 (1980), pp. 141–60.

geometrical progression as they rise."[62] In 1816, Jefferson had involved himself in sponsoring the translation and publications of more of Tracy's works, including his *Treatise on Political Economy*, published in 1817, and he introduced the book with a prospectus on Tracy's political economy, including the principles he himself drew from the work. Regardless of the objects of taxation, Jefferson suggested, in a note to the publisher, Joseph Milligan, once what to be taxed was decided upon the policy is "to be equally and fairly applied to all. To take from one, because it is thought that his own industry and that of his fathers had acquired too much, in order to spare to others" who had not been as industrious, "is to violate arbitrarily the first principle of association, 'the guarantee to everyone of a free exercise of his industry, and the fruits acquired by it."[63] The best remedy for overgrown estates was a law of equal inheritance, concluded Jefferson, but a policy of "extra-taxation" in the service of redistribution was a violation of natural right.

Tracy's *Treatise on Political Economy* was part of larger and never completed project, *The Elements of Ideology*, which he intended to be a systematic philosophical work and a fleshing out of some of the basic principles of the *Ideologues*, an intellectual circle in post-revolutionary France that included other economists such as Jean-Baptiste Say. In the wake of the French Revolution, Tracy was not alone in finding himself shaken by the inadequacy of previous political and economic thought for understanding what had just happened. Enlightened attention to the power and significance of public opinion by the previous century's leading minds now seemed only a prelude to the raw, direct, and violent power of ideas in an angry and frantic public mind.[64] The goal of Tracy's project was to extend the inquiries of political economy and political philosophy to psychology, and he applied a Lockean empiricism and sensationalism in the service of a theory of individual behavior in society. Tracy's conjectural history began not with modes of production but with states of mind, and he posited a natural linkage between personality and property that configured the individual as naturally self-possessed.[65] Possession made no sense without a sense of self, distinct from the sense of

[62] Jefferson to Madison, October 28, 1785, *The Papers of Thomas Jefferson*, Vol. 8, p. 682.

[63] Jefferson to Joseph Milligan, April 6, 1816, "Prospectus on Political Economy," *The Complete Jefferson*, Saul K. Padover, ed. (New York: Duell, Sloan, and Pearce, 1943), pp. 372–3.

[64] See Knott, *Sensibility in the American Revolution* (Chapel Hill: University of North Carolina Press, 2009).

[65] Tracy, *A Treatise on Political Economy*, p. 55.

others, and that distinction made no sense without a feeling of possessing one's self. Tracy was reconfiguring the human subject for commercial society from the bottom up.

The "animated being" depicted by Tracy was a creature of sense and desire possessed of little more than the liberty of the will to satisfy its wants. Everything else was convention, and for Tracy even the capacity to distinguish between justice and injustice first had to flow from the exchange of goods and sentiments.[66] "Mutual understanding" was an essential part of the creation of society, for it was only in the security of possessing one's self and one's possessions that human beings could begin to agree with one another on certain rights, restrictions, and responsibilities to protect that security. The implication of this history for Tracy was clear: "Society is purely and solely a continual series of exchanges. It is never anything else, in any epoch of its duration, from its commencement the most unformed, to its greatest perfection."[67] From this series of exchanges society grows and matures as nothing else besides the process of exchanging, and so the moral imperative of life in society became the rules of participating in this process. The growth of society could produce remarkable things: "On the whole surface of the land habitations have been constructed from distance to distance, in favorable positions, for the use of those who cultivate the ground and attend to its produce. These habitations have been surrounded with enclosures and plantations, that render them more agreeable and more useful." The useful labor and the production of useful things feeds "a population really astonishing, the individuals of which have the use of a perfected language" with which to conduct the business of society, the business of making, buying, and selling.[68]

By such means was value created, the use of money introduced, and the society and all of the individuals exchanging in it made satisfied and secure. And most crucially, by such means was the mass of exchanging individuals to be governed by the very practice of exchanging. The laws of society created and disciplined the proper use of land and language – the government of men proceeded securely by way of the government of use. Jefferson's own experience as an increasingly indebted slave owner, who would go on to speak of his participation in domestic manufacturing through the establishment of a nail factory at Monticello manned by enslaved young boys, certainly must have

[66] *Ibid*, pp. 86–7. [67] *Ibid*, p. 95. [68] *Ibid*, pp. 98–9.

played a role in making Jefferson more sensitive to federal taxation policy, and so open to liberalizing economic arguments and political economy as a basis for analysis, particularly the political economy of slavery.

But how he was thinking about commerce and empire informed and was in turn shaped by his own attention to intellectual practice, and that attention was a concrete site in which to theorize the practices of others, a crystallization of the politics of that theorizing. "He had been a great reader," Jefferson wrote of Montesquieu to William Duane, and commonplaced everything he read. At length he wished to undertake some work into which he could bring his whole Commonplace book in a digested form. He fixed on the subject of his Spirit of Laws & wrote the book."[69] Tracy's *Commentary and Review*, Jefferson asserted, would correct the manifold inconsistencies and "false inferences" to be found in such a book. Jefferson was not only taking Montesquieu to task for the spirit of system, a spirit he had no problem celebrating in Tracy, but for working from and indeed leaving his audience with a commonplace book. In a remarkable shift in his theorization of the politics and history of intellectual practice, from using his own commonplace books as jumping off points for legal and political reflection and action, Jefferson set up an implicit critique and contrast between the old humanist's method and Tracy's depiction of him as out of date for failure to recognize the power of the printing revolution. In the case of Jefferson, this adjustment would map directly on to a parallel shift in his thinking about law, from assemblage to code and that in the service of projecting empire over a great expanse of territory.

However one squares Jefferson's intellectual development here, the most important thing to note is the starkness with which Jefferson comes to articulate his vision of an empire of laboring, property-owning men expanding successfully and in imagined relative tranquility across the space of the North American continent. In his mirroring of the Native American societies as naturally primed for consensual participation in the empire of liberty, governed as that empire would be not by a powerful state but by the very communicative networks that made the empire free, Jefferson carved out conceptual space to assume the participatory consent of others or exclude them not only from participation but from any legal personality and civic acknowledgment

[69] Jefferson to William Duane, August 12, 1810, *Papers of Thomas Jefferson, Retirement Series*, Vol. 3, p. 6.

at all.[70] And in doing so he arrived at something else that was new in the history of political thought: a particular kind of liberal and commercial argument for violence and conquest, one that proceeded by way of an intellectual project geared toward disciplining the plurality and historicity of use. The substantive liberties of not only subject peoples but the settler beneficiaries of the empire itself were heavily narrowed down as a result.

JURISPRUDENCE, EMPIRE, AND JURISDICTION

In his first inaugural address, delivered after the tumultuous public debate and contested result of the election of 1800, Jefferson had summoned the image of a "rising nation, spread over a wide and fruitful land, traversing all the seas with the rich productions of their industry, engaged in commerce with nations who feel power and forget right."[71] In Jefferson's mind, the problems posed to republicanism by its being so spread out remedied themselves through the fact of an engaged and virtuous public. The federal government was the strongest one on earth, Jefferson assured his listeners, because it was the only one "where every man, at the call of the law, would fly to the standard of the law, and would meet invasions of the public order as his own personal concern."[72] He would go onto say in his second inaugural address, retrospectively defending the Louisiana Purchase, and echoing the earlier arguments of Madison in Federalist 10: "who can limit the extent to which the federative principle may operate effectively. The larger our association, the less it will be shaken by local passions."[73] Breaking past the traditional boundaries of participatory politics that characterized the ancient republics, Jefferson provided a nationalist vision with which to sustain the vital principles of republican polities across large amounts of territory.

Still, Jefferson had to account for the presence of distinct peoples on much of that same territory or just beyond its borders. Part of the responsibility of the government sustained by the taxes of an expanding settler society, Jefferson reasoned, was to "extinguish the native right of

[70] On communicative networks in imperial governance, see James Tully, "Communication and Imperialism," *Public Philosophy in a New Key, Volume II: Imperialism and Civic Freedom* (Cambridge: Cambridge University Press, 2008), pp. 175–9.

[71] Jefferson, "First Inaugural Address," Vol. 33, p. 148. [72] *Ibid*, p. 149.

[73] Jefferson, "Second Inaugural Address," *Writings*, Merrill D. Peterson, ed. (New York: Library of America, 1984), p. 519.

soil within our limits" as well as to "extend those limits." With regards to the Native Americans themselves, Jefferson reported again in his second inaugural that he viewed them with the "commiseration their history inspires." Given the inevitable overflow of settlers into their land, Jefferson suggested, it was only acting in accord with the dictates of humanity to "teach them agriculture and the domestic arts" that were in his view the only hope for Indians to establish means for future subsistence."[74] Protected by law at the outset of this adventure, the Native Americans would, in theory, naturally take up their status as committed and propertied fellow cultivators of the earth.

Jefferson drew an explicit contrast between the energetic bustle of the expansive agricultural and commercial nation with the revival of traditionalism that was becoming more popular among various Native American tribes at the very moment of his ascension to the presidency. Efforts to "enlighten them on the fate which awaits their present course of life, to induce them to exercise their reason, follow its dictates, and change their pursuits with the change of circumstances" had run into the obstacles of "interested and crafty individuals" who were inducing many to return to the nearly forgotten customs of their ancestors rather than adopt the civilization program Jefferson had retained and expanded from the Washington administration. The result of these revivals was "a sanctimonious reverence for the customs of their ancestors, that whatsoever they did, must be done through all time; that reason is a false guide, and to advance under its counsel in their physical, moral, or political condition is perilous innovation." Operating in the early modern historiographical paradigm of barbarism, where the barbarian was he who had society and customs but not the means to change either, Jefferson painted Native Americans as mentally encircled by their own history. This image was in stark contrast to that of the idealized white citizens of Jefferson's imagined republic, who, in theory, were no longer compelled to work on the materials of their history as revolutionaries, having freed themselves to pursue the historical dynamism characteristic of commercial society. The goal, for Jefferson, was to entice Native Americans into leaving behind what history they had and mix themselves with the stronger and unitary force of the history of the United States, a force for which Jefferson was now the primary and most powerful partisan and ideologist. He would even compare the

[74] *Ibid*, p. 520.

leaders of the Indian cultural revival to the Federalist clergy who had opposed his election: "they, too, have their anti-philosophers."[75]

As President, Jefferson was in communication with agents of the government in the Indian Territory, as well with Native American leaders. He maintained a consistent program of encouraging the development of private property and bringing Native American agricultural production thus produced into the networks of American continental commerce. The land necessary for the expansive agrarian republic, replicating itself over new territory, compelled Jefferson to pursue any means necessary to extinguish native title through purchase and the forceful encouragement of smaller tracts of private property for cultivation. The fact that Jefferson continued to insist on purchase rather than covering doctrines of conquest or discovery, points us to the essential role that the concept of the natural historical progress enabled by commerce played in justifying expansion policy. Sufficient and productive usage of land provided an argument, but even that argument would have been incomplete without the enveloping assumption that whether they knew it or not Native Americans would come to desire and benefit from their tutelage in civil society at the hands of the United States government. This assumption added a new ideological component to the history of European legal theory in its justification of colonization in the Americas. If commerce was the process through which Native Americans would necessarily enter a higher stage of social development, in Jefferson's vision, it was political economy and print culture that made possible the thinking of such a vision and its attempted implementation.[76]

Promoting individual agriculture and commerce went hand in hand with extinguishing native title through the fundamentally commercial activity of purchasing land. Such a policy would enable Native Americans to "to live on much smaller portions of land, and indeed will render their vast forests useless but for the range of cattle," as Jefferson wrote to his agent from the War Department, Benjamin Hawkins.[77] While the Indians learned how to cultivate small tracts of land

[75] *Ibid*, p. 521.

[76] Michael Mann has developed the linkage between early national liberal capitalism and the genocidal violence of Jeffersonian expansion policy; see Mann, *The Sources of Social Power: The Rise of Classes and Nation-States, 1760–1914* (Cambridge: Cambridge University Press, 1993), ch. 5, and *The Dark Side of Democracy: Explaining Ethnic Cleansing* (Cambridge: Cambridge University Press, 2004), pp. 92–3.

[77] Jefferson to Benjamin Hawkins, February 18, 1803, *Papers of Thomas Jefferson*, Vol. 39, p. 547.

productively, America could feed white settler thirst for more land, and this would in turn produce a "coincidence of interests," a "commerce" that would be as good for Native Americans as it was for the white citizens of the United States. The theory at work here was one of universal benefit, not merely from paternalist charity and philanthropy (although that clearly is present), but from the progress of commerce. "The ultimate point of rest & happiness for them is to let our settlements and theirs meet and blend together, to intermix, and become one people," for "this is what the natural progress of things will of course bring on."[78] Commerce created a plane for the establishment of coordinating sentiments within the (expanding) boundaries of the nation. The course of this development was natural and therefore compelling, necessary and undeniable. The United States, in turn, would become a nation unified by its cultivation of private property, converting agricultural surplus and the land from which it was drawn into the commodity form. As such, not only was the nation the harbinger of mankind's natural historical progress; it was the instrument for the implementation of that very process.

The potency of this nascent American nationalism and sense of national history as a force of wider historical development can be seen in how Jefferson addressed Native American delegations during his presidency. Universally, Native Americans were "children" in these addresses and he and the other leaders of the United States their "fathers." He assured Handsome Lake, the leader of a religious and cultural revival among the Seneca in western New York that establishing private property and allowing such property to be moveable would be beneficial to his people.[79] To the Cherokee, who by and large adopted the civilization program put to them and had already begun precisely the local and self-sufficient agricultural and household manufacturing envisioned by American policy makers, Jefferson outlined the general sketch of their subsequent history. "When a man has enclosed and improved his farm," Jefferson taught, he will want the fruits of his labor to be enjoyed by his family rather than others, and when a "man has property," he will need to be protected by the law in the holding of that property. "You will find it necessary then to appoint good men, as judges, to decide contests between man and man, according to reason

[78] *Ibid.*

[79] Jefferson to Brother Handsome Lake, November 3, 1802, *Papers of Thomas Jefferson*, Vol. 38, pp. 628–31.

and to the rules you establish."[80] While precisely what rules are to be set up is left for them to decide, Jefferson offers them the services of American advisors, but more significant is the assumption that property and its demands will by and large dictate those laws as a matter of natural course. Native Americans for Jefferson now inhabited the linear and flattened world of continental commerce and political economy, and it was a world of unavoidable economic interdependence that they shared with and as a result would eventually become indistinguishable from their fellow producers in the western United States.

Enforcing this vision of commerce, and its attendant unifying force, was crucial for implementing the empire of liberty. "To promote this disposition to exchange lands," among the Indians, Jefferson wrote to William Henry Harrison, the governor of the Northwest Territory, Americans "would be glad to see the good and influential individuals among them run in debt, because we observe that when these debts get beyond what the individuals can pay, they become willing to lop them off by a cession of lands."[81] In a rather perverse ideological twist, after a decade and a half of decrying the plans of Alexander Hamilton to draw the body of the public as well as the state governments into greater economic dependence on the federal structure through mechanisms of credit, Jefferson oversaw the establishment of trading houses at borders with Native nations to encourage the taking on of personal debt among the purportedly newly and freely independent cultivators that would be made out of the disparate plurality of Native peoples the United States found standing in the way of its own extension. In time, Jefferson reasoned, the Indians will either incorporate themselves into the body of the nation or be forced out west. The former, he asserted, "is certainly the termination of their history most happy for themselves." Jefferson went on to impress on Harrison that it was vital for the United States to cultivate good relations with the Indians during this transitional time, for "it is best they should see only the present age of their history."[82] Arguing that Native Americans had not developed the powers of historical consciousness necessary to see too far beyond the present, and so they would naturally and willingly let themselves become subjects of American commercial and demographic prowess, Jefferson plotted the eventual

[80] Jefferson to the Chiefs of the Cherokee Nation, January 10, 1806, *Writings*, p. 561.
[81] Jefferson to William H. Harrison, February 27, 1803, *Papers of Thomas Jefferson*, Vol. 39, p. 590.
[82] *Ibid*, p. 591–2.

fading of a distinctly Native history into that of the United States. Again, the idea of commerce made republican empire possible, and the trappings and forces at work in drawing peoples into dependence on the marketplace were the calculated instruments through which the implementation of that empire would take place.

The ideas of commerce and extended continental empire employed by Jefferson increasingly led him to articulate and really believe that not only was American conquest of the west inevitable, but that this inevitability was secured in the certainty of its ultimate appeal to Native peoples. In 1813, at the height of conflict with Britain as well as their Native American allies, Jefferson wrote to Alexander von Humboldt, the traveling German botanist and philosopher, with whom he and the American Philosophical Society had been in contact previously. "They have seduced the greater part of the tribes within our neighborhood, to take up the hatchet against us," he informed Humboldt, "and the cruel massacres they have committed on the women and children of our frontiers taken by surprise, will oblige us now to pursue them to extermination, or drive them to new seats beyond our reach."[83] Americans had offered peace through assisted development, legal protection, and the exchange of goods and sentiments appropriate to a commercial relationship, and by this logic, those tribes that chose differently brought righteous violence upon themselves. What is at work here, as Michael Rogin established in his study of Jacksonian ideology, is at once a paternalism reflective of the insecurities of the settler project and the mask that benevolent arguments from commerce and improvement pulled over destructive violence and conquest.[84] The result is a particular kind of rage at those that do not conform to the fantasy of uniformity and order, even if to do so, as Jefferson had made quite clear, would lead to the death of their history.

The ideological imperatives of the empire of liberty led Jefferson to deny the constituted and complex histories of peoples who, in having distinct histories, would potentially live and judge differently. As with the case of enslaved or formerly enslaved African Americans, the security

[83] Jefferson to Alexander von Humboldt, December 6, 1813, *Papers of Thomas Jefferson: Retirement Series*, Vol. 7, p. 30; see Sandra Rebok, *Humboldt and Jefferson: A Transatlantic Friendship of the Enlightenment* (Charlottesville: University of Virginia Press, 2014).

[84] Michael P. Rogin, *Fathers and Children: Andrew Jackson and the Subjugation of the American Indian* (New York: Random House, 1988).

of the settler subject and his liberty, to say nothing of that of its planter-theorist, rested uncomfortably in the face of collective and individual bodies and their histories whose subjection, as Walter Johnson has shown, was the very stuff out of which that liberty was made.[85] The practical theorization of Jeffersonian democracy went hand-in-hand with nervous attention to figures whose form of life troubled the calculable uniformity of its juridical space, and the inevitability of the spread of its history.

A shift from the historical and institutional focus of his revolutionary constitutionalism to print culture and political economy as organizing structures in Jefferson's thought had significant jurisprudential implications, both in Jefferson's thought and for the legal history of American expansion policy more broadly. Recent scholarship on the Atlantic and imperial dimensions of the American founding has emphasized the roots of settler concepts of liberty in the intellectual tradition of natural jurisprudence, and in particular, in the Lockean conceptualization of legally recognizable title to land being directly related to the land's appropriative cultivation.[86] Within this framework, the operating logic of Anglo-American imperialism on the North American continent had been an argument that Native Americans had not established sufficient title to their lands by failing to cultivate those lands and establish relations of individual property holding among themselves. Larger conceptual frameworks of course played a role in this process, as early modern European developments of the Roman *ius gentium* into modern use as the law of nature and nations provided a vocabulary of rights and responsibilities that could be expected of the peoples of the world and in turn used to conquer, subdue, or combat those found to be in

[85] Walter Johnson, *Soul by Soul: Life Inside the Antebellum Slave Market* (Cambridge, MA: Harvard University Press, 2000); *River of Dark Dreams: Slavery and Empire in the Cotton Kingdom* (Cambridge, MA: Harvard University Press, 2013).

[86] Barbara Arneil, *John Locke and America: The Defense of English Colonialism* (Oxford: Oxford University Press, 1996); James Tully, "Rediscovering America: The Two Treatises and Aboriginal Rights," Tully, *An Approach to Political Philosophy: Locke In Contexts* (Cambridge: Cambridge University Press), ch. 5, pp. 137–76; Christopher Tomlins, *Freedom Bound: Law, Labor, and Civic Identity in Colonizing English America, 1580–1865* (Cambridge: Cambridge University Press, 2010); Aziz Rana, *The Two Faces of American Freedom* (Cambridge, MA: Harvard University Press, 2010); Craig Yirish, *Settlers, Liberty, and Empire: The Roots of Early American Political Theory* (Cambridge: Cambridge University Press, 2011); Lisa Ford, *Settler Sovereignty: Jurisdiction and Indigenous People in America and Australia, 1788–1836* (Cambridge, MA: Harvard University Press, 2011); Andrew Fitzmaurice, *Sovereignty, Property, and Empire, 1500–2000* (Cambridge: Cambridge University Press, 2014).

violation of its maxims.[87] That being said, the settler aspects of the basis of empire in British North America from the seventeenth to the nineteenth centuries are usually taken to stand in contrast to the jurisprudential disputes and legitimating frameworks that characterized earlier Spanish conquests in the Americas. While the colonization of British North America can be understood as predicated on the natural duty of individual members of society to work the land, and law itself in this framework was taken to be a product of the compacts that arose out of mutual needs for security in their justly held possessions, Spanish conquest, on the other hand, held in check to a certain extent by the deliberations of Francisco de Vitoria and his students in the school of Salamanca, took cognizance of the Native peoples they encountered as peoples, who retained some level of corporate sovereignty over themselves before conquest and therefore some collective legal identity after conquest, a legal fact that imposed certain rights and responsibilities on the conqueror as well as the conquered.[88]

[87] Craig Yirush, *Settlers, Liberty, and Empire: The Roots of American Political Theory, 1675–1775* (Cambridge: Cambridge University Press, 2011), pp. 29–80; Tomlins, *Freedom Bound*, pp. 111–90.

[88] Tomlins, *Freedom Bound*; Andrew Fitzmaurice argues for an even sharper distinction, emphasizing the historically progressive and developmental character of the commercial justifications of empire that built on the Lockean framework of cultivation and use from the eighteenth century onward, particularly in the Anglo-American context, contrasting Vitoria's concern to note that the Indians were not natural slaves by Aristotelian standards, nor simply savages who left their lands unused and unoccupied (indeed, as Fitzmaurice establishes, the Roman law doctrine of *terra nullius* was of minimal significance to early modern debates on the legal legitimacy of conquest, where the fact of at least minimal occupation on the part of the Indians was rarely doubted). It seems significant, however, that for Vitoria, the criteria of sufficient use and commercial exchange were hardly exclusive of one another; indeed, communicative exchange, partnership, and trade were types of use that could be and in fact were by Vitoria and others evaluated for efficiency relative to rival claims of Spanish "travelers." James Tully has argued that the distinction between conventional and appropriative/contractual traditions of theories of property is overstated, and that Locke shares a broader sociological account of law and property with the a natural jurisprudence tradition that included Vitoria; see Tully, *An Argument About Property: John Locke and His Adversaries* (Cambridge: Cambridge University Press, 1980). Vitoria opened a communicative if not quite a commercial argument for empire, resting as it did on estimations of the linguistic and cultural capacity for use of land, language, and law; see Fitzmaurice, *Sovereignty, Property, and Empire, 1500–2000*, pp. 22, 33–170; on Vitoria's legal theory and its applications in the Americas more broadly, see Robert A. Williams, Jr. *The American Indian in Western Legal Thought: The Discourses of Conquest* (Oxford: Oxford University Press, 1990); Anthony Pagden, *The Fall of Natural Man: The American Indian and the Origins of Comparative Ethnology* (Cambridge: Cambridge University Press, 1982); *Spanish Imperialism and the Political Imagination* (New Haven: Yale University Press, 1990); *Lords of All the World: Ideologies of Empire in Spain, Britain, and France, c. 1500–1800* (New Haven: Yale

The jurisprudential basis of Jeffersonian expansion policy, far from being merely a logical outgrowth of basically if not exclusively Lockean conceptualizations of natural property rights and proprietary cultivation, depended on a fusion of these normally contrasting traditions of empire. Certainly, as is clear from Jefferson's own efforts to encourage private cultivation among Native groups within US territorial boundaries, an argument from rights of settlement was an important aspect of early nineteenth-century thinking on the legal legitimacy of expansion and empire. Equally important however was a conjoined emphasis on use and exchange that echoed earlier Spanish concerns with natural obligations of communication as a basis for framing relations with the Indians. Vitoria himself, in his discourse on the American Indians of 1539, had reviewed the possible theoretical justifications for Spanish dominion in the Americas, had refuted rights of conquest asserted on the grounds of Papal mandate, Christian mission, or right of discovery, arguing that it was indisputable that Native Americans legitimately occupied their land. The natural law of "partnership and communication," Vitoria asserted, was the only legitimate basis of Spanish conquest.[89] By the law of nations, the Spanish had the right to travel and dwell in the Americas and to do so freely, and had equal rights to trade in the Americas and with the Native Americans so long as no harm was done in these exchanges, and that resources or goods held in common among the Natives could be equally and lawfully used and even cultivated and possessed by the Spanish. Finally, Vitoria concluded, failure on the part of Natives to respect these and others rights was just cause for war, in which case all of the rights of war and conquest could be legitimately asserted. To secure the peace and safety of their rights to travel, trade, and exchange, war and the rights of war were held to be legitimate responses on the part of the Spanish. Resistance not simply to appropriation but communication and exchange invited just war, according to Vitoria, the rights of which included "plunder, enslavement, deposition of their former masters, and the institution of new ones."[90] And once just war

University Press, 1995); Anthony Anghie, *Imperialism, Sovereignty, and the Making of International Law* (Cambridge: Cambridge University Press, 2005); Annabel Brett, *Liberty, Right, and Nature: Individual Rights in Later Scholastic Thought* (Cambridge: Cambridge University Press, 1997); *Annabel Brett, Changes of State: Nature and the Limits of the City in Early Modern Natural Law* (Princeton: Princeton University Press, 2011).

[89] Francisco de Vitoria, "De Indis, in Vitoria," *Political Writings*, Anthony Pagden and Jeremy Lawrence, eds. trans. (Cambridge: Cambridge University Press, 1991), p. 278.

[90] *Ibid*, p. 283.

to protect the natural right of communicative activities had begun, Vitoria argued, citing the Roman Digest, "everything captured in war belongs to the victor." This was a powerful and profoundly historically significant theoretical basis for thinking about the legal subjectivities of Native Americans.

Whatever Vitoria's intention was in framing his discourse as he did, whether it was to critique Spanish imperialism or work his way to justifying in whatever way he could, or something in between, he left political theory regarding the European relationship to the Americas with an important conceptualization of communicative exchange as an instrument of empire. The assertions of Jeffersonian expansion policy and the articulation of Jeffersonian republicanism in national political discourse made extensive use of conjoined arguments from commerce and communication. As discussed in this and the previous chapter, not only did Jefferson feel compelled to take stock of Native capacities for use of the resources of land, language, and law and find them wanting, configuring an impoverished legal and historical subjectivity that made out of Native history fit material for forceful refashioning; he plotted an argument for republican empire where rights of expansion and assimilation followed from and through the activity of commercial exchange, an exchange that was forced and resistance to which constituted legal grounds for total war. Either Native Americans peacefully assimilated themselves completely into the legally uniform plane of commerce extending itself over the continent or they invited what Jefferson was comfortable discussing as wars of annihilation, and the choice they faced in Jefferson's terms was that simple. It is particularly important to note here that neither the theory of conquest elaborated by English jurists in the seventeenth and eighteenth centuries to formulate the legal status of the British North American colonies nor the settler and proprietary theory of possession articulated independently by Locke sufficiently explain or anticipate the articulated basis of Jeffersonian expansion policy. As Jefferson's treatment of Native Americans makes clear, not only was commercial empire newly and more energetically violent and imperial; it was all the more powerful as an ideological force for its rhetorical supplanting of the violence of conquest and settlement with the proscribed consent and free participation in the exchange of words and things.

By way of conclusion, the political and jurisprudential implications of Jefferson's particular theorization of commercial empire can be seen in his involvement in disputes over the legal conquest of New Orleans and partisan conflict over the legal basis of expansion. The subsequent history of law and expansion in the antebellum period illustrates the significant transformations in Jefferson's legal and constitutional thinking, and how impactful these transformations proved to be. Jefferson appointed William Claiborne the territorial governor of New Orleans and the surrounding area, and in that capacity Claiborne exercised civil and military jurisdiction until such time as a process similar to that outlined by the Northwest Ordinance had taken place, implementing republican governmental structures along lines compatible with the United States Constitution. Over the course of his presidency, the troubles Jefferson encountered in imposing that process led his administration and Congress to be more aggressive and direct in their policy, maintaining a military government and becoming more concerned to impose common law jurisdiction in replacement of both Spanish and French civil law. The degree to which fragments of Roman law, and the Spanish and French iterations of it, continued in force was a matter of great anxiety and dispute both in New Orleans and at the level of the federal government. What was at stake was the status of standing legal orders within newly acquired territory, and the boundaries of the rights of the sovereign in supplanting local law with the normative law and institutions of the empire.

Perhaps the most crucial legal question brought up by expansion into the west was that of the applicability of the English common law in American jurisdictions. In response to the growing assertion in US Supreme Court decisions that the common law as naturally part of the existing law of the United States, Jefferson wrote to Edmund Randolph in 1799 that this was an "audacious, barefaced and sweeping pretension to a system of law for the US" because it was done without the formal adoption of the legislature. Continuing to see constitutionalism as characterized by a "legislated constitution," Jefferson argued that since the beginning of British colonial settlements, what existed of the common law existed only insofar as the "organs" constituted for declaring the will of the nation, by which he meant the colonial assemblies, had formally adopted those components.[91] "The law being law only because it is the will of the nation," the law is not changed, Jefferson urged, by a change in the state.[92] Just as the commercial treaty with France was still valid after

[91] On the concept of the legislated constitution, and the importance of deliberative bodies to constitutional interpretation in time, see Jeremy Waldron, *Law and Disagreement* (Oxford: Oxford University Press, 1999).

[92] Jefferson to Edmund Randolph, August 18, 1799, Vol. 31, p. 169; on the concept of the nation in Jefferson's foreign policy, see Peter Onuf, *Jefferson's Empire: The Language of American Nationhood* (Charlottesville: University of Virginia Press, 2000); Brian Steele,

the French Revolution, a position Jefferson argued in his position as Secretary of State to no avail, the laws in use from the colonial period were still valid after the American Revolution. What made such laws valid was their conscious and publicly acknowledged adaptation and subsequent embodiment in the nation rather than the authoritative continuity of inherited laws and legal traditions.

Despite the fact that "our laws, language, religion, and politics and manners are so deeply laid in English foundations, that we shall never cease to consider their history as part of ours," as Jefferson wrote to William Duane, or, as he would write to Albert Gallatin about judges, "a man first & thoroughly initiated into the principles of one system of law, can never become pure & sound in any other," it was nevertheless the case, in Jefferson's view, that the republic needed to be able to represent this influence to itself, to make it changeable by making it tangible and legible.[93] When James Madison read Peter Stephen Du Ponceau's *A Dissertation on the Nature and Extent of the Jurisdiction of the Courts of the United States*, published in 1824, he wrote the author with sharp skepticism of the assertion that the common law was a part of the law of the United States. If the authors of the Constitution had intended any such thing, Madison cautioned, they would have assuredly made it explicit, but in fact they did not. "On sound principles," he continued, "no change whatever in the state of the law can be made but by the Legislative authority."[94] Jefferson and Madison were both sensitive to any imputation that the laws of the American republic were made legitimate and authoritative by their heritage in the history of English law and politics.

Republican narratives of the revolution emphasized the historical actuality of the consenting activity of the people to the laws by which they were governed, and Federalist and constitutional nationalist jurisprudence challenged that narrative in several ways. First and foremost, for Jefferson in particular, the organic continuity of law asserted by Du Ponceau, among others, minimized the politics of discontinuous lawmaking and new use of inherited historical material, undermining the entire edifice of Jefferson's theorization of revolutionary republican constitutionalism. Just as importantly, the folding of practices of use within

Thomas Jefferson and American Nationhood (Cambridge: Cambridge University Press, 2012); Francis D. Cogliano, *Emperor of Liberty: Thomas Jefferson's Foreign Policy* (New Haven: Yale University Press, 2014).

93 Jefferson to William Duane, August 12, 1810, and Jefferson to Albert Gallatin, September 27, 1810, *The Papers of Thomas Jefferson: Retirement Series*, Vol. 3, pp. 5, 125.

94 Madison to Peter S. Du Ponceau, August 1824, *Writings*, pp. 805–6.

ongoing processes of inheritance and transmission challenged not only Jefferson's theorization of law but his articulation of the legitimacy of expansion policy. That challenge was twofold: the narrative of continuity configured the U.S. government as an inheritor of the rights and responsibilities of the conqueror according to conquest theory, which undermined the freer power of removal Jefferson and later Jackson expected to follow from purchase and the extension of American settler cultivation and commerce into western territory. Secondly, and relatedly, the assertion of continuities of legal cultures threatened the legal uniformity of the plane of commerce asserted as vital to safely and legitimately extending republican governance over extensive territory. Partisan conflicts over jurisdiction and expansion brought about fundamental tensions in the longer history of justifying and implementing that expansion.[95]

[95] In the 1823 Supreme Court decision *Johnson & Graham's Lessee* v. *M'Intosh*, John Marshall made use of the doctrines of discovery and conquest to argue that while cessions of Indian land, even by private purchase, were subject to the jurisdiction of the federal court system, Indians themselves had no standing to sue in federal court on account of their subject status and diminished legal rights. In subsequent cases dealing with federally organized Cherokee communities in Georgia, *Cherokee Nation* v. *Georgia* and *Worcester* v. *Georgia*, Marshall adapted his use of the theory of discovery, which as he articulated it was in effect the theory of conquest elaborated by Blackstone, arguing that the Native Americans as original occupants relenting to British and later American conquest constituted distinct and dependent nations within the boundaries of the United States, and as such were in a heavily diminished but nevertheless legally recognizable and reciprocal, treaty-bound relationship with the federal government, given exclusive power of dealing with Native Americans by the U.S. Constitution itself; see John Marshall, Opinions in *Johnson* v. *M'Intosh*, *Cherokee Nation* v. *Georgia*, *Worcester* v. *Georgia*, in *Writings*, Charles A. Hobson, ed. (New York: Library of America, 2010), pp. 575–96, 731–6, 753–79. In the recounting of the history of sovereign conquest rather than settler actions, however, Marshall's decision rebuked the basis for the Jeffersonian and Jacksonian visions of expansion, the idea that, all unpleasantness aside, the cession of Indian land was either a matter of the willing and free exchange of moveable property or of removing Indians from the space required for the willing and freely exchanging activities of others. See Eric Hinderaker, *Elusive Empires: Constructing Colonialism in the Ohio Valley, 1763–1800* (Cambridge: Cambridge University Press, 1997); Tully, *An Approach to Political Philosophy: Locke in Contexts*, ch. 5; Paul A. Passavant, *No Escape: Freedom of Speech and the Paradox of Rights* (New York: New York University Press, 2002); Gary Lawson and Guy Steidman, *The Constitution of Empire: Territorial Expansion and American Legal History* (New Haven: Yale University Press, 2004); Lindsay G. Robertson, *Conquest by Law: How the Discovery of America Dispossessed Indigenous Peoples of Their Lands* (Oxford: Oxford University Press, 2005); Robert J. Miller, *Native America, Discovered and Conquered: Thomas Jefferson, Lewis and Clark, and the Manifest Destiny* (Lincoln: University of Nebraska Press, 2008); Bethel Saler, *The Settlers' Empire: Colonialism and State Formation in America's Old Northwest* (Philadelphia: University of Pennsylvania Press, 2014); Deborah A. Rosen, *Border Law: The First Seminole War and American Nationhood* (Cambridge, MA: Harvard University

Jefferson asserted the right of the United States in lawfully purchased or conquered territory to establish American sovereignty and common law in all new territories in which consent could be procured, and later leaders like Andrew Jackson would directly challenge the inheritance of the powers of the Crown on the part of the U.S. government in relation to Native Americans.

Du Ponceau, like Jefferson understanding his jurisprudence as an extension of his enthusiasm for comparative ethnography and linguistics, told law students in his work that "we live in the midst of the common law, we inhale it at every breadth, imbibe it at every pore; ... it is interwoven with the very idiom that we speak, and we cannot learn another system of laws without learning at the same time another language."[96] As American sovereignty and population moved west, Du Ponceau argued, so went the jurisdiction of the common law, just as the settlers of the British colonies had extended the reach of British law, sovereignty, and empire. The American Revolution had not disturbed the organic and unbroken quality of particular cultural, legal, and linguistic histories, and nor would American expansion into the west. In his *Dissertation*, Du Ponceau took time to suggest that the amalgamation of civil and common law taking place in Louisiana was unproblematic, because whether the local inhabitants knew it or not, their usage of French civil law amounted to their possession of a customary and therefore common law. The efforts of his friend Edward Livingston to produce a code were surely welcome and would go a long way in settling the uncertain jurisdiction in the Orleans territory, Du Ponceau suggested, but even with codification would come disputes over meaning.[97] He argued for a philosophical jurisprudence inherited from continental legal learning, necessarily at home with a pluralistic and comparative framework for legal adaptation and change over time, and so safely applied to the common law of the United States.

Press, 2015). On the primary role of purchase to the cession of Native American lands to British and then American settlers, see Stuart Banner, *How the Indians Lost Their Land: Law and Power on the Frontier* (Cambridge, MA: Harvard University Press, 2005); on the theory of conquest and its relation to the question of Native American land title, see Aziz Rana, *The Two Faces of American Freedom* (Cambridge, MA: Harvard University Press, 2010); Yirush, Settlers, Liberty, and Empire.

[96] Du Ponceau, *A Dissertation on the Nature and Extent of the Jurisdiction of the Courts of the United States* (Philadelphia: Abraham Small, 1824), p. 91.

[97] *Ibid*, pp. 81–2.

The favorable mention of Edward Livingston was a legacy of the intense legal battle that raged from 1810–1811 over the matter of the federal seizure of what came to be called the New Orleans Batture, and the episode provides an appropriate coda to the tensions inherent in the Jeffersonian vision of expansion and jurisdiction. Livingston had been a Democratic-Republican in New York where he befriended Du Ponceau, and having been caught up in political scandal not of his own making, he moved to New Orleans immediately after the Louisiana Purchase. There, he proved a political obstacle to the goals of the territorial governor, Claiborne, and through him the Jefferson Administration and ultimately Jefferson himself. Livingston, who had to fight accusations and rumors of his attachment to Aaron Burr (by that point not exactly one of Jefferson's favorite people), had been a passionate enemy of judicial power for his entire political career, and he stoked fears that federal imposition of common law rules with regard to real property was an attempt to conquer and usurp property, including land and slaves, held by locals under their inherited legal traditions.[98] His repeated efforts at alternative codification were meant to introduce a clear and concise framework where he and others would be relatively free to stake out new property for themselves. While Jefferson had initially instructed Claiborne to respect local legal customs and proceed gradually, objections to Livingston's codifications and frustrations at his successes in thwarting constitutional goals of setting up a common law court system compelled Jefferson and Congress to pursue increasingly aggressive and ultimately futile efforts to expunge and fully Americanize the civil law legal culture of the territory. When Livingston claimed a right of first

[98] George Dargo, *Jefferson's Louisiana: Politics and the Clash of Legal Traditions* (Cambridge, MA: Harvard University Press, 1975). Mark Fernandez has corrected the traditional understanding of the contest as a "clash of legal traditions," arguing that Livingston was pursuing his own vision of Americanization; see "Edward Livingston, America, and France: Making Law," in Peter Kastor and Francois Weil, eds. *Empires of the Imagination: Transatlantic Histories of the Louisiana Purchase* (Charlottesville: University of Virginia Press, 2009), pp. 268–98; the account given here owes much to the above and to Peter J. Kastor, *The Nation's Crucible: The Louisiana Purchase and the Creation of America* (New Haven: Yale University Press, 2004). The Louisiana Purchase was negotiated by Edward Livingston's older brother, Robert Livingston, who had been a member of the committee charged with drafting the Declaration of Independence, and had served as the Chancellor of New York before being appointed Minister to France by President Thomas Jefferson. Edward Livingston, or his part, would go on to serve under Andrew Jackson at the Battle of New Orleans, later becoming a U.S. Senator from Louisiana, and then Secretary of State and Minister to France during Jackson's presidency.

possession to an exposed riverbed (a batture) in the Mississippi River, he was ultimately challenged on Jefferson's orders.

Livingston sued Jefferson personally, leading Jefferson to write and publish an extended memo on the legality of his actions according to the civil law in effect in New Orleans at the time. Aside from serving as a performance of his legal erudition (most of the pamphlet and the surrounding correspondence with his own attorneys on the issue aimed to instruct them on how to proceed in court), the pamphlet and the context that produced it mark a telling episode in the history of Jefferson's forays into the history of law, jurisprudence, and jurisdiction. Neither the civil nor the common law in any iteration, Jefferson asserted, gave grounds for claims of private appropriation on what was until specifically granted public property, nor did either grant rights of alluvial holding within the limits a city.[99] The size and commercial importance of the Mississippi River, Jefferson asserted, made the idea of having every municipality with adjoining territory capable of deciding its own procedures of use and possession absurd: "it is certainly for the good of the whole nation to assimilate as much as possible all it's parts, to strengthen their analogies, obliterate the traits of difference, and to deal law and justice to all by the same rule and measure."[100] Finally, Jefferson moved to refute the pursuit of an injunction against the government from the Superior Court in the New Orleans territory, as an injunction was a power of Chancery jurisdiction and the power of that jurisdiction did not exist in the territory, according to Jefferson. Congress had authorized the court system and temporary government there according to statute that relied on the Northwest Ordinance of 1787 and which mandated common law jurisdiction in the territories. While Congress had left standing laws in force until they were altered by the territorial legislature, Jefferson admitted, it had granted no powers of Chancery courts to the regular operations of justice in this or any other territory.[101] Roman and later civil law maxims of equity and natural right, while perhaps correctly part of the meaning of equity in civil law courts, had no standing in a dependent territory and under a superior jurisdiction claimed by an imperial sovereignty.

Whatever the merits, chancery would have allowed much greater consideration of civil law arguments from absolute right of occupancy

[99] Jefferson, *The Proceedings of the Government of the United States in Maintaining the Public Right to the Beach of the Mississippi, Adjacent to New Orleans, against the Intrusion of Edward Livingston* (New York: Ezra Sargeant, 1812), pp. 30, 40.

[100] *Ibid*, p. 50. [101] *Ibid*, pp. 71–5.

and dominion made by Livingston, and Jefferson was compelled to argue in response that the underdeveloped constitutional structure in the territory did not contain within itself the powers to entertain arguments from equity and exercise chancery jurisdiction. He won the argument, but his administration never succeeded in its persistent efforts to remake the legal landscape of the New Orleans territory. Moving away from the beginning of his career as a practitioner and theorist of law who came out of a century-long fight on the part of Virginia elites to assert the local powers of police and chancery jurisdiction as contained in the lawmaking sovereignty of the colonial assemblies, Jefferson now turned to argue that the newly constituted territorial assembly lacked the power to establish such markers of local sovereignty. He combated one effort at codification with what amounted to another. In justifying empire, Jefferson had refused to see and take into account the complex histories of the inhabitants of the North American continent. In his articulation of a naturally self-ordering and uniform plane of expanding society, the particular historicity and acknowledgment of practices of transmission and representation as a necessary part of constitutional practice had faded from view.

6

The Discipline of Recollection

In retirement, Jefferson took up a famously extensive correspondence with John Adams after years of embittered silence in the wake of their ideological conflict and political rivalry. He attended to his own recollections of his life and career, organizing his papers and records, copying and archiving correspondence, and in his last years composing a short autobiography that was nominally for the use and reference of his family. He once again pursued in earnest the copying and printing of his collection of the manuscript copies of the laws of colonial Virginia, opening his library to any who could make use of it, including an Irish radical, Jon Burk, who used them to write a history of Virginia, George Ticknor, a young and aspiring antiquarian from Massachusetts who had been sent by Adams to Monticello, and William Waller Hening, who based his collection and publication of Virginia's *Statutes at Large* in large part on Jefferson's authoritative collection.[1] As had been the case for most of his adult life, Jefferson corresponded with young men on the arts of reading, and studying law in particular. In these projects and more, Jefferson was attending to problems in the politics of historical representation, and how these representations were transformed and in turn contributed to the transformation of ways of thinking about law and constitutionalism.

[1] On Jefferson's retirement, see Dumas Malone, *The Sage of Monticello* (New York: Little, Brown, 1981); Merrill D. Peterson, *Thomas Jefferson and the New Nation* (Oxford: Oxford University Press, 1970); *Adams and Jefferson: A Revolutionary Dialogue* (Oxford: Oxford University Press, 1978); Kevin J. Hayes, *The Road to Monticello: The Life and Mind of Thomas Jefferson* (Oxford: Oxford University Press, 2008).

He was once again purposefully taking stock of histories as transmitted and assembled, and examining the possibilities and implications of their reassembly.

Two projects in particular bear out this attention: his composition of rules of parliamentary procedure for the US Senate, and his construction of a heavily edited version of the New Testament. These series of texts illustrate Jefferson at his most eccentric and his most engaged with experimentation in the use of history. But along with the wider trajectory of his intellectual practice late in his career and in his retirement, up to and including the founding of the University of Virginia, these projects went on within what were by the early nineteenth century rigidifying boundaries of racial subjectivity. As Jefferson gave more and more attention to the dynamic and experimental historical, textual practices that had been typical of his life as a radical and eccentric theorist of law and constitutionalism, he did so increasingly within a shrinking zone of protected self-management. He made, unmade, and remade texts in the space of his study, but his thinking went on largely within the confines of particularized and anxiously guarded regimes of historical subjectivity, regimes that Jefferson himself had played and would continue to play no small part in building, maintaining, and policing. Even late in life, his thinking about law and constitutionalism was predicated on the occluding work of securing and guarding the boundaries of the historical subjectivity he saw at the center of his constitutional project.

Jefferson experimented with representing to himself and to others the potentialities of the transmitted histories at play in all of these seemingly divergent arenas of private and public life. His preparation of the manual for parliamentary procedure in the United States Senate, his extractive and secular editing of the New Testament, his attention to publishing the collections of Virginia records he had amassed, and his designs for his home at Monticello and the "academical village" of the University of Virginia each in their own way reworked the materials of historical representation. At the same time, Jefferson carried out these projects with a certain degree of political impotency. His own withdraw to Monticello and his repeated celebration of the happiness of private as opposed to public life sat in stark contrast to his continued insistence that freedom required participation in and preparation for public affairs. The withdraw to what he called his "*sanctum sanctorum*," or his "holy of holies," his acquisition of an additional library for retirement after sale of his main library to Congress in 1814, and his "seeking refuge in the histories of other times," as he wrote to William Duane, complimented the limiting of his historical and political vision to the white men of Virginia.[2] All of these textual projects took place within an ossified space of guarded historicity.

INSTITUTIONS OF ASSEMBLY

Almost immediately after retiring, Jefferson turned to the establishment of local tribunal governments, or ward republics, as necessary conduits for popular political participation. "I have indeed two great measures at heart, without which no republic can maintain itself in strength," Jefferson wrote to John Tyler in 1810. He intended to press Virginians for a plan of "general education, to enable every man to judge for himself what will secure or endanger his freedom," and to "divide every county into hundreds" so that every child would be within reach of a public school, and every adult would be in reach of electing officers to form a "corporation to manage all its concerns, to take care of its roads, its poor, and its police by patrols," as well as "jurors to serve where requisite."[3] Education and political participation were the wellsprings of a vital republic, and Jefferson thought that the law needed to guarantee them. Only then, Jefferson reasoned, could sovereignty be broken up and dispersed across the federal republic. "The way to have good and safe government," Jefferson wrote to Joseph Cabell in 1816, is to "divide it among the many" for liberty became threatened when power was concentrated in a single body. Thus would the system of the ward republic "form a gradation of authorities, standing each on the basis of law," for only "where every man is a sharer in the direction of his ward republic, or of some of the higher ones, and feels he is participator in the government of affairs, not merely at an election one day in the year, but every day; when there shall not be a man in the State who will not be a member of one of its councils, great or small," will the citizen be sufficiently attentive to the maintenance of his liberty and that of the public.[4] This imagined citizen was not just a buyer or seller. Clearly, Jefferson had made another turn in thinking.

[2] Jefferson to William Duane, April 4, 1813, *The Papers of Thomas Jefferson: Retirement Series*, J. Jefferson Looney, ed. (Princeton: Princeton University Press, 2010), Vol. 6. p. 53.

[3] Jefferson to John Tyler, May 26, 1810, *Papers of Thomas Jefferson: Retirement Series*, Vol. 2, pp. 420–1.

[4] Jefferson to Joseph C. Cabell, February 2, 1816, *Papers of Thomas Jefferson: Retirement Series*, Vol. 9, pp. 436–7; see Hannah Arendt, *On Revolution* (New York: Penguin, 2006), p. 227; on the implications of Arendt's arguments about council democracy, see Dana Villa, *Public Freedom* (Princeton: Princeton University Press, 2008); Jason Frank,

Jefferson's interest in the development of the ward republics came out of his experience of partisan politics as much as from his attempt to theorize the institutions of self-governance. In response to his enforced embargo of British trade in American ports, Jefferson told Joseph Cabell, "I felt the foundation of the government shaken under my feet by the New England townships. There was not an individual in their states whose body was not thrown with all its momentum into action."[5] He went on to surmise that the broader public outside of Federalist New England was in support of the measure, but that they lacked the institutional means to voice organized political opinion. The accuracy of Jefferson's optimistic faith in the popularity of his embargo is doubtful at best, but his experience of having the "foundations of the government" over which he presided shaken to the core left him with an even greater sense of urgency for the need of common citizens (his common citizens) to be able to participate in politics. In stark contrast to John Adams' understanding of a polity governed by laws and not men, Jefferson suggested to John Taylor that a republic is "a government by its citizens in mass, acting directly and personally, according to the rules established by the majority; and that every other government is republican, in proportion as it has in its composition more or less of this ingredient of the direct action of the citizens."[6] The way to incorporate this principle within a federal and extensive republic was to create multiple orders of spaces and times where the citizen felt that they were part of the government.

To Jefferson, the principle of including within the structure of the government room for the direct action of the citizens was a partisan one. "This is a game," Jefferson had written of politics in the 1790's, "where principles are the stake."[7] What was at stake was the degree to which fidelity to the spirit of

Constituent Moments: Enacting the People in Postrevolutionary America (Durham: Duke University Press, 2010).

[5] *Ibid*, p. 437; on the politics of the Embargo Act of 1807, see Drew McCoy, *The Elusive Republic: Political Economy in Jeffersonian America* (Chapel Hill: University of North Carolina Press, 1980); Burton Spivak, *Jefferson's English Crisis: Commerce, Embargo, and the Republican Revolution* (Charlottesville: University of Virginia Press, 1988); on how the idea of the ward republic might be seen to fit more comfortably into Jefferson's political thought, see distinctly: Richard K. Matthews, *The Radical Politics of Thomas Jefferson: A Revisionist View* (Lawrence: University of Kansas Press, 1986); David N. Mayer, *The Constitutional Thought of Thomas Jefferson* (Charlottesville: University of Virginia Press, 1994); Jean M. Yarbrough, *American Virtues: Thomas Jefferson and the Character of a Free People* (Lawrence: University of Kansas Press, 1998).

[6] Jefferson to John Taylor, May 28, 1816, *Papers of Thomas Jefferson: Retirement Series*, Vol. 10, pp. 86–7.

[7] Jefferson to John Taylor, June 4, 1798, *Papers of Thomas Jefferson*, Vol. 30, p. 389.

the revolution required planning for and instituting the capacity of the people to participate in law and politics. For Jefferson, this was an uncertain and problematic but necessary bet on his own ability to design institutions and a legal culture that produced the particular textually activated mode of subjectivity he understood as appropriate to constitutionalism in a democratic republic. Like his earlier plans for Virginia constitutional reform, Jefferson envisioned in the proposals for ward republics the fostering of a culture of active political participation, made possible by a critically engaged approach to the textual material that instituted civil history.

In his letter to Samuel Kercheval in 1816, Jefferson again laid out the advantages of implementing a system of ward republics, returning to the constitutional skepticism he had expressed to Madison while in France, and offering his strongest statement of the particularly material textuality he wanted to see fostered as a necessary part of constitutionalism: "Some men look at constitutions with sanctimonious reverence, and deem them like the arc of the covenant, too sacred to be touched. They ascribe to the men of the preceding age a wisdom more than human, and suppose what they did to be beyond amendment."[8] Jefferson insisted that to surrender the freedom of constitutional action and change was to make a terrible mistake. He recommended once again that Virginia should follow in the example of other states and not fear constitutional revision, and embrace the freedom "to correct the crude essays of our first and unexperienced, although wise, virtuous, and well-meaning councils. And lastly, let us provide in our constitution for its revision at stated periods."[9] Jefferson's plans for the participatory republic were thus related to a series of textual projects. They amounted to what John Dunn calls a "democratization of prudence, a spreading out of the burden of judging and choosing soberly about political questions."[10] Jefferson's various projects of representing the constructed character of fundamental texts suggested a radically alternative way of using founding documents as "American scripture," for it was in their materiality and availability for use that such documents could be what he called in his inaugural address "texts of civic instruction."[11]

[8] Jefferson to Samuel Kercheval, July 12, 1816, *Papers of Thomas Jefferson: Retirement Series*, Vol. 10, p. 226.

[9] *Ibid*, p. 227.

[10] John Dunn, *Interpreting Political Responsibility* (Princeton: Princeton University Press, 1990), p. 214.

[11] See Pauline Maier, *American Scripture: Making the Declaration of Independence* (New York: Knopf, 1997); Jefferson, "First Inaugural Address," *Papers of Thomas Jefferson*, Barbara B. Oberg, ed. (Princeton: Princeton University Press, 2006), Vol. 33, p. 151.

HISTORY IN THE ASSEMBLY

Jefferson approached the problem of ward republics as he did other political and constitutional projects, insisting on the viability of the sometimes ancient and always constituent origins of the tradition and authority of the institutions and practices of law. His use of the term "hundreds" directly tied his theory of the ward to a discourse of ancient constitutionalism that Jefferson had used as inspiration for his proposals for the revolutionary constitution of Virginia, and that had characterized British Whig and oppositional historiography for the previous two centuries. The inscription of debates about the antiquity of parliament and the historical character of rules and customs into the text of the printed manual on parliamentary procedure was a singular episode in the history of Jefferson's experimentation in a kind of public and political historiography. As Secretary of State, Vice President, and later President, Jefferson had kept private records of cabinet meetings, diplomatic conversations, and collected printed ephemera from bustling partisan presses in order to construct an alternative historical representation to what he thought was dominant Federalist historiography. That cluster of ideas included the power and importance of George Washington as a political symbol, and the proven wisdom of concentrating national power in a central government and of emulating British political economy. Jefferson's parliamentary notes and manual were of a piece with his effort to craft an alternative historical imaginary, but in this particular case Jefferson returned to his earlier reading of common law precedent and parliamentary history, and did so in texts that were intended for direct use in the institutions of government.[12] Once again, Jefferson was understanding and responding to political context in an early modern humanist mold, consciously tinkering with representations of history by assembling new representations of eccentric counter-histories.

In various drafts of his manual of parliamentary practice for Congress, Jefferson directly engaged historical controversies over the antiquity of Parliament and the relevance of Norman and pre-Norman English constitutional history for understanding and interpreting seventeenth- and

[12] Thomas Jefferson, *The Complete Anas of Thomas Jefferson*, Franklin B. Sawvel, ed. (New York: Round Table Press, 1903); Joanne Freeman, *Affairs of Honor: National Politics in the New Republic* (New Haven: Yale University Press, 2001); Matthew E. Crow, "Jefferson's 'Anas' and Autobiography,"*A Companion to Thomas Jefferson*, Francis D. Cogliano, ed. (Oxford: Wiley-Blackwell, 2011), pp. 477–90.

eighteenth-century political conflict.[13] By recording and representing what he thought he could know of the role of village and national councils in medieval English political structure as part of what made up the history of the principles and practices of assemblies, for example, Jefferson deliberately contradicted the authoritative narratives advanced by David Hume's *History of England* as well as John Adams' *Defense of the Constitutions of the Government of the United States of America*. In his desire to minimize the reach of Hume's influence, Jefferson went so far as to request American publication of John Baxter's 1801 abridged and "corrected" edition of Hume's *History*. While Jefferson had recommended the *History of England* to younger readers and admitted devouring it as a student, his life in political combat had left him less tolerant of the historiographical support to established institutional order that he read Hume as purposefully providing through his extended depoliticizing of the ancient constitution.[14] The issue for Jefferson was precisely Hume's skepticism of the political status and use of historical materials. That being said, it would be a mistake to assume that Jefferson's divergence from Hume and his use of the language of ancient constitutionalism amounted to a "vulgar Whiggism" that simply ignored the skeptical, scientific achievements of what Duncan Forbes called Hume's "establishment history."[15] Jefferson turned to what one could call a kind of disestablishment history.

For Hume, those who professed the unproblematic continuity of components of ancient constitutionalism within the extended development of the British Constitution spun narratives that were not only historically and philosophically obtuse but politically dangerous as well. The dominance of the Whig party in politics had solidified the hegemonic character of the Whig narrative of its own ascendancy as the restoration and modern perfection of British liberty. While "in some particulars" the

[13] On the development of parliament and parliamentary privilege, see John Robert Maddicott, *The Origins of the English Parliament, 924–1327* (Oxford: Oxford University Press, 2010); on subsequent development of parliamentary privilege, see Josh Cafetz, *Democracy's Privileged Few: Legislative Privilege and Democratic Norms in the British and American Constitutions* (New Haven: Yale University Press, 2007).

[14] Jefferson to William Duane, August 12, 1810, *Papers of Thomas Jefferson: Retirement Series*, Vol. 3, pp. 4–6; Jefferson to Thomas Skipwith, August 3, 1771, *Papers of Thomas Jefferson*, Vol. 1, pp. 76–81; on Jefferson's reading of Hume, see Douglas L. Wilson, "Jefferson vs. Hume," *The William and Mary Quarterly*, Vol. 46, No. 1 (January 1989), pp. 49–70.

[15] Duncan Forbes, *Hume's Philosophical Politics* (Cambridge: Cambridge University Press, 1975), p. 264.

Whig ascendancy had been "advantageous to the state," Hume reasoned, it "has proved destructive to the truth of history, and has established many gross falsehoods."[16] Hume was well aware that at times throughout British history, narratives containing various degrees of mythical content, whether civil or spiritual, had played an essential role in organizing law and politics. Modern experience, however, demonstrated the dangers of ignoring the political effects of the stories people told themselves. The passions of party and faction, when planted in the fundamental constituting narratives of civil government, seized the minds of the public and politicians alike, and could tear the entire fabric of society apart. Whig historians like Paul de Rapin-Thoyras or William Petyt were not only incorrect to assert the continuity of principles of ancient constitutionalism across the long and complicated history of British institutions; they were providing an unnecessarily precarious, and therefore potentially destructive picture of the status of liberty in the modern political order.[17]

Influenced by the work of Henry Spelman and John Brady, Hume found the Norman invasion and subsequent reigns of William the Conquer and Edward I had fundamentally changed the structure of English law and society by introducing feudal laws regarding the possession and transmission of land.[18] Along with the observation that as a result of the feudal revolution nobles technically held their land in a baronial capacity in the King's dominion, Hume articulated a great deal of skepticism as to the historical reality of a pre-Conquest parliamentary democracy that survived to become the royal council of nobles and finally Parliament. What came after, Hume asserted against the overarching Whig narrative, was of an entirely different character than what had come before. It was bad history, bad philosophy, and even worse politics to pretend that the reported meeting of the village chiefs in Saxon England had gone on to force the Norman kings into acknowledging the power of

[16] David Hume, *The History of England, from the Settlement of Julius Caesar to the Revolution of 1688* (Indianapolis: Liberty Fund, 1985), Vol. 6, p. 553.

[17] See Pocock, "Hume and the American Revolution: The Dying Thoughts of a North Briton," and "The Varieties of Whiggism from Exclusion to Reform: A History of Ideology and Discourse," *Virtue, Commerce, and History: Essays on Political Thought and History, Chiefly in the Eighteenth Century* (Cambridge: Cambridge University Press, 1985), pp. 25–142, 215–310, *Barbarism and Religion, Volume 2: Narratives of Civil Government* (Cambridge: Cambridge University Press, 1999), pp. 163–240.

[18] On the "Brady Controversy," see Pocock, *The Ancient Constitution and the Feudal Law: A Re-Issue with Retrospect* (Cambridge: Cambridge University Press, 1987), pp. 182–251.

a parliament in the British Constitution. It was equally absurd to posit that such meetings were fitting subjects for retrieval and redemption after nearly a millennium of history and under conditions of the modern state, growing populations, and global commerce.

The history of England as told through an accurate, skeptical history of the British Constitution revealed the gradual development of a "prodigious fabric" from which none of its component ideals, practices, and events could be separated while preserving the integrity of that fabric.[19] "In each of these successive alterations," of periodic social structures, Hume asserted, "the only rule of government which is intelligible or carries any authority with it is the established practice of the age and maxims of administration which are at the time prevalent and universally assented to." Established practice was the product of a long and complicated history that was possible to narrate but the various strands of which were impossible to disentangle. As Hume continued:

> Above all, a civilized nation like the English, who have happily established the most perfect and most accurate system of liberty that ever was found compatible with government, ought to be cautious in appealing to the practice of their ancestors, as certain rules for their present conduct. An acquaintance with the ancient periods of their government is *chiefly* useful by instructing them to cherish their present constitution, from a comparison or contrast with the condition of those distant times. And it is also *curious* by showing them the remote, and commonly faint and disfigured, originals of the most finished and most noble institutions, and by instructing them in the great mixture of accident which commonly concurs with a small ingredient of wisdom and foresight in erecting the complicated fabric of the most perfect government.[20]

Like Jefferson's other great constitutional and historiographical nemesis of eighteenth-century Britain, William Blackstone, Hume narrated a history of the slow stitching together of multifaceted strands of change and continuity. It was the very complexity of this process that lent the resulting "fabric," a word Hume shared with Blackstone, its great authority. The purpose of the study of history, for Hume, was to appreciate the immense complexity of history and caution against pursuing the desire to disentangle that history.

At stake in Hume's reading of the past and in the reading of Hume's history was not so much what happened but how to interpret records of what happened and what the civic status of these records and

[19] Hume, *History of England*, Vol. 1, p. 455.
[20] Hume, *History of England*, Vol. 2, p. 525.

interpretations would be. "The ancient Saxons," Hume admitted, "like the other German nations, where each individual was inured to arms, and where the independence of men was secured by a great equality of possessions, seem to have admitted of a considerable mixture of democracy into their form of government."[21] The question was to what extent such ancient liberty and its apparent foundations in the operation of a kind of agrarian law mattered after the Norman Conquest. Even before the conquest, the expansion of Saxon settlement "produced a great inequality in property" that tended to encourage the establishment of a more aristocratic form of government. It was well known, and admitted to an extent even by Hume's Whig interlocutors, that the conquest "threw more authority into the hands of the sovereign, which, however, admitted of great control; though derived less from the general forms of the constitution, which were inaccurate and irregular, than from the independent power enjoyed by each baron in his particular district or province."[22] In the Saxon constitution, the consolidation of property in the hands of large landholders had already undermined the power of the democratic practices used in local governance. The most revolutionary aspect of the conquest was the agreement among the nobility to become barons owing payments to the King in the form of taxes and military service in exchange for an acknowledgment of their rights of usage in the land, the establishment of feudal relations between the barons or lords and their dependents, and the granting of their freedom to participate in the deliberations of the King's council. It was a question, then, of how to interpret the fact that after the conquest, the King called his council into being.

For Hume, the King created what would become Parliament as an act of sovereign will. The body of nobles who would compel John I to sign the Magna Carta therefore had little or nothing to do with the deliberative councils that had apparently existed at multiple levels of Anglo-Saxon society previously. An important part of this claim was the fundamental role that royal sovereignty and the establishment of feudal relations between manorial lords and various classes of laboring servants had played in the subsequent development of the British constitution. The establishment of a relatively reliable political order and laws protecting persons and property had been the social basis for the encouragement of the personal liberty that would later support the unparalleled civil liberty enjoyed by subjects of the British Constitution. That modern liberty had

[21] *Ibid*, p. 524. [22] *Ibid*, pp. 524–5.

its origins in the raw power of a conquering monarch and the anxiety of an armed aristocracy was only the penultimate example of the mixture of accident and human nature of which so much of recorded history consisted. In Hume's eyes, those who trumpeted the cause of liberty were ignorant of the actual historical causes behind what liberty they enjoyed, and therefore mistakenly thought they and anyone else would want or could know how to live under the conditions of a primordial, barbarian, often hotly contested and violent political order of English ancient liberty.

John Adams cited Hume's *History* as well as many of Hume's essays in a similar historiographical effort to dismiss the desire for an ancient, more demanding and participatory form of liberty found in radical political arguments on both sides of the Atlantic. In his *Defense of the Constitutions of Government of the United States of America*, Adams responded to Turgot's critique of the reliance of the majority of American state constitutions on the British mixed and bicameral model. While in the years leading up to the revolution, Adams had gone as far as Jefferson and James Wilson in finding the authority of the British Constitution in the American colonies to be a matter of willful adoption on the part of the colonists, in his *Defense* he put forward an extensive historical argument that followed Hume in comparing the balance and protection of the British Constitution favorably with the gothic constitutions of the Saxons, the classical confederacies of Greece, and the Roman republic.

For Adams, the possible willingness of Americans to walk away from their inheritance of British institutions in favor of a chimera of popular, democratic constitutionalism was a frightening prospect. What would Cicero and Tacitus say, Adams warned, if the Americans, at the advice of the great philosophers of the age, had abandoned the model of the most free, solid, and durable government in history, and instead opted to "set up the governments of ancient Goths and modern Indians?"[23] Following Hume, Adams found the established levels of society, the maintenance of a balance between the naturally existing elements of monarchy, aristocracy, and democracy, and the protection of private property achieved by the passage of the British Constitution through its complex history to be principles with which modern polities could not do without while maintaining freedom and stability at the same time. Confronted with the accusation that American leaders had by and large uncritically adopted

[23] John Adams, *A Defense of the Constitutions of Government of the United States of America, Against the Attack of M. Turgot in his Letter to Dr. Price* (Philadelphia: Budd and Bartram, 1797), Vol. 1, p. xix.

British models instead of seeing to the potential of their revolution, Adams responded by offering a vast history of the superiority of balanced constitutional order. In his own right, Adams was aware of the degree to which constitutionalism was a historiographical enterprise and that therefore constitutional strife was in part a struggle over the modes of reading, interpreting, and representing constitutional text and history that would prevail in practice.

Jefferson's composition of his *Parliamentary Pocket-Book* and the *Manual for Parliamentary Practice* directly engaged him in the historiographical issues at stake in the narratives advanced by Hume and to a lesser extent, Adams. Indeed, at some later point in life, Jefferson filled the last entry of his legal commonplace book with selections from Hume's *History*, collecting several examples of warnings against taking the myth of the people as the origins of all just power too seriously.[24] The recording of such sentiments were proof, for Jefferson, that Hume was a worthy adversary. Just as he had in his legal critique of Blackstone, Jefferson took up an occasion of drafting new rules to display, if only to himself at first, the assembled, palimpsest character of texts that instituted and guided the boundaries and course of political action in a republic. While the *Manual* was published in 1800 and revised in 1812, the pocket-book was a record of reading Jefferson had kept throughout his life, a commonplace book of parliamentary law, procedure, and constitutional principle.

At the end of his tenure as Vice President from 1797–1801, in which he had been the president pro-tempore of the Senate, and before his election to the Presidency, Jefferson wrote to George Wythe about the collective need for a parliamentary manual in both houses of Congress. "I had, at an early period of life, read a great deal on the subject, & commonplaced everything I read," Jefferson wrote on parliamentary law. "This commonplace has been my pillar but there are many questions of practice on which that is silent," he regretted, and he had written to his old law professor for assistance in procuring accurate information for specifics.[25] Like an ancient law, Jefferson told Wythe that his erudition on the subject had fallen into "desuetude," and needed to be recovered. It was under the tutelage of Wythe that Jefferson had learned to use his reading and note-taking, his "commonplacing," as a site for historical investigation and

[24] Jefferson, *Legal Commonplace Book*, Thomas Jefferson Papers, Special Collections, Library of Congress, Series 5, #905.

[25] Jefferson to George Wythe, February 28, 1800, *The Papers of Thomas Jefferson*, Vol. 31, pp. 400–1.

thinking through the entire accessible history of a given usage. Jefferson sent Wythe copies of his notes, and Wythe seemed to pick up on the nature of the project. In response, he wrote to Jefferson encouraging him to eventually publish the piece, calling for the collection of precedents and historical references in Greek.[26] The appreciative and playful response of Wythe registered not only the mutually appreciated humanistic performance of the linguistic and legal erudition he shared with this prize student but the manner in which Jefferson had gone about investigating and representing the history of parliamentary activity.

The commonplace book of parliamentary law eventually became what Jefferson called the *Parliamentary Pocket-Book*, a manuscript that was copied and circulated among friends and in Congress but not printed at the time.[27] Jefferson wasted no time in making the historiographical stakes of his text clear: the opening entries identify the three estates, the King, Lords, and Commons, noting that the Lords included the "lords Spiritual as well as temporal, not as Spiritual persons by reason of the Temporal baronies annexed to their bishoprics," and noting further that Parliament had the right to operate "*excluso clero*," without the formal representation of ecclesiastical authority.[28] Jefferson, in effect, constructed a narrative of the origins of parliamentary power in the British Constitution in the early entries. That narrative depended on an archaeological mode of reading the origins of the institutions in question that Jefferson had practiced throughout his life. While "it had been useful for the kings of England by their charters to give to towns a right of sending members to parliament" Jefferson acknowledged, the commons eventually "declared the elections void which were made by the prince's charters." Citing the statute books, the English handbook *Lex Parliamentaria* (the most heavily cited source in the text) and the work of the seventeenth-century royalist antiquarian Henry Spelman, Jefferson's entries acknowledge the fact, inconvenient for traditional Whig historiography, that both before and after the Conquest the King had called into being England's

[26] George Wythe to Jefferson, April 23, 1800, *The Papers of Thomas Jefferson*, Vol. 31, p. 539.

[27] Jefferson shared the manuscript with John Beckley, a political supporter, Clerk of the House of Representatives, and whom Jefferson appointed as the first Librarian of Congress in 1802; Beckley returned the manuscript along with a copy of his notes to Jefferson, see Beckley to Jefferson, March 15, 1798, *The Political Writings of John James Beckley*, Gerard W. Gawalt, ed. (Washington, DC: Library of Congress, 1995), pp. 141–6.

[28] Thomas Jefferson, "Parliamentary Pocket-Book," *Jefferson's Parliamentary Writings*, Wilbur Samuel Howell, ed. (Princeton: Princeton University Press, 1988), p. 47.

highest deliberative body. What was in question was not that this happened, or whether it mattered, but why it happened and thereby how it mattered. Jefferson applied a hermeneutic principle that he had developed and practiced as a young attorney, legal researcher, and draftsman of legislative text.

In the erudition self-consciously performed in the text, Jefferson displayed the aristocratic possession of a sufficient library and depth of reading. At the same time, his excavations and representations aimed to restore the contents of the archive and legislative record to open, contemporary vision and use. "In the Saxon government," the third entry begins, "there was an appeal from the lesser assemblies of the people to the greater." Appeals could go from the "courts of manners & Tythings to the Wapentakes or Hundred Courts, from these again to the Folkmotes or County cts., and from these to the Witenagemote or Parliament."[29] Building on reading he had done as a reader of the law and recorded in his legal commonplace book, Jefferson began his pocket-book on parliamentary procedure with attention to what could be known of the assembly practices at work in ancient and medieval English history. Fragments get combined and appear as reassembled, but are never stitched back together completely. The pieces and passages Jefferson assembled were an attempt at holding and representing a history, or histories, and without the aid and organization of tradition.

What interested him most was his finding that common men appeared to have maintained certain elective and deliberating powers, and that however rigid the gradation of assemblies at different levels of society, the higher assemblies retained appellate jurisdiction above and beyond the rulings of judges. Citing Spelman, *Lex Parliamentaria*, and the Saxon Chronicle, Jefferson noted in the fourth entry: "Among the Saxons no officer Civil, Military, or Ecclesiastical could be appointed without the free election of those over whom he was to preside," and further noted that Bishops continued to be elected after the Conquest.[30] As he had written in his early essay, "Whether Christianity is a Part of the Common Law," recorded in his legal commonplace book, and which he circulated again to a young law student in 1814, Jefferson emphasized the fact that at the origins of the British constitutional edifice the laity could be found to have played a significant role. He

[29] Jefferson, "Parliamentary Pocket-Book," *Jefferson's Parliamentary Writings*, p. 47.
[30] Jefferson, "Parliamentary Pocket-Book," *Jefferson's Parliamentary Writings*, p. 48.

was drawing on his earlier reading in law and legal history, and his long-held and extensive records of that reading.

In the narrative that Jefferson spun as his pocket-book proceeded, a parliament and its members retained privileges that guaranteed their special status and role as debating legislators. Matters of parliament were not ruled by the common law, and the laws of parliament protected speech in the assembly from regulation. Indeed, as Jefferson detailed the privileges of parliaments, he translated from the law-French of Sir Robert Brooke that "where any matter is against reason and yet the party has no remedy at the Common law he shall sue for remedy" in parliament, and noted that this power had over the course of its history been transferred to the High Court of Chancery.[31] Jefferson was again discussing equity. In calling attention to the degree to which ancient parliaments had been concerned to keep temporal and spiritual power distinct, and in the equitable jurisdiction of the highest legislative body, Jefferson sought alternatives to Hume's argument that clerical learning in theology and Roman law stood at the root of subsequent British law and constitutionalism. He was drawing on narratives of ecclesiastical history that emphasized the elective and deliberative role of the laity in the ancient English political world.

The *Parliamentary Pocket-Book* and the later *Manual* were histories of usage intended as guides for present and future action. A studied awareness of the historicity of usage is apparent in the substance of both texts and even more so in the manner in which Jefferson went about composing them. The pocket-book contained several references to parliamentary laws that were no longer in formal use, and included in its entries "desuetude," a parliamentary bill or declaratory act in protest to the King that had not gone into effect but remained on the books in a general condition of "Non-Usage."[32] When Jefferson referred to desuetude, both with regard to laws and his own reading and writing, he referred specifically to the kind of reading of the law appropriate for the action of the representative constitutional body against the privileged and executive ordering work of the central state, electing to brandish the intellectual identity of an early modern antiquary as a modern politician.

Once Jefferson persuaded himself that his parliamentary manual could be published, he set about converting the pocket-book into a reliable and

[31] Jefferson, "Parliamentary Pocket-Book," *Jefferson's Parliamentary Writings*, p. 63.

[32] See Jefferson, "Parliamentary Pocket-Book," *Jefferson's Parliamentary Writings*, pp. 63, 117.

useable guide for practice in the everyday life of Congress. The process of conversion entailed drawing American practice as it had developed in its first decades from within the long history of the British Parliament and the English common law. As Jefferson wrote of rules of Parliament in the preface to the published editions of the *Manual*, "I have here endeavored to collect and digest so much of these as is called for in ordinary practice, collating the Parliamentary with the Senatorial rules, both where they agree and where they vary."[33] Jefferson's notes for the compilation of the manual bear out his account of the endeavor. On forty-eight page faces of note cards, many pasted together, Jefferson organized his thoughts on the history and law of Parliament, drawing material especially on protecting parliamentary privileges from the threat of abuse by the Crown or a majority party.[34] The notes, composed around 1800, exhibit Jefferson's awareness of his task as one of compiling and assembling, of representing the complicated history of the origins of American constitutionalism in British institutions and practices.

Listing notes on Parliament under Roman numerals and notes on the Senate under Arabic numerals, Jefferson began with Parliamentary precedents along the lines of the pocket-book and gradually connected them to subsequent parliamentary or later congressional history. As he corrected mistakes or sought to reorder the organization of the categories, he crossed out entire passages, sometimes added extensive marginal notes, and often pasted new paper over the older writing. In the latter case, if he totally covered up a previous passage, he made sure to continue at the point that the last visible original material left off. In most cases, however, he pasted smaller pieces of paper along the top or side margin of the original writing, adding supplementary or further material to what he had written originally. In almost every example of pasting additional writing space into the manuscript, the new add-on served to physically link historical connections between parliamentary practice in the original

33 Jefferson, "Manual for Parliamentary Practice," *Jefferson's Parliamentary Writings*, p. 355.

34 Jefferson, *Manual for Proceeding in the Rules of the Senate of the US*," Manuscripts Division, Huntington Library, San Marino, CA, HM 5986; the manuscript, listed as two attempts at drafts of different components of the manual, is, according to the editor of Jefferson's parliamentary writings, more like four distinct documents that had been crudely taken apart and put back together after Jefferson's death by the executor of his estate, Henry Randall. While there is repetition of some entries across the forty-eight pages of the manuscript, there are also several points where at least part of the text seems put together accurately; see Howell, "Editor's Introduction," *Jefferson's Parliamentary Writings*, pp. 342–5.

and congressional practice in the supplement. A true palimpsest, in the notes for the manual, like his earlier commonplace books or some of his revolutionary-era legislative drafts, Jefferson constructed a space on which to make readable the character of constitutional history as an assemblage of usages built up over time.

The first edition of the *Manual* was published in 1801, and it was only after his presidency that Jefferson responded to a request for an updated and revised edition, printed with the text of the U.S. Constitution at the end of the expanded but smaller, truly pocket-size book in 1812. Both editions followed the outline of the rough notes in listing congressional rules by Arabic numerals under parliamentary precedents listed by Roman numerals, and both editions included extensive references to both original and secondary sources pertaining to the period before the Norman Conquest, through the treatises and parliamentary journals of late medieval and Renaissance England, and on into the seventeenth, eighteenth, and at least in the 1812 edition, nineteenth centuries. To the front of the *Manual*, Jefferson attached quotations in the form of an essay on the importance of adhering to rules.[35] As strict observance of the rules was the only means of guiding action in deliberative bodies, protecting the will of the majority as well as the rights of the minority, Jefferson could nevertheless only write and establish such rules in a manner that revealed them to be the products of a history of political deliberation.

There was a distinct and explicit connection between Jefferson's own collection of the histories that made up his parliamentary history and that history's subject matter and intended use in constituted deliberative assemblies. In the section on privilege in the *Manual*, Jefferson cited the 1621 protest of the Commons to James I, where the lower house expressed outrage at the attempts of the King to harass or control members opposed to his increasing claims to absolutism.[36] Furthermore, out of political frustration with James at home and a more global fear of a European Catholic restoration threatening England, the Commons declared that the "liberties, franchises, privileges, and jurisdictions of Parliament are the ancient undoubted birthright and inheritance of the subjects of England." Hume wrote in his *History* that upon hearing of the protest, the King sent for the journals of the Commons and in front of his

[35] Jefferson, "Manual for Parliamentary Practice," *Jefferson's Parliamentary Writings*, p. 357.

[36] Jefferson, "Manual for Parliamentary Practice," *Jefferson's Parliamentary Writings*, p. 362.

council tore out the text of the declaration.[37] For Hume, the episode and its context illustrated the grave danger of the imprudent wielding of politically charged historical narratives, and he found both sides to be equally guilty. The King, for his part, had with "so rash and indiscreet a hand, torn off that sacred veil which had hitherto covered the English constitution." Doing so was bad for the royal prerogative and the health of the constitution. By contrast, with both James and Hume, Jefferson included reference to the remonstrance of the Commons in his historical guidelines of parliamentary practice and law.

In his imprudence, Hume asserted, James had let the cat of the public "discoursing of state affairs" out of the bag. Jefferson not only used the protest of the Commons to include the enumerated rights of parliamentary privilege, but in citing the protest, he kept it in represented, recorded memory both within and outside the walls of Congress. The question that such constitutional moments and their legacies in subsequent civil history brought up, for both Hume and Jefferson, was to what extent public judgment and participation in political action was a legitimate part of constitutionalism. For Hume, the fundamental issue of the execution of Charles I and really of the entire English Civil War was whether "the people, in any case, were entitled to judge" their sovereign.[38] Jefferson was preoccupied in later years with designing a constitutional culture and a corresponding textual environment that could nurture a people in their capacity to judge in common affairs. It was a question, for Jefferson, of what particular pieces of history were doing or could be made to do in the present, of what the collected histories of institutions and polities would need to look like to be useful and historical in a republic.

SCISSORS AND PASTE

That question also shaped Jefferson's thinking about religion, and more specifically, what he could do with religion and its history. Discussions of Jefferson's religious views have usually centered on the nature of his theological beliefs and to what extent those beliefs informed his constitutional views on the separation of church and state.[39] It is important to

[37] Hume, *History of England*, Vol. 5, p. 92. [38] *Ibid*, p. 544.

[39] On Jefferson and religion, see Charles B. Sanford, *Thomas Jefferson and His Library: A Study of His Literary Interests and of the Religious Attitudes Revealed by the Relevant Titles in His Library* (Hamden: Archon Books, 1977), and *The Religious Life of Thomas Jefferson* (Charlottesville: University of Virginia Press, 1984); Edwin S. Gaustad, *Sworn on the Altar of God: A Religious Biography of Thomas Jefferson* (Grand Rapids:

appreciate both the radicalism of Jefferson's secularism and in particular his secular criticism, and the dependence that his political theory and criticism had on a close engagement with religion as a historical phenomenon. Jefferson did not think about the divine subjects of theological inquiry, at least as they pertained to him and those he acknowledged as fellow citizens, outside of the history of law and institutions in which public representations of God took place, and his engagement with religion needs to be understood in this framework. Jefferson barely had a theology outside of his conceptualization of theological inquiry as a form of critical and skeptical ecclesiastical history. The material projects in which Jefferson engaged with religion and its history prodded and reworked conceptual distinctions between sacred and secular.

Part of Jefferson's presidential and retirement attention to religion and to Christianity in particular came directly out of his political experience. In the course of the election of 1800 and for most of his two terms in office, Federalist clergy had portrayed Jefferson as an atheist, a leveler, and a French philosopher, an associate of Thomas Paine and a threat to the very foundations of the republic.[40] Clement Clark Moore, later author of *The Night before Christmas*, in 1804 published *Observations upon Certain Passages in Mr. Jefferson's Notes on*

Eerdmans, 1996); David L. Holmes, *Faiths of the Founding Fathers* (Oxford: Oxford University Press, 2006); Peter S. Onuf, "Jefferson's Religion: Priestcraft, Enlightenment, and the Republican Revolution," *The Mind of Thomas Jefferson* (Charlottesville: University of Virginia Press, 2007). On the separation of church and state, see Merrill D. Peterson and Robert C. Vaughan, eds., *The Virginia Statute of Religions Freedom: Its Evolution and Consequences in American History* (Cambridge: Cambridge University Press, 1988); Daniel L. Dreisbach, *Jefferson's Wall of Separation Between Church and State* (New York: New York University Press, 2002); Philip Hamburger, *Separation of Church and State* (Cambridge, MA: Harvard University Press, 2002); Frank Lambert, *The Founding Fathers and the Place of Religion in America* (Princeton: Princeton University Press, 2003)

40 On the Federalist political and theological critique of Jeffersonian democracy, see Linda K. Kerber, *Federalists in Dissent: Imagery and Ideology in Jeffersonian America* (Ithaca: Cornell University Press, 1970); James C. Turner, *Without God, Without Creed: The Origins of Unbelief in America* (Baltimore: Johns Hopkins University Press, 1985); Marshall Foletta, *Coming to Terms with Democracy: Federalist Intellectuals and the Shaping of American Culture, 1800–1828* (Charlottesville: University of Virginia Press, 2001); Colin Wells, *The Devil and Dr. Dwight: Satire and Theology in the Early American Republic* (Chapel Hill: University of North Carolina Press, 2002); Bryan Waterman, *Republic of Intellect: The Frinedly Club of New York City and the Making of American Literature* (Baltimore: Johns Hopkins University Press, 2007); Catherine O'Donnell Kaplan, *Men of Letters in the Early Republic: Cultivating Forums of Citizenship* (Chapel Hill: University of North Carolina Press, 2007).

Virginia, which argued that Jefferson's *Notes* revealed him to be a feeble but willing wielder of irreligion and false philosophy. Jefferson's conjectures of the deep time and natural history necessary to make sense of the creation of mountains and the discovery of seashells in those that surrounded Monticello, as well as his postulation of the original and natural distinction of races all threatened the Biblical narrative of creation and its promise of universal salvation for a fallen and singular humanity. His successful efforts at disestablishment in Virginia and his comment that his neighbor's religious opinions were of no consequence to him evidenced for Moore a dangerous contempt for religious authority. Jefferson's anti-clericalism and his wider approach to the question of the civic status of religious authority stemmed from a life-long engagement with issues of ecclesiastical institutions and practices of scriptural interpretation.

As a student, Jefferson had carried out an extensive reading in the realm of ecclesiastical law. His fragmentary "Notes on Episcopacy" and on heresy testified to his knowledge of the history of ecclesiastical institutions and the importance of that history to the laws and identity of Anglican Virginia. His early essay on "Whether Christianity is Part of the Common Law," which he copied from his legal commonplace book and sent to Thomas Cooper in 1814, and his arguments with Wythe over the nature of ecclesiastical law in his cases as a young attorney would not have been possible without fairly extensive reading in ecclesiastical law and history.[41] He owned and read Eusebius and Bede, the latter of which was particularly important to Jefferson as a source on early English history and language, and he read the work of Origen, Jerome, and Erasmus as scholars of the history of the early church and as examples of biblical textual scholarship and translation. At several points in his life he engaged closely with Milton's poetry and political writings. He recommended Gibbon's *Decline and Fall of the Roman Empire*, in which the spread of Christianity played a significant role, and he further recommended the Protestant ecclesiastical histories of Conyers Middleton and Johann Lorenz von Mosheim.[42] He owned and read the antiquarian Paulo Sarpi's politically realist historical work, the *History of the Council of Trent*, Gilbert Burnet's *History of the Reformation*, and Henry Spelman's *History of Sacrilege* and *The*

[41] Jefferson to Thomas Cooper, February 10, 1814, *Writings*, pp. 1321–9.
[42] Jefferson to Peter Carr, August 10, 1787, *Papers of Thomas Jefferson*, Vol. 12, pp. 14–19.

Beginnings of Monastic Life.[43] He corresponded with and took inspiration from the Unitarian scientist and philosopher Joseph Priestley, whose *Harmony of the Evangelists in Greek* (1777) and *History of the Corruptions of Christianity* (1782) Jefferson admired, and whom Jefferson urged, unsuccessfully, to undertake his own extractive reading of the Gospels.[44] In short, Jefferson sustained wide reading in the history of the church from one end of his adult life to the other.

As with his reading in constitutionalism, throughout his life Jefferson's interest in ecclesiastical history lay in the constituent and lay role in the founding of the early church, and the corruptions introduced by the withering of the common management of the Christian community. Mosheim, a German Lutheran and along with Middleton Jefferson's most oft-recommended ecclesiastical historian, began his work with the history of "ministers, rulers, and form of government" in the church. This was a civic history of religious institutions. "When we look back to the commencement of the Christian church, we find its government administered jointly by the pastors and the people," but, Mosheim continued, "in the process of time, the scene changes, and we see these pastors affecting an air of pre-eminence and superiority, trampling upon the rights and privileges of the community, and assuming to themselves a supreme authority both in civil and religious matters." This "invasion of the rights of the people," as Mosheim called it, was carried out finally to the extent of establishing a monarchy in the form of the Papacy.[45] Thus did the church take on the worst characteristics of its enemy, a form of Roman paganism where the priests showed little interest in cultivating "the people in virtuous conduct," a necessity in a republic, and instead insisted that only "the rites and institutions which the people have received by tradition from their ancestors" was necessary for the "true worship of the gods."[46] Mosheim's work narrated a failure of civic virtue that stemmed from an usurpation of the right to participate in the management of the common

[43] E. Millicent Sowerby, ed., *The Catalogue of the Library of Thomas Jefferson* (Washington, DC, 1953), Vol. 2, pp. 286–96.

[44] Jefferson to Joseph Priestley, January 29, 1804, *Writings*, pp. 1141–3; Jefferson was ultimately disappointed in Priestley's attachment to the divinity of Christ and Christian millenarianism; on Priestley and Jefferson, see Pocock, "Religious Freedom and the Desacralization of Politics: From the English Civil Wars to the Virginia Statute," *The Virginia Statute for Religious Freedom*, pp. 43–73.

[45] John Lawrence [Johann Lorenz] von Mosheim, *An Ecclesiastical History, Antient and Modern, from the Birth of Christ, to the Beginning of the Present Century*, Archibald Maclaine, trans. (London: T. Cadell, 1782), Vol. 1, p. 4.

[46] Mosheim, An Ecclesiastical History, p. 29.

affairs on the part of the clergy.[47] The Lutheran Mosheim established a republican historical critique that was not simply a plea for *sola scriptura* or salvation by faith alone, and he implicitly questioned any historically constructed hierarchy of governance by fleshing out a radical historical alternative.

Jefferson came to see ecclesiastical history in similar terms. While Jesus had taught an unparalleled code of morals, a code that surpassed the classical philosophers in its instruction of our duties to one another as well as to ourselves, the "Platonising successors" to the Christians of the first century after Christ had "found it necessary to disavow the primitive Christians, who had taken their principles from the mouth of Jesus himself," Jefferson wrote to John Adams. Jefferson could only hope in the future for "restoration of the primitive simplicity of its founder."[48] The language of restoration echoed the spirit of Jefferson's interest in ancient constitutionalism and the historical understanding at work in his enthusiasm for the establishment of the ward republics, and the parallel was not mere coincidence. In the history of colonial and revolutionary law recounted in the *Notes on the State of Virginia*, Jefferson had detailed the laws placing the responsibility for the care of the poor and the governance of other community affairs with the twelve vestry members of the local parish.[49] As Jefferson articulated what he envisioned as the

[47] See Pocock, *Barbarism and Religion, Volume 5: Religion: The First Triumph* (Cambridge: Cambridge University Press, 2011), ch. 6; on ecclesiastical historical scholarship, see Girolamo Imbruglia, "My ecclesiastical history': Gibbon between Hume and Raynal," *Edward Gibbon: Bicentenary Essays*, David Wormersley, ed, (Oxford: Voltaire Foundation, 1997), pp. 73–102; Felicity Heal, "Appropriating History: Catholic and Protestant Polemics and the National Past," Ian W. Archer, "Discourses of History in Elizabethan and Early Stuart London," John Spurr, "A Special Kindness for Dead Bishops: The Church, History, and Testimony in Seventeenth Century Protestantism," Andrew Starkie, "Contested Histories of the English Church: Gilbert Burnet and Gilbert Collier," in Paulina Kewes, ed. *The Uses of History in Early Modern England* (San Marino: Huntington Library, 2006), pp. 105–28, 1–22, 307–46; on the politics of ecclesiastical or denominational conflict and the assertion of its great significance, see the work of J.C.D Clark, *The Language of Liberty: Political Discourse and Social Dynamics in the Anglo-American World* (Cambridge: Cambridge University Press, 1994), *English Society, 1660–1832*, Second Edition (Cambridge: Cambridge University Press, 2000); on the development of Biblical historical criticism, see Jonathan Sheehan, *The Enlightenment Bible: Translation: Scholarship, Culture* (Princeton: Princeton University Press, 2005).

[48] Jefferson to John Adams, October 12, 1813, *Papers of Thomas Jefferson: Retirement Series*, Vol. 6, p. 549.

[49] "The poor, unable to support themselves, are maintained by an assessment on the titheable persons in their parish. This assessment is levied and administered by twelve persons

design and operation of the ward republics, he ascribed precisely the same functions to the council of the local hundred, or ward. In effect, Jefferson imagined the ward republic as an institution what would supplant the church as the center of local collective interaction and governance of the common affairs, and in that imagining histories of the radical communities of the early church provided no small amount of inspiration, as such histories had before. In fact, to take Jefferson at his word on the design and practice of the ward republic system, citizens would still be in many cases required to participate in some council or another of their government just as their attendance at public worship had been regulated by law in the colonial period.

Jefferson's isolation of examples of various modes and moments of democratic governance modeled the exemplary mode of history championed by one of his great intellectual heroes, Lord Bolingbroke. History, Bolingbroke wrote in his *Letters on the Study of History*, is the most proper field of study to "train us up in private and public virtue." In short, he continued, "history is philosophy teaching by examples."[50] Its purpose was to "prepare us for action and observation;" history was "conversant about the past" rather than the past itself.[51] The study of history, for Bolingbroke, served as a tribunal for the actions of statesmen of the past and provided models, inspiration, and caution to the statesmen of the present. Crucial actors, events, and moments lent themselves to the special attention of the aspirant participant in directing the course of human events. For Jefferson, the exemplary mode dovetailed well with the historical skepticism he read and recorded from Bolingbroke's philosophical works in his literary commonplace book as a young man. Jefferson had taken down extended entries on the unreliability of ancient testimonies regarding miracles and other things violating what human reason knew of the laws of nature. The necessity of contemporary witnesses, using contemporary materials, made ancient history little more in Bolingbroke's eyes than a "thread of dark and uncertain traditions."[52] Good history could not go beyond philosophical scrutiny of what one had of the

in each parish, called vestrymen, originally chosen by the housekeepers of the parish, but afterwards filling vacancies in their own body by their own choice," *Notes on the State of Virginia*, p. 140.

50 Lord Bolingbroke, "'Letter 3,' Letters on the Study and Use of History," Isaac Kramnick, ed. *Historical Writings* (Chicago: University of Chicago Press, 1972), p. 25.

51 Bolingbroke, "'Letter 3,'" p. 29.

52 *Ibid*; see Jefferson, *Jefferson's Literary Commonplace Book*, Douglas L. Wilson, ed. (Princeton: Princeton University Press, 1989), pp. 24–55.

original materials. Only after sifting through the long history of assembled and mediated narratives could the student arrive at the original material from which the prime historical exemplar could be drawn.

Jefferson applied the tools of both civil history and the skeptical, natural story of religion to the origins and development of Christianity. "Fix reason firmly in her seat, and call to her tribunal every fact, every opinion. Question with boldness even the existence of a god," Jefferson had written to Peter Carr from Paris in 1787, "because if there be one, he must more approve of the homage of reason, that that of blindfolded fear. You will naturally examine first the religion of your own country. Read the bible then, as you would read Livy or Tacitus."[53] Just as in reading civil history or law, Jefferson encouraged students in whom he had confidence to use their reading as a site for the unraveling of constituted narratives. "I forgot to observe when speaking of the new testament," he continued, "that you should read all the histories of Christ, as well as those of whom a council of ecclesiastics have decided for us to be Psuedo-evangelists pretended to inspiration as much as the others, and you are to judge their pretensions by your own reason, & not by the reason of those ecclesiastics."[54] The history of the transmission of narratives concerning Christ and the origins of the church, to which as with any history of transmission Jefferson paid sustained and careful attention, was a history of developing hierarchies in the authority to define and interpret the contents of the canon, and it was a history narrated in the works of Bolingbroke, Mosheim, Middleton, Hume, and Voltaire that Jefferson recommended to his nephew.

Understanding that all historical narratives were texts assembled from other texts, sources, and traditions, Jefferson approached the history of religious authority through the method and the medium of the commonplace book. In a commonplace book, the material assemblage of tradition could be represented and potentially sifted through, disassembled, and reassembled in the present. The penultimate example of Jefferson at play among the authoritative narratives of history is the "Jefferson Bible." Jefferson made two attempts at assembling a reconstituted narrative of the life and teaching of Jesus, extracted from the four canonical gospels. The first, the "Philosophy of Jesus," consisted of clippings from two editions of the New Testament of the King James

[53] Jefferson to Peter Carr, August 10, 1787, *Papers of Thomas Jefferson*, Vol. 12, p. 15.
[54] *Ibid*, p. 17.

Bible that Jefferson assembled in February of 1804. The second, the "Life and Morals of Jesus," or what is today the Jefferson Bible, consisted of new extractions from the Greek, Latin, French, and English versions placed side-by-side and bound in a leather folio volume. While he frequently discussed the former in private correspondence with trusted interlocutors, the latter, probably composed around 1820, remained completely private until Jefferson's death in 1826. Both texts illustrate the radicalism of Jefferson's reading carried out to a kind of logical extreme, and both are indicative of the political tensions that in part made up the mind of their compiler.

Jefferson's title page of the "Philosophy of Jesus" declared it to be "an abridgment of the New Testament for the use of the Indians unembarrassed with matters of fact or faith beyond the level of their comprehension."[55] The reference to Indians at the front of the compilation registers the political context in which Jefferson composed the first edition of his eclectic gospel. At the time approaching the inauguration of his second term as President, Jefferson and his administration were confronting a rising tide of ethnic consciousness, infused with the spirit of religious revival and cultural recovery, and constituting a vitalized and unanticipated recollection of Native history. The rise to prominence of leaders like Handsome Lake among the Seneca threatened the expected compliance with American expansion and Americanization programs championed by the Jefferson administration. As we have seen, Jefferson increasingly depicted Native Americans as barbarous, as members of a polity who for several historical reasons had forgotten or never taken up the capacity to change their inherited laws and customs. Like the Jews among whom Jesus moved as a reformer, in Jefferson's formulation, the Native Americans had surrendered their capacities for public liberty to the uncritical acceptance of the authority of tradition inherited from their ancestors. Creatures of custom needed to be dealt with on a basic level, according to their limited capacities, and the "Philosophy of Jesus" is an example of Jefferson's usage of the idea of the Native American as a kind of empty vessel on which progressive social experimentation could beneficially take place.

One of the major entries in the "Philosophy," not included in the later "Life" was the extended passage from the Gospel of Matthew detailing

[55] Dickinson W. Adams, ed. *Jefferson's Extracts from the Gospels: The "Philosophy of Jesus" and "The Life and Morals of Jesus,"* (Princeton: Princeton University Press, 1983), pp. 28, 55.

the lineage of Jesus from King David.[56] In Jefferson's vision of them, the Native Americans were really the only people in his potential audience for whom prophecy, bloodline, and tradition would be impressive indicators of sacred power and authority. The image of the Native American played an important part in Jefferson's thinking about religion, even during his presidency, as Christian missionaries were encouraged to combat the tide of Native religious revivals. The "Philosophy of Jesus" makes sense as a part of the history of Jefferson's textual and linguistic configurations of Native American historical subjectivity. While Jefferson directed the "Philosophy" at least potentially at an external audience and a more calculable and ordered temporality, he directed the "Life" to almost no one but himself. The shift to describing the United States as an expansive commercial society, examined in the previous chapter, went hand in hand with Jefferson's turn to relative isolation in retirement and the reinforcing of boundaries of historical subjectivity.

Understandably, given his political experience, Jefferson was largely unwilling to share anything about his personal religious views outside of private correspondence with a select few. It was thus increasingly in a narrow discursive world that Jefferson's work on these materials of constituted history took place. In the earlier text Jefferson fundamentally reordered the story of the New Testament, beginning and concluding with the events of the early life and later death, but in between he presented less a biographical narrative and more a series of doctrines culled from across the preaching career of Jesus. In contrast, the "Life and Morals" presented a more biographical and historical account, beginning with the taxation and census decree of Caesar Augustus and ending with the trial, death, and burial of Jesus. The overall text of the "Life" represented to its assembler a work of linguistic and philological erudition as well as a civil history of the life of Jesus.

Insofar as their actual selections are concerned, the texts of both Jefferson's volumes of extracts are quite similar. Still, there were significant differences. Besides the inclusion of the Davidic lineage of Jesus in the earlier text but not in the latter, in the "Life" Jefferson extended the narrative of the death and burial. Whereas the "Philosophy" had ended with Matthew 27:50, "Jesus, when he had cried again with a loud voice, yielded up the ghost," literally concluding at the second the mortal and human Jesus dies, the "Life" went on to include Matthew 27:55–56, John

[56] Jefferson, "The Philosophy of Jesus," *Jefferson's Extracts from the Gospels*, pp. 60–1 (MS pp. 2–3).

19:31–34, 38–41 with a fragment of John 19:42, and the last sentence of Matthew 27:60. The last page and half of the "Life" narrated the successful efforts of Joseph of Arimathea and Nicodemus to procure, clean, and customarily prepare the body for burial, as well as their selection of a burial space, so that the last sentence of the text is as follows: "There laid they Jesus, and rolled a great stone to the door of the sepulchre, and departed."[57] Jefferson concluded the more extensive extraction from the Gospels, not with the passing of Jesus but with his anonymous monument, the sepulcher. What the would-be reader was left with was an inscription not simply of the mortality of Jesus, but with the blank slate of the memorial to the life of Jesus, and thus with a hint at the degree to which the history of Christianity was a history of power struggles carried out through collective efforts at naming and locating the authority to circumscribe the meaning and future usage of that memorial.

Another section of the text, included in both the "Philosophy" and the "Life," provides context for Jefferson's final attention to the monumentality of the life of Jesus. From Matthew 23, Jefferson recorded the preaching of Jesus against the scribes, who were readers and transcribers of the Law, and the Pharisees. "Woe unto you, scribes and Pharisees," Jesus said, "hypocrites! for ye pay tithe of mint, and anise, and cummin, and have omitted the weightier *matters* of the law, judgment, mercy, and faith."[58] The italicized "matters" of the English translation placed rhetorical emphasis on what the scribes and Pharisees ignore, the spirit of justice and equity that should govern the interpretation and application of the sacred texts over whose meaning the scribes and Pharisees exercise political control. Jefferson's extraction goes on:

27. Woe unto you, scribes and Pharisees, hypocrites! for ye are like unto whited sepulchres, which indeed appear beautiful outward, but are within full of dead *mens'* bones, and of all uncleanliness.

28. Even so ye also outwardly appear righteous unto men, but within ye are full of hypocrisy and iniquity.

29. Woe unto you, scribes and Pharisees, hypocrites! because ye build the tombs of the prophets, and garnish the sepulchres of the righteous,

30. And say, if we had been in the days of our fathers, we would not have been partakers with them in the blood of the prophets.

[57] Jefferson, "Life and Morals of Jesus," *Jefferson's Extracts from the Gospels*, p. 297 (MS p. 82).

[58] *Ibid*, p. 257 (MS p. 62).

31. Wherefore ye be witnesses unto yourselves, that ye are the children of them that killed the prophets.

32. Fill ye up, then, the measure of your fathers.

33. Ye serpents, ye generation of vipers! how can ye escape the damnation of hell?[59]

In the Temple no less, Jesus preached against the power of those who dawn the mantle of the law but fail to see to its promise of justice. Power works by polishing and policing the ruins of its own history. The obsession with the clean, white outward appearance of the monumental tombs is a desperate attempt to mask, from one's self as much as others, the rot at the very heart of the authority and tradition these sepulchres are meant to communicate to their living viewers. For Jefferson, this self-deception was just as real in his day as it was in that of Jesus and the Apostles. In the repetition of the sepulchre motif, Jefferson builds on his fundamental critique of clerical authority. Unlike the sacred authority communicated by the polished monuments, the tomb of Jesus was simply blank, making no claim on future use and understanding, surrendering to the inevitability of subsequent history. Underneath the edifice of tradition presented as an unbroken line of development, Jefferson's extractions aimed at restoring the moments of beginning, transmission, and fragmentation to memory, to the history of usage, and thereby to the potential for new usage. The "Jefferson Bible" was a deliberate, carefully constructed critique of efforts to remove meaning from the sphere of dynamic projects of retrieval and exploration.

Jefferson confronted such questions in the realm of civil as well as sacred and ecclesiastical history. Indeed, his extractions from the gospels formed part of a larger project of trying to forestall, eliminate, or walk back the making sacred and absolute of what could be shown to be temporal and political. When reading the gospel, one needed to be aware of two competing stories in "the history of a personage called Jesus," Jefferson had written to Peter Carr, referencing the *persona*, the legal, scriptural, and historical construction of Christ's own subjectivity. The first story was the orthodox view that Jesus was the Son of God, born of a virgin, who over the course of his life and death "suspected & reversed the laws of nature at will." A second reading belonged to those "who say he was a man of illegitimate birth, of a benevolent heart, an enthusiastic mind, who set out without

[59] *Ibid.*

pretensions to divinity, ended in believing in them, & was punished capitally for sedition by being gibbeted according to the Roman law."[60] Jefferson continued with the citations to the law books in which the applicable criminal laws on whipping and crucifixion in the Roman civil code could be found. Needless to say, a narrative of the life of Jesus centered around the unfortunate historical possibility that he believed he was the Son of God and was legally, if not justly, executed for the politics implied by that belief was hardly one stemming from a traditional religious faith.

Over the course of his own life, Jefferson would grow to praise the life of Jesus and refuse the suggestion that such a great teacher and practitioner of our worldly duties, our duties to one another, could have ever truly believed himself to be the Son of God. Nevertheless, as both the "Philosophy" and the 'Life" attest, he continued to see the events surrounding the life and death of Jesus of Nazareth as events which took place in a secular history of law, politics, and philosophy. Jesus was in this narrative a victim of the combination of the political force of religious certainty and the muscular arm of the state. The life of Jesus could thereby serve as an exemplar to the judgment of those who theorized the relationship between text, history, and authority.

In his extracts from the gospels, Jefferson was operating with the conceptual tools of both a natural, philosophical mode of history and those of a more civil history to understand the offices and institutions that arose from the events described in the Gospels and the writing and canonization of the Gospel texts themselves. The philosophical basis of Jefferson's approach to the New Testament was the kind of skepticism that led him to recommend Hume's *Essays*, including the deeply skeptical "On Miracles," in the section of a reading list on religion. It was the kind of materialist, empirical skepticism that led him to declare his admiration of Epicurus and Epictetus. Indeed, as Jefferson wrote to William Short in 1819, he planned to translate Epictetus together with the teachings of Epicurus, culled from the seventeenth-century materialist and Epicurean philosopher Pierre Gassendi's *Syntagma philosophicum*.[61] For Jefferson, getting the history of the Gospels right was in large part a matter of clipping the miracles out of the narrative and taking account of the fragments that were left to

[60] Jefferson to Peter Carr, August 10, 1787, Vol. 12, p. 16.

[61] Jefferson to William Short, October 31, 1819, *Writings*, p. 1431; on the recovery and influence of ancient materialism, empiricism, and skepticism in early modern philosophy, see Richard Popkin, *The History of Scepticism, from Savonarola to Bayle*, revised and expanded edition (Oxford: Oxford University Press, 2003).

consider, of consciously stripping texts and concepts of their authoritative force as Scripture and restoring them to history as scriptures, as writing.

Anthony Grafton has discussed the turn away from the critical historical arts of the early modern antiquaries in the increasingly rationalizing period of the eighteenth century, citing Bolingbroke's exemplary mode of history as a crucial example of the new history and indicative of what was lost in the transition.[62] In Jefferson's hands, the relationship between politics, reason, and erudition was a complicated one, amounting to an imperfect and transforming distillation of humanist textual practice into a politics of recollecting and redemptive use. Neither Bolingbroke nor Jefferson were historians as much as students of history, or more precisely, students of the study of history and its uses. What concerned Bolingbroke the most about the study of history was its use by the young political actor in the formation of the self and the capacity for judgment. Following Bolingbroke, what concerned Jefferson the most about the study of history, perhaps even more than Bolingbroke, was the status of narratives of civic identity and the fact that such narratives themselves had a history. In his various textual projects, Jefferson worked on the materials of authoritative and sacred histories. This work consisted of a mode of reading and writing that restored the open availability at the founding moment of what would later become untouchable or unquestionable, removed from principles of accessibility and potentiality. Capable of erudition with respect to ancient languages and texts, Jefferson's reading life led him to be attuned to histories and politics of usage. Both Bolingbroke and Jefferson were keenly aware of the politics of historical representation, and understood historical critique of these representations as an especially important kind of historical study and thought. Jefferson's work stripped away what he saw as the history through which the texts had become canonical, sacred, and authoritative, restoring them, at least potentially, to the profane and civic usage of the laity.

SPACES OF RECOLLECTION

For all of his worldliness, contempt for religious authority, and commitment to the separation of church and state, Jefferson gave a great deal of attention to matters of religion, its place in politics, and its history. That

[62] Anthony Grafton, *What Was History? The Art of History in Early Modern Europe* (Cambridge: Cambridge University Press, 2007), pp. 251–4.

attention grew out of his study in the law, and that study informed an ethic of textual practice. In the entrance hall of Monticello, Jefferson placed a copy of a rare portrait of Jerome, *Saint Jerome in Meditation* by Hendrick Goltzius (1558–1617).[63] While it is difficult to say to what extent copies of Goltzius' work would have been available to Jefferson as a consumer of reproductions in Paris, or whether the copy was made after another copy or an engraving, it is important to note that the Goltzius portrait departs significantly from more famous Renaissance and early modern images of Jerome. One of Goltzius' chief inspirations, Albrecht Dürer, had engraved Jerome in his study, illuminated by the divine light and in the company of the legendary lion from whose paw Jerome had removed a thorn and cleaned the wound.[64] In the meditative image that Jefferson owned, Jerome is alone in the dark with a book, looking askance as if he remained troubled by his readings and the thoughts they generated, even after a lifetime of unparalleled learning.

Many early modern images of Jerome tried to capture his struggle to balance his professed inability to leave behind the Latin classics with his commitments as a Christian scholar. Jerome had famously recounted a vision of being called before a judge and denounced as a Ciceronian, compelling Jerome to promise he would no longer read the pagan authors of pre-Christian Greece and Rome.[65] The legacy of Jerome in such representations was of a man torn between the eloquence and achievements of classical, especially Roman culture, and the life of faith. Jefferson's image maintains sole focus on the subjective experience of Jerome, without depictions of the miracles he had performed as a saint. This Jerome was a reader and thinker, a man who worked with and on texts. The portrait of the translator and compiler of the Latin Vulgate is indicative of the complex world of historical representation occurring in the halls of Monticello. If Jefferson ever felt spiritually torn by his editing of the New Testament or his love of ancient philosophy, he gave little

[63] Susan Stein, *The Worlds of Thomas Jefferson at Monticello* (New York: Harry N. Abrams, 1993), p. 143.

[64] On images and representations of Jerome, see Eugene F. Rice, Jr. *Saint Jerome in the Renaissance* (Baltimore: Johns Hopkins University Press, 1985). Depicting Jerome without his miracles was a hallmark of Erasmus' *Life of Jerome*, which Jefferson did not own, but he did own several other works by the Catholic humanist, including his new Latin translation of the New Testament, on Erasmus and his work on Jerome; see James Kearney, *The Incarnate Text: Imagining the Book in Reformation England* (Philadelphia: University of Pennsylvania Press, 2009), ch. 1.

[65] Megan Hale Williams, *The Monk and the Book: Jerome and the Making of Christian Scholarship* (Chicago: University of Chicago Press, 2006), pp. 25–6.

indication of it. At the same time, the Jerome that Jefferson presented to himself and to guests was a human being, acting in secular time, a reader, a writer, a translator, and an assembler of texts of history, and so the presence of Jerome in Jefferson's domestic display is a crucial register of the dense historicity that Jefferson as an assembler and disassembler of texts inhabited. Even so, for Jefferson, the recognized boundaries of that weighty yet playful space of historical imagination and representation became more rigid as he sought to define and control the reach and usage of a revolutionary politics he had helped to theorize and create.

The portrait of Jerome hung alongside busts of philosophers such as Voltaire and Turgot, statesmen including Alexander Hamilton, Native American artifacts, the addresses and animal skins from the Lewis and Clark expedition, pieces of Jefferson's fossil collection, and maps of the North and South American continents. Jerome in Jefferson's world at Monticello was thus part of an exhibition of contiguous histories and multiple temporalities. Jefferson's projects of configuring and thinking through the challenges of temporality took place at the center of a plantation where the time of labor was rigorously measured and enforced by the figures of the master and his overseer.[66] Jefferson's own garden and farm books, kept over the course of his life, attest to his calculating attention to his own estate and the people who inhabited it, and the inscription of the lives of the slave community in tables and charts of birth, productivity, and death provide an explicit contrast to the fluid historicity with which Jefferson located himself by recording his own activities of reading, writing, and rewriting.

In the withdrawn and buried context of the worlds Jefferson constructed for himself at Monticello, one of his most important projects was the preservation and publication of Virginia historical records. Along with supporting the writing of histories of the state going back to its colonial origins, Jefferson made his library open to the use of William Waller Hening, who was then compiling his *Statutes at Large; being a Collection of All the Laws of Virginia*, still the authoritative source on early Virginia legal history. Offering to ship his collections of the printed laws dating from 1682, Jefferson informed Hening in 1807 that the manuscript copies of the earlier laws, dating from 1622, would not bear

[66] See Thomas M. Allen, *A Republic in Time: Temporality and Social Imagination in Nineteenth-Century America* (Chapel Hill: University of North Carolina Press, 2008), pp. 54–8; Kariann Akemi Yakota, *Unbecoming British: How Revolutionary America Became a Postcolonial Nation* (Oxford: Oxford University Press, 2011), pp. 3–10.

movement and could only be copied by Jefferson or Hening himself at a table in Monticello. A careful archivist, Jefferson all the same gave Hening his full support, noting that the purpose of the collection of the laws was to "save all those for the Public which were not then already lost, in the hope that at some future day they might be republished. Whether this be done by public or private enterprise, my end will be equally answered."[67] Jefferson had hoped earlier that the state or a benefactor would agree to publish them, perhaps compensating his labors in collecting and archiving them, but his earnestness to get the volumes in print led him to embrace the first trustworthy opportunity. That earnestness stemmed in part from Jefferson's real fear that some of the records would be lost or destroyed. Another cause of the urge to get the laws in print, however, was Jefferson's growing anxiety regarding the status of Virginia and his place in it. Amid economic stagnation, soil depletion, failures of public investment in infrastructure, education, and industry, Virginia was no longer the political and economic leader of the states, nor was it any longer the most populous. As a heavily indebted slave owner, Jefferson was anxious about the capacity of southern and western states to protect the economic basis of their leaders' liberty as well as their purchasing power from tariffs protective of American manufacturing in the North. He was increasingly fearful for Virginia's economic security and viability.

The great project of Jefferson's retirement, the establishment of the University of Virginia in Charlottesville, grew in large part out of his concerns for the protection of a provincial identity and the political economy of slave labor that had supported this identity over time. As the university was nearing its completion in 1821, Jefferson wrote to James Breckinridge that his hopes for the future were dampened by the line separating slave and free states in the Missouri Compromise, which amounted to "a speck in our horizon which is to burst on us as a tornado, sooner or later."[68] Jefferson was famously nervous and prescient about the threat that slavery and the resulting division between the North and South posed to the peaceful survival of the Union, but that did not mean he was entirely conciliatory. "If," Jefferson wrote, "as has been estimated,

[67] Jefferson to William Waller Hening, January 14, 1807, *Writings*, p. 1171.

[68] Jefferson to James Breckenridge, February 15, 1821, *Writings*, p. 1452; on racial conflict and economic trouble in Virginia in this period, and the politics of both, see Alan Taylor, *The Internal Enemy: Slavery and War in Virginia, 1772–1832* (New York: Norton, 2013).

we send three hundred thousand dollars a year to the northern seminaries, for the instruction of our own sons, then we must have there five hundred of our sons, imbibing opinions and principles in discord with those of our own country," by which, of course, he meant Virginia. Those in the legislature who doubted the necessity of supporting the University were in Jefferson's eyes ignoring the larger situation regarding the vitality of the state. "This canker is eating on the vitals of our existence," Jefferson wrote of sending Virginians to schools in the North, "and if not arrested at once, will be beyond remedy."[69] Recalling the embodied language of the *Notes*, where he had described dependent labor as a festering sore on the body politic, and African Americans themselves as creatures of their bodily passions, Jefferson saw the inculcation of Federalist or Northern political, intellectual, and economic values as similarly a danger to the minds and bodies of the Virginia leadership class. Proper, native cultivation needed to be implemented, and soon.

Set in a neoclassical environment that blended civil and natural histories like the *Notes on the State of Virginia*, the curriculum of the University of Virginia would need to include ancient and modern languages, mathematics, physics, chemistry, mineralogy, botany and zoology, and medicine. In addition to these, the students would study government, political economy, natural jurisprudence, and "History, being interwoven with Politics and Law," municipal law, ideology, grammar, ethics, rhetoric, *belles lettres* and the fine arts.[70] In line with his goal for the university as an almost monastic space of rigorous civic formation in close quarters, Jefferson defended the secular character of the institution, which was indeed the first university not to include or have been founded as a school of divinity. "We have proposed no professor of divinity," Jefferson wrote in the report to the commissioners of the university, going on to explain that metaphysics, theology, and the "laws and obligations these infer" will be the concern of the professor of ethics. In addition, the "developments of these moral obligations, of those in which all sects agree," will be joined by "a knowledge of the languages, Hebrew, Greek, and Latin," the goal being that "a basis will be formed common to all sects."[71] Religious education at the secular public institution would be an education in the history, ethics, and politics of religions combined with a study of the original languages in

[69] Jefferson, *ibid.*
[70] Jefferson, "Report of the Commissioners for the University of Virginia," pp. 462–3.
[71] *Ibid*, p. 467.

which the sacred texts and canons of Judaism and Christianity had been expressed and transmitted across time. For Jefferson, the category of the religious, being a matter of ethics, of the consequences of belief for behavior in the public realm, took place squarely within the boundaries of the civic and the temporal. A common space of critical study and engagement would control the danger of political and social life being reduced to questions of opinions about God or the nature of the liturgy, gradually encouraging the public recognition and careful maintenance of this common space.

At times, Jefferson took his skeptical and historical understanding of religious discourse and its relationship with secular thought and institutions to nearly Erastian lengths.[72] In a letter to Peter Carr about the curriculum of the university, Jefferson wrote of three departments or graduate schools; one for the fine arts, one for the sciences, and finally one for "Theology and Ecclesiastical history' as well as "Law, Municipal and Foreign."[73] The admittance of "theology and ecclesiastical history" to the graduate curriculum, while never instituted, in Jefferson's vision accomplished nothing less than the bringing of the sacred transmission of ecclesiastical authority within the borders of the civic, the temporal, and the secular. In response to the claim by some that the secular nature of the university was an attack on religion, Jefferson later reported to Thomas Cooper that the committee had compromised by allowing religious leaders to each establish an independent "professorship of their own tenets, on the confines of the university," such that they could use the library and make use of the university, be in contact with their flock among the student body, all while remaining structurally and financially independent of the university itself.[74]

In Jefferson's eyes, the partisans of the integrity of the university as a secular institution had gotten the better end of the deal. "By bringing the sects together, and mixing them with the mass of other students, we shall soften their asperities, liberalize and neutralize their prejudices, and make the general religion a religion of peace, reason, and morality."[75] In

[72] On Erastian politics in early modern England, see Mark Goldie, "Priestcraft and the birth of Whiggism," *Political Discourse in Early Modern Britain*, Nicholas Phillipson and Quentin Skinner, ed. (Cambridge: Cambridge University Press, 1993), pp. 209–31; Eric Nelson, *The Hebrew Republic: Jewish Sources and the Transformation of European Political Thought* (Cambridge, MA: Harvard University Press, 2010).

[73] Jefferson to Peter Carr, September 7, 1814, *Papers of Thomas Jefferson: Retirement Series*, Vol. 7, p. 639.

[74] Jefferson to Thomas Cooper, November 2, 1822, *Writings*, p. 1465.

[75] *Ibid.*

Jefferson's framework for education, the "general religion," the public philosophy, was a historically constituted and civic thing, and while a great part of its history was indebted to the history of religion, it was all together too precious and fragile a thing to be left in the hands of the clergy or any other form of sacred authority. Admitting theology to the common space of public education exacted the price of re-conceiving it as the civil history of ecclesiastical institutions and the various misrepresentations that had characterized denominational conflict.

Jefferson imagined education, his own and that of others, as formation in the discipline of study necessary for an active participant in government. "Education begets habits of application, of order, and the love of virtue; and controls, by the force of habit, any innate obliquities in our moral organization," he wrote, outlining the overarching goals of an education at the University of Virginia.[76] Just as one could not expect to get better results out of a wild and uncultivated tree that produced sour and bitter fruit, Jefferson confidently reported, "we know that the grafting art implants a new tree on the savage stock... Education, in like manner, engrafts a new man on the native stock, and improves what in his nature was vicious and perverse into qualities of virtue and social worth."[77] Like Jefferson's own reading and writing in his notes for his manual on parliamentary procedure, intellectual development consisted in attending to collected materials, and like his editing of the New Testament, education for political life was a heavy pruning of the old and experimenting with the possibilities of new growth. The governing metaphor at work here, however, was not that of human work on the artificial surfaces of a page but that of the gardener's work on the vegetative growth of his seeds. The naturalistic language reinforced Jefferson's biological distinction of the sons of Virginia.

Education was the unique tool of historical dynamism that in Jefferson's vision was the fundamental quality of the republic. "What, but education, had advanced us beyond the condition of our indigenous neighbors? And what chains them to their present state of barbarism and wretchedness, but a bigotted veneration for the supposed superlative wisdom of their fathers," asked Jefferson. The Native Americans exhibited the "preposterous idea that they are to look backward for better things, and not forward, longing, as it should seem, to return to

[76] Jefferson, "Report of the Commissioners of the University of Virginia," p. 461.
[77] *Ibid.*

the days of eating acorns and roots, rather than indulge in the degeneracies of civilization."[78] Slaves of their own custom rather than their own bodies, to Jefferson Native Americans were the barbarous, historically stationary people against which the movement of the American nation through continental space and developmental time could be measured. The blind worship of tradition, Jefferson argued, was the "genuine fruit of the alliance between Church and State," again using his configuration of Native Americans in time as an opportunity to take a shot at those in his own polity he considered backwards-looking.[79] And again, Jefferson could thus imagine his own project, in this case the University of Virginia and the "country" it served, as the spear point of a linear, directional force of historical time. The "bad fruit" Jefferson saw in the lives and history of the Native Americans only reinforced his desire to support the genetic improvement of the budding plants that settler stock could produce.

Jefferson's racial theorizing with regards to the purpose of the university was nowhere more apparent than in his plans to have Anglo-Saxon be one of the major languages of instruction. In the report on the university, Jefferson and his fellow committee members (although it is almost certain that this was Jefferson's idea) listed Anglo-Saxon as a modern rather than an ancient language. "It is in fact that which we speak," Jefferson assured the board, for the language had undergone change over time like any other language. Fortescue-Aland, from whose work Jefferson recorded entries in his legal commonplace book, "has well explained the great instruction which may be derived" from a study of Anglo-Saxon "to a full understanding of our ancient common law, on which, as a stock, our whole system of law is engrafted."[80] The vitality and continuity of the law

[78] *Ibid*, pp. 461–2.

[79] *Ibid*, p. 462; on the seeming paradox of Jefferson's depiction of Native Americans and his own embrace of Anglo-Saxon as a linguistic heritage, see Peter Thompson, "Judicious Neology: The Imperative of Paternalism in Thomas Jefferson's Linguistic Studies," *Early American Studies*, Vol. 1, No. 2 (Fall 2003), pp. 187–224, and "Aristotle and King Alfred in America," in *Thomas Jefferson, The Classical World, and Early America*, Peter Onuf and Nicolas P. Cole, eds. (Charlottesville: University of Virginia Press, 2011), pp. 193–218.

[80] Jefferson, "Report of the Commissioners of the University of Virginia," p. 466; see also Jefferson to J. Evelyn Denison, November 9, 1825, *Writings*, pp. 1502–5; on Jefferson and his enthusiasm for Anglo-Saxon, see Stanley R. Hauer, "Thomas Jefferson and the Anglo-Saxon Language," *Papers of the Modern Language Association*, Vol. 98, No. 5 (October 1983), pp. 879–98; Thompson, "Judicious Neology: The Imperative of Paternalism in Thomas Jefferson's Linguistic Studies," pp. 187–224.

flowed from the vitality and continuity of the language in which it had originally been written, and both the language and the law could, allegedly, be traced to the virtues of the ancient Britons and Anglo-Saxons themselves. Study of the Anglo-Saxon language would "form the first link in the chain of an historical review of our language through all its successive changes to the present day," and "will constitute the foundation of that critical instruction in it which ought to be found in a seminary of general learning."[81] Only within the tightly intertwined lineage, language, and law that had supposedly survived intact across a long stretch of history could Jefferson imagine the capacity to critically look at the history of the language one spoke.

That the positing of the unproblematic survival of an Anglo-Saxon language and constitution through the long history of British constitutionalism went against two centuries of historical study with which he had repeatedly engaged never appears to have bothered Jefferson. In his "Essay on the Anglo-Saxon Language" that he had composed in 1798 as an enclosure with a letter, and which he sent out again to another correspondent in 1825, Jefferson deliberated on the benefits of studying Anglo-Saxon, the methods of doing so, and the principles to be kept in mind by the student so inclined. "Although since the Norman Conquest it has received vast additions and embellishments from the Latin, Greek, French, and Italian languages," Jefferson wrote of Anglo-Saxon, "yet these are but engraftments on its idiomatic stem; its original structure and syntax remain the same."[82] To show the continuity of Anglo-Saxon, Jefferson in his "Essay" lined up in columns sentences from the first chapter of the Book of Genesis, providing Anglo-Saxon, Anglo-Saxon in modernized alphabet, and the requisite passages from the King James Bible.[83] Unlike the "Life and Morals of Jesus of Nazareth," though, here the cuts are implicitly and automatically sutured by the security of race. Only race in Jefferson's vision could keep history and judgment organized, and it was thus only race that could allow him to say that unlike their predecessors in the Glorious Revolution, Americans had avoided having to hunt through musty parchments, and instead had found the principles of right engraved on their hearts.[84]

[81] Jefferson, "Report of the Commissioners of the University of Virginia," p. 466.

[82] Jefferson, "Essay on the Anglo-Saxon Language," *The Complete Jefferson*, Saul K. Padover, ed. (New York: Duell, Sloan, and Pearce, 1943), p. 57.

[83] *Ibid*, pp. 876–82.

[84] Jefferson to John Cartwright, June 5, 1824, *Writings*, pp. 490–6.

That Jefferson expressed such enthusiasm for keeping the language of his "barbarous ancestors" in the curriculum while depicting Native Americans as barbarians who had surrendered the capacity to remake their own history is a telling marker of the tensions surrounding his various historical, textual projects. Jefferson found Americans exceptional in their potential for projects of making and remaking themselves and the fundamental texts that had constituted their history, but the safety of this ideological projection came to require, for Jefferson, the policing of the racial boundaries of his vision and its applicability. Jefferson sought to secure himself and his vision from the impulse of revolt with the barrier of race and the support it was meant to lend to the carefully constructed and anxiously guarded, fleeting experience of his own historicity.

Conclusion

Jefferson wrote in the preface to his *Manual of Parliamentary Practice* that he had composed the manual for congressional, public, and his own use, as well as "to deposit with the Senate the standard by which I judge and am willing to be judged."[1] This was a perfect image of Jefferson's unique experience and theorization of history, caught up as his thinking was in the political valences of modes of organized memory and their use in informing further judgment and action. His keen awareness of having participated in events that were already becoming inscribed in texts, images, and institutions that were going to be used by others shaped his continuing concern for the politics of personal and collective memory.

In retirement at his estates at Monticello and Poplar Forest, he assembled his final two textual projects, his autobiography and his journals of cabinet political activity from his time as Secretary of State.[2] Both texts, the Autobiography and the "Anas," as the notes were called, narrate Jefferson's life in public, and taken together with later notes on politics account for his political career up to and through the years of his presidency. While the autobiography was purportedly written for the reference of his family, Jefferson's awareness of its potential value to others is unmistakable throughout the text, for the brief account represents his career in Virginia and early congressional politics through to

[1] Jefferson, "Manual of Parliamentary Practice," *Jefferson's Parliamentary Writings*, Wilbur Samuel Howell, ed. (Princeton: Princeton University Press, 1988), p. 355.

[2] See Matthew E. Crow, "History, Politics, and the Self: Jefferson's 'Anas' and Autobiography," *The Blackwell Companion to Thomas Jefferson*, Francis D. Cogliano, ed. (Oxford: Wiley-Blackwell, 2012), pp. 477–90.

his time in France, glossing over his troubled tenure as governor during the revolutionary war and partisan political conflict concerning the French Revolution. At the same time, Jefferson recounts the promise of his original draft of the Declaration of Independence and proposals for legal and constitutional reform in Virginia, becoming the first of many to hold out the potentiality of the revolution as a way of problematizing what it became, and in the process being compelled to gloss over the subjective tensions and insecurities that connected theory and practice. Indeed, as Peter Onuf points out, Jefferson remembered a much more direct role for himself over the course of his life in attempts to end slavery than appears to have actually been the case.[3] The "Anas" and other notes with which it was posthumously published offer a kind of private and insider record of Jefferson's self-styled republican resistance to Federalist politics, documenting in cabinet conversations and correspondence the potential corruption of the republic, and engaging in a political fight for historical memory calculated for the long-term.

At the very least, these texts illuminate the close relationship between Jefferson's own subjectivity and performative acts of self-representation with his thinking about historical subjectivity, his self-constitution with the constitution he shared with others. For the most part bereft of personal matters, covering up as much as they reveal, both texts communicate an understanding of self as ultimately inseparable from the arena where speech and action are recognized by others, and where these actions are written down to be used in the self-constituting acts of untold others in the course of human events. In a similar spirit, Jefferson's chosen epitaph for his tomb, usually remarked upon for its humility in not mentioning his political offices, inscribes his memory in his inscriptions, the texts that would be used and the institutions in which they would be transmitted for further use. His claim to be the "author of the Declaration of Independence, the Virginia Statute for Religious Freedom, and Father of the University of Virginia" asserts nothing less than authorship, and does so after a lifetime of exploring ways of approaching texts and institutions where authorship, founding, and paternal inheritance were not

[3] Peter Onuf, *The Mind of Thomas Jefferson* (Charlottesville: University of Virginia Press, 2006), pp. 213–14; Jefferson suggests he authored an amendment for gradual abolition to the slavery bill that was part of the 1779 legal reform project, but that amendment was never submitted to the Assembly; see "Bill 51: A Bill Concerning Servants," *The Papers of Thomas Jefferson*, Vol. 2, pp. 470–3, and Jefferson, "Autobiography," *Writings*, Merrill D. Peterson, ed. (New York: Library of America, 1984), p. 44.

useful categories of analysis.[4] The inscription on the gravestone marks tensions and ambiguities that characterized Jefferson's thinking over the course of his life, a life caught, not uniquely but glaringly between the play of texts, subjects, and their uses and the anchoring of the right to fully participate in that play in a cultivated capacity to do so, a capacity guaranteed, it was hoped, by the security of mastery and self-ownership.

If there is a lesson here, perhaps it is only this: that at some point the freedom to play and the capacity to possess come into conflict, and the one must overwhelm the other, or, in the course of human events, people find time and space to explore what histories they have been participating in making, and where those histories might intersect or be available for intersection with those of others. Old and new histories alike might be rethought and remade, and so in turn might laws and constitutions. With Jefferson, it is possible to conclude that history, to be useful to life in the present, must be recollected and shared. What historical practice can communicate, among other things, is the hope of forms of life unalloyed to the bindings of the strictly sovereign and possessive use of history, or histories, natural and civil.[5] In moments, it has seemed to me, Jefferson understood this, and feared its implications.

As Jefferson anticipated, his thinking and the distillation of that thinking in text and image had a life beyond his own. The boundaries and possibilities of his theorized subjectivity are at once asserted and contested in the work of the authors of the Declaration of Sentiments of 1848. His vision of a cultivated and reflective cultivator becomes crystalized in Lincoln's addresses to labor, and the settler promise of what Lincoln called the "profitable and agreeable combination of labor with cultivated thought" in agriculture.[6] John Dewey went on to write that "equality denotes the unhampered consequences which each individual member of the community has in the consequences of associated action. It is equitable because it is measured only by the need and capacity to utilize..."[7] Jeffersonian ideas centered around the combination of work, thought, and a constitutional culture of equitable use are both examples

[4] Jefferson, "Epitaph," Writings, p. 706.

[5] Friedrich Nietzsche, "On the Use and Abuse of History for Life," *Untimely Mediations*, R.J. Hollingdale, trans. (Cambridge: Cambridge University Press, 1983), pp. 57–124.

[6] Abraham Lincoln, "Address at Wisconsin State Agricultural Society," (1859) *Selected Writings, 1859–1865*, Don E. Fehrenbacher, ed. (New York: Library of America, 1989), p. 99.

[7] John Dewey, *The Public and its Problems: An Essay in Political Inquiry*, Melvin L. Rogers, ed. (University Park: Penn State Press, 2012), p. 123.

and component parts of a history of "modifiable and altering human habits" that "generate political phenomena."[8]

What J.G.A. Pocock calls "the persistence of Jeffersonian values" in American political and intellectual history, within and beyond the agrarian republican tradition, is unmistakable.[9] But just as unmistakable is the Jeffersonian resonance in the postmodern question of whether the remnants of his thinking have outlived their usefulness for any kind of meaningfully democratic politics. To that question this book offers not an answer, but hopefully along with some tools with which to think about law, history, and politics, it does offer a warning. To cut up and toss out histories is a powerful and surprisingly weighty political act. It is an act that can encourage a belief that one is acting untrammeled, a master directing the flow of histories in political time. In dispensing with pieces of history, there is a risk of losing the ability to keep that history in view for perpetual interrogation, for acts of critical reflection and recollection, and for use, use against a history of the violence of empire and its circumscription of people, of peoples, and their histories.

Jefferson's thinking can be put to such use in modifying and altering this history still. What his thought points to is the exclusionary as much as the ameliorative promise of historical constructions of law, politics, and history, and so the power involved in the life of that constructing activity today. What is worth recollection here is the idea that a constitution is in large part the establishment of space where these constructions are assembled and reassembled collectively in time. Pocock writes of such constructions:

> Thomas Jefferson once remarked that the trouble with being a slave-owner was that you could not behave decently in that role even if you wanted to: but then there must be a history of your wanting to, as well as of your not being able to. Such a history can be written from the slave-owner's point of view, if not actually by him. The history written by or for the slave will probably emphasize the bad faith of the slave-owner's position, to the point where even his best intentions will be presented as inauthentic. It seems possible to ask, however, whether or how often the Master is obsessed with his own role to the point where he cannot see himself outside it, and needs to be emancipated from this

[8] *Ibid*, p. 43.

[9] J.G.A. Pocock, "Cambridge Paradigms and Scotch Philosophers: A Study of the Relations Between the Civic Humanist and the Civil Jurisprudential Interpretation of Eighteenth Century Social Thought," *Wealth and Virtue: The Shaping of Political Economy in the Scottish Enlightenment*, Istvan Hont and Michael Ignatieff, ed. (Cambridge: Cambridge University Press, 1983), p. 244.

tunnel vision. The alternative is that he can see himself outside it, and needs to be told that he can only escape from it by giving it up.[10]

Indeed, Jefferson worked himself into just such a tunnel vision of history, and it is in the confrontation with other histories that departures from the tunnel can be imagined. But it is important to account for the Jeffersonian insight that this is probably not enough. It is not so much recognition or acknowledgment of one's self and others but the historical, and that is to say material and institutional conditions for such activities to be practiced in the first place that is at issue, and has been for some time.

What the consideration in this book on Jefferson's thinking about law and history holds on to is an image of work on the past, articulated succinctly by Franz Kafka in his short manuscript, "The Problem of Our Laws," the hope "that a time will eventually come when the tradition and our research into it will jointly reach their conclusion, and as it were gain a breathing space."[11] Historical practice, in this light, is a gate to that space. This would be a study of law and history attuned to the transformative work of civic practice and use, and to such an extent that the lines between history and its study begin to fade. Jefferson took it upon himself to make subjectivity safe for the founding of a racially homogenous, propertied politics. Perhaps it is our task to refound by returning the founding to potentiality, to usability, even to a kind of play, and in doing so return the concept of use itself to contemporary visibility by caring for the plurality and historicity of its forms, and most of all, by decoupling it from its historically Jeffersonian yoking to ownership and mastery. We live in the midst of distinctive but intertwined histories, and those histories are caught up in a dialectic of possession and revolt. Here, now, we have some amount of freedom in how we decide to use them, and that is the art of recollection.

10 Pocock, "The Politics of History," *Political Thought and History: Essays on Theory and Method* (Cambridge: Cambridge University Press, 2009), p. 251.

11 Franz Kafka, "The Problem of Our Laws," (New York: Pocket Books, 1979), p. 156; see Kafka, "The New Advocate," *Kafka's "The Metamorphosis" and Other Writings*, Helmuth Kiesel, ed. (New York: Continuum, 2002), pp. 59–60; Walter Benjamin, "Franz Kafka: On the Tenth Anniversary of His Death," *Selected Writings, Volume 2, Part 2, 1931–1934*, Harry Zohn, trans. Michael W. Jennings, Howard Eiland, Gary Smith, eds. (Cambridge, MA: Harvard University Press, 1999), p. 815.

Index

For EU product safety concerns, contact us at Calle de José Abascal, 56–1°,
28003 Madrid, Spain or eugpsr@cambridge.org.

www.ingramcontent.com/pod-product-compliance
Lightning Source LLC
LaVergne TN
LVHW101459200926
848483LV00001B/169
9781107161931